PRAISE FOR *VIVA VEGAN!*:

"*Viva Vegan!* hits the mark. Celebrating her Venezuelan roots—and Latin culture as a whole—the NYC-based chef has not simply veganized Latin-food . . . . Instead, she presents unique dishes infused with Latin flavors . . . Thirteen well-organized chapters of recipes cover everything from quintessential condiments to more versions of rice and beans than you ever thought possible." —VEGNEWS

"In Romero's kitchen, firm tofu is turned into a chewy, smoky pan-fried 'vegan stunt-double' for *chicharrón*, the fried pork rinds popular in the Caribbean, while ceviche is reimagined with mushrooms or heart of palms." —NEW YORK DAILY NEWS

"Loaded with attitude to show that vegan cooking can be an absolute blast and doesn't have to rely on faux meats and pretend cheeses to taste good. . . . " —PORTLAND OREGONIAN

"[Romero] comes to the rescue of cooks whose imagination limits their vegan output, and vegans who would like more Latin dishes on their menus. There is a great selection of dishes that everyone will enjoy . . .' Crepes with Un-Dulce de Leche and Sweet Plantains' are swoon-worthy . . . Bottom Line: Would I buy *Viva Vegan!*? Sí." —BLOGCRITICS.ORG

"What sets Romero's recipes apart from other vegan fare is her reliance on standard kitchen ingredients—not creepy faux meats . . . Her recipes ultimately rely on fresh ingredients, creating healthier, lighter versions of otherwise traditionally heavy meals." —SACRAMENTO BOOK REVIEW

PRAISE FOR *VEGANOMICON*:

"Spending time with [Moskowitz's] cheerfully politicized book feels like hanging out with Grace Paley. She and her cooking partner, Terry Hope Romero, are as crude and funny when kibitzing as they are subtle and intuitive when putting together vegan dishes that are full of non-soggy adult tastes. . . . Do look for an excellent roasted fennel and hazelnut salad, bok choy cooked with crispy shallots and sesame seeds, hot and sour soup with wood ears and napa cabbage and a porcini-wild rice soup they say is 'perfect for serving your yuppie friends.'" —NEW YORK TIMES BOOK REVIEW

"Exuberant and unapologetic . . . Moskowitz and Romero's recipes don't skimp on fat or flavor, and the eclectic collection of dishes is a testament to the authors' sincere love of cooking and culinary exploration." —SAVEUR

"[T]his slam-bang effort from vegan chefs Moskowitz and Romero is thorough and robust, making admirable use of every fruit and vegetable under the sun." —PUBLISHERS WEEKLY

"Full of recipes for which even a carnivore would give up a night of meat." —SAN FRANCISCO CHRONICLE

"It's no shocker that the very same urban chefs who had you inhaling vegan butter-cream frosting during your free time have crafted the next revolution in neo-vegan cuisine." —PHILADELPHIA CITY PAPER

"*Veganomicon* not only offers tons of mouth-watering ways to put 'veg' back into your vegan diet with actual produce, but also tutorials that gave me confidence to start improvising on my own." —BUST

"*Veganomicon* is user-friendly, packed with tips and instructions for a wide range of cooking techniques." —NEW YORK SUN

"The *Betty Crocker's Cookbook* of the vegan world . . . It's one more step in the quest to prove that vegan food really doesn't taste like cardboard when you know what you're doing." —BITCH

"Seriously good with broad appeal." —WASHINGTON POST

PRAISE FOR *VEGAN PIE IN THE SKY*:

"Isa. Terry. Pie. Those three words are pretty much all you need to know . . . One of the most highly anticipated vegan-baking tomes since *Vegan Cupcakes Take Over the World*. Or *Vegan Cookies Invade Your Cookie Jar*." —VEGNEWS

"Bursting with an 'anyone-can-do-this' approach and a defiant 'non-vegans-won't-be-able-to-tell-the-difference' attitude, they provide dozens of recipes for classic fruit pies, cobblers, crisps and cheesecakes . . . this mouthwatering collection of desserts will satisfy even the most reluctant reader." —KIRKUS REVIEWS

"Whether you want to prepare a down-home favorite or something a lot more uptown, *Vegan Pie in the Sky* has the recipe you need. The variety is excellent." —TECHNORATI.COM

"With recipes for every pie you can think of, and several you'd never even thought to try, this cookbook is destined to become a go-to guide for home bakers everywhere." —SAN FRANCISCO BOOK REVIEW

VEGAN
EATS
WRLD

Also by TERRY HOPE ROMERO

Viva Vegan!

With Isa Chandra Moskowitz

Veganomicon

Vegan Cupcakes Take Over the World

Vegan Cookies Invade Your Cookie Jar

Vegan Pie in the Sky

VEGAN
EATS
W🌐RLD

250 International Recipes for Savoring the Planet

TERRY HOPE ROMERO

Da Capo Press/Da Capo Lifelong Books
A Member of the Perseus Books Group

Copyright © 2013 by Terry Hope Romero
Photographs by Isa Chandra Moskowitz
Illustrations by John Stavropoulos

Editorial production by *Marra*thon Production Services.
www.marrathon.net
Designed by Lisa Diercks
Set in Tisa, Tisa Sans, and Mr. Moustache.

Cataloging-in-Publication data for this book is available from
the Library of Congress.

First Da Capo Press edition 2012
ISBN: 978-0-7382-1486-3 (hardcover)
Also available as an electronic book.

Published by Da Capo Press
A Member of the Perseus Books Group
www.dacapopress.com

Da Capo Press books are available at special discounts for
bulk purchases in the U.S. by corporations, institutions, and
other organizations. For more information, please contact
the Special Markets Department at the Perseus Books Group,
2300 Chestnut Street, Suite 200, Philadelphia, PA, 19103, or
call (800) 810–4145, ext. 5000, or e-mail special.markets@
perseusbooks.com.

To Vegans Everywhere

Past, Present & Future

contents

what if the world was vegan?

*D*o *not* try to imagine if suddenly, overnight, the entire population of Earth went vegan. That's not what this book is about.

So instead, let's imagine this: what if the great cuisines of the world evolved over time centered on a 100 percent plant-based way of life?

There are brilliant and scholarly environmentalists, economists, and all around do-gooders that have pumped hundreds of brain-hours into telling us how our health and environment would be better off if the whole planet didn't consume animal products. I'm a chef and a cookbook author, and those details are beyond my world of measuring flour, shopping lists, banging together pots and pans (that's an actual cooking technique, you know), and occasionally blogging.

But I do have one heck of an imagination.

This is the story, in the form of a rather heavy little cookbook, of a vegan history that has never existed, but is alive today, inspired by all of the great cuisines that ever were. Many of these foods already go into wholesome everyday vegan meals. The hummus you smeared on a breakfast bagel, the falafel pita stuffed with roasted eggplant downed for lunch between classes, the red curry with tofu shared with a friend for dinner, a seitan taco devoured from a forward-thinking food truck, a weekend family meal gathered around homemade potato pierogi. All of these foods didn't just imagine themselves into being; they started their lives elsewhere on a part of the planet likely very different from the one where you're probably reading this paragraph right now.

This is 2012, and meatless, dairy-free meals have cast aside the American-centric confines that once defined them. Instead of a side of brown rice, wan unseasoned tofu (a cold and naked spectacle in too many salad bars of the early 1990s), and sun-leeched alfalfa sprouts, we can freely indulge, nourish ourselves, and save the planet by reinventing vegan food. It's as easy as borrowing from all the cuisines of the world, that's all.

I mentioned in my previous vegan ethnic opus, *Viva Vegan!*, that meat is just meat, but the true building blocks of cuisines across the planet are the spices, herbs, and grains—from basmati rice to buckwheat, coconut to caraway seeds. That's still my food philosophy and my motivation for creating these recipes. Thinking about the plant-based ingredients of the cuisines of our world, you can guess which I'm referring to: cilantro, lime, coconut milk, lemongrass (Thai or Vietnamese) . . . garlic, toasted sesame oil, soy sauce, scallions (Korean) . . . pinto beans, tomatoes, chipotles, corn (Mexican). Yes, there are fine nuances between the Thai and Vietnamese, but it becomes clear: wherever it's eaten, meat basically remains the same—it's plant foods that transport

our senses. Apply those flavors to vegan staples such as seitan or tofu and even straight-up vegetables, and the possibilities? If not endless, pretty darned expansive.

AMERICAN FOOD IS WORSE THAN EVER. AMERICAN FOOD IS BETTER THAN EVER.

You see the headlines in your RRS Feed (or old-fashioned newspaper) every day: American food is at peril. Seems like there is a new documentary every few weeks about the trouble with corn, wheat, soy, meat, sugar, coffee, chocolate, fast food, slow food, really slow food. "Pink slime" derived from ground beef gone rogue . . . *pink slime!* . . . is making the headlines as I write this in March of 2012, and regardless if you eat tofu pups or foot-long hotdogs, the notion that *somebody with influence over our food* imagined that this is acceptable eats is stomach–churning. We're in trouble from the moment we open a box of cereal in the morning up until digging into a dish of ice cream at night.

What's our best defense against this unsavory serving of bad food news? Knowing that the old-fashioned art of cooking—flavorful, fresh, and often whimsical cooking—can withstand whatever modern hazards threaten our everyday bread. Part of that is embracing (instead of fighting against) our own changing, evolving palates. Americans—meatless Americans I'm especially looking at you—don't want to settle anymore for the bland, beige, barely-edibles of their childhoods (unless you're a vegan kid right now, and you're probably eating the most diverse vegan diet to date). Both omnivores and meat-eschewing vegetarians and vegans are feeling increasingly more comfortable with the ever-evolving immigrant influences on American food. Despite all the terrible developments in food around us, this is also an exciting time for American cuisine.

As any new vegetarian or vegan can tell you, when you cut out a big portion of the old way of eating, you seek out other things to eat. And while almost everyone has heard about veggie burgers, many Americans can comfortably say they crave quinoa, fresh cilantro, flaking filo vegan spinach pies, Vietnamese pho noodle soup, and authentic soft corn tortilla tacos on a regular basis. And nearly everybody by now knows guacamole like an old friend.

While vegetarian and vegan food needs may be meatless, we also crave these flavors more than ever. To the vegan curious who happen to be reading this: never mistake a rejection of eating animals as a rejection of really good-tasting food. This book is about just that; we can have it all.

VEGAN CUISINE DOESN'T LIVE ON A MAP. IT LIVES AND GROWS IN IDEAS.

These recipes channel the flavors of the regions they hail from, but I've also taken some big liberties with regard to what is "authentic." My cooking style has changed, and after working with over 100 active recipe testers from all over North America and beyond, I know creativity and necessity always trump a slavish adherence to "tradition." Years after *Veganomicon* was first published, I now regularly cook with less oil and more vegetables, and along with this, my increased passion for spices and ethnic ingredients translates into dishes that are lighter but steeped in flavor. And while traditional favorites are represented here, I had my fun with mash-ups too: South American quinoa plays the role of tourist in Middle Eastern cuisine when tossed with traditional ingredients such as dates, pistachios, or sumac powder. Why not spike a flourless chocolate cake with

warming, intriguing Ethiopian berbere? My massaman curry hack may not taste like the one from your favorite Thai restaurant, but it's damned good, satisfies the human need for peanut butter curry, and makes killer leftovers.

Vegan cuisine right now is being created by a community that's linked not by language or ethnicity but by ideas. From the first hummus I mashed in high school to the roasted artichoke paella made before finishing this introduction, the years watching my food community grow make me proud—most of all, the willingness of vegan foodies to push beyond what's expected of them and want something more. Evolving and in constant flux, vegan food is getting better, and we're better people for it. The more we open our plates to food from around the world, the more likely we'll view others outside of our culture as people just like us!

SECRETLY, THIS IS A COOKBOOK ABOUT NEW YORK CITY. QUEENS, TO BE EXACT.

In a single day I can eat crisp South Indian dosas for breakfast, slippery pad Thai noodles for lunch, snack on piping-hot Colombian rice and bean empanadas, and enjoy a Korean stone bowl bibimbap garnished with kimchi for dinner. My savvy travel agent that never sleeps? The New York City subway system.

This cookbook has a secret . . . it's not just an international cookbook in the old-fashioned sense; it draws inspiration from the teeming avenues, bodegas, and restaurants of Queens, New York City. From the Latino and Asian markets of Jackson Heights (one of the most ethnically diverse places in the world) to the Greek and Mediterranean stores and Middle Eastern bakeries of Astoria, Queens, these neighborhoods and others cradle an astonishing array of cultural food windows. *Viva Vegan!* owes its existence to the intricate patchwork of Latin American markets in Queens; my weekly shopping trips for *Viva Vegan!* recipes of plantains and dried chilies were fueled by stops for dosas, chaats, dumplings, and wok-seared noodle stir-fries. After over a year of being immersed in a world of vegan latino recipes, I knew I had to complete my food infatuation by bringing home my favorites inspired by Asian, European, African, Mediterranean, and Middle Eastern cuisine.

The ambitious international cookbooks of the past also inspired me, from a childhood of browsing through books from the likes of Betty Crocker to James Beard. Beard's unabashedly kitschy *Fireside Cookbook* is a window to another America on the tipping point past pot roasts and boiled potatoes. Polish, Chinese, and French flavors stamp the American classics of those times, but today Thai, Japanese, Ethiopian, Lebanese, and perhaps more than ever Mexican—just to name a few cuisines—have left a huge impression and created a nonstop craving for sushi, tacos, and green curry on our American palates right now. With so much exciting flavor and the explosion of "foodie culture" online, in pop-up restaurants, and in farmers' markets, American vegan cuisine has leveled up like never before, and I'm thrilled to see what shape it will take 5 months to 15 years from now. From my almost daily shopping trips in Queens to my Latin-American heritage (which includes a healthy dash of Polish), I present to you my vision of a new cuisine without borders.

So what if the world was vegan? *Your* own cooking is the answer to that question; fire up the stove and make a green curry, simmer a date tagine stew, or hold a freshly made corn tortilla piled high with chile-braised jackfruit in your hand. Chart your course in the great, growing map of vegan food history.

HOW TO USE THIS BOOK

Open it up, flip through the pages, pick a recipe that sounds yummy. Cookbooks should be more user-friendly than ever, but sometimes all these new recipes can be a little overwhelming, especially if you're browsing while hungry!

And there may be some information (ingredients, techniques, and so on) that is unfamiliar to you. If you're new to cooking in general, *sweating* a skillet of onions may sound weird, while experienced chefs might be new to the wonders of pandan leaves or sumac.

With that in mind, you may notice frequent references to the Kitchen Cartography section in the front of this book. If this were a website I'd provide hotlinks, but a book being older tech, I'll provide page references. As the chapter name suggests, it's my way of mapping out the four sections—techniques, ingredients, shopping lists, and kitchen equipment—that you may find helpful.

LEARNING HOW TO COOK?

Even cookbook authors were once new chefs. If you're relatively new at cooking, or maybe are really good at making one or two things but want to expand your repertoire, it's easy to get started. Look for recipes with fewer pots or pans, relatively basic steps, and ingredients that are not too out of the way. Beginner doesn't always mean done in 5 minutes; making gyoza dumplings may require a little extra time to assemble, but the procedure is straightforward and simple to get the hang of.

In fact, I've made it even easier for you—recipes that are especially friendly to newbie chefs are marked with this **123**.

THE KEYS TO THE KITCHEN

The recipes in this book are labeled with a few mysterious icons. Well, mystery no more! Consult this list when deciding on a dish that needs to be low fat, or quick and easy, gluten free, etc. Many of the recipes will be more than one of these things.

45 Under 45 minutes from start to finish. Does not include preparing other recipes needed for the final recipe or presoaking of beans or nuts

Majority of cooking time is inactively on the stovetop or in the oven, so you can relax

$ Cheaper ingredients, especially when seasonal produce is used

123 Try this if you're a kitchen novice: recipe has fewer steps beyond chopping or prepping the ingredients or is straightforward in putting together

LOW FAT Recipe has 1 tablespoon or less of added oil, no nuts, no avocado

G No wheat or barley. Be sure to use gluten-free soy sauce in these recipes (such as gluten-free tamari) when soy is mentioned in the ingredients.

S No tofu, tempeh, miso, soy sauce. Margarine may be listed, so be sure to use a soy-free vegan margarine. As of this writing Earth Balance has a product in its line of vegan "buttery spread" that is soy free.

VEGAN
EATS
WRLD

PART 1

KITCHEN CARTOGRAPHY

MAPPING YOUR WAY TO A BRAVE NEW VEGAN CUISINE

Cooking is not only what you do with the stove and pot and a bag of groceries but it's an organic process from the moment you read a recipe and until the last clean dish is stacked away (no matter who washes the dishes!).

BEFORE COOKING

You don't need a map of India or Tibet or Poland to make great curries, momo dumplings, or pierogi. The only map required is a solid recipe. But like a map, a recipe demands your attention and study before starting the voyage. Mistakes can be avoided before they ever happen: if you can't stand eggplant, then that vacation on Baba Ganoush Island should be spent elsewhere. The careful reading of a recipe—before you're standing in front of the stove—can reveal questions or potential issues before you even make a shopping list. Below is a checklist to help you jumpstart your next recipe trip.

➔ Read the entire recipe before you even enter the kitchen. *Then* read it again.

➔ Make a mental checklist of the ingredients, and compare to what you may already have in the pantry and refrigerator.

➔ Jot down a quick list of ingredients to buy, including ingredients that may be in need of restocking. Double check your memory: if you haven't seen a can of tomato paste since yesterday but recall buying one last June, pick up another can at the store and avoid the heartache of going without when it's needed most. For the tech-minded, email or text yourself a list, or download one of the many excellent (and free) grocery apps for smartphones (*Evernote* is my current favorite note-making app that's a champ for making grocery lists and recipe notes.)

➔ Take note of how long the recipe may take to prepare, unless you're cooking on a leisurely weekend day with all the time in world. Even if a recipe mentions how long it should take, review the steps and check with yourself how long it may *actually* take you. I can dice carrots and celery in under 3 minutes, you can chop it all in 1, and the guy next door needs 10 minutes to find carrots in a packed refrigerator. A teacher once told me to estimate how long it will take to do something, then multiply it by three. (Sue, you're still right after all these years!)

➔ Make another mental note of the cooking tools and equipment needed, especially if it's beyond a pot and a wooden spoon.

➔ Make sure to understand the cooking terms used. Deglazing, folding, and sweating have nothing to do with deconstructed pottery, laundry, or baking a dozen peach pies without air conditioning in August. Knowing these basic techniques will make your cooking better and more efficient. Consult "Cooking Terms" on page 6 for an explanation of all of those and more.

Everything in Its Place (Including Your Mess)

An international cookbook is great excuse to talk about mise en place, *French for literally "putting in place" and the mantra of chefs and cooking students everywhere. Having once been a cooking school student myself, I thought mise en place a touch too control freakish: setting aside chopped vegetables, measured ground spices, spoonfuls of oil, and minced garlic in their own little bowls seemed fussy and a waste of time.* Then.

Well, it still seems somewhat anal, but the calmness of mise en place is now a thing I've embraced years later. Life is complicated already (social media, taxes, Tivo), why not exercise some controlled simplicity in the kitchen? If you find yourself stressing over stir-frys or tearing apart the cupboard for cumin as a pot of curry boils over, consider mise en place the never-takes-a-sick day, 24–7, DIY personal assistant in the kitchen.

Make your own mise en place more exciting by purchasing a set of colorful plastic or vinyl nested bowls in sizes ranging from 2 cups to tiny ⅛-cup pinch bowls. I have a set of tiny, 1 tablespoon, bright yellow flexible silicon measuring cups for holding ground spices or salt; I love how these bendy, "pinchable" bowls are ideal for streaming spices and salt into bubbling soups or food processors.

Making a stir-fry? Then you'll automatically assemble a mise en place. This style of fast, high-heat cooking demands ingredients that are chopped and ready to go. There's no time to stop and dice when bite-size nuggets of food cook in under 2 minutes in a searing hot wok.

Lastly, a small or medium-size mixing bowl for throwing out vegetable scraps is alarmingly useful. You don't need a signature $20 Rachael Ray garbage bowl. Anything will do, including the previous paper or plastic packaging for mushrooms or tofu. Just get that waste out of your face, and instantly feel like a Zen kitchen master.

Stop and Chop

There are infinite techniques for slicing vegetables, but the most useful one is the simple dice; slicing things into little cubes. For more on what knife is best suited for your needs, see **Kitchen Equipment** (page 26).

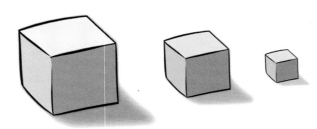

Use these illustrations to guide you when dicing and chopping vegetables, tofu, and seitan. Perfect squares or rectangles are not required, but a little finesse goes a long way: minced garlic versus slices of garlic can make the same recipe taste and look remarkably different. Basic knife skills will make you faster and more confident in the kitchen and make the most out of cooking investments like a nice chef's or santoku knife.

Dice, an illustrated guide:

Below is the most basic of diced vegetables: an onion. This fast, finger-friendlier method can be used to dice anything from an eggplant to a tomato, potato or rutabaga.

Mince, an illustrated guide:

Mincing is just dicing taken to a new, ethusiastic level; the result are tiny (1/16-inch or finer) bits. Mincing is used to make tiny bits of intensely flavored ingredients such as garlic, ginger, or herbs; these fine flecks distribute flavor evenly in food. Use this technique with fresh herbs for fluffy mounds of parsley or cilantro.

Special exciting bonus slice: the baton.

Better known as the french-fry shape, you'll apply this to more than just potatoes, including carrots, celery, apples, or whatever.

How to Chop a Mushroom

Slices or dices, experimenting with the cut of juicy mushrooms can make all the difference.

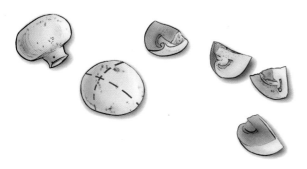

Garlic Wrangling

Fresh garlic is wonderful. Use it when you can; the following should help you get a little closer to more of it in your recipes!

SHAKING YOUR WAY TO LOTS OF SUDDENLY PEELED GARLIC

A method that took the internet by storm last year uses two metal mixing bowls to rapidly peel lots of garlic. Place one or more whole heads of garlic in a bowl, cover with another bowl (ideally one bowl should be slightly nested in another), hold on tight, and shake, shake, shake it like a Shake Weight on fire. The insane friction of the garlic against the hard metal bowls will remove most, if not all, of the papery skin. Best performed on very fresh garlic with dry peels. For peeling just a few cloves, try shaking them in a stainless steel martini shaker.

SMASH! PEEL!

Smashing a single, unpeeled clove of garlic is the faster way to remove the peel. Simply lay the flat side of your chef's knife on a clove and give it a fast, hard rap with side of your closed fist. Lift off the knife and lift away the peel from the smashed clove.

SALTED GARLIC PASTE

A little jar of freshly made garlic paste is a fast method of scooping fresh garlic into recipes.

To make, take a few of those freshly unpeeled cloves, place them in a mortar and pestle, and sprinkle with a healthy pinch of sea or kosher salt. Use the mortar and pound into a chunky paste. This shouldn't take very long, about 2 to 3 minutes. Store in a small, tightly covered container in the fridge. Use within 2 weeks.

Use in any recipe that calls for garlic. 1 teaspoon equals 1 clove of garlic. Store the paste in the fridge and use 1 teaspoon for every clove.

One Clove Equals One What?

Some garlic cloves can be almost as large as Brazil nuts, others as teeny as anemic almonds. As you can see, there's little consistency in writing "1 clove" of garlic. However, after rigorous, unscientific online polls, most seemed to prefer me saying "1 clove garlic" instead of "1 teaspoon minced garlic." But if you require precision garlic, the average clove of garlic equals about 1 rounded teaspoon of minced garlic in these recipes.

DURING COOKING

This is when it all comes together. A few tweaks or special attention can make all the difference when preparing a special dish or everyday meal.

Highs and Lows

Pay close attention to what high, medium, and low heat are on your particular stovetop. I've watched lots of people cook and one of the most common, easy to remedy mistakes is using too much heat for too long; for instance, frying delicate ingredients like garlic on high heat for more than a minute is courting bitter burned garlic sadness.

On most stoves, both electric and gas, 6 o' clock on the dial (usually numbered "5") is a steady **medium heat**, tending a little bit toward low. This is the ideal temperature if you like nonstick pans, since they should never be used for high-heat cooking (although see "Green Nonstick Pans" on page 28). **Low heat** is a 2 to 1, with anything after that being very low heat indeed. This is mostly used for long simmers of soups and some sauces. **Medium-low** heat hovers between medium and low, at about 3 to 4.

Medium-high heat, ranging from about 6 to 8, is best suited for use with cast-iron and stainless-steel pans. A solid **high heat** ranges around 9 and as far as the dial can go: this is useful in short bursts for stir frying and wok cooking.

Cooking Terms

You may be an expert chef or a beginning carrot scraper, so let's spend a few moments on the following cooking terms to ensure we're speaking the same language throughout the remainder of the book. These terms are used repeatedly through the book.

BRAISE

A classic cooking technique if there ever was one, braising is a combination of three steps: browning, deglazing, and just enough sweating to render things tender. The resulting food will have a gently browned exterior, an interior that's tender and maybe a little juicy. A great cooking technique for mushrooms, eggplant, tofu, or any dense, moist food.

BROWN

Browning is simply frying pieces of food at a high temperature in a little oil, but not necessarily cooking them all the way through, to give the outside a pleasing, golden brown sheen.

DEGLAZE

Deglaze is still the coolest-sounding cooking term that elevates anyone from cook to chef in just two syllables. Deglazing occurs when a small amount of liquid is poured into a hot pan after a sauté. The action of adding liquid to a hot pan will make it rapidly simmer, dissolving tasty bits of caramelized sugars and fats from the bottom of the pan into the liquid, infusing it with flavor. You can speed this along by constantly stirring the liquid, releasing

---

Step It Up

More complex recipes can be broken down into stages, steps than can be stretched over a few hours or even days. Below are a few recipes that should be done in advance if you have the time, either refrigerated or frozen for later.

➲ Thai curry pastes (refrigerated or frozen). Make double or triple batches of curry paste and store for later!

➲ *Laksa Curry Paste*, page 216 (refrigerated or frozen)

➲ Pastry dough for *Jamaican Curry Seitan Patties* (page 213), rolled and cut into circles (refrigerated or frozen)

➲ *Basic Dumpling Dough* (page 171), unrolled, stored in a plastic wrapped ball (refrigerated)

➲ Any chutney, salsa, yogurt sauce, or condiment (up to 3 days in the refrigerator)

➲ Washed, chopped raw veggies, stored in airtight plastic, glass containers, or zip-top plastic bags (up to 3 days in the refrigerator). Especially great for stir-fries and soups for weeknight meals.

more browned bits from the pan into the liquid.

Two excellent things happen by deglazing a pan. First, this process infuses the final dish with more umami flavors. This also does double duty of cleaning the bottom of the pan; rather than scrub off those (flavor-packed) browned bits of food when it's time to clean, these flecks are put to good use. Your pan is cleaner, you food tastes better, everybody high five!

Any liquid can be used to deglaze a pan, and wine is traditionally favored because just a little can enhance any dish. Vegetable broth is an acceptable substitute for deglazing.

FOLD

Folding is a slightly refined kind of mixing. Rather than just stirring the spoon round and round a batter or dough, the action is to dig the spoon deep underneath the food, then lift up and away to bring the ingredients in the bottom of the bowl to the top. A wide rubber spatula or wooden spoon comes in handy here. Folding is especially useful when adding ingredients to a batter toward the end of the mixing stage when you just want to blend them into a mixture without stirring the hell out of it, such as adding nuts to a delicate cake batter.

KNEAD

Kneading is the process of pushing and pressing dough. Even if you've never kneaded anything before, you've seen it in action. Watch your cat the next time she settles into a comfy spot; cats are natural born kneaders. Or if you lack a cat watch the staff at your local bakery for tips.

SAUTÉ

This little French word defines how we use the stovetop. Sautéing is just the action of moving around food in a hot pan, gently swirling it around until it's browned and ready to serve. Usually some liquid fat is used to sauté food, but we can be sneaky and use wine, broth, or water in addition to oil or vegan butter to cut down on the total added fat for many recipes. Sautéing can be done in any manner of pans, including stainless steel, cast iron, or aluminum. I also use "fry" as a kind of shorthand for sauté; chances are if you already fry your food, you've been sautéing things all along.

Stirred, Not All Shook Up for Fearless Stir-Frying

Did you read what I said about mise en place on page 3? Well, even if you didn't, I'll sum it up again, but this time it's not an option for stir-frying with a wok.

Stir-fry dishes rely on a few principles to make them fast, effective, and flavorful:

→ A very hot wok. Preheat it for 2 to 3 minutes until the surface is almost smoking.

→ Uniformly chopped morsels of food. This ensures even, fast cooking with high heat.

→ Don't crowd the wok. Smaller batches means better final dishes that cook faster.

→ The bridge between small batches and better dishes: vegetables sliced and spices, sauces, and liquids measured out and set aside in small cups or bowls (it's that mise en place again!).

Follow these principles, and suffer no more from burned garlic or mushy broccoli or undercooked eggplant. Dishes will taste more like your favorite restaurant meals, because they already do this, only on a bigger scale than you (unless like a restaurant, you stir-fry 30 pounds of diced broccoli every night).

A Less-Oil or No-Oil Sauté

Cooking with less or no oil is simple business; you can convert almost any stovetop recipe into a reduced-oil recipe (or sometimes eliminate it all together) by replacing the oil with a flavorful liquid such as wine or vegetable broth with any of these three methods.

→ Pour about double or triple the amount of wine or broth (in place of oil) into a preheated pan and bring to a bubbling simmer. Then sauté as usual but keep an eye on the bottom of the pan; if it looks dry, stir in another 1 to 2 tablespoons of liquid and continue until done.

→ If using vegetable broth, stir up a small, concentrated batch from bouillon for the biggest flavor boost (about 1 cup should last for two to three pans of sautéed vegetables).

→ Inexpensive boxed wine may not be your first choice for drinking, but it is great for cooking. Store wine in the refrigerator for longer shelf life.

→ Use less oil in a sauté. Start with half the amount of oil in a recipe, brown the food, *then* build on with wine or broth to finishing the cooking process. This is essentially braising your food, but with much less liquid.

→ A good method for soups is using only broth or wine for sautéing vegetables *before* adding the oil. When the soup is done, drizzle a small amount of high-quality cold-pressed oil such as extra-virgin oil or nut oil over the food. This is a great way to stretch out flavorful, expensive oils with low smoking points. You'll get all of the flavors of the oil as it blossoms on top of the hot food but with a minimum amount.

SIMMER

Simmer refers to the gentle, easy, not-quite-boiling of liquid foods. Simmering is usually done at a medium or low level of heat. The bubbles in a simmered food are small and the liquid never reaches a rolling boil. Simmering a curry or soup or stew for a long time breaks down firmer ingredients and helps the flavors to fully develop.

STIR-FRY

Stir-frying may seem like sautéing, but it differs in that it always involves high heat, very short cooking times, and constant, active stirring. A big skillet can work, but truth be told, stir-frying is much more fun, easy, and better tasting in a wok. So go get a wok already (see pages 29–30 for more on woks)!

SWEAT

Sweat and food only collide when talking about this technique. To sweat a high-water content food (such as mushrooms, zucchini, or eggplant), briefly brown it first over high heat, then cover the pan. Then lower the heat slightly: as the water in the foods releases, the food will practically steam itself, *voilà!*

WHISK

A high-speed stirring technique, whisking uses a little extra elbow grease and maybe even a whisk (though sometimes a fork will do). Whisking is excellent for blending together oil and vinegar for a salad dressing or creating other emulsions.

AFTER COOKING, CHILL OUT

Soups, sauces, and saucy foods taste better when not served boiling, blazing hot: let them stand for 5 to 10 minutes to cool down just slightly. Searing heat prevents your tongue from tasting what's going on with food. Even a blazing hot stir-fry fresh from the wok benefits from a minute or two of rest.

Leftovers for Later

To extend the shelf life of leftovers or any cooked food, let it cool on a kitchen countertop so that it is no longer boiling hot before packing it away in the refrigerator.

Sticky Business

Dishes and pans with baked-on crust from tasty sauces or marinades need just a little more TLC (but not much more) than your dinner plates. Fill them to the top with hot, soapy water and leave them be for at least 2 hours; you've just made a meal so it's time to relax already! Drain and scrub, or if desired sprinkle the insides with a thin layer of baking soda before scrubbing with a plastic mesh scrubbing pad.

INGREDIENTS

Many specialty ingredients are explained in their respective recipes, but this glossary features some of the stand-out ingredients for your browsing pleasure. For easier shopping, consult the **Shopping Lists** that begin on page 23.

Ethnic Market Ingredients

These are some of the more notable ethnic ingredients featured in these recipes. Regarding ethnic origin, there is a lot of overlap: semolina flour is used in Indian and Middle Eastern dishes beyond the Mediterranean; olives are enjoyed in southern Europe, western Asia, and South America; and basmati rice is treasured by people all over the world. But for the sake of convenience, I've listed each ingredient once.

Browse through this list between reading recipes if there's something new to you; when it's time to go shopping, consult the ethnic shopping lists on pages 24–25.

Mediterranean

FARRO

An ancient Mediterranean wheat that's received new attention in the latest wave of updated Italian cuisine. Chewy and flavorful, if you're a fan of bulgur wheat this is a natural addition to your pantry. I adore it in soup, where it holds its texture much better than mushy pasta.

OLIVE OIL

While you should use the best-quality extra-virgin oil you can afford, this doesn't mean you need the stuff that's bottled like wine and spirals upward past $30. A nice 32-ounce bottle in the $8 to $12 range from Trader Joe's or at the natural store or ethnic market is fine. If you must, sauté foods with inexpensive canola oil, then save the extra-virgin olive oil for drizzling just a little on top of cooked foods right before serving; you'll taste the olive oil fully. Store olive and all oils in a dark, cool kitchen cabinet.

OLIVES

Skip the tasteless canned black olives from California. Greek Kalamata olives, with their purple-grey flesh and meaty, salty texture, are super-flavorful, all-purpose black olives. For a great all-purpose green olive, supermarket Manzanilla olives will do the trick.

SEMOLINA FLOUR

Ground from hard durum wheat, this gritty, golden flour looks similar to cornmeal. I use it in Indian and Middle Eastern desserts for its thick, pudding-like texture when boiled and the pleasing sandy texture it lends to cookie dough.

Middle Eastern

ALEPPO PEPPER FLAKES

Bright red, shiny flakes from a special sun-dried Syrian pepper that is a moderately spicy, slightly sweet, tangy, and habit forming: This is my go-to pepper before cayenne pepper or red pepper flakes, especially for pizza. Aleppo pepper adds not just heat, but a warm, fruity flavor to soups, salads, breads, and grilled foods.

BULGUR WHEAT

While almost any natural food store carries cracked or whole bulgur wheat, you'll find the greatest variety and most authentic tasting at Middle Eastern and Mediterranean grocery stores, including fine grain #1 for delicate kibbe and chunky, large grain #3 for pilafs. This bulgur is peeled and has a mild taste and fluffy texture compared to bitter "bulk bin" unpeeled bulgur wheat.

EGYPTIAN SMALL BROWN FAVA BEANS (FUL MEDAMES)

These brown little fava beans are an ancient staple eaten in Egypt for breakfast but are filling and tasty any time of day served with pita or rice, salad, and good olive oil. Not to be confused with regular large fava beans, which have a greenish color and a flattened bean shape; these are too large, tough and bitter to be used as a replacement for small brown fava beans. (See page 152 for more on these beans.)

ORANGE FLOWER WATER AND ROSE WATER

Look for orange flower water and rose water in the baking aisle of gourmet stores or in the dry goods section of Indian and Middle Eastern markets. Orange flower water does not taste like oranges; it has a light floral scent which, when combined with agave nectar, gives it a honeylike aroma. Be sure to buy a food-grade (not cosmetic-grade) flower water. There's no substitute for either, so just leave them out of a sweet recipe or increase the amount of vanilla or almond for a different flavor.

RAS-EL-HANOUT

You feel like you're doing something particularly smart when buying a spice blend whose name translates to "best in the shop"! Used in Persian cuisine, ras-el-hanout can be a complex, heady mix of up to twenty different spices. Try rubbing it into tofu or seitan before marinating or grilling, or stir into rice before boiling.

SUMAC POWDER

My favorite single Middle Eastern spice, this pretty maroon powder is made from a sharp, tangy berry with fruity notes and a mysterious hint of salt. Some claim that lemon juice can be substituted for sumac powder, but it doesn't come close. Find yourself some sumac powder and soon no salad (especially one with cucumbers, tomatoes, onions, and parsley) will taste complete without it.

ZA'ATAR

Used to flavor bread, za'atar is a Middle Eastern spice blend that usually features thyme, sesame, and tangy sumac. This spice blend may be found in Middle Eastern groceries, often sold in large bags perfect for heaping on warm bread drizzled with olive oil, its traditional use, or even sprinkled on baked potatoes or fries for an unexpected twist. Za'atar has a coarse texture, a greenish-brown color, and a rich nutty, herbal aroma.

European

SHALLOTS

Tasting like a cross between onions and garlic but with a high sugar content, shallots play a big role in

European and Asian cuisines. Shallots look a little like tulip bulbs, with several fat cloves held together by a root stem at the bottom. In this book, 1 shallot refers to one of these individual cloves.

To use a shallot, separate the bulb from the bunch and slice off the tip. I like to slice the shallot in half, which helps give me something to grab onto when removing the peel.

To freeze shallots, first separate and peel the bulbs and trim away root and top ends. Slice into paper thin circles and freeze in tightly sealed plastic bags as directed for lemongrass (see page 17).

Latin American and Caribbean
ALLSPICE BERRIES (PIMENTO BERRIES)
Single out one spice to represent Jamaican cuisine, and it has to be the pimento berry, more commonly known as allspice. You can grind it yourself from the whole, brown, pea-sized berries or just use a fresh bottle of ground allspice for making Jamaican curry powder and jerk sauce.

CHIPOTLES IN ADOBO SAUCE
Chipotle is a generic term for any smoked, dried Mexican pepper, but often it's red jalapeños that have undergone the process. Canned chipotles that have been stewed in a thick, rich tomato sauce (adobo sauce) are easy to use and bursting with smoky chipotle flavor. A small 6-ounce can will last through many marinades and sauces.

Try this method for preparing canned chipotles for easy use in recipes. Puree the chipotles with sauce (a food processor is fine) until smooth and keep refrigerated. To temper the heat of the chipotles, slice them open on a cutting board and use the tip of a knife to scrape away the seeds, then puree. Use in recipes or try it as a thick, spicy chipotle sauce that's great on scrambled tofu, sandwiches, or as a bracing hot sauce for tortilla chips.

CILANTRO
Cilantro is used the world over in tropical and semi-tropical cuisines, an essential element of many Latin, Indian, and Southeast Asian dishes. Dried cilantro is flavorless; it's a waste of money and space, so avoid it. Store fresh cilantro tightly wrapped and stashed away in the vegetable bin of the refrigerator and use within 3 days for best color and flavor.

MASA HARINA
A Mexican corn flour made from corn kernels that have been soaked in limewater (not lime juice, but a solution of calcium hydroxide), then dried and ground into a fine corn flour. When mixed with warm water it instantly forms a smooth dough; in this book we'll use it to make homemade tortillas that make unforgettable tacos. Masa harina is cheap and plentiful wherever Mexican grocery products are sold. *Do not* substitute regular cornmeal for masa harina, it simply won't work.

MEXICAN DRIED CHILE PEPPERS
Don't underestimate the power of a dried chile pepper! Dried Mexican chile peppers bring a whole world of intense, nuanced flavors cheaply and conveniently.

There are so many varieties to choose from, but I find it useful to divide chile peppers into two camps: large, slightly soft, darker-colored chilies such as ancho, mulato, or guajillo that are moderately hot and good for most any use. Hot and zestier are bright red chilies with a thin, brittle skin such as costeño, chile de arbol, or little pequin chilies. For the fullest flavored sauces, use a combination of two or more chilies.

As a rule of thumb, dried chilies are first stripped of seeds, then lightly toasted in a skillet, and lastly soaked in hot water until soft to prepare them for recipes. Dried chilies should be stored in a dry, dark

The Care and Feeding of Fresh and Dried Chile Peppers

Fresh chile peppers, despite their best attempts to stop you, must be eaten. Humans have been cultivating them for thousands of years, and no matter how many times they make us cry we can't resist their deliciousness.

➔ Store fresh chile peppers loosely wrapped in the refrigerator and use within 2 weeks. Or freeze whole washed and dried fresh chilies and use within 6 months. When you're ready to use them, they don't need much thawing time at all. Work with chilies while still slightly frozen for easy slicing; thawed peppers will be mushy.

➔ Removing the seeds from fresh chilies can tame their heat, but even more so if you remove the internal whitish pith that attaches the seeds to chile's insides. This pith contains the highest level of capsicum, the irritating chemical that makes chilies hot. Remove that and the seeds and you've more than halfway tamed that tiger.

➔ If you're particularly sensitive to chilies, wear rubber gloves (though admittedly most chefs or home cooks I know, myself included, don't bother with special chile-handling gloves). If you go bare-handed handling chilies, take care to never rub your eyes or blow your nose right away (if you forget, you'll soon be reminded why it's a bad idea).

➔ For a fast substitute for dried chilies in sauces, use about 2 teaspoons of chile powder per generous ounce of dried chilies and add the powder along with tomatoes or vegetable broth in the recipe. For best results, skip the generic grocery store chile powder and look for single chile powders such as ancho, guajillo, or chipotle.

place in a tightly covered container and will last for many, many months.

PLANTAINS

The bigger, starchier cousins of bananas, plantains must be cooked before eating. Green plantains have a mild, starchy flavor. Set aside green plantains for 4 to 6 days and the peels will turn yellow and black and inside the flesh will ripen and become sweet and soft. For the purposes of this book, we'll boil chunks of plantain in stews like a starchy vegetable, or fry green plantains into thick, sturdy chips for dipping with a fast mole sauce.

Asian, General Ingredients

CHILI GARLIC SAUCE

This bright red sauce bursting with chile and garlic goodness is essential. You have a lot of choices in your typical pan-Asian grocery store; sambal oelek, Sriracha, and just chili garlic sauce are the most common finds. Chunky and flecked with chile seeds, sambal oelek is Malaysian in character. Smooth Sriracha is of Thai origins, and chili garlic sauce sort of falls in between Southeast Asian cuisines. Sample them and pick your favorite; but they are fairly similar, exploding with bright red chile heat, tangy vinegar, and sharp garlic. All are delicious, versatile and utterly habit forming.

CHINESE BLACK VINEGAR

Sometimes referred to as "Chinese balsamic," this is a sweet, inexpensive and nuanced black vinegar that's equally good in recipes or sprinkled on top just before serving (especially good sprinkled along with Sriracha on noodles). Makes a fast dipping sauce combined with a thin soy sauce.

CHINESE SESAME PASTE

Made from unhulled toasted sesame seeds, this

grainy, grayish-brown paste has a smokier, earthier flavor than its Middle Eastern cousin, sesame tahini. Use this for authentic-tasting Chinese sesame noodles.

CHINESE SHAOXING COOKING WINE

An inexpensive Chinese rice wine that adds just the right hint of boozy sweetness to marinades and stir-fries. A big bottle will last many recipes. Sherry is a decent substitute; some sherry wines are filtered with animal products, so look for unfiltered sherry.

DRIED SHIITAKE MUSHROOMS

Dried shiitake mushrooms are versatile and inexpensive and add loads of umami flavor to vegetarian broths, soups, and when rehydrated, even stir-fries and stewed dishes.

When shopping for dried shiitakes, first determine what the ultimate use will be and then decide how much you want to spend. In most cases, the higher the price, the better quality the mushroom. For broths where the mushrooms will be discarded, opt for thinner, cheaper mushrooms. If you're planning on consuming the mushrooms after soaking (thinly slice into chewy morsels), purchase the thicker, rounder caps with deep cracks. These thicker mushrooms have been allowed to grow longer and develop a richer, more concentrated flavor.

Occasionally cheap dried mushrooms will have a little bit of grit trapped underneath the caps. Soak in hot water until tender, then gently squeeze but don't stir the liquid. The grit will drift off the caps and to the bottom of the bowl. You can also strain the soaking liquid and reuse it as stock for an added dash of umami flavor to soup broth.

FRESH WHEAT NOODLES

Irresistible and affordable, refrigerated fresh wheat Asian noodles cook lightning fast and make superior stir-fried noodles. Always check the ingredients to avoid eggs; sometimes egg-free noodles are tinted with yellow food coloring, but these are probably best avoided if you're avoiding artificial ingredients.

HOISIN SAUCE

Hoisin is another excellent Chinese seasoning sauce that also makes an appearance in Vietnamese cuisine in these recipes. Usually it's vegan friendly, but read labels and if possible purchase a brand without artificial colors and flavors.

SPRING ROLL WRAPPERS

Not to be confused with rice paper wrappers, spring roll wrappers are typically made with wheat flour. Usually they can be found in the frozen section, often available in two sizes. While often fried, these wrappers bake up crisp and browned with a good spritzing of cooking oil spray.

TOBAN DJAN GARLIC BEAN SAUCE

In the vast palate of Chinese cooking sauces, toban djan has become a favorite of mine. It features abundant garlic, chilies, salt, and hearty broad beans mashed together and then fermented for a pungent paste that's essential for ma-po tofu. Many subtle differences lurk in different brands; try first a jarred brand such as Lee Kum Kee, then canned varieties and taste the difference; some are more garlicky, others hotter or saltier. It's okay to even use more than one brand in a recipe for a well rounded, spicy-as-hell dish. There are multiple spellings for this sauce, including *tobanjan* and *doubanjiang*.

VEGETARIAN STIR-FRY SAUCE

Once commonly called vegetarian oyster sauce, I've seen it increasingly labeled as vegetarian stir-fry sauce. It's a thick soy- and wheat-based sauce that adds a full-bodied, robust flavor to not just stir-fries but all kinds of sauces, and in emergencies makes a decent dipping sauce. Read those labels, and if possible avoid brands with added MSG.

WONTON WRAPPERS

Wonton wrappers can have a wide variety of additional ingredients beyond flour and water; if you read labels carefully, it is possible to find egg-free wrappers. The biggest, freshest selection can be found in Chinese markets. Round wrappers are the most common, but large square "Shanghai" style are my favorite for larger dumplings. Or use vegan gyoza wrappers (see page 15) if no egg-free alternative is available.

Indian and Sri Lankan

BLACK MUSTARD SEEDS

Worth a mention of their own, black mustard seeds are essential for Indian curries. When sautéed over high in oil or even in a dry pan, mustard seeds will sizzle and pop. For best results cover the pan as the seeds heat to avoid a hot mustard seed in your eye!

FRESH CURRY LEAVES

These glossy, pointed green leaves don't taste like curry on their own but have a complex, earthy flavor that adds depth to Indian and Sri Lankan dishes. Sautéed or simmered, curry leaves become tender and edible. Best used fresh (don't bother with dried curry leaves, they're flavorless), and they can be frozen to drop into curries as needed. To store curry leaves, wash and wipe dry, then keep in a zip-top bag in the refrigerator for up to a week and use before they turn black and soggy. Freeze curry leaves the same way, but don't thaw; toss frozen curry leaves directly into a hot pan to preserve the color and flavor.

FROZEN GRATED COCONUT

Freshly grated coconut is a wonderful part of Indian and Sri Lankan cuisine, but it's awfully time-consuming to crack open and scoop out the inside flesh of whole coconuts. Enter the best convenience food ever: freshly grated coconut that's been packed into 1-pound (or more) bags and frozen. Frozen coconut may be found in Indian and Southeast Asian grocery stores.

Allow solid frozen bags to thaw in the refrigerator overnight, or cover unopened bags with hot water for an hour or so, occasionally kneading the bag to break up large clumps. Once thawed, break apart the coconut and fluff it up with a fork. Just as fresh and tasty as the ground stuff, you may find other reasons to use it beyond the Sri Lankan recipes in this book.

SEV AND INDIAN PUFFED RICE

Sev are chickpea flour noodles fried to be crispy and golden; they come in a range of thicknesses and shapes. Indian puffed rice is different from the stale-tasting American cereal: it's made from long-grain basmati, crisp and full of toasted flavor. There are really no good substitutes for these ingredients, but they are cheap and plentiful in any Indian grocery store. In this book I use them to make the best chaat (Indian street food) of all, behl puri.

And while you're hunting for sev (often stocked in the snack foods aisle), look for colorful premixed behl puri sev and puffed rice blends; there are many to choose from. These may include other goodies including roasted dahl, different shapes of sev (thick and thin), tiny "chappati" crackers, and spices; just to name a few things that will make for a different behl puri every time. Have fun and try a few!

TAMARIND

An intensely sour, bean pod–shaped fruit with a dark brown pulp that grows in towering trees, tamarind is consumed in tropical countries the world over. For the purposes of this book we'll use it primarily in Indian cuisine. Tamarind is most commonly available (and easiest to use) either in sticky blocks of pulp (with and without seeds), or a thick jelly-like paste. In pulp form, tamarind needs to be soaked in hot water, then kneaded to strain out the fibrous debris, so you may prefer to use the fiber-free concentrated form. The only caveat: tamarind concentrate quality can vary and be considerably stronger tasting than self-strained pulp. See **Tamarind Date Chutney** (page 59) for a detailed explanation of handling tamarind pulp and concentrate.

WHOLE SPICE SEEDS

Coriander, cumin, fenugreek, black mustard seeds, star anise, and familiar black peppercorns are all useful whole spices that can be economically purchased at Indian groceries. Often these seeds are enhanced by gently toasting before grinding for recipes. Store spices in a cool spot in the kitchen an air-tight container (large metal tins rule!) and use within 6 months for the freshest flavor.

Korean

GLASS NOODLES

A whole family of intriguing Korean noodles is made from the starch of an Asian yam. When boiled, these hard, pearl-grey twigs transform into chewy, springy, nearly transparent noodles. Occasionally these need to be trimmed into manageable lengths before cooking, but some varieties come presliced into 10-to 12-inch lengths. Cook with plenty of freshly boiled water for about 6 to 8 minutes or until transparent and chewy.

GOCHUGARU

Gochugaru is special: sweet, spicy, and fruity, these shiny soft red flakes are essential for kimchi and many stews and sauces. Don't substitute cayenne pepper or red pepper flakes; these chilies are too hot and bitter and won't taste right.

Look for large bags of Korean red pepper in Korean markets. It's often labeled "for kimchi." Oddly enough it may be labeled a product of China, but believe that you can't make proper Korean food without it.

GOCHUCHANG

One of my favorite Korean ingredients, this is a gleaming red paste made from grain-fermented red chile peppers. It's sweet, spicy, and tangy; diluted into a creamy sauce it's an essential condiment for Korean bibimbap but tastes great dolloped on veggie burgers or grilled tofu. If you love Sriracha, you will absolutely adore gochuchang!

KOREAN GARLIC SOYBEAN PASTE

Similar to miso, garlic soybean paste is mellower, less salty, and somewhat sweet (similar to white miso). Diluted with a few drops of water it can be used as a condiment to be slathered onto grilled foods and folded in crisp lettuce leaves.

Japanese

DAIKON

Looking like a giant, plump white carrot or parsnip, daikon is actually a very mild radish. It has crisp, white flesh with a faint peppery aroma. It's enjoyed both raw, pickled, and lightly stir fried.

GYOZA WRAPPERS

A convenient and usually vegan premade wheat dough wrapper for fast and easy dumplings, gyoza wrappers are acceptable for making most any kind of Asian dumpling in a pinch. Typically these are sold frozen in little stacks of fifty or more; thaw completely before attempting to separate. If you can't find vegan wonton wrappers, gyoza skins make a good substitute.

KABOCHA SQUASH

Also called kabocha pumpkin or Japanese pumpkin, this squash already has many fans in North America thanks to its intensely sweet, slightly starchy flesh, quick cooking times, and edible skin. Available in natural markets and in Asian markets where it's often sold cut into smaller chunks for added convenience.

MIRIN

Mirin is a golden Japanese rice cooking wine with a full body and generously sweet character. It goes particularly well with sweet vegetables and dipping sauces, and paired with miso in marinades.

MISO

The famous fermented soybean paste of Japanese cuisine is almost mainstream; it's full of protein and important enzymes and should never be boiled to protect all those important nutrients. For the purposes of this book, shop for mild, pale golden shiro (white) miso.

PANKO BREAD CRUMBS

These popular Japanese-style breadcrumbs are crunchier and larger than standard Western bread-crumbs. Often used as a coating for deep fried foods, they also respond well to baking to form a crisp golden coating around foods.

RICE VINEGAR

You may already have a version of this mildly acidic vinegar in your pantry. When shopping for rice vinegar in Japanese markets, be sure to purchase plain, unseasoned vinegar and avoid vinegars that may have added sweeteners, salt, or artificial flavors.

SEAWEED (HIJIKI, NORI)

Seaweeds play an important role in many popular Japanese dishes. For the purposes of this book, you'll need a small package of each of the following:

Hijiki: Purchased dried, these wiry black threads must be soaked in water to plump them up before using in recipes. They have a pronounced flavor that's a little sea-like and a little bit earthy. They have a lot of texture and work well blended with tofu.

Nori: The most familiar of the bunch, these glossy greenish-black sheets are usually seen holding sushi rice together. They can also be snipped into thin shreds for topping snack foods and soups.

SOBA NOODLES

Grey, perfectly straight soba noodles are made from buckwheat flour, sometimes with other additions such as yam flour or green tea powder. Fast cooking, filling, and nutritious, soba noodles are great in soup or salads.

Thai and Southeast Asian

If you're luckily within traveling distance of a Southeast Asian market (Thai, Vietnamese, etc.), most of these items will be cheap and easy to find. The second best option is a large, well-stocked Chinese supermarket; some of these markets feature much more beyond Chinese products and carry a healthy assortment of Thai, Vietnamese, and Filipino grocery and produce items.

GALANGAL ROOT

Not always easy to find but worth the trouble, fresh Thai galangal root makes Southeast Asian curry pastes taste authentic. It looks similar to ginger, only with a thinner, yellowish peel with a flush of pink. Galangal root tastes entirely different: it's pungent, earthy and has notes of mustard seed, hot white pepper, and tropical, floral citrus.

The root is woodier and tougher than fresh ginger, but you'll only need a fraction of the amount in recipes; a small 2-inch chunk will last through many curries. Peel a small piece about the size of the tip of your thumb for the curry paste. Store fresh galangal tightly wrapped in plastic in the refrigerator and use within 2 weeks.

GREEN ASIAN PAPAYA

The star of Thai green papaya salad, these hard, dark green papayas are somewhat smaller than their fully developed cousins with bright orange flesh. The hard, crisp flesh is pale green and somewhat watery. Some Thai markets sell it preshredded, but shredding a whole green papaya isn't too much trouble. Peel it first with a Y-shaped vegetable peeler (see page 30), slice in half, scoop and discard the seeds, and either shred it by hand with the largest holes of a box grater or use the shredding disk of your food processor.

LEMONGRASS

An essential element in Southeast Asian cuisine, fresh lemongrass are long, narrow, pale yellow-green stalks with a woody core and a refreshing sweet citrus aroma. Fresh lemongrass will have firm, tightly bound leaves.

Lemongrass can be used two ways: either the long stems are steeped in simmering broth and discarded before serving, or the inner core of the stalks are sliced paper thin to be eaten (a third way is pureeing into curry pastes, where the texture no longer matters so much). The texture of lemongrass can be very fibrous, and in the case of soup you may prefer to simmer whole stalks and discard if you don't want all that fiber. If using the whole stalks, pound the stalks with the dull edge of a chef's knife before adding to a soup; this will diffuse the flavor into the broth.

To slice lemongrass, steady a stalk on a heavy wooden cutting board and using a very sharp heavy chef's knife, cut off the bottom ¼ inch from the stem and trim about 3 or 4 inches from the top. Holding the stalk firmly on a cutting board, slice as thin as possible, ⅛ inch or thinner if you can. You'll have a little pile of fine circles; if desired pull them apart with your fingers.

Refrigerated fresh lemongrass will eventually dry out, and its long shape can make it awkward to store, so I prefer to chop and freeze fresh lemongrass immediately. I usually prepare six or more stems at a time, packing sliced lemongrass into small zip-top plastic bags and squeezing out any air. Keep frozen until ready to use. Don't thaw the lemongrass, just add directly to a soup or curry paste.

Freezing Fresh Herbs

I'm a huge fan of prepping and freezing some basics that you'll use time and time again. When prepping for a stir-fry there's nothing like reaching into the freezer for a handful of prepared lemongrass, garlic, or shallots. Half an hour in the kitchen now will save you hours of prep for weeks; give it a try! These methods are perfect for when you've lugged home a sack of goodies from the ethnic market and need to find space in the kitchen.

I usually chop up a bundle of lemongrass (five to seven stalks), a pound of shallots, and wash, dry, and strip the leaves off a bag of fresh curry leaves in one frenzied session. Then I tightly pack these ingredients into small snack sized zip-top bags and freeze immediately. Writing the date on the bags is helpful, as is the name of the ingredient if it's one you're not super-familiar with.

But if you don't want to bother with preparing fresh lemongrass, look for jars of sliced, brined lemongrass in gourmet or Asian markets.

PALM SUGAR

This minimally refined sugar is made from the sweet sap of a tropical palm; it's sold in little cakes and should be grated or chopped fine before use. It's similar in flavor to light brown sugar, which makes a good substitute.

PANDAN LEAVES

Also known as *bai toey, rampe, lá dúa,* or *screwpine,* pandan is a wide, long green grass with a sweet aroma hinting of vanilla, toasted nuts, and citrus. The most commonly available form outside of Southeast Asia is frozen pandan; it keeps well and the leaves can be torn off and added to curries or simmered in puddings; the leaves are too tough to be edible, but are sometimes used as a garnish in Sri Lankan curries. Pandan can also be purchased in an easy-to-use (and store) extract. Use ½ teaspoon as a substitute for a single 10- to 12-inch frozen pandan leaf.

SHALLOTS

Shallots are used with great enthusiasm in Southeast Asian cooking. Fried shallots are a Thai specialty, sweet crumbles that are great sprinkled into salads or soups or dusted on curries before serving. Look for small jars of ready-to-use fried shallots in Thai or Southeast Asian markets. Shallots really shine when cooked until golden brown to bring out their remarkably sweet, pungent flavors. For more about shallots, see the European ingredients list, page 25.

THAI APPLE EGGPLANT

Ranging from the size of a peach to an apricot, these round, pale green or lilac Thai "apple" eggplants can be eaten raw; they have a very mild flavor and a snappy crunch. I use them in Thai curries in this book added a minute or two before a curry is done to warm them slightly but preserve their intriguing texture.

THAI BASIL

An Asian basil with increasing popularity in Western cuisine that gives many Southeast Asian dishes a distictive fresh spicy basil aroma and flavor. It can still be difficult to find outside of Asian markets, though, so in a pinch use slightly less fresh sweet basil in a recipe. If you have a patch of dirt outside to call your own that gets plenty of sun, try growing some!

THAI GOLDEN MOUNTAIN SAUCE

Not exactly a soy sauce, this complex seasoning sauce is essential if you love pad kee mao, that addictive and flexible spicy noodle and vegetable dish (see recipes on pages 223 and 226). If you're attempting to replicate a beloved stir-fry dish from your favorite Thai restaurant and can't quite get the flavor quite right, try adding a splash or two of Golden Mountain . . . it might be just what the sauce doctor ordered.

THAI SOY SAUCES AND SEASONING SAUCES

Discovering Thai soy sauces opened up a whole new world of Thai cooking for me. Yes, you can make tasty Thai dishes with the Kikkoman stuff, but seeking out Thai sauces will really bring your game to a new level of authenticity—your pad thai and noodle dishes will taste much more like your favorite dishes from your local Thai eatery.

Most of these sauces are made from a base of soy, wheat, salt, and maybe sugar and a smattering of preservatives. I've found these sauces to be vegan, but always read the label to make sure you're not accidentally purchasing something with sneaky fish sauce. Browsing the aisles of your local Thai or Chinese grocery may reveal a mind-bending selection of sauces. I rely on just a few for homemade Thai dishes.

Mushroom Soy Sauce: A delightful twist on regular soy sauce, this soy sauce infused with shiitaki mushroom essence is bursting with layers of umami flavor. Use it in place of regular soy sauce in Chinese and Thai dishes.

Thai Thin Soy Sauce: Sometimes called "white" soy sauce, this Thai soy sauce is worth your precious time to find. Unlike standard Japanese-style soy sauces, this delicate sauce has a thin, light consistency and a clean, sharp, salty flavor without sweetness. It's my favorite substitute for fermented fish sauce in Southeast Asian cuisine. Simply switching out supermarket soy sauce for Thai sauce helps bring an authentic edge to stir fry dishes.

Thai Sweet Soy Sauce, Thai Black Soy Sauce: I've grouped these two together because they both resemble molasses, are nearly black, and have intensely sweet and salty flavors. If you don't want both bottles of these sauces taking up space, choose one (I would opt for the sweet soy sauce), but if you're feeling generous go for both. Sweet and black soy sauce have their own nuanced differences, and you'll need both for authentic tasting homemade Pad See Ew (flat rice noodles sautéed in sweet soy sauce).

African

COUSCOUS

These little hand-rolled grains of quick-cooking pasta are a nearly effortless—they are a convenient alternative to rice and an essential companion to Moroccan dishes. Israeli large-grained couscous is a tasty variation of couscous, but not my favorite for use with tagines or African cuisine. Whole wheat couscous is a tasty, whole-grain substitute for regular couscous.

MILLET

This ancient grain is a popular foodstuff in many African cuisines; after cooking, it has an interesting texture that's simultaneously crunchy, fluffy, and tender. Quick to prepare, the flavor is enhanced by lightly toasting in a little oil before boiling.

TEFF FLOUR

A light grey, whole-grain flour ground from the tiny teff seed that's packed with fiber and protein. In this book teff flour is used only for a hack of the injera crepes of Ethiopian cuisine (see page 206). Buckwheat flour is an earthy, whole grain substitute for teff and has a similar greyish color.

Natural Grocery Ingredients

Formerly known as "health food" stores, natural food stores have become a common sight in urban areas (even many big box supermarkets boast a natural foods aisle). The following ingredients are easier to find at such stores, if only for the security of knowing you're buying organic. In the case of tofu, you may want to source this from a well-known brand in a natural food store that is made from GMO-free soybeans.

Coconut Milk, Canned

You'll see "canned" when referring to coconut milk in these recipes, mostly due to the increasing popularity of coconut-based beverages that are flooding the nondairy milk market. When a recipe lists "canned coconut milk," reach for the thick, fatty, delicious stuff in cans imported from Thailand (the best quality I've found so far is Thai). Don't substitute it with the beverage designed for pouring on cereal or in coffee!

Thai canned coconut milk is excellent for both savory curries and desserts. If you're reducing the amount of fat intake in your diet, it's okay to use

Cornstarch vs. Stir-Fry

Cornstarch: it can do wonders in baking and stir-frying, but add too much and it recalls the sludgy, greasy Chinese takeout of childhood memory. For casual vegetable stir-fries I usually skip it entirely, preferring the clean flavors of vegetables paired with the simple soy or vinegar based-sauces.

But sometimes a touch of cornstarch can transform an ordinary pile of vegetables into something worthy of a properly made Chinese dish. Try this technique the next time you're craving a silky, slightly clingy sauce to surround stir-fried veggies and tofu (I especially like this technique with eggplant, bok choy, or a mix of Asian greens).

In a 2-cup liquid measuring cup (the sort shaped like a little pitcher), whisk together ¼ cup of cold water and 1 teaspoon of cornstarch. In the last 2 minutes of the stir-fry, pour only half over the stir fry. (Using this simple cornstarch slurry toward the last few minutes of cooking eliminates a lot of the guesswork and commitment of throwing it in with the soy sauce or other liquid flavorings.) Continue to stir-fry until the sauce thickens and lightly coats the vegetables. If you want it thicker, add the remaining liquid and cook until thickened. Fully cooked cornstarch won't taste powdery. Use this sauce in addition to other seasoning ingredients in the stir-fry, such as soy sauce, vinegar, or sweeteners.

reduced-fat coconut milk; good reduced-fat coconut milk can be found in Thai brands or even the reduced-fat coconut milk from Trader Joe's. Don't expect recipes made with this stuff to be exactly like full-fat coconut milk dishes, but they will be tasty all the same.

Cooking Oils
Keep it simple; the primary oils in your pantry should be neutral-tasting canola oil, olive oil, maybe another mild oil like grapeseed, and for frying, peanut oil (or high-heat canola oil for those with peanut allergies). Always buy cold-pressed, minimally refined oils, which is why you're better off buying these from natural food stores. Unrefined coconut oil is a saturated vegetable fat that when used sparingly adds rich flavor and texture to foods. I splurge occasionally on a luxury oil such as avocado; its velvety consistency adds a special lushness to **Cultured Cashew Spread with French Herbs** (page 94).

Cornstarch, Non-GMO and Organic
Cornstarch is still the cheapest and easiest-to-use thickener for sauces or as a binder in vegan baking. Skip the grocery store stuff and opt for organic brands made from non-GMO sources; Whole Foods, Trader Joe's, and online on Amazon are good places to seek out organic cornstarch.

Garbanzo Bean (Chickpea) Flour
Garbanzo beans (also known as chickpeas) can be ground up into a smooth, golden flour that adds protein and rich umami flavor to seitan dough and batters and is useful as a thickener in stews. It's a common ingredient in Indian food. Look for high-quality garbanzo bean flour in natural food stores or in Indian markets called "besan gram" flour. Don't substitute other bean flours (such as soy) for garbanzo bean flour.

Lemon and Lime Juice

Unless specified, bottled lemon and lime juice is perfectly acceptable to use in these recipes. I'm busy, you're busy, and who the heck has time to juice lemons, especially when the end result will be cooked. I try to use organic citrus juices whenever possible.

Nondairy Milks (soy, almond, rice, etc.)

With so many options for cow-less milks available, use what the recipe suggests or ultimately use your favorite. Almond, soy, coconut-based milk (not to be confused with canned coconut milk), rice milk, and sometimes hemp milk are my current favorites.

Never use old-fashioned powdered nondairy creamer in any vegan recipe. It was designed only for use in coffee decades ago and is full of nasty fake ingredients. Just never touch it, period.

Seitan

The super-trio of vegan proteins—seitan, tempeh and tofu—are special because not only are they great sources of protein, but in theory you could make all of these yourself at home, therefore escaping the label of factory-made "fake meat," at least in my book.

While you may need a fairly elaborate setup to make your own tofu, making homemade seitan is stupidly easy and fast, especially if it's steamed or baked "cutlets" of seitan (my favorite method of all time). You'll find a recipe on page 49. There's also no shame in purchasing seitan; it will probably be more expensive than either tempeh or tofu, but sometimes the convenience pays for itself. In the United States, Westbrae and White Wave make a few varieties of water-packed seitan in chunks, flakes, and ground form.

Soy Sauce

Crack open any vegetarian cookbook from the '70s through the '90s (and in some cases, even today), and you'll see the particular kind of Japanese soy sauce known as tamari as a common ingredient, even in non-Asian dishes. Sometimes it's practically in everything, even dessert (ugh).

While modern vegan cooking doesn't require tamari to be in everything, soy sauce still plays an important role, especially in seasoning soy foods. In this book you'll see soy sauce primarily used in Asian recipes and in making homemade seitan. In some instances I'll ask you to purchase ethnic-specific soy

Gotta Get It Gluten Free

If you avoid gluten you're probably already adept at making substitutions. Or maybe you just want to make something gluten free for a friend. Over the course of testing these recipes, a few gluten-free substitutions came in handy:

↻ Try substituting finely pulsed Rice Chex cereal to replace panko breadcrumbs

↻ Gluten-free regular breadcrumbs can be used in place of regular breadcrumbs in any recipe

↻ In place of any soy sauce, use gluten-free tamari (the end result won't taste the same, but it should still be tasty). But steer clear of recipes that call for vegetarian stir-fry and hoisin sauce, as these contain wheat; as a substitute use 2 teaspoons of tamari plus 1 teaspoon of agave nectar per tablespoon of sauce. Consider using a cornstarch slurry (page 20) to thicken up the dish if it's a stir-fry.

↻ Use a packaged gluten-free baking mix in place of wheat flour; if you'd rather bake from scratch, both the *Ethiopian Chocolate Flourless Torte* (page 340) and *Italian Cashewcotta Cheesecake* (page 337) are naturally gluten free.

DIY Tofu Pressing

Why press tofu at all? Physically pressing tofu down for an extended period of time helps remove some of the excess water. The resulting tofu is firmer, making it easier to slice or stir-fry and hold together. Pressed tofu also mops up marinades for more flavorful tofu. Try pressing tofu for any of the recipes in this book and taste the difference. The exception to the tofu rule is silken tofu, which is best only gently drained before pureeing for use.

To press a block of firm, or extra-firm tofu, slice tofu in half, then slice each half again. One last time slice each piece in half; you should have eight pieces of tofu of the same thickness for a typical 1-pound block of tofu.

Layer a large cutting board with clean kitchen towels or paper towels, then arrange the tofu slices on top in a single layer (the slices can touch, it's okay). Top with another towel, then another cutting board. Securely place a few heavy things on top to press (thick books, large cans or jars, lazy cats). Press for a minimum of 20 minutes to up to an hour. The tofu will seep out water as it presses, so take care to prop this arrangement near the sink on a slight angle.

If constructing an oversized Jenga tower in your kitchen doesn't sound like much fun, consider purchasing a tofu press. For more on tofu presses, see page 31.

sauces (Thai and Chinese sauces, for instance), but if I just ask for soy sauce, you can use a fairly generic Japanese brand such as Kikkoman or an inexpensive Chinese-style thin soy sauce.

Note: while I love old-school vegetarian hero Bragg's Liquid Seasoning as much as the next guy, it is *not* a substitute for soy sauce. Save it for your next lentil casserole vegan potluck (it's perfectly fine used there), but don't use it in Asian dishes.

Tempeh

This dense, toothsome, fermented soybean cake with flavor notes of mushroom and fresh yeast has escaped its Indonesian origins and run wild over the foodscape of vegan cuisine for years. Tempeh tastes best first steamed, then marinated and either braised or grilled.

Natural food stores and gourmet markets now stock varieties that include all kinds of ingredients for flavor and texture including millet, wild rice, herbs, vegetables, rice, and barley. Go nuts and use any kind of flavored tempeh for the recipes in this book.

Tofu

This book uses several kinds of tofu for different effects in entrees, sauces, toppings, and dessert. Almost all of these can be found in natural food stores and pan-Asian grocery stores. Use the kind of tofu suggested in each recipe. Generally, the softer the tofu, the greater the concentration of water it contains.

Firm, extra-firm, and super-firm tofu: All are excellent tofu for roasting, grilling, and marinating in savory dishes. Pressing tofu will help the tofu taste better and greatly improve the texture. Super-firm tofu is a more recent style of tofu that's so dense you can skip the pressing step and go straight to marinating it (after draining it first).

Soft tofu: This tender tofu is good for scrambles and blended up for creamy toppings. Not to be confused with silken tofu, it has a slightly grainy texture with compact curds like firm tofu.

Silken tofu: soft, firm, and extra-firm varieties: Silken is a special style of tofu, most often seen in Japanese and Korean cuisine. It has a delightfully delicate, custard-like texture that's perfect for making desserts and creamy sauces and may be used in savory dishes in Asian cuisine. It comes in soft, firm, and extra-firm varieties and can be purchased in special shelf-stable boxes; the most common brand of this kind of silken tofu found in the United States is Mori-Nu. In a pinch you can use firm silken tofu in place of soft and extra-firm silken tofu.

If a recipe calls for silken tofu, don't substitute it with regular soft tofu; the texture is too grainy, the flavor too beany, and the final dish won't be the same.

Vegetable Broth and Vegetarian Bouillon Cubes and Pastes

If you have the time to make your own vegetable broth, then feel free to skip this info. But if you're like the rest of us, packaged vegetable broth and vegetarian bouillon pastes are a huge time-saver and add essential richness and depth to soups, stews, curries, and sauces.

Generally I recommend tasting a wide selection of broths to find the one you like the best. Unfortunately many vegetable broths (those available in cans or shelf-stable boxes) don't taste very good and have overly bitter or cabbagelike flavors. They do have the advantage of having a few low sodium offerings, if that's a feature that's important to you.

What I prefer are broths made from bouillon cubes and pastes. These products generally have stronger, sharper flavors with richer umami notes.

My favorite brand is Better Than Bouillon, which currently offers an organic vegetable paste and two meatless vegetarian "chicken" and "beef" flavors that make an excellent base for soups and sauces. These pastes also have the advantage over boxed broths and cubes in that you can prepare as little or as much as you need by whisking a small amount of paste into hot water. Made to taste, I usually use a third less in a recipe than the recommended amount of paste, or make an extra concentrated small batch for reduced-fat sautéing (page 7).

Regarding broth and salt: purchased vegetable broth can be salty, and this affects the total amount of salt needed in a recipe. Taste your broth before using; if it's very salty you may not need to add any salt at all; I find this especially true with sauces or seitan recipes. If it tastes like it could use some salt, start with the suggested amount and add more toward the end of cooking.

SHOPPING LISTS

When shopping at ethnic markets and natural food stores, having an all-purpose shopping list or two kept on hand can make dinner out of a handful of impulse purchases.

No doubt you have a store or two in your neighborhood that blends a few ethnicities, so you might be able to combine a few shopping trips in one stop. Ingredients also can overlap ethnicities (green papaya appearing in Chinese and Thai markets, for instance).

Photocopy and keep a list in the glove compartment of your car, or folded and tucked away into your reusable shopping bags. Or even better, download the PDF from my site **veganlatina.com** to your phone and be ready when the opportunity for Thai soy sauce or curry leaves strikes.

INDIAN

Produce:
Cilantro
Fresh curry leaves
Frozen grated coconut (freezer isle)
Mangoes, unripe

Spices:
Black mustard seeds
Black peppercorns
Cardamom pods, green or black
Cardamom seeds
Coriander seeds
Cumin seeds
Dried Indian chile peppers

Dry Goods:
Atta flour for chappati and paratha
Basmati rice, white or brown
Cashews
Dried beans: split red lentils, chickpeas, pigeon peas, etc.
Dried, unsweetened grated coconut
Garbanzo (besan) flour
Pistachios, without shells
Puffed rice (for bhel puri)
Sev (fried chickpea noodles for bhel puri)

CHINESE AND SOUTHEAST ASIAN

Produce, Fresh and Frozen:
Asian eggplants
Asian greens: gai lan, bok choy, napa cabbage
Garlic chives
Frozen pandan leaves
Green papaya
Long green beans

Prepared Sauces, Vinegars, and Oils:
Black vinegar
Chinese Shaoxing cooking wine
Chinese white sesame paste
Dried shiitaki mushrooms
Hoisin sauce

Peanut oil
Toban djan chile bean sauce
Toasted sesame oil
Vegetarian stir fry sauce

Noodles, Rice, and Such:
Fresh, refrigerated eggless wonton wrappers
Fresh, refrigerated eggless wheat noodles
Frozen spring roll wrappers (check for vegan ingredients)
Short-grain sweet (sticky) rice

SOUTHEAST ASIAN (THAI OR VIETNAMESE) AND FILIPINO

Fresh produce:
Canned or frozen unsweetened jackfruit
Fresh galangal root
Shredded or whole green papaya
Thai apple eggplants

Sauces and Dry Goods:
Filipino coconut or palm sap vinegar
Filipino soy sauce
Golden Mountain seasoning sauce
Jasmine rice
Mung bean threads (or noodles)
Pandan extract
Round rice paper sheets
Thai canned coconut milk
Thai black soy sauce
Thai thin soy sauce
Thai sweet soy sauce

JAPANESE AND KOREAN

Produce and Refrigerated:
Asian eggplant
Asian pear
Gyoza wrappers (check for vegan ingredients)
Mung bean sprouts
Napa cabbage (for kimchi!)
Refrigerated or frozen udon noodles
Scallions

Dry Goods:
Dried seaweed: aonori, kombu, hijiki
Dried soba and udon noodles
Gochugaru (Korean red pepper powder for kimchi)
Miso, shiro (white)
Panko crumbs (check label for vegan ingredients)
Plain rice wine vinegar
Short grain sushi rice
Toasted white sesame seeds

LATINA AND CARIBBEAN
Produce and Fresh Goods:
Avocado
Cilantro
Fresh corn tortillas
Jicama
Limes
Plantains

Dry goods:
Canned chipotles in adobo sauce
Dried Mexican chile peppers (ancho, guajillo, pequin),
    whole or powdered
Masa harina
Quinoa

MEDITERRANEAN, MIDDLE EASTERN, AFRICAN
Dry Goods and Frozen:
Aleppo red pepper flakes
Baharat spice blend
Berber spice blend
Bulgur wheat, peeled #3 large grain and fine grain #1
Couscous, regular or whole wheat
Dried bay leaves (the best are from Mediterranean
    markets)
Frozen or refrigerated filo (also spelled phyllo) dough,
    especially #10 thick country-style
Greek oregano (more flavorful than supermarket
    oregano)
High-quality dried dates (such as majoul or medjool)
    and apricots
High-quality extra-virgin olive oil

Miskos #2 hollow tube pasta (for Greek pastichio)
Pistachios, without shells
Pomegranate molasses
Ras-el-hanout spice blend
Really fresh pita bread (from folder-thin Lebanese pita
    to thick to puffy Isreali-style and everything
    in between)
Small brown Egyptian fava beans (ful medames)

EUROPEAN
Fresh or Refrigerated:
Bulk or refrigerated sauerkraut
Fresh brown mushrooms
Fresh dill

Dry goods:
Belgian ale
Red wine vinegar
Rye flour

NATURAL FOOD STORES
Refrigerated:
Plain soy or coconut yogurt, preferably unsweetened
    for savory dishes
Organic Tofu
    Super-firm
    Extra-firm
    Medium and soft
    Silken, soft through extra-firm varieties
Tempeh
Vegan margarine, nonhydrogenated
Vegan mayonnaise

Dry Goods:
Garbanzo bean flour (if you want a smaller bag than
    what's sold in Indian markets)
High quality, nonhydrogenated shortening
Millet
Nutritional yeast flakes
Organic quinoa
Teff flour
Vital wheat gluten flour (for seitan)

KITCHEN EQUIPMENT

Years of living, cooking, and eating in teeny little urban kitchens has made me somewhat ruthless when it comes to kitchen equipment. If it can't do its primary function and a few side jobs with aplomb, it's not worth the time and money. Same goes for most ethnic cookware; you can cook like you've traveled the world without owning a comal for tortillas, a paella pan, or a Thai sticky rice pot. *Do* consider a wok though, if you don't already have one.

Read along if you're building your kitchen from the ground up, or even if there's only a wok-shaped hole in your heart.

Knives

Do yourself a favor: Stop chopping vegetables with an old steak knife stolen from your mom's kitchen drawer and get yourself a real knife. A hard-working, decent-quality chef's knife can be purchased for the price of a movie ticket and dinner, so you can keep up your Himalayan pink salt habit *and* have a good-quality knife that will last for years, if not forever.

→ A chef's knife is the large, single-edged knife you've seen in a million cooking shows and horror movies, typically having a blade that's 8 to 10 inches long. Don't bother with anything smaller (or larger) than that for your first chef's knife.

→ A good-quality chef's knife should have a tang, an extension of the blade, that runs the entire length of the handle. On most good knives you can see the tang, a long metal line, extending down the entire handle. Cheap knives will feel a somewhat light in your dominant hand, will not have a tang in the entire handle, and typically have a flimsy-feeling blade. Go for knives that feel heavy and have a solid, dense handle; a heavier knife means you need to work less when chopping veggies.

→ Avoid chef's knives with a serrated edge; usually seen on cheap knives, they make it virtually impossible to resharpen the blade. Direct your hard-earned cash towards a knife with a smooth edge and not seen on late-night television infomercials.

→ Good, inexpensive brands include: Cuisinart, Kitchen Aide, Calphalon, even IKEA's 360+ line. Check out discounted home supply stores with ample kitchen sections such as Marshall's, T. J. Maxx, World Market, and Home Goods and look for a good-quality knife at a discounted price.

→ It's better to purchase the knives you need separately and avoid packed knife sets. This ensures you'll own only the ones you need and better-quality ones at that. Plus you won't end up with the clutter

Sensational Santoku Knives

It's hard not to feel lust at first sight with the pretty colors and gorgeous finishes of santoku knives, the Japanese parallel to the chef's knife. Before you succumb to your want, there's something very key to keep in mind: the cutting technique is very different from a chef's knife—instead of a rocking motion, santoku knives use a rapid up and down chopping motion. It's a different school of knife technique that should be observed when using these knives.

A santoku knife isn't necessary if you're already proficient with a regular chef's knife, but they offer a cleaver-like advantage for attacking big, thick vegetables such as winter squash and hefty root vegetables. I also found that a less-expensive santoku knife can be a fun entry-level knife, especially if you're an old hand with a chef's knife.

Board of Cutting? Slice It Up on Better Cutting Surfaces!

For serious cooking, a dedicated cutting surface that will be kind to your cutting surfaces and your knives is essential.

There are two schools when it comes to cutting boards: wood or plastic. There's also paper and cardboard, but more on that later.

Both wood and plastic have their advantages and drawbacks. Wood looks nice, and bamboo in particular can take a beating without beating up the edge of your knives. They cannot be washed in a dishwasher and need a certain amount of TLC with the occasional oiling to prevent cracking. Some studies have shown that bacteria tend to not reproduce as rapidly on wood surfaces as they may on plastic.

Plastic cutting boards are cheap, can be tossed in the dish washer, and don't require much care. They can look rather drab, and not as pleasing after years of use (unlike wood, which can look better with time and care). But by all means avoid those thin, oddly foldable vinyl cutting mats. They're terrible for knife edges and are unpleasant to cut on. Same goes for glass cutting boards.

There are also interesting cutting boards made from recycled, compressed materials such as paper, cardboard, wood pulp, plastic yogurt cups, and other postconsumer materials. They typically have a smooth matte finish, can be washed in a dishwasher, are fairly resistant to bacteria and odor, are easy on knife edges, and seem to have the best of both wood and plastic worlds. They're a little pricey, but their modern looks, durability and low maintenance make them an exciting new choice in the wild world of cutting boards. As you can probably guess, I love these technologically advanced boards.

Regardless of your choice of cutting board, to keep it from swimming around the counter top while you're chopping (a sure way to cut yourself), lay a folded dish towel under the board or in a pinch, a damp paper towel. This will keep it stable and slide-free.

of knives you won't use (like that deboning knife, not so essential for slicing tofu).

→ The mantra of so many of great chefs: a few knives can prepare everything. A chef's knife OR santoku knife (see the previous page for more on santoku knives) is good for everyday use. A little paring knife is handy; consider a "bird's beak" hooked blade if you like your vegetables precision trimmed. If you purchase lots of rustic bread with thick crusts, consider a heavy bread knife with a well made, scalloped edge; after you slice the bread, you can effortlessly slice tomatoes if your chef's knife is a little dull.

→ Now that you have a nice knife, learn how to use it. I give you some basic shapes/slicing and dicing info on page 4. The basic motion of using a chef's knife is a rocking motion, starting from the back of the knife and rocking over and on top of food. This is done relatively fast; celery is the classic practice veggie when learning knife skills. Don't lift the knife up and down from the cutting board, just rock it rapidly over food and let the knife do the work. If you're unsure what this looks like, do an internet search for a demonstration of basic chef's knife technique.

→ Get your knife regularly sharpened. My recommendation: once again, the internet is your friend and can guide you to a kitchen store or hardware store near you that will do the job for you. Very likely they can do it quickly and efficiently at a respectable price. Unless you have a lot of time on your hands or want to seem more menacing at parties ("just before talking to you, I was sharpening my knives in the basement . . ."), leave knife sharpening to the pros. Or if you do want to learn to sharpen your own knives, a Japanese whet stone and water (instead of messy oil) are a good start, but I strongly suggest taking a knife-sharpening class to get real hands-on instruction from a professional. That and load up your computer queue with lot of movies, because it's going to take some time to get that knife as sharp as the day you bought it on your own.

⊙ Interesting fact: a steel (that long swordlike thing that sometimes comes with a chef's knife), is not so much for sharpening the edge of the knife but helping keep the blade straight.

Skill-et, Measure It, Strain It, Steam It
SKILLETS AND SAUCEPANS
You don't need an army of pots and pans, just one of the following: a large 10- to 12-inch skillet (preferably with a lid), two sauce pans (2 quart and 3 quart, with lids), and a really big soup pot (at least 4 quart, 6 or 8 is better). A big, cast-iron Dutch oven (just a big squat pot with a lid) is optional but very useful. The rest as they say is gravy. Here's my take on the common materials they're crafted from.

CAST IRON
Ultra heavy duty and hardier working, a properly seasoned cast iron pan will outlive you and generations to come. It's kind of impressive to imagine that in a world of disposable stuff! For more on cast-iron cookware, see page 33.

CARBON STEEL
Love the durability of cast iron but not the weight? Consider carbon steel pans, a heavy-duty, unfinished, dark grey steel that requires a little bit of seasoning (just like cast iron), but conducts heat more efficiently and usually weighs a little less. Often imported from France, these are high-quality pans that don't come cheap but can last a lifetime and when properly seasoned are even better at preventing food from sticking than nonstick pans. My crepe pan is a French carbon steel pan and it's given me years of free flying crepes and pancakes.

STAINLESS STEEL
The choice of professional chefs, shiny stainless steel pans are the important *other* pan in your kitchen besides cast iron. Stainless steel pots and one deep, 12-inch skillet (preferably with a lid) are fantastic for simmering tomato soups and acidic, wine-based sauces, as the nonreactive nature of stainless steel won't give acidic foods an off-flavor or color that cast iron may. There are expensive fancy brands (All Clad) and mid-range (Cuisinart), but the IKEA 365+ line has a range of affordable, tough stainless-steel sauté pans and pots that look nice and are nearly pro grade.

"GREEN" NONSTICK PANS
Nonstick cookware can be a sticky situation; it offers the convenience of easy cleaning and the promise of low-fat cooking; it's virtually everywhere and unavoidable and is commonly used on low-cost pans and bakeware. But it can be loaded with really nasty chemicals, most notably PFOA and PTFE, two chemicals that have been putting a serious strain on the environment and our bodies. If overheated (ironic, since this a coating put on cookware!), these chemicals release fumes that have been shown to kill birds, and you know what they say about the canary in the coal mine. . . .

With that, I've been avoiding nonstick pans and pots for years. But recently there have been developments in "greener" nonstick that don't have these chemicals. I'm a fan of well-seasoned cast iron, which does as good a job or better at nonstick cooking as any nonstick cookware. But if you must use nonstick, shop for these updated nonstick pans (and as always, never use metal utensils on nonstick cookware). While the jury is still out on how great these pans are, they seem to do a decent enough job for a little while, but seem to lose a degree of non-stickiness over time and can't stand up to constant use like uncoated cookware can.

PYREX (TEMPERED GLASS) LIQUID MEASURING CUPS

Nice to look at and hard working, these heat-tempered glass liquid measuring cups and dishes will serve you for years to come. Start your collection with 2-cup and 4-cup liquid measuring cup, plus a basic 9 x 13-inch rectangular pan.

FINE WIRE MESH STRAINERS

Get a selection of sizes; often they can be purchased bundled together in diameters of 2, 5, and 7 inches. Essential for rinsing quinoa and my favorite accessory for the mess-free steaming of sticky rice!

STEAMER SETUP

Steaming is an easy, fast, and valuable method of cooking food. Make a note of which cooking method (wok, rice cooker, pasta pot) you already use and build your steamer setup around it.

→ Asian bamboo steamers that are designed to be fitted over a wok or similar wide pot. Cheap and nice to look at, but they can be cabinet space hogs in small kitchens.

→ Some rice cookers (usually the more affordable ones) come equipped with steaming baskets. Perfect if you already want to buy a rice cooker and are looking for a useful extra feature.

→ My own standby: A large stainless steel pasta pot fitted with a small steamer basket inside, the sort that hovers at least 6 inches from the bottom of the pan. Look for 8- to 12-quart 4-piece pot sets that come with a lid and a few steamer baskets, usually a smaller one for steaming food well above the water and a deeper basket that serves as a colander. Overstock and Amazon are great places to look for nice deals on these setups. I promise you'll use it all the time, and when not steaming stuff you can boil sticky-free pasta or make a huge batch of soup!

I'm not crazy about those fan-like steaming trivets that can be fitted inside a pan, as they leave too little space between the water and your food; properly steamed food should never touch water. Listen to me and get yourself a great big pasta multipot!

My motto: if you can get by in the kitchen with what you already have (and it's not a total pain in the butt that prevents you from seriously steaming food), then keep using it!

WOK ON BUY

Avoid cheap, nonstick woks. Standard nonstick pans are not designed for high-heat cooking, and since a wok is all about high-heat cooking, this unholy mix should be avoided. See the Carbon Steel Wok section on page 33 for details on how to season affordable, hard-working carbon steel woks for years of nonstick cooking.

→ Cast-iron woks have the nonstick advantages of other cast-iron pans, but can be expensive, extremely heavy, and cumbersome to use. If you want to be able to flip your food around a wok like a pro, skip these woks in favor of affordable and authentic carbon steel.

↪ 14 inches is the standard "home" size for woks, but I prefer a slightly smaller 12-inch wok for tight kitchen spaces. You'll appreciate the extra space on your cramped stove range that this petite wok provides, perfect for families of three or fewer.

↪ Perhaps it's a personal preference, but I recommend flat-bottom woks in favor of rounded-bottom woks that need a ring for support, especially if your stovetop is electric. A flat-bottom wok works great on a gas range, too. Also pass on woks that come with 16 pieces of other stuff. That's just more kitchen flair you'll need to store and sort. Less is more.

↪ A wok with a lid is handy, but I bet you already have a lid from a 10- or 12-inch pan that if you ask it nicely would be more than a happy to lend itself to your wok.

Grate It, Mash It
Y-SHAPED VEGETABLE PEELER

The easiest to hold and maneuver over bumpy root vegetables, Y-shaped peelers are superior to old-fashioned handle peelers. Purchase these in a bundled three-pack on Amazon or any kitchen supply store. A plain blade is a good multipurpose peeler, and a serrated blade is good for taking off the tough skins of winter squash.

Y-SHAPED JULIENNE PEELER

This special Y-shaped peeler deserves its own mention. It's a fabulous little tool for transforming an ordinary carrot, daikon, or even unripe mango or papaya into perfect little matchsticks, great for garnishes, salads, soups, or stir-fries. Fast, easy to use, and almost no cleanup compared to food processors or mandolins, run out and get one if you don't already have one.

Wok Talk

For years I resisted purchasing a wok; I thought I could live without and get similar results in a cast-iron pan. Well, after caving in and finally buying one, I realized what I was missing. The large, convex shape and high heat–conducting materials (always carbon steel) really will make your stir-fries taste authentic, and the speed and ease of cooking will lure you into making curries, stews, scrambled tofu, and the occasional fried dumpling in the wok too.

For wok beginners, shop for a wok made from carbon steel. Carbon steel is reasonably light, conducts high heat beautifully, and when properly seasoned will develop a naturally nonstick finish. Carbon steel woks are reasonably priced, too; browse online stores like World Market and Amazon for well-made and authentic woks. For more on the care, feeding, and usage of carbon steel woks, see page 33.

MANDOLIN

A mandolin is just a flat board with a sharp blade stuck in the center, made for running vegetables across its surface for paper-thin slices of potato or shreds of carrot or cabbage, to name a few uses. Available at a range of prices, from simple Japanese models to more elaborate American brands with a selection of removable blades. While I love using a julienne peeler for quick small jobs, I whip out the mandolin for larger tasks like shredding up a head of cabbage for soup or a bundle of daikon for pickles.

MICROPLANE GRATER

A flat, handheld grater that's perfect for grating

lemon zest, ginger, nutmeg, even garlic or any firm food into fine particles. Cheap and easy to store, you'll find plenty of uses for it.

MORTAR AND PESTLE

Possessing old-fashioned chic and hard-working sensibilities, a mortar and pestle still has a place in modern kitchens. It makes beautiful garlic paste in minutes, and if you're feeling really industrious, it will pound spices and fresh herbs into curry pastes with intriguing textures; use this for curry pastes instead of a food processor and see for yourself (and get a free upper-arm workout as a bonus).

POTATO MASHER

Another oldie but goodie, potato mashers get the job done quickly and cheaply. Also great for tender beans, squash, or potatoes in soup or stews.

Plug It In: Appliances

IMMERSION BLENDER

Also called a stick blender or submersion blender, this is a blender in a handy stick form that will get you through pots of hot creamy soups, curry pastes, dressings, sauces, and even smoothies without the hassle of cleaning up a blender pitcher or food processor. Even if you already own a standard blender, you'll find scores of uses for this handy kitchen appliance.

Shop for models that come with bells and whistles like a mini food processor bowl, a wide blade for blending hot soups in pots, a whisk for dressings and sauces, and a pitcher or cup for dressings and smoothies.

As with any appliance, but especially hand-held blenders, always unplug before cleaning or changing the blades.

The Pressure's On: The Tofu Press Comes of Age

The good old days of tofu pressing weren't always so good. First, bring out the cutting boards and the paper towels or scramble through the drawers looking for clean kitchen towels. Assemble something akin to a giant Jenga tower with these boards, towels, cookbooks, 20-ounce cans of tomatoes, jam jars, cinder blocks, or whatever on top of the tofu. Wait for 30 minutes and pray that the jiggly tofu foundation doesn't rebel against this oppressive regime and send the tower tumbling. And if all goes well, there's still a puddle of tofu juice sliding onto the floor.

Up until recently I subjected my tofu to such barbarity. And this method still works. But curiosity drove me to want something better for *both* me and my pressed tofu.

I caved and got a tofu press. An internet search will reveal a few options; as of this writing I own a Tofu Xpress press, but there are other interesting designs available, including simpler presses with fewer moving parts (meaning less stuff to break). Of all the few single-use appliances in my life, this one is a keeper.

If you consume tofu at least two times a week, go and buy one already. The quality of the pressed tofu is superior to anything made under a pile of reading material. It soaks up marinades and stands up to stir frying with unparalleled vigor. And when I want to play Jenga, the cookbooks and canned tomatoes can stay the hell out of my tower.

Seasoning a Brand New Carbon Steel Wok

1. Admire that mirror-like silver shine on that brand new wok for the first and final time. Once seasoned, your new wok may look old, but its purple-black finish will grow on you with its rustic cool.

2. Wash the outside and inside of the unseasoned wok with mild soap, warm water, and a plastic or steel wool scrubber pad. Rinse well and wipe the wok down completely dry. This is also the only time you'll probably use soap on your wok. Don't skip this step though! You absolutely need to remove the machine oils from the factory from both the outside and inside of the wok; leave it on and your food will taste like the bottom of a factory floor.

3. Heat the wok over high heat. Occasionally tilt and rotate the wok on the burner until the metal turns a yellowish-grey or grey-blue color. It will develop mostly on the bottom two-thirds of the wok, so if possible rotate the wok on its side occasionally to help heat up the sides. Keep doing this for about 10 to 15 minutes. Be careful, the wok will be very hot throughout the seasoning process.

4. Remove the wok from the heat. Crumple up a paper towel and dip one end in high-heat vegetable oil, such as refined peanut oil. Securely grab it with long-handled metal tongs and rub it over the entire surface of the inside of the wok; be generous and coat everything. Optionally, rub a light coating of oil over the outside of the wok only once, but be sure to wipe any residue away before heating.

5. Return the wok to the stove over medium-low heat. Heat for 10 minutes, occasionally rotating the wok. Turn off the heat and use a clean paper towel (held by tongs or a silicon baking mitt) and wipe down the insides thoroughly to remove as much brown residue as possible. During the seasoning process, the wok will darken in color, ranging from brownish-grey to blackish-blue.

6. Repeat oiling the inside of the wok again, heating for 10 minutes over medium-low heat, and wiping down another two to four times. The wok is ready when no brownish-black residue can be wiped away from the insides.

FOOD PROCESSOR

This is another appliance that can get as expensive or complex as money can buy, but sometimes the cheapest, simplest models are best. Avoid the overly elaborate processors with multiple bowls and parts in favor of simpler appliances with a single, generous 6-cup bowl and a few blades including a basic chopping blade and a shredding dish for the fast shredding of carrots and other hard vegetables.

COFFEE GRINDER, AKA THE PERFECT SPICE GRINDER

There's no need to shop for spice grinders when the best ones available are humble electric coffee grinders. These do a better job than most spice mills ever could and are relatively cheap ($20 or less) and low maintenance. Make sure the grinding jar and top can be thrown in the dishwasher for no-hassle cleanup between grinding jobs. If you love your coffee and freshly ground spices, consider a dedicated coffee mill just for spices.

HANDHELD MIXER AND STANDING MIXERS

Whichever you prefer. For the recipes in this book a handheld mixer will get the job done, but if you and your KitchenAid cannot bear to be parted, go right ahead.

CARBON STEEL WOK

Real woks, the carbon steel kind, are a great example of a timeless cooking vessel that with a little bit of forethought will last forever. Light, cheap, and great at conducting high heat quickly and efficiently, a well-used carbon steel wok will develop over time a naturally nonstick coating.

Cast-Iron Cookware

Cast-iron cookware is hipper than ever: it lasts forever, it's easier on the environment than nonstick, its ability to retain and distribute heat in an even and lengthy manner make it fantastic for beautifully browned foods, and it makes you feel like a badass using it.

However, there sometimes feels like an aura of mystery and snobbery around its care and usage. Cast iron was originally the cookware of pioneers, explorers, and other salt-of-the-earth folk, so don't let this high-minded prattle about 20-hour season-

Wok Maintenance

A newly seasoned wok may require a repeat of the seasoning every three to four uses, but just one or two oiling/heating/wiping sessions should do it. As the seasoned finish develops, you may only need to do this every few months, or maybe never.

While the wok is still new, you may have the occasional recipe that's a little sticky and requires a steel scrubber or a touch of warm soapy water to clean. If so, lightly season it again as described.

When your wok is really well seasoned, nothing will stick to it for long. For most dishes, I rinse with hot water and quickly scrub down the insides with a bamboo cleaning whisk, which is a stiff, hardy brush made from bamboo sprigs that does a fantastic job at scrubbing away sticky food debris from the surface of a well-cured wok without soap. When done scrubbing, rinse the bamboo brush with hot water and set aside to completely dry before storing.

If the patina inside the wok looks a little worn out in spots, repeat the seasoning process one or two times. And remember, the best way to maintain a wok is to use it all the time!

ing with artisanal bacon drippings put you off from using this excellent cooking medium. Here are my short and sweet tips for becoming an iron woman or man in the kitchen.

PURCHASE PRESEASONED COOKWARE

Ignore the snobs that say you must have a 100-year-old skillet passed down from your lumberjack ancestors and that it can only be seasoned using free-range lard. You can purchase wonderful, perfectly blackened brand new preseasoned cast iron online, in many kitchen supply stores, and at bargain prices at discount home-goods stores. The hard work has already been done for you with preseasoned cast iron; your job is now to expend a little effort to keep its good looks going. The difference is immediately apparent; unseasoned cast iron has a dull grey finish and preseasoned skillets and pots have a black finish with a subtle sheen. In the United States, Lodge cookware is a popular choice for preseasoned cast iron that requires minimal care.

Follow the manufacturer's directions for the initial "pre-preseasoning" of preseasoned pans. This may involve the first (and only time) of washing it with soap to remove the factory coating of oil from the surface. Afterwards, use a solid vegetable shortening instead of animal-based fats the first time you grease the pan (in the manufacturer's instructions for the first use of the pan). You'll be using only a thin layer and wiping it off, so don't worry that you'll be eating tons of this. For this initial seasoning, liquid vegetable oils are generally not recommended as they can oxidize into a sticky film on the surface of a pan. However, the more you use your pan, the less of a concern this will be (see "Use It or Lose It" below).

You can scrub a seasoned cast-iron pan once in a while after frying up a sticky dish (tofu with sweet marinades, for instance), but only if you lightly reseason it immediately after. Dry the wet pan over a hot stove, and when it cools down enough to handle, rub the surface with a thin coating of vegetable shortening or flaxseed oil.

Use It or Lose It

A seasoned finish on cast iron, like your muscles and your brain, gets better with use, but dimishes if neglected. While there is some truth to the notion of most vegetable oils eventually becoming sticky when used to season cast iron, it's mainly due to rubbing it with these oils and then not using the pans for days or weeks. Use your cast-iron pans every day, or even every other day, and its nonstick properties will be enhanced. That means the best way to keep cast iron well seasoned is to keep cooking with it! Frying oily foods once in a while can help; what better excuse to make the occasional treat of tostones or fried pierogi other than "my cast iron pan *needs* this"?

PART 2

THE RECIPES

CHAPTER 1

spice blends

American grocery-store shelves are alive with spice combinations; chipotles, curry powder, and unusual mash-ups of herbs and spices run wild like never seen before. I promise you can cook any recipe in this book and never have to grind a thing in your coffee mill other than beans for your morning brew. But, if the cheap and plentiful spices at an Indian grocery store make you daydream of freshly toasted garam masala, or you need to make a Jamaican vegetable curry right now, or if the secret to authentic-tasting Ethiopian food keeps eluding you, step right in.

I understand if making spice blends from scratch can seem overwhelming, but believe that it takes mere minutes to grind up fresh and uber-fragrant blends. The **Spiced Buttery Oil** (page 44) is an advanced move in spice blends; *niter kibbe* is the "masala" submerged in flavor-transporting fats that give Ethiopian food its depth and richness. These homemade mixes should be used within 3 months, but when properly stored, they're so fresh even months after they'll still taste better than store-bought blends.

For all you recycling fans: old glass spice bottles are perfect for storing your blends. Make sure the bottle is clean and absolutely dry before filling. After washing, I like to position bottles upside down on top of the radiator; the hot air dries the insides of the bottle perfectly in no time at all. A dedicated blast with a hot hairdryer works, too.

All of these spice blends are **45**, **$**, **123**, **G**, **S**. With the exception of the Olive Oil Harissa Paste and Spiced Buttery Oil, the rest are **LOW FAT**.

Garam Masala

MAKES ALMOST ½ CUP

My all-time favorite spice blend: good Indian curry powders can be purchased ready to go, but fragrant homemade garam masala makes anything (even dessert) irresistible and warming. And I love the slightly coarse, rustic texture of this homemade version.

I use a mixture of ground spices and whole spices, which are cheap and plentiful in Indian groceries. Some better-stocked Indian markets may even stock prepackaged whole spices for garam masala, sometimes including whole sticks of cinnamon and both green and black cardamom. These are convenient, but at home you'll need to sort out the seeds for even toasting (see note).

Working with cardamom pods is easy: with your fingers or the tip of a sharp paring knife, open the cardamom pods and remove the seeds. I usually find it easiest to slice each pod horizontally, break open the pod, and shake out the seeds. Discard the empty pods.

If you don't care for picking apart cardamom pods, look for cardamom seeds in the spice isle of your Indian grocery.

If you do purchase a package of whole-spice garam masala, empty the bag on a large dinner plate and set aside any large chunky spices (cardamom pods, star anise, bay leaves, cinnamon sticks) from the small seeds (cumin, fennel, coriander, cloves). Toast the fine seeds together, then toast the large spices in individual batches. This will ensure the spices are evenly toasted.

14 green cardamom pods, or 1 teaspoon of cardamom seeds

4 bay leaves

3 tablespoons coriander seeds

2 tablespoons fennel seeds

2 tablespoons cumin seeds

2 tablespoons whole cloves

1 tablespoon black peppercorns

1 teaspoon ground cinnamon

½ teaspoon ground nutmeg

Most garam masala blends feature both small green cardamom and bumpy pods of black cardamom. This recipe uses just green cardamom, but if you prefer, use half green and half black pods, or add up to six pods of black cardamom along with all of the green cardamom.

1. Remove the seeds from the cardamom pods (see instructions above).

2. In a skillet over medium heat, toast the bay leaves for 45 seconds, flipping once and pressing into the pan until fragrant, lightly toasted and brittle. Remove immediately from the pan and crumble into a bowl. Add the cardamom seeds, coriander, fennel, cumin, cloves, and peppercorns and toast for about 2½ minutes, stirring occasionally. Remove seeds immediately when fragrant and fennel seeds have darkened slightly.

3. Grind the bay leaves, toasted spices, and ground cinnamon and nutmeg in a clean coffee grinder as fine as possible. Store in a clean, dry glass jar and cover tightly. Keep in a dark, cool kitchen cabinet and use within 3 months for the best flavor. This makes enough to refill a 1-ounce/30-gram glass spice jar.

Jamaican Curry Powder

MAKES ABOUT ⅔ CUP

Authentic Indian-style curry powders may be easy to find these days, but Jamaican curry powder can be difficult to come across outside of West Indian communities. There are countless recipes for Jamaican curry, but almost all feature allspice berries for that uniquely West Indian flavor. It's up to you how spicy; make this curry powder fiery with lots of chile powder or leave it out altogether for a mild, aromatic blend.

*Try using this spice blend in the Indian curries in this book; instantly transform the Indian **Okra Masala** (page 281) into a Jamaican treat with a helping of this curry powder!*

> 3 tablespoons coriander seeds
> 2 teaspoons fenugreek seeds
> 4 teaspoons whole allspice berries
> 1 tablespoon cumin seeds
> 12 whole cloves
> 6 star anise pods
> 2 teaspoons black or mixed peppercorns
> 1 tablespoon ground turmeric
> 1 tablespoon ground ginger
> 2 teaspoons garlic powder
> 2 teaspoons ground cinnamon
> 2 to 5 teaspoons ground cayenne pepper
>   (optional)

Look for whole allspice berries—round, dark-brown seeds about the size of a tapioca pearls—in Latin American groceries or anyplace that stocks Caribbean spices. As with any spice mixture, store this in a tightly sealed glass container in a cool, dark cabinet and use within 3 months for the best flavor.

1. In a small skillet over medium heat toast the following whole spices, one spice at a time: coriander seeds, fenugreek seeds, allspice berries, cumin seeds, cloves, star anise, and peppercorns. Most of the whole spices will toast within 1½ to 2 minutes at the most, with the star anise taking slightly longer. Watch the spices carefully to make sure they don't burn; when the spices become fragrant and lightly browned, it's time to transfer them to a small bowl.

2. Grind all of the toasted whole spices together in a spice grinder or clean coffee mill as fine as possible. Add the remaining ground spices and pulse a few times until everything is combined. Store the spices in a clean glass jar, tightly sealed (this recipe will comfortably fill a 3.81-ounce/108-gram glass bottle three-quarters of the way).

Add one or both of the following to your curry powder along with the ground spices and proceed as directed: 1 tablespoon dried thyme, 1 teaspoon ground nutmeg.

East Indian–Style Curry Powder: For an East Indian–style blend, follow the recipe above for *Jamaican Curry Powder*, omitting the allspice and garlic powder. Increase the coriander seeds to 4 tablespoons total and the cumin seeds to 4 teaspoons total and add 1 tablespoon of fennel seeds, toasted in the manner of the other spice seeds. Grind as directed.

Toasted Rice Powder

MAKES ½ CUP

Toasted rice powder is a subtle ingredient in many Asian cuisines; I like using it for a crunchy, nutty topping on Southeast Asian salads and rice. Making it at home is a snap—it takes 10 minutes or less. Store unused rice powder in a tightly covered container in a cool place and it will last nearly forever . . . but if it has been forever, it's easy and fast enough to make a fresh batch!

⅔ cup white short-grain rice (sushi or sweet rice is okay), uncooked

1. Over medium heat, pour rice into an ungreased cast-iron skillet or wok. Stir rice occasionally and toast until light golden brown, about 5 to 7 minutes; to ensure the rice doesn't burn, remove it from the pan before it turns overly dark as the rice will continue to toast a minute or so after it's removed from a heat source. Pour the rice onto a plate and spread grains to help speed up cooling.

2. When the rice is cool enough to handle, grind in a blender or food processor into as fine a powder as you can get it. Depending on the power of the blender this can take 1 to 4 minutes; a Vitamix-type blender is especially good at making a very fine powder. The rice powder will be somewhat gritty and that's okay. Store completely cooled powder in a tightly covered glass or plastic container.

Sichuan 5-Spice Powder

MAKES 2 TABLESPOONS

One of the most versatile of Asian spice blends, just a pinch of this sweet and mouthwatering blend transforms tofu and seitan into an exquisite Chinatown-style treat.

1 rounded tablespoon fennel seeds
1 rounded tablespoon Sichuan peppercorns, outside husks only
5 large star anise pods
8 cloves
1 teaspoon ground cinnamon

Sichuan peppercorns are not related to pepper at all, but are an entirely different species. All of the mildly pungent, slightly citrusy flavor resides in the outer husks of the fruit, not in the tough black seeds. For best results take your time and discard all of these seeds; they don't have any flavor and will only add an undesirable, gritty texture to your blend. Only the outer husk should be used in the best-quality 5-spice powder.

1. In a small skillet over medium heat toast the following whole spices, one batch at a time: fennel seeds, Sichuan peppercorns, star anise, and cloves. Most of the whole spices will toast within 1½ to 2 minutes at the most, with the star anise taking a little longer. Watch the spices carefully to make sure they don't burn; when the spices become fragrant and lightly browned it's time to transfer them to a small bowl.

2. Grind all of the toasted whole spices together in a spice grinder or clean coffee mill as fine as possible; make sure the star anise is completely ground. Add the ground cinnamon and pulse a few times until everything is combined. Store the spice blend in a clean glass jar, tightly sealed. And you guessed it, use within 3 months for the best flavor.

White Peppercorn 5-Spice Powder: Substitute whole white peppercorns for the Sichuan pepper and proceed as directed. An alternative to using Sichuan pepper; while not too authentic, the white peppercorns' sharp dry heat will produce a slightly hotter and mildly bitter 5-spice.

Roasted Chile Pepper Harissa Paste

MAKES ABOUT 1 CUP OF HOT SAUCE PASTE

*This Lebanese-inspired condiment is thick, fiery, and fresh tasting. Use the freshest red chile peppers and dollop this lively harissa on **Baked Punky Pumpkin Kibbe** (page 261) or **Pistachio Date Quinoa Salad** (page 89) or stir into the **Cashew Yogurt Sauce** (page 65) for a creamy, bright pink sauce to serve with rice.*

No gas burner for roasting peppers? Spread the whole chilies on a baking sheet and roast at 450°F until the skins are browned and blistered, about 10 to 12 minutes. Cover and let steam as directed in the recipe.

½ pound fresh hot red chile peppers (serrano, Thai, red jalapeños, whatever you can find)
2 teaspoons fennel seeds
1½ teaspoons coriander seeds
1 teaspoon cumin seeds
1 tablespoon tomato paste
1 tablespoon lemon juice
1 tablespoon olive oil
2 teaspoons chopped garlic
¼ teaspoon sea salt

1. Over a gas burner, roast chilies until most of their skins are charred and blistered. My favorite way to roast small chilies is roasting them whole in an ungreased cast iron pan over high heat, until the skin is charred. When chilies are roasted, transfer to a bowl and cover tightly. Cool for 10 minutes; the steam with will help loosen their skins. Meanwhile, in a small pan over medium heat roast the fennel, coriander, and cumin seeds for about 1½ minutes or until fragrant, then grind in a clean coffee mill to a fine powder.

2. When chilies are cool enough to handle, remove as much of the charred skin as possible and discard the stem end. If desired, remove some of the seeds to temper the heat of the final sauce; the more seeds left in the chilies, the hotter the harissa. Puree chilies with ground spices, tomato paste, lemon juice, olive oil, garlic, and salt until smooth. Serve immediately or store in a tightly covered container in the fridge for up to 2 weeks.

olive oil Harissa paste

MAKES ABOUT ¼ CUP

This earthy, smoky harissa is made from a combination of whole ground spices and convenient purchased ground cayenne. It's a hot yet richly flavorful sauce (at least for seasoned hot sauce fans), but you can temper it by reducing the amount of cayenne . . . or boost it for an even more intense paste. A little dab will do ya in any sandwich, swirled in soy yogurt sauce, or in marinades.

> 1 tablespoon cumin seeds
> 2 teaspoons fennel seeds
> 2 teaspoons coriander seeds
> 1 teaspoon caraway seeds
> 4 teaspoons ground cayenne pepper
> ½ teaspoon sea salt
> 2 tablespoons olive oil

1. In a small skillet over medium heat toast the cumin, fennel, coriander, and caraway seeds until fragrant, about 1½ to 2 minutes. Transfer to a clean coffee mill and grind to the finest powder you can.

2. Add the cayenne and salt to the coffee mill and pulse a few times to combine with the ground spices. Empty the spices into a small bowl and drizzle with olive oil. Use a fork to stir the oil into the spices, then transfer the paste to a small glass or plastic container. Cover tightly and store at room temperature in a cool, dark place. Use within 2 months.

persian 7-spice Blend (Baharat)

MAKES 2 TABLESPOONS

Baharat is a fragrant blend of sweet spices that enhances many Middle Eastern dishes, especially rice or roasted seitan; to our Western palates this warm, mild blend may remind us of the foods of fall.

> 6 green cardamom pods or ¼ teaspoon cardamom seeds
> 2 tablespoons black peppercorns
> 2 tablespoons cumin seeds
> 1 tablespoon coriander seeds
> 10 cloves
> 2 teaspoons ground cinnamon
> 1 teaspoon ground nutmeg or mace

1. Remove the seeds from the cardamom pods (see instructions on page 39).

2. In a small skillet over medium heat, toast together the black peppercorns, cumin seeds, coriander seeds, and cloves for about 2½ minutes. Watch the spices carefully to make sure they don't burn; when the spices become fragrant, it's time to transfer them to a small bowl.

3. Grind all of the toasted whole spices together in a clean coffee grinder as fine as possible. Add the remaining ground spices and pulse a few times until everything is combined. Store the spices in a clean glass jar, tightly sealed. Use within 3 months for the best flavor.

berbere spice blend

MAKES OVER ½ CUP

Berbere spice blends, along with spiced "butter," are the soul of so many Ethiopian stews. Berbere can range from mild to fiery; I like mine with hot paprika, but a blend of both hot and sweet is a good basic berbere blend.

> 6 green cardamom pods or ¼ teaspoon cardamom seeds
> 6 allspice berries or ½ teaspoon ground allspice
> 1 tablespoon coriander seeds
> 2 teaspoons cumin seeds
> 2 teaspoons fenugreek seeds
> 1 teaspoon black peppercorns
> 6 whole cloves
> 3 tablespoons ground hot or sweet paprika
> 2 teaspoons ground ginger
> ½ teaspoon ground turmeric
> ½ teaspoon ground cayenne pepper
> ½ teaspoon salt
> ¼ teaspoon ground cinnamon

1. If using the cardamom pods, open them with your fingers or the tip of a sharp paring knife and remove the seeds. Slice each pod horizontally, break open the pod, and shake out the seeds. Discard the empty pods.

2. In a skillet over medium heat toast together the cardamom seeds, allspice berries (if using ground allspice, don't toast, add directly to the coffee mill), coriander, cumin, fenugreek, peppercorns, and cloves for 2 to 2½ minutes, stirring occasionally. Remove seeds immediately when fragrant and fenugreek seeds have darkened slightly.

3. Grind the toasted spices with the paprika, ginger, turmeric, cayenne, salt, and cinnamon in a coffee grinder as fine as you can make it. Store in a clean, dry glass jar in a dark, cool place and use within 3 months for the best flavor.

spiced buttery oil (niter kebbeh)

MAKES ABOUT 1 CUP, ENOUGH FOR ALL THE ETHIOPIAN RECIPES PLUS A LITTLE EXTRA

This gently spiced cooking oil gives Ethiopian dishes that uniquely layered range of flavors. This is the stuff that makes Ethiopian food so irresistible!

Usually made with clarified butter, I like to use a combination of vegan margarine with a mild oil to help balance the saltiness of the vegan butter (as of this writing, unsalted vegan margarine does not exist). Simmer up a batch, keep it chilled in the fridge, and it will last for months for many spontaneous Ethiopian creations.

As this niter kebbeh *simmers, some foam may rise to the top. I found that a good deal of the salt collects in the foam, so go ahead and skim some of it off for a less salty oil.*

1-inch piece peeled ginger, sliced into
    ¼-inch pieces
½ cup (8 tablespoons) of vegan margarine
½ cup grapeseed or peanut oil
1 small red onion, roughly chopped
4 cloves garlic, smashed
Two 3-inch cinnamon sticks
½ teaspoon fenugreek seeds
½ teaspoon ground turmeric
8 cloves

1. With the butt end of the knife handle (that's the very end of the knife, proving that everything indeed has a butt), pound the ginger slices a few times to bruise them; they'll release more flavor during the simmer. In a small saucepan over medium heat, melt the margarine and stir in the oil. Stir in the remaining ingredients and simmer for 2 minutes. A layer of yellow foam will form on top of the niter; use a spoon to skim off as much foam as possible, but don't worry if some remains. Reduce the heat to low and continue to simmer for 10 minutes, then turn off the heat. Stir a few times during the simmer.

2. Cool the niter kebbeh for 15 minutes, then pour through a metal strainer into a plastic container. Use a spoon to press down on the solids to release as much oil as possible; discard the solids. Store chilled until ready to use.

CHAPTER 2

The Three Protein Amigos: Tofu, Seitan & Tempeh

Tofu (made from soy), seitan (made from wheat gluten), and tempeh (also made from soy but with a taste and texture entirely different from tofu), are the great chameleons of the meatless culinary world: marinate, grill, or roast, and they'll take on the character of any cuisine on the planet. And prepared with care, they can satisfy the deepest "meaty" cravings for both seasoned vegans and die-hard omnivores.

A Quick Primer on Our Protein Pals

Tofu, seitan, and tempeh deserve our attention because unlike store-bought faux meats (tofu pups, veggie chicken strips, and so on), you *could* make all three of these in your own home—in theory, that is. Which is why I don't bother making either of them, but I do make my own seitan. The seitan I make at home is an easy steamed seitan (featured in this chapter) that I hope you'll also enjoy making yourself.

These are not high-tech factory foods; this protein power trio has ancient roots in traditional cuisines and can be made from whole plant foods. But for our purpose we'll give them passports and send tofu, tempeh, and seitan packing on a tour of cuisines throughout the world.

TOFU

Tofu is an ancient food that originated in China and that's also a huge part of Japanese, Korean, and other Asian cuisines. It has a delicate texture enhanced by pressing out some of the excess moisture (see tofu pressing, pages 22 and 31).

Tofu is made in a process similar to how soft cheeses are made; instead of animal milk, soy milk is combined with a natural enzyme derived from seaweed or calcium to create tender soy curds. These soy curds are gathered up and pressed; depending on the pressing process tofu can be firm and grainy (like ricotta), or perfectly smooth and delicate (like fine custard). The final resulting soy milk "cheese" must be stored in water.

SEITAN

This "meat" made from wheat is a boon for those seeking chewier, firmer protein. Unlike tofu, the sturdy texture of seitan holds up where tofu and tempeh crumble. Seitan is the only one of the protein trio I make myself; if you can knead bread dough, you can make seitan.

Even more forgiving than bread, seitan doesn't require rising or messing with yeast. In the good old days of seitan making, cooks made the gluten dough through an arduous process of kneading, rinsing, and boiling whole wheat flour dough for hours. Modern home cooks (that's you holding this book, even if you've yet to make seitan) now use a flour called vital wheat gluten. Vital wheat gluten flour (once reserved for professional bakers to help loaves rise higher) is a concentrated wheat flour with much of the starch removed. Creating a firm, starch-free dough takes minutes instead of hours! If you consume gluten, fast homemade seitan is an exciting food to work into your recipe rotation.

TEMPEH

Tempeh is also made from soy, but please don't confuse it with tofu. Tempeh is made from whole soybeans that have been cooked, pressed, and fermented. The result is a firm soybean cake with a complex, nutty, mushroom-like flavor. Tempeh responds best to braising, grilling, and roasting. For best results tempeh should be steamed, and then marinated, allowing the pores in the cake to expand to better drink up marinades.

seitan coriander cutlets

MAKES 4 LARGE CUTLETS, ENOUGH FOR 2 ENTREE RECIPES

These flavorful seitan cutlets blend well with a wide range of cuisines, especially with the Middle Eastern, African, Indian, and Mediterranean recipes in this book. Baking gives it a chewier texture, ideal for grilling and long simmers in any tagine stew, but if you prefer plump, moist loaves of seitan, steam them using the same steps as **5-Spice Seitan** *(page 51).*

1½ cups cold vegetable broth

2 cloves garlic, peeled, pressed or grated with a Microplane grater

3 tablespoons soy sauce

1 tablespoon olive oil

3 tablespoons tomato paste

1¾ cups vital wheat gluten flour (one 10-ounce package, see page 52 about brands)

¼ cup nutritional yeast

¼ cup chickpea flour

1 teaspoon ground coriander

½ teaspoon ground cumin

1. Preheat oven to 350°. In a 1-quart measuring cup or bowl, whisk together vegetable broth, garlic, soy sauce, olive oil, and tomato paste. In a separate mixing bowl, stir together vital wheat gluten flour, nutritional yeast, chickpea flour, coriander, and cumin. Form a well in the center and pour in the broth mixture.

2. Use a wooden spoon or rubber spatula to stir the ingredients together; as the flour absorbs the broth, a moist dough will rapidly form. When all of the broth is absorbed, use both hands to fold the dough in a kneading motion for 2 to 3 minutes. Let the dough rest for 10 minutes, then divide into four equal pieces.

3. Tear away four pieces of foil about 12 inches wide. Spray the dull side of each piece of foil lightly with olive oil or canola oil cooking spray. Shape a piece of dough into an oval on the oiled side of the foil and pat it down to a thickness of about ¾ of an inch. Fold foil as directed for **5-Spice Seitan**. It's very important to leave some space in the foil pouch; as it bakes, the seitan will expand and if the foil is too tight, it might burst through the pouch!

4. Place the foil packages side by side directly on a baking rack positioned in the center of the oven. Bake for 32 to 34 minutes; seitan should be firm to the touch. Remove from the oven and cool, still wrapped in foil, on the kitchen counter for 45 minutes before using. For best flavor and texture, cool the seitan to room temperature, keep it wrapped in the foil, store in a tightly covered container, and chill overnight. If desired, freeze seitan and use within 2 months; to defrost, leave in the refrigerator overnight. This recipe takes well to variations. Omit the ground coriander and cumin and add the following when mixing the dry ingredients.

Herbes de Provence Seitan: Add 1 tablespoon of dried, crumbled Herbes de Provence blend.

Curry Seitan: Add 2 teaspoons of any curry powder from purchased Indian Madras style, **Jamaican Curry Powder** (page 40), or any homemade blend.

Garam Masala Seitan: Add 2 teaspoons of garam masala spice blend, either purchased or homemade (page 39).

Mediterranean Seitan: Add 2 teaspoons of dried, crumbled oregano plus 2 teaspoons of dried, crumbled rosemary. Increase garlic to 4 cloves total.

savory Baked Tofu

MAKES 8 SLICES OF TOFU, SERVING 2 TO 4 PER RECIPE

Seasoned, pressed tofu is homemade fast food: flavorful and chewy, these lightly seasoned cutlets slide into sandwiches and, when diced, into stir-fries, stews, and even salads. Roast a double or quadruple batch; stored in a tightly covered container it can last 10 days or more. This particular marinade works well with any Asian dish; see below for marinades with Mediterranean, African, and Eastern European twists on the theme.

> 1 pound extra-firm or super-firm tofu
> 3 tablespoons soy sauce
> 2 tablespoons canola or vegetable oil
> 1 tablespoon agave nectar or maple syrup
> 2 teaspoons lemon juice
> ½ teaspoon garlic powder
> ¼ teaspoon ground cayenne pepper

1. Press tofu for 20 minutes up to an hour, following directions on pages 22 and 31. Slice the tofu as directed for pressing.

2. About 20 minutes before you're ready to bake the tofu, preheat oven to 425°F. In a glass or ceramic 9 x 13-inch pan, whisk together the remaining ingredients. Place tofu into marinade in a single layer and flip a few times to coat each side. Bake for 20 minutes, remove from oven and flip each piece of tofu. Bake for an additional 20 to 24 minutes or until almost all of the marinade is absorbed and tofu slices are golden brown.

Super-firm tofu is an exciting new variation on firm tofu that lives up to its name; look for it in natural food stores. It's so firm you can pass the pressing step entirely and go directly to marinating and baking.

Mediterranean Baked Tofu Marinade

*This citrusy baked tofu loves to be served with Latin foods, too. Use the following marinade for 1 pound of tofu, prepare as directed for **Savory Baked Tofu** (page 50).*

> ½ cup orange juice
> ½ cup white wine
> 2 tablespoons lemon juice
> 2 tablespoons olive or vegetable oil
> 2 teaspoons dried oregano
> 1 teaspoon garlic powder
> 1 teaspoon ground Mexican chile powder
>   (optional but good for Mexican dishes)
> 1 teaspoon sea salt

African Baked Tofu Marinade

This flavor of baked tofu also pairs well with Middle Eastern foods. Use the following marinade for 1 pound of tofu, prepare as directed for **Savory Baked Tofu** (page 50).

¼ cup orange juice
⅓ cup vegetable broth
2 tablespoons lime juice
2 tablespoons olive or vegetable oil
3 cloves garlic, minced
2 teaspoons freshly grated ginger
1 teaspoon ground coriander
1 teaspoon hot chile sauce or ½ teaspoon ground cayenne pepper
1 to 2 teaspoons of *Persian 7-Spice Blend* (page 43), optional
1 teaspoon sea salt

Eastern European Baked Tofu Marinade

Use the following marinade for 1 pound of tofu, prepare as directed for **Savory Baked Tofu** (page 50).

¼ cup white wine, mild-flavored beer, or vegetable broth
2 tablespoons olive or vegetable oil
2 teaspoons white wine or apple cider vinegar
2 teaspoons sweet ground paprika
1 teaspoon garlic powder
1 teaspoon sea salt
½ teaspoon ground black pepper

5-Spice Seitan

MAKES 4 PORTIONS OF SEITAN, ENOUGH TO
SERVE 4 TO 6 IN RECIPES

I love steamed seitan; it's fast and the prep won't take over your kitchen compared to boiling the seitan dough. This 5-Spice Seitan is my favorite multipurpose Asian seitan and is great in Chinese, Korean, and Southeast Asian cuisine. The dense texture is perfect for slicing into delicate, thin slices; sliding into a zesty marinade; or browning in a cast iron pan. Replace the Chinese spices with other spice blends to change the ethnicity of your seitan to fit into other cuisines.

1½ cups cold vegetable broth
2 cloves garlic, peeled and pressed or grated with a Microplane grater
¼ cup soy sauce
1 tablespoon peanut or grapeseed oil
1 teaspoon freshly grated ginger
1¾ cups vital wheat gluten flour (one 10-ounce package, see page 52 about brands)
2 tablespoons nutritional yeast
¼ cup chickpea flour
2 teaspoons *Sichuan 5-Spice Powder* (page 41) or store-bought Chinese 5-spice powder
½ teaspoon ground white pepper

1. In a 1-quart glass measuring cup or bowl, whisk together vegetable broth, garlic, soy sauce, peanut oil, and ginger. In a separate bowl, stir together

vital wheat gluten flour, nutritional yeast, chickpea flour, 5-spice powder, and white pepper. Form a well in the center and pour in the broth mixture.

2. Use a wooden spoon or rubber spatula to stir the ingredients together; as the flour absorbs the broth a moist dough will rapidly form. When all of the broth is absorbed, use both hands to fold the dough in a kneading motion for 2 to 3 minutes. Let the dough rest for 10 minutes, then divide into four equal pieces.

3. Tear away four pieces of foil into squares about 12 inches wide. Place each piece of dough in the center of each foil square and shape the dough into a flattened oval shape. To seal a packet for steaming, bring the two opposing ends of the foil together and fold over the top by ½ inch, then fold once more to form a tent over the dough. Fold and seal tight the remaining ends; the result should be a foil pouch with an ample amount of space above the dough (see illustration). The seitan will expand as it steams, so it's important to leave some space in each foil pouch. Repeat with remaining seitan portions.

4. Set up a steamer (see "Steamer Setup" on page 29) and steam the seitan for 30 minutes; take care that the seitan does not touch the water during the steaming. The loaves will have expanded in size and should feel semi-firm; if not, continue to steam for another 5 minutes. Remove seitan (do not remove the foil), and let cool on the kitchen counter for 30 minutes before using, or store in a tightly covered container in the refrigerator for up to a week. For best flavor and texture cool the seitan to room temperature first, keep it wrapped in the foil and store

in a zip-top plastic bag or similar air-tight container and chill overnight. If desired, freeze seitan and use within 2 months; to defrost, leave in the refrigerator overnight.

Thai and Vietnamese Seitan: Reduce the 5-spice powder to ½ teaspoon. Increase ground white pepper to 1 teaspoon.

Middle Eastern Seitan: Omit 5-spice powder and replace with **Persian 7-Spice Blend** (page 43).

The brand of vital wheat gluten flour will make a difference in any homemade seitan. Bob's Red Mill flour gives me a consistent result, but Arrowhead Mills Vital Wheat Gluten makes great seitan, too. Try different brands and see which you prefer. FYI, Some recipe testers outside of the United States had different results with their local wheat gluten flours; testers in the United Kingdom reported that they typically have to add much less total liquid to their flour—up to ½ cup less.

chorizo tempeh crumbles

Use this marinade for spicy, chorizo-like crumbles for Mexican dishes. Prepare saucy chorizo tempeh for eating with rice and beans, or let it simmer for a drier tempeh for use in tacos or quesadillas.

8-ounce package tempeh
2 tablespoons peanut oil
1¼ cups vegetable broth
3 cloves garlic, finely minced
3 tablespoons soy sauce

2 tablespoons tomato paste

2 teaspoons smoked sweet or hot paprika

1½ teaspoons Mexican chile powder
    (see page 11)

½ teaspoon liquid smoke

1. Dice the tempeh into ½-inch chunks. In large skillet, preheat the peanut oil over medium heat. Stir in the tempeh and fry for 3 minutes or until the edges of the tempeh are lightly browned.

2. In a 2-cup liquid measuring cup, whisk together the remaining ingredients. Pour into the skillet, increase the heat to medium-high, and bring the liquid to a rapid simmer. Cover the pan and simmer for 5 minutes. Uncover the pan and continue to simmer the tempeh, stirring occasionally, for another 5 to 8 minutes. Depending on how saucy you prefer the chorizo tempeh, serve it when it's saucy and moist or continue to simmer until the liquid has been absorbed by the tempeh for drier crumbles.

Chinese Tempeh Sausage Crumbles

MAKES ABOUT 2 CUPS

Crumbled, braised tempeh is a respected vegan substitute for crumbled sausage in the universe of vegan cuisine. Tempeh greedily drinks up tasty marinades and speedily transforms into toothsome, savory, sausagey morsels; in this instance the sweet and garlicky flavors of Chinese sausage. A unique rose-scented cooking wine also flavors this sausage,

but since this can be difficult to locate we'll use brandy or common, inexpensive Chinese Shaoxing rice cooking wine.

*Stir these sticky crumbles into Chinese rice dishes including **Chinese Sticky Rice with Tempeh Sausage Crumbles** (page 305) or any vegetable stir-fry. Or better yet, sprinkle onto a mound of freshly cooked rice and serve with sautéed green vegetables for a complete weeknight meal.*

8-ounce package tempeh

2 tablespoons peanut oil

1 cup vegetable broth

3 cloves garlic, minced

3 tablespoons soy sauce

2 tablespoon brandy, Chinese Shaoxing
    wine (see page 13), or Chinese rose wine

2 tablespoons brown sugar

1 tablespoon natural ketchup

1 teaspoon *Sichuan 5-Spice Powder* (page 41)
    or store-bought Chinese 5-spice powder

½ teaspoon liquid smoke

1. Dice the tempeh into ½-inch chunks. In a large skillet, preheat the peanut oil over medium heat. Stir in the tempeh and fry for 3 minutes or until the edges of the tempeh are lightly browned.

2. In a 2-cup liquid measuring cup, whisk together the remaining ingredients. Pour into the skillet, increase the heat to medium-high, and bring the liquid to a rapid simmer. Simmer the liquid, stirring occasionally, until it's completely absorbed by the tempeh, about 8 to 10 minutes. The tempeh will turn golden brown and look sticky; continue to stir the tempeh for another minute until most of the liquid has been absorbed. Remove from the heat and use in recipes immediately, or eat with plain boiled rice and vegetables.

Lemon and Olive Chickpea Seitan

MAKES 4 LARGE LOAVES, ENOUGH FOR 2 ENTREE RECIPES

*The addition of pureed, cooked chickpeas here makes for a tender and pleasantly grainy seitan. The lemon and olives go great with Middle Eastern and Mediterranean cuisines, and this is my seitan of choice for making **Gyro Roasted Seitan** (page 253). For best results, prepare the seitan the night before; the flavor and texture need a proper amount of rest to blossom.*

¼ cup lemon juice

1 tablespoon olive oil

3 cloves peeled garlic

1 cup cooked chickpeas, either canned
    or homemade, rinsed and drained

1¼ cups cold vegetable broth

Finely grated zest of 1 lemon

¼ cup nutritional yeast

1 teaspoon crumbled, dried thyme

1 teaspoon crumbled, dried oregano

1 teaspoon sea salt

1½ cups vital wheat gluten flour
    (see page 52 for info about brands)

½ cup Kalamata or black oil-cured olives,
    pits removed and finely chopped

1. In a food processor, pulse the lemon juice, olive oil, and garlic until smooth. Add the chickpeas and pulse for about a minute to form a thick paste; don't make it as smooth as hummus—keep it somewhat grainy. Pulse in the vegetable broth, lemon zest, nutritional yeast, thyme, oregano, and salt for 20 seconds. Stream in the vital wheat gluten flour and pulse, occasionally stopping to push down the mixture with a rubber spatula. Once all of the flour is added, pulse a few more times to form a thick, moist dough. Add the olives and pulse just enough to chop in the olives but not completely mince them into microscopic bits.

2. Tear away four pieces of foil into squares about 12 inches wide. Sprinkle a little extra wheat gluten onto a work surface and scoop out the dough. Knead the dough for 1 minute, then divide into four equal pieces. Place each piece in the center of each foil square, then shape the dough into a flattened oval shape. Wrap as directed for *5-Spice Seitan* (page 51), and repeat with remaining seitan portions.

3. Steam and cool as directed for *5-Spice Seitan*. If desired, freeze seitan and use within 2 months; to defrost, leave in the refrigerator overnight.

Mushroom Seitan: Omit the lemon juice and olives. Sauté 8 ounces of fresh, finely chopped mushrooms in 1 tablespoon of olive oil until reduced in size by half and very tender, about 10 minutes (for tips on how to chop mushrooms, see page 5 in the ***Kitchen Cartography*** section). To evenly cook the mushrooms, occasionally cover the pan you're cooking them in to lightly steam them. Add the sautéed mushrooms instead toward the end of pulsing the dough in the food processor. Use this seitan in Eastern European dishes.

Arabic Olive Seitan: Omit the dried oregano and thyme and use 1 tablespoon of ***Persian 7-Spice Blend*** (page 43) or ras-el-hanout spice blend (see page 10).

CHAPTER 3

pickles, chutneys & saucier sauces

C hile pastes, chutney, pickles, and sambals—across the globe, everyone craves that something extra dabbed on, dipped in, or nibbled with our favorite foods. Sometimes that extra thing—for example, the kimchi, which must orbit any Korean meal, or malluma, an addictive Sri Lankan medley of greens, coconut, and chilies—is the epicenter of a great meal.

Gently fermented via natural means or blended with fresh ingredients right before the main attraction, this worldly collection of special sauces and essential sides make even the most humble sandwich or plate of veggies and tofu a five-star feast.

Fast Lane Cabbage Kimchi

MAKES OVER 4 CUPS

Kimchi, *the hauntingly spicy, crunchy, and garlicky fermented Korean cabbage "salad," is so much more than a condiment—it's a lifelong habit that kimchi fans swear by.*

Alas, sometimes you need kimchi and need it now, so learn to make quick-fix kimchi at home and a whole world of this ridiculously healthy Korean delicacy can be yours. Though not fermented in the traditional sense, the bright red, peppery brine bathing the cabbage improves with time; if you don't gobble it all up now, let it rest in the refrigerator for a few days and it will indeed ferment slightly, for a bubbling edge similar to authentically aged kimchi.

*The must-have ingredient for this kimchi is Korean-style red pepper powder, also known as gochugaru. Used generously in many Korean reci-*pes, gochugaru's flavor is hot but not blazing (on a scale of 1 to 10, I'd give it a 4), with smoky, fruity notes. There's really no substitute for gochugaru; supermarket red pepper flakes (the kind you'd sprinkle on pizza), ground cayenne pepper, or ground-up Thai or Indian dried chile peppers are all far too hot and bitter. Hot and spicy kimchi needs gochugaru to have the authentic sweet and spicy goodness.*

Yet gochugaru-free kimchi does exist; I've included a mild, green variation if you can't find Korean red pepper or eat spicy foods; it's refreshing, cooling, and a must for fans of fresh ginger.

> 2 pounds Napa cabbage (about 1 small head cabbage), washed and outer leaves removed
> ½ cup kosher salt
> 1 large bunch scallions (6 scallions), ends trimmed and sliced into 1-inch pieces
> 1 large carrot, peeled and grated or sliced into matchsticks
> ⅓ cup rice vinegar
> ¼ cup chopped fresh garlic
> 2 tablespoons finely minced fresh ginger
> ½ cup Korean red pepper powder (gochugaru, see page 15)
> 2 tablespoons roasted sesame seeds
> 1 teaspoon brown sugar or agave nectar (optional)

1. You have two options for slicing the cabbage: for an easy-to-serve kimchi, slice the cabbage in half, then remove the core at the base of the cabbage. Slice each half into thirds, lengthwise, then cut each piece into 2-inch sections. Repeat with remaining half.

2. For a more authentic presentation, don't remove the core from the cabbage and instead slice in half, then slice each half in half once more. When ready to eat, slice each section into bite-size pieces.

When I Say Pickle...

Just to be clear, when I'm talking about pickles in this book, I'm referring to the fine art of refrigerator pickles. These are not long-term vegetables requiring months of suspended animation in a jar; these are fresh, easy pickles marinated in your refrigerator and designed to be eaten up within a few days. All of these pickles (with the exception of kimchi and preserved lemons) are best consumed within a week of making them.

Pick a Jar for Proper Pickles

Before starting any of these refrigerator pickles that need to be stored in a glass jar, hunt around your kitchen cabinets or your recycling bin for a proper jar to keep your pickles in. Make sure you also locate a lid for the jar that has a tight, secure fit. It's tempting to use pasta sauce jars for pickles, but the mouths of these jars are awkwardly small and make fishing out chunky vegetables a chore. Use repurposed wide-mouth jars from past cucumber pickles, sauerkraut, and applesauce for more pleasing homemade pickling.

Retaining the core will hold together the long pieces of cabbage; these sections can then be sliced into stacks and presented in a neat little pile.

3. After slicing the cabbage, place it in the largest mixing bowl you have or use a huge soup pot. Sprinkle with kosher salt and vigorously rub salt into every leaf. Let cabbage sit for 1 hour, then rinse thoroughly with cool water. Drain cabbage and shake off as much liquid as possible and return to the big bowl. Add the scallions and the carrot.

4. In a food processor pulse together vinegar, garlic, ginger, red pepper powder, sesame seeds, and brown sugar, if using, to form a thick paste. Drain the cabbage of any additional liquid that may have collected. Empty the paste onto the cabbage and use your hands to massage the paste onto each cabbage leaf. Pack the kimchi into gallon-size plastic zip-top bags or really big glass jars (two 1-quart wide-mouth jars or larger) to almost the top. Press out any extra air from the bag and seal. Let stand at room temperature for 1 hour before eating. The longer the kimchi rests, the more the flavors will deepen.

5. If you want to stimulate a little fermentation, leave the bag or jar of kimchi on the kitchen counter overnight. If your kitchen is very cold, you can even extend this an additional day; afterward keep the kimchi tightly sealed in the refrigerator for up to 3 weeks.

Replace the cabbage with the following vegetables, or use a combination of two or more. The paste mixture will coat 2 to 2½ pounds of vegetables.

Daikon Kimchi: Use uniform, angled slices of daikon in place of cabbage. Or try any radish or small turnip: Japanese salad, watermelon radish, even French breakfast radishes! Salt the daikon or root veggies and proceed as directed for cabbage.

Cool Ginger Kimchi: This red pepper–free variation is a great alternative if you simply can't find Korean red pepper or don't like spicy food. Omit the red pepper powder. Increase the fresh ginger to 3 tablespoons total. I love adding one Asian pear, core removed, sliced in half and sliced into ¼-inch-thin half moons for deliciously sweet and crunchy contrast.

As your kimchi ages day by day, it will get juicier and more flavorful. "Old" or ripe kimchi that's soft and watery is ideal for stew or chopping up and using in kimchi jeon (savory kimchi pancakes) or as a filling for dumplings. The juices also make a great broth for soup and a liquid binder for the pancakes.

preserved lemons, two ways

Why bother with preserved lemons at all? Lemon fans take note: because there's nothing quite like their unforgettable briny, tart, and ultra-lemony flavor. A teaspoon or two of finely minced preserved lemon peel wakes up any recipe, and this ingredient is especially fitting in Middle Eastern stews, salads and vegetables.

Here are two methods for preserving lemons, one for the impatient foodie and one for the traditionalist with time on their side. The fast-track lemons make softened, salty lemons that can be used within a day. The next day, pack the leftover lemons into jars (or start them in jars with the "slow" recipe) for authentically preserved lemons that will continue to develop in exquisite flavor and texture for months to come. Once chilled, after about 3 months the preserved lemons will develop a slippery and viscous texture. That's okay, even desirable! Just rinse away the goo (or add it to stews or tagines, it's loaded with flavor), discard the pulp (or throw it back into the jar to add more juice to the remaining lemons), and mince the rind as fine as possible. Because you'll be eating the outside rind of the lemon, be sure to use organic lemons for this recipe. Purchased organic lemon juice is also recommended; because it won't be consumed fresh, it's okay to skip the additional work of squeezing half a dozen fresh lemons for extra juice.

12-Hour Freezer Lemons

*I'm a fan of food writer Diane Rossen Worthington's method for preserving lemons for the fast-track foodie: freezing lemons helps soften the cell walls of the rind, similar to the preserving process. After thawing, the rind is ready to mince and add to any dish. These lemons are ready to use right out of the freezer but can be further enhanced with additional preserving techniques; pack any unused lemons into a large glass jar and store in the refrigerator as directed for **Slow Down Preserved Lemons** (recipe follows).*

> 1 pound organic lemons (about 6 to 7
> small lemons)
> ½ cup lemon juice
> Plenty of kosher salt, at least ½ cup

1. Firmly roll each lemon a few times with your palm on a hard surface; remove any tough stem nubs from ends. Use a sharp knife to partially slice each lemon into quarters lengthwise, stopping ¼ inch from the bottom. The lemons should still be in one piece and hold together at one end.

2. Gently open up the partially quartered lemons and stuff as much salt as possible into the centers all the way to the bottom and rub the salt into the outside peel. Place lemons into a 1 gallon plastic zip-top bag, sprinkle with any remaining salt and pour in the lemon juice. Press out all the air from the bag and seal; if desired, wrap in another bag to prevent

any leaking. Massage the bag of lemons with your hands for about a minute, then freeze for at least 12 hours or overnight.

3. When ready to use a lemon, remove from the freezer and let thaw on the kitchen counter; when it's softened slightly, it's ready to use. To speed the process, place the lemon in a securely zipped bag and drop into a bowl of hot water. To use a lemon, rinse and remove the seeds and the pulp. The softened rind is the part of the lemon that's used in recipes.

4. If you have any frozen lemons remaining you can continue to freeze them for up to 6 more weeks. Or consider packing them into a jar to further preserve them (boosting their flavor and texture) as directed for *Slow Down Preserved Lemons*.

Slow Down Preserved Lemons

A traditional recipe for preserved lemons, truly the slowest of slow foods. The actual number of lemons is a guideline: first, find yourself a large wide-mouth jar (1 liter is my favorite size), and then estimate how many small lemons can be packed inside.

For fancy preserved lemons, tuck 3 bay leaves, 6 to 8 whole cloves, a teaspoon of cayenne pepper, and a few cinnamon sticks into the jar while packing in the lemons.

> 1 pound organic lemons (about 6 to 7 small lemons)
> ½ cup organic lemon juice
> Plenty of kosher salt, at least ¾ cup

1. Prepare and salt lemons as directed for freezer lemons, except pack lemons firmly into a clean wide-mouth jar, sprinkle with any remaining salt, and then pour the juice over the lemons. Twist the

lid onto the jar and leave in a cool, dark place for 2 weeks, occasionally turning the jar upside down to redistribute the juices. After 2 weeks, move the jar to the refrigerator, remembering to turn the jar upside down once a week.

2. To use a preserved lemon, tear away a section and brush away the salt. Remove the pulp and seeds; I like to squeeze the juices of the pulp into the jar of lemons, adding more juice and flavor to the lemons in the jar. Discard the pulp (it's tough and not so flavorful), and mince the softened rind as finely as possible for use in recipes. After 3 months, the lemon juice may appear murky and the lemon skins will have a jellylike texture; that's perfectly fine, just rinse in a little cool water before using. Or instead, use the lemon "goo" in marinades—it's bursting with preserved lemon flavor.

Tamarind Date Chutney

MAKES ABOUT 1½ CUPS

*A good friend to **Cilantro Chutney** (page 61), Tamarind Date Chutney is that brown sweet and sour sauce served with nearly every South Indian meal. It has a thin consistency, perfect for drizzling over Indian breads, samosas, or, beyond Indian cuisine, empanadas, rice, beans, or even fries. Most restaurant tamarind chutneys lean toward the very sweet side, so I've kept the amount of sugar fast and loose for you to adjust depending on your taste buds; you may enjoy a more tart chutney when given the chance to prepare it yourself. Tamarind chutney is delicious served alongside any curry, with any Indian*

bread or finger food, and is an essential ingredient in the best snack of them all, **Bhel Puri** (page 96).

While I prefer using tamarind pulp, I've included instructions for making this with Indian tamarind concentrate; for best results, look for light brown, creamy-looking tamarind concentrate instead of the thick, black, syrupy concentrate (which is too strong for this chutney).

Tamarind pulp is sold in 1-pound solid, dark brown blocks wrapped in plastic; if possible use Indian tamarind pulp without seeds, as it will yield a smoother, darker chutney. I prefer this to dried tamarind pods (no peels to remove), and it comes with or without seeds (check the package to see if the seeds have been removed). With or without seeds, both contain lots of fibrous material and need to be strained.

DATES

½ cup dates, pits removed

1 cup hot water

CHUTNEY

1 pound tamarind pulp, with or without seeds

1 cup plus ½ cup hot water

1 teaspoon cumin seeds

1 teaspoon fennel seeds

6 to 8 tablespoons dark brown sugar

1 tablespoon lime juice

½ teaspoon ground cayenne pepper or more to taste

½ teaspoon sea salt

1. Place the dates in a small bowl, cover with hot water, and set aside to soak for 20 minutes. Unwrap the tamarind pulp block, place in a mixing bowl, and add 1 cup of hot water. Let it stand for 20 minutes. While the pulp is soaking, toast together the cumin and fennel seeds in a small dry skillet over medium heat for 1 to 1½ minutes until fragrant. Remove from heat and pulse in a clean coffee grinder to a fine powder. Empty the ground spices into a blender, then add the brown sugar, lime juice, cayenne, and salt.

2. Fit a 2-cup metal mesh strainer over a small bowl. When the pulp feels soft and squishy, use one hand to knead the pulp. Knead the pulp for about 2 minutes to loosen the pulp from the seeds (if present) and other fibrous stuff. When the pulp looks creamy and most of the tamarind is a soft goo, use a rubber spatula or your fingers to press a small portion of pulp through the strainer, working the pulp over a few times to extract as much strained tamarind as possible. Occasionally scrape under the strainer to free any pulp into the bowl. Discard the remaining matter in the strainer and continue working batches of pulp through the strainer until it's all been pressed through.

3. Drain the dates and add to the blender, then add the strained tamarind pulp and ¼ cup of the hot water and pulse into a smooth sauce. Continue to add more water to the chutney, a tablespoon at a time, until a very thin and pourable consistency is reached. Taste and add more sugar if desired. Store the chutney in a tightly covered container in the fridge.

Tamarind Chutney using Tamarind Concentrate

Less messy and much faster, tamarind concentrate is convenient but may taste different from chutney made with tamarind pulp. Look for tamarind concentrate that's light brown and creamy instead of the black, syrupy kind (see tamarind in the Ingredients section, page 14).

DATES

½ cup dates, pits removed

1 cup hot water

CHUTNEY

½ cup tamarind concentrate

½ cup hot water

⅔ cup dark brown sugar

1 tablespoon lime juice

½ teaspoon sea salt

½ teaspoon ground cumin

½ teaspoon ground fennel

½ teaspoon ground cayenne pepper

1. Soak the dates as directed in **Tamarind Date Chutney** (page 59), then drain and add to a blender.

2. Add the remaining ingredients and pulse into a smooth sauce. If a chutney with a thinner consistency is desired, drizzle in a little warm water and pulse.

cilantro chutney

MAKES ABOUT 1½ CUPS

Cilantro Chutney is a simple but stimulating Indian chutney that enhances so many great Indian meals. It's also essential for my favorite Indian street food, Bhel Puri (page 96). Cilantro Chutney is also strikingly similar to many Latin American salsas and is right at home served alongside tacos or beans and

rice. The dried, unsweetened coconut adds a hint of sweetness but does not make it overly "coconutty."

Look for unsweetened, finely grated coconut in Indian markets and natural food stores. Use Thai or Indian green chilies or small serrano peppers. Remove the seeds from the chilies for a milder chutney.

2 cups cilantro leaves, lightly packed

¼ cup dried grated coconut

3 cloves garlic

1 to 2 green hot chile peppers

1¼ teaspoons *Garam Masala* (page 39), or store-bought garam masala

2 tablespoons lime juice

¾ teaspoon sea salt

¼ cup water

1. In a food processor or blender combine the first seven ingredients plus half of the water. Pulse until as smooth as possible; if the chutney seems very thick, dribble in a little extra water at a time until a pourable consistency is reached; it should resemble a thin pesto sauce. If necessary, add more water, a teaspoon at a time.

2. Store in a tightly covered container in the refrigerator until ready to use; if possible let the chutney sit for 30 minutes before serving to allow the flavors to blend.

Cilantro Mint Chutney: Replace ½ cup of the cilantro with mint.

pickled red onions

MAKES ABOUT 1½ CUPS

If you're going to make only one pickle in your life-time, these sweet and sour onions are it. In less than 30 minutes, these crunchy, neon-pink onion strands are ready to garnish tacos, sandwiches, burritos, soups, or rice and beans.

*While a traditional companion to Mexican food, try the variations with Indian and Middle Eastern flair. Serve Pickled Red Onions with **Deluxe Tofu Vegetable Mafe** (page 160) as a tangy foil for this rich, peanuty stew.*

> 3 cups red onions, sliced ¼ inch thin
> 3 tablespoons red wine vinegar
> 1 teaspoon sea salt

1. Place red onions in a large metal colander in a sink. Boil 3 cups of water, pour over the onions, and shake the colander to get rid of any excess water. Place the onions in a glass or plastic mixing bowl, toss with vinegar and salt, and set aside to marinate, stirring occasionally. Onions are ready to eat after about 30 minutes.

2. Store the onions along with their pickling juices in a tightly covered container in the fridge. Pickled onions can last for weeks in the refrigerator, so you may want to double or triple the batch.

Indian Pickled Onions: Add 1 teaspoon each toasted mustard seeds (toast in a dry skillet over high heat for 1 minute or until they start to pop) and toasted fennel seeds. For additional spice, stir in 1 teaspoon of ground cayenne.

Middle Eastern Pickled Onions: Toast 2 teaspoons of coriander seeds and gently crush using a mortar and pestle (see page 31); they don't need to be a powder, just slightly crushed. Stir into the onions along with the marinade.

star anise daikon pickles

MAKES ABOUT 1 PINT

*Tangy, sweet, and heady with star anise, this fast Southeast Asian–style pickle mix is perfect for the **bahn mi** sandwiches in this book (page 109) and also for tacos, salads, or tofu hot dogs topped with sweet Asian chili sauce. These pickles are also fantastic piled onto a steaming hot bowl of **Sizzling Seitan Pho Noodle Soup** (page 220)!*

> ½ pound daikon radish (about one slender 10-inch radish)
> ¼ pound carrots (about 2 large carrots)
> 6 large green jalapeño or serrano chilies, stems removed
> 1 cup rice vinegar
> ½ cup sugar
> ¼ cup kosher salt
> 1 teaspoon whole peppercorns, black or mixed color
> 4 whole star anise

1. Scrape the daikon and carrots to remove the outer peel and slice into long matchsticks no thicker than ¼ inch: I use a mandolin (see page 30) for this but you can take your time and use a chef's knife. Or even better, use a Y-shaped julienne peeler (page 30). Slice the chilies in half, remove the seeds (or keep them in for really hot pickles), and slice into very thin slivers. Toss everything together and pack into a clean, dry, 1-pint glass mason jar.

2. In a small saucepan, bring to a gentle boil the vinegar, sugar, salt, peppercorns, and star anise and boil for 2 minutes. Stir to dissolve the sugar and salt and then pour everything over the vegetables in the jar, including the star anise and peppercorns. Cover very tightly and chill for 30 minutes before using. Store tightly covered and chilled.

green Tahini sauce

MAKES ABOUT ½ CUP

Classic sesame tahini sauce gets a fresh green glow from cilantro and parsley. Good with any Mediterranean or Middle Eastern cuisine that could use a touch of rich, velvety, dairy-free creaminess.

    ¼ cup sesame tahini paste
    1 tablespoon lemon juice
    3 cloves garlic
    ¼ teaspoon salt, or to taste
    6 tablespoons warm water, plus extra
        as needed
    3 tablespoons chopped cilantro leaves
    3 tablespoons chopped flat-leaf parsley

1. In a food processor or blender, pulse together the tahini, lemon juice, garlic, salt, and water into a creamy sauce. Scrape down the sides of the food processor as necessary. Add the chopped cilantro and parsley and pulse a few more times until the leaves are very finely chopped.

2. If a thinner sauce is desired, dribble in a little extra water until the sauce has reached desired consistency. Serve immediately or store in a tightly covered container in the refrigerator. The sauce will thicken slightly as it stands; add a few teaspoons of water to loosen up the tahini if needed.

whipped garlic dip (Toum)

MAKES SLIGHTLY LESS THAN 1 CUP

Garlic lovers, step right up; you'll find any excuse to slather this powerful Lebanese condiment on anything. Outside of using your bare fingers, dipping the edge of pita bread into this creamy dip is the most direct way eat more toum immediately. Traditionally, raw garlic is used—if you're a hardcore garlic-phile, by all means make it that way—but the less devoted maybe want to blanch the garlic to tame the sharpness. Garlicky doesn't begin to describe this dip!

Toum is similar to Greek skordalia (page 93), but even more garlicky; the potato, if anything, is just a backdrop (sometimes bread is used, too). Adding a little potato is an option. Without it, it's a creamy sauce; adding it, it's a pastelike dip. Prepeeled garlic cloves are a fantastic time saver, but if you insist on peeling your own, see page 5 to quickly shake your way to faster peeled garlic.

2½ ounces fresh garlic, about 16 peeled
    garlic cloves
2 tablespoons chilled lemon juice
½ rounded teaspoon sea salt, or more to
    taste
3 tablespoons cold mild vegetable oil such
    as grapeseed or light olive oil
¼ cup cooked, mashed and cooled starchy
    white potato (optional; see note)

To prepare the mashed potato, peel, dice into 1-inch cubes, and boil a small russet baking potato until tender, about 10 minutes. Drain and mash with a fork or press through a potato ricer (page 93) for perfectly smooth potatoes. Chill before using.

1. Chop the garlic into pieces about ½ inch thick or slightly thinner and place in a glass or metal mixing bowl. Boil 2 cups of water and pour over the garlic; steep the garlic for 1 to 1 ½ minutes. Drain the garlic in a metal mesh sieve and rinse with plenty of cold water to cool it off. Shake the sieve to remove as much water as possible from the garlic.

2. In a food processor pulse together the garlic, lemon juice, and salt into a creamy paste. Use a rubber spatula to frequently push the chopped garlic down the sides of the bowl. Stream in 1 tablespoon of oil at a time until the toum is white and creamy. If using, pulse in the mashed potato, 1 tablespoon at a time to create a thick paste. You may not need to use all of the potato if the toum reaches a desired consistency without it. Taste and add more salt if desired.

3. Chill the toum for at least 20 minutes before serving. Toum will mellow out slightly as it chills.

Quick toum: For faster toum, replace cooked potato with mashed potato flakes. Add 1 tablespoon at a time until a thick, creamy paste is achieved.

Toasted Hazelnut Crunch Dip (Dukka)

MAKES ABOUT 1½ CUPS

Dukka is a nuanced Egyptian blend of roasted nuts and toasted spices. Often served as a dip, chunks of pita or any bread are first doused with olive oil and then dipped into dukka. I add smoked salt because it tastes awesome, but if you can't find it, use sea salt.

*It's hard to just have a single dip of dukka, so this recipe makes a generous amount. You'll find many excuses to use it; sprinkle it onto salads, tagines, curries, quinoa, even vanilla ice cream for an unexpected nutty twist. While bread is traditional, I love it served with sticks of jicama as a refreshing, lower-calorie snack (keep some sticks packed in a tightly covered container covered with water for immediate dukka dipping enjoyment). Or serve elegant **Roasted Pumpkin Salad with Dukka** (page 91) for an exciting alternative to hummus.*

1 cup whole raw hazelnuts
½ cup shelled green pistachios or blanched,
    slivered almonds
2 teaspoons cumin seeds
2 teaspoons fennel seeds
2 teaspoons coriander seeds
1 teaspoon caraway seeds
1 teaspoon black peppercorns
Pinch of red pepper flakes or 1 whole dried
    red chili pepper
½ teaspoon smoked salt or sea salt

1 large jicama

1 tablespoon lemon juice

Or

Fresh, thick pita or crusty bread and good olive oil

1. Preheat oven to 325°F and spread hazelnuts onto a rimmed baking sheet. Roast for 10 to 14 minutes until the skins have cracked and the nuts appear to be light golden brown. Remove from oven and pour hazelnuts into a roughly textured kitchen towel. Twist the towel around the nuts and massage the towel for a few minutes to loosen the skins off the hazelnuts; before opening up the towel shake gently a few times. Most of the skins should be released from the hazelnuts; pick out the hazelnuts, transfer to a food processor, and discard the skins. Roast the pistachios or almonds for 6 to 8 minutes until toasted and add to the hazelnuts.

2. In a small skillet over medium heat toast the cumin, fennel, coriander, caraway, and peppercorns until fragrant, about 2 minutes. If you're using a whole dried chile pepper, toast it along with the seeds. Pour the toasted spices (and whole dried chile if using) into a spice grinder and pulse a few times. Don't grind into too fine a powder; a slightly gritty texture is best. Add the ground spices to the nuts along with the red pepper flakes (if using) and smoked salt and pulse until the dukka has a sandy consistency. The dukka is done! For an average appetizer serving for 4, pour about ½ cup into a small, shallow serving bowl.

3. Serve with hearty bread or thick "pocketless" pita and a small dish of good olive oil. To serve with jicama, peel the jicama with a Y-shaped peeler (page 30) and slice into sticks about ½ inch thick. Toss with the lemon juice and serve with a serving dish of dukka for dipping.

Try adding 1 to 2 teaspoons of the following seeds; roast with the other spices.

Flax Seed Dukka: whole flax seeds

Black Cumin Dukka: black cumin (nigella seeds)

Sesame Seed Dukka: sesame seeds

Black Sesame Seed Dukka: black sesame seeds

Store in a tightly sealed container in the refrigerator to keep the oils in the nuts fresh and tasty.

cashew yogurt sauce

MAKES ABOUT 2 CUPS

*Enhance plain soy (or coconut) yogurt with the creamy sweetness of cashews, or serve as a tasty sauce alongside Indian curries and Middle Eastern dishes, or use as a basis for **Cucumber Tzatziki** (page 66), a luscious Greek-style dip perfect with warm pita bread or along with **Seitan Gyro Roll Ups** (page 112). Make sure to use unroasted, unsalted cashews only; roasted cashews won't taste right.*

½ cup unroasted whole cashews, soaked for 1 hour or longer until completely soft

1½ cups plain soy or coconut yogurt

2 teaspoons olive oil

2 cloves garlic

¾ teaspoon salt

1. Drain the cashews and place them in a blender. Pulse the cashews with ½ cup of soy yogurt and the olive oil until as smooth as possible. Pour into a small mixing bowl and add remaining yogurt.

2. Using a mortar and pestle (see page 31), grind together the garlic and salt to form a smooth paste, then stir into yogurt mixture. Cover and chill completely before serving or using in recipes.

cucumber tzatziki

½ cup unroasted whole cashews, soaked for 1 hour or longer until completely soft

1½ cups plain soy or coconut yogurt

2 teaspoons olive oil

4 cloves garlic

¾ teaspoon salt, plus additional for sprinkling cucumbers

½ pound of cucumbers

2 heaping tablespoons finely chopped fresh dill

1. Drain the cashews and place them in a blender. Pulse the cashews with ½ cup of soy yogurt and the olive oil until as smooth as possible. Pour into a small mixing bowl and add remaining yogurt.

2. Using a mortar and pestle, grind together the the garlic and salt to form a smooth paste, then stir into yogurt mixture.

3. Peel the cucumbers and grate on the large holes of a box grater, then sprinkle the cucumbers with a little sea salt. Layer a few strong paper towels on top of one another, pile in the cucumber and gently twist the top of the towels together to form a bundle. Squeeze the cucumber sachet over the sink to remove as much liquid as possible, taking care not to tear the paper towels.

4. Stir the grated cucumber into the yogurt sauce along with 2 heaping tablespoons of finely chopped fresh dill. Pour into a dish and chill until completely cold. Serve alongside Greek dishes or with pita bread brushed with olive oil and grilled.

tomato dill apple raita

MAKES ABOUT 2½ CUPS

Use this zesty and cooling soy yogurt sauce with any savory rice dish or grilled item for a proper Indian-thali style feast. Making it a day in advance will enhance the summery sweet and herbal flavors.

2 cups plain soy yogurt or coconut yogurt

2 cloves garlic

½ teaspoon sea salt

10 fresh basil leaves

1 tablespoon fresh mint, finely chopped

1 large tomato, seeds and core removed and finely chopped

2 tablespoons lime juice

1 green apple

1 teaspoon black mustard seeds

½ teaspoon ground cayenne pepper (optional)

1. Pour soy yogurt into a mixing bowl. Peel the garlic and use a mortar and pestle to pound it (see page 31), along with the sea salt, into a paste (see salted garlic paste, page 5). Stir into yogurt. Roll up the basil leaves and with a chef's knife slice them into the thinnest ribbons possible; stir these along with the mint, tomato, and lime juice into the yogurt mixture.

2. Remove core from apple, don't peel, and with the large holes of a box grater, shred the apple and immediately stir into the yogurt mixture.

3. Sprinkle the mustard seeds into a preheated small skillet over medium-high heat. Toast the

seeds, stirring occasionally, until they pop, any-where from 1 to 3 minutes. When the seeds begin to pop, cover the pan (and keep hot mustard seeds out of your eyes). As soon as the popping slows down, remove from heat and immediately pour the seeds into the yogurt mixture, add cayenne, and stir. Taste mixture and if necessary season with more salt and lime juice. Pour into a serving bowl, cover with plastic wrap, and chill for 30 minutes until ready to serve.

MOCK NUOC Cham

MAKES ABOUT 1 CUP

*Oh, that heavenly sweet and tangy sauce that gar-nishes Vietnamese cuisine is a must for the **Seitan Bo Bun** salad (page 234). This recipe makes plenty of sauce, ideal for your next Vietnamese cooking marathon.*

> 3 tablespoons finely shredded carrot
> ½ cup lime juice (bottled is fine, since you must simmer the sauce)
> ¼ cup water
> 6 tablespoons sugar
> 2 tablespoons finely minced fresh red hot chile pepper
> 4 teaspoons finely chopped garlic
> 1½ teaspoons sea salt
> Sprinkle of sesame seeds
> A few fresh mint leaves, rolled and sliced into paper-thin ribbons (optional)

1. To shred the carrot on the finest holes of a box grater, or use a Y-shaped julienne peeler (page 30) for delicate, perfectly shaped shreds.

2. Combine lime juice, water, sugar, chile pepper, garlic, and sea salt in a small saucepan and bring to a rolling boil over medium heat.

3. Reduce heat, stir and simmer for 10 to 12 minutes until liquid has thickened to the consistency of a thin syrup. Remove from heat and stir in sesame seeds. Let cool to room temperature and stir in shredded carrot before serving. Garnish with mint right before serving.

Miss the Fish Sauce?

For a fermented, salty flavor, use 4 teaspoons of Thai thin soy sauce (see page 19) in place of salt. Don't use regular supermarket soy sauce; it tastes too strong and will make the sauce a dark color.

Chickpea Parmigiana Topping

MAKES ABOUT 2 CUPS

A technique borrowed from Ethiopian cuisine trans-forms humble chickpea flour into salty, tender golden crumbles that resemble coarsely grated Parmigiano-Reggiano cheese. Like finely grated cheese, these crumbles dissolve on contact with hot, moist foods

and add a sharp, lemony, and salty coating perfect for Mediterranean recipes. Best enjoyed sprinkled directly onto soups, like my **White Bean Farro Soup with Chickpea Parmigiana** (page 122), immediately before serving, or on hot pasta or **Mostly Mediterranean Eggplant Parmagiana** (page 273). Store Chickpea Parmigiana in a tightly covered container in the fridge, and always use a clean, dry spoon to serve.

> 3 tablespoons olive oil
> ½ cup chickpea flour
> ¼ cup lemon juice
> ¼ cup water
> 1 teaspoon sea salt

1. Over medium heat in a small saucepan preheat the olive oil, then pour in the chickpea flour. Use a rubber spatula to mash the flour into the oil and stir constantly to toast the flour for about 2 minutes. The flour should turn a darker shade of yellow and look slightly damp.

2. In a measuring cup, whisk together the lemon juice, water, and salt. Pour into the flour; it will sizzle and splatter a little. Stir constantly until a firm ball of dough forms and pulls away from the sides of the pan, about 3 minutes. Remove from heat and spread the dough onto a dinner plate. Use the spatula or your fingers (once the dough cools slightly) to press and smear the dough into a thin layer over the surface of the plate. Transfer the plate to the refrigerator and chill for 15 minutes.

3. Once the dough feels completely cool, remove from the refrigerator and drag a large fork through the dough. Continue to press the fork through it while also stirring and fluffing up the crumbs. The more you work the dough with the fork, the finer the crumbs will be. Continue for 3 to 5 minutes until it's very fine and crumbly. The crumbs

are ready for use. Or pour them into a container and chill another 20 minutes for slightly firmer crumbs.

4. For best results, sprinkle crumbs generously over hot soup or pasta just before serving. The crumbs will dissolve on hot, moist food. To keep crumbs fluffy, use a fork to fluff up before serving.

Rhubarb cranberry chutney

MAKES ABOUT 2½ CUPS

Tangy, tongue-tingling rhubarb is a favorite of mine for homemade stovetop chutneys. Many of the testers enjoyed using this sweet and sour chutney as an alternative to cranberry sauce for Thanksgiving, but I make it for all kinds of Indian meals (rice and breads are my favorite) or tuck it into a sandwich spread with cashew-based vegan cheese spread.

> 2 teaspoons coriander seeds
> 1 teaspoon black mustard seeds
> 1 pound rhubarb stems, cut into ½-inch-thick slices
> 1 cup dried cranberries
> ¾ cup plus 2 tablespoons sugar
> ⅓ cup apple cider vinegar
> 1 star anise
> One 3-inch stick of cinnamon
> ½ teaspoon ground cayenne pepper (optional, for a spicier chutney)

1. Gently crush the coriander seeds using a mortar and pestle (see page 31). In a heavy 3-quart pan, toast the mustard seeds over high heat. When they start to pop, stir in the crushed coriander and toast for 30 seconds, then add remaining ingredients. Stir a few times with a wooden spoon and simmer for 15 minutes, then reduce heat to medium-low and continue to simmer, stirring occasionally, for 20 to 25 minutes, until rhubarb has broken down and mixture resembles a thick sauce. The mixture will continue to thicken as it cools.

2. Remove star anise and cinnamon stick before packing into a tightly covered glass container and storing in the fridge until ready to serve.

coconut Chile Relish (pol sambol)

MAKES 2 CUPS

This coconut condiment can spark a lifetime love affair with Sri Lankan food and is hearty enough to enjoy as a side dish, too. All coconut-based curries can be enhanced by the addition of this chewy, tart, spicy mash.

Made with frozen grated coconut, pol sambol is relatively fast to prepare. Look for the frozen grated coconut and curry leaves in Indian grocery stores (see page 14 for more about frozen grated coconut). If you can't find curry leaves, just omit them entirely. When working with fresh curry leaves (see page 14), don't chop them, always leave curry leaves whole.

Curry leaves are soft and edible and do not need to be removed from a dish before serving.

2 cups (about ½ pound) grated coconut, frozen or fresh
1 large ripe tomato, core and seeds removed and finely chopped
1 small red onion, peeled and finely diced
6 fresh or frozen curry leaves, left whole
2 tablespoons lime juice
4 cloves garlic, minced
2 to 4 teaspoons ground cayenne pepper (use even more if you love spicy food)
1½ teaspoons ground black pepper
1¼ teaspoon sea salt

1. In a mixing bowl, combine coconut, tomato, onion, and curry leaves. In a measuring cup whisk together lime juice, garlic, cayenne, black pepper, and sea salt and pour over coconut. Use a fork or your fingers to thoroughly mix. Warm a large stainless steel skillet over medium heat and add this mixture.

2. Stirring frequently with a wooden spoon, cook just until the mixture has a slightly dried-out consistency and is fragrant, about 5 minutes. Don't cook long enough to toast the coconut, only just enough so that the mixture is no longer damp. This is important if using frozen coconut. Remove from heat and let cool; serve at room temperature with curries. Store chilled in a tightly covered container for up to a week.

Tonkatsu Sauce

MAKES ABOUT ¾ CUP

*Many Japanese fast foods must be accompanied by this salty, sweet condiment that may remind you just a little of a Japanese spin on barbeque sauce. A must for panko-crusted foods, or try brushing it on hot **Savory Baked Tofu** (page 50) during the last few minutes of baking. Look for vegetarian Worcestershire sauce (it doesn't contain any anchovies!) in natural food stores.*

⅔ cup all natural ketchup

2 tablespoons vegetarian Worcestershire sauce

2 tablespoons dark brown sugar

1 tablespoon shoyu soy sauce (see page 16)

1 tablespoon mirin cooking wine (see page 16)

1½ teaspoons dry mustard powder

1. In a small saucepan whisk together all the ingredients until the mustard powder is completely blended into the sauce. Simmer over medium heat for 2 minutes, stirring occasionally. Serve warm or at room temperature. Keep leftover sauce chilled, stored in a tightly covered container.

Mexican Dried Chile Salsa

MAKES ABOUT 2½ CUPS

Here's a dark red, smoky salsa that's destined for greatness on tacos, rice and beans, chips, or other Mexican edibles. Depending on the chilies, it can be quietly piquant to tongue-blistering, so heed my advice regarding chile selection. A good beginner-level version can use ancho chilies for a mellow, dark red salsa with hints of wood smoke and berries. Toasting and plumping the chilies in boiling water removes bitterness, and roasting the tomatillos enriches their tart flavor.

If tomatillos are in short supply, substitute green regular tomatoes, or look for canned tomatillos where Mexican groceries are sold. If using canned tomatillos, skip the broiling step and add them (along with the juices) directly into the blender along with the rest of the ingredients.

3 ounces dried Mexican chile peppers, either one kind or a combination

1 pound tomatillos, papery husks removed

1 small red or white onion, peeled and diced

1 tablespoon lime juice

3 cloves garlic, peeled

1 teaspoon sugar or ½ teaspoon agave nectar

1 teaspoon salt, or to taste

1. In a large sauce pan bring 1 quart of water to boil. Have ready a medium-size glass or metal heat-resistant bowl. Heat a cast-iron skillet over medium heat. While the skillet is heating slice open the dried chilies, remove the stems and seeds, and spread the chilies so that they can be easily flattened when pressed down with a spatula. Place in a heated skillet and toast for a minute, pressing and frequently flipping over the chilies. Watch carefully to prevent the chilies from burning. Remove skillet from heat and place chilies in a heat-resistant bowl. Pour boiling water on top and soak for 10 minutes to soften chilies. Drain and discard the water.

2. Preheat the oven broiler to high and get ready a 10- to 12-inch cast-iron skillet. In a mixing bowl cover the tomatillos with hot water and slosh around to remove the soapy residue on the skins. Drain, pat tomatillos dry, and arrange in the skillet. Broil for 6 to 8 minutes, stirring occasionally, until the skins have turned a dull green and are beginning to char and split. Turn off the oven, remove the tomatillos from the heat, and cool for 5 minutes. Transfer the roasted tomatillos and their juices to a blender or food processor. Add the drained chilies and remaining ingredients. Puree into a thick salsa, but don't make it too smooth; leave a little bit of chunky texture.

3. Store in a tightly covered container in the fridge; the flavor develops as it sits. Use within 2 weeks.

Large ancho, guajillo, or pasilla chilies are deep red chilies with varying degrees of mild heat that make a good beginner's salsa. If you crave more heat, sneak in dried chili de arbol—a small, bright red chile—or small-but-feisty piquin chilies, or long, glossy costeño chilies. Look for an assortment of dried chilies sold in plastic bags in Mexican groceries.

sour Dilly cream

MAKES 1 CUP

A tangy cream is an essential partner for many Eastern European dishes. This is my fast go-to cream for something zippy and smooth for swirling into soup or drizzling on a dumpling.

If there's a vegan faux sour cream product you love to use, just whip it up with chopped dill, garlic, and salt for a special Eastern European garnish. Sour cream (vegan or otherwise) was never my thing, but I love this blend of plain soy yogurt with a touch of vegan mayo. Use a thick, rich vegan mayonnaise in this recipe for the best flavor.

¾ cup plain soy yogurt
¼ cup thick vegan mayonnaise
1 clove garlic, minced
Pinch of sea salt
3 tablespoons finely chopped dill

1. In a food processor or in a large measuring cup using an immersion blender, pulse together the yogurt, mayonnaise, garlic, and salt until smooth. Pulse in the dill a few times. Keep chilled until ready to serve.

spicy sesame tomato sambal

MAKES ABOUT 1 HEAPING CUP

This sesame-based sambal is inspired by the smoky sambals that complement the momo dumplings from my favorite Tibetan and Nepalese restaurants, but it's versatile enough to dab on any dumpling or slather on a veggie burger. Go ahead and adjust the red chile to your own heat tolerance, or make it hotter, tough guy.

2 teaspoons cumin seeds

2 teaspoons coriander seeds

3 to 5 teaspoons red pepper flakes or dried red Thai chile peppers

⅓ cup sesame seeds

2 plum tomatoes, core and seeds removed

2 tablespoons tomato paste

2 cloves garlic, peeled

3 tablespoons rice vinegar

1 tablespoon agave nectar

1 tablespoon toasted sesame oil

¾ teaspoon sea salt

1. Toast the cumin seeds, coriander seeds, and red pepper flakes over medium heat in a skillet until fragrant, about 1½ minutes. Pour spices into a clean coffee mill and pulse until powdered, then pour into a food processor. Toast the sesame seeds until fragrant, stirring frequently, about 2 minutes, then pour into the food processor along with the spices.

2. Add the remaining ingredients to the food processor and pulse everything into a pasty sauce, scraping down the sides of the food processor occasionally. Taste the sambal, and if desired season with more salt or vinegar. Store in the refrigerator in a tightly covered container.

Tomato Dill Sambal: A delicious variation of this sambal, great for samosas and Middle Eastern foods. Pulse 2 tablespoons of finely chopped fresh dill into the sambal.

spicy kale coconut relish (malluma)

MAKES ABOUT 2 ½ CUPS

My favorite Sri Lankan sambol, this cooling saladlike creation is a joy to eat piled on top of any hot curry or rice pilaf. Common kale is minced very fine, standing in for the traditional gotu kola used in Sri Lanka, but some recipe testers enjoyed chopping the leaves by hand into larger pieces for a more substantial side dish. See page 14 for more about frozen grated coconut.

1 pound leafy kale

¼ cup grated frozen grated coconut, thawed
at room temperature

1 plum tomato, core and seeds removed and
finely chopped

3 tablespoons lime juice

1 teaspoon ground cayenne pepper (or more
for a spicier sambol)

1 teaspoon sea salt

1. Tear stems away from kale leaves and discard. In a salad spinner wash kale and spin dry. Use a food processor to finely chop kale, pulsing it in small batches, then transfer it to a glass or plastic mixing bowl. Add coconut and tomato.

2. In a measuring cup whisk together lime juice, cayenne, and salt. Pour over the kale and use your fingers or a fork and thoroughly mash the dressing into the sambol. Cover with plastic wrap and let stand at room temperature for an hour to allow the flavor to develop. Serve at room temperature and refrigerate any leftovers. Store tightly covered and consume within 2 days.

CHAPTER 4

salads, spreads & sandwiches

A light meal or a starter to the main course, there's a world of salads, spreads, and finger foods that have inspired me and stretch well beyond the concept of appetizer. How often is it that the little things before the entrée are the most memorable parts of a meal . . . so why not make them the entire meal? When served two or three together, they can create a rich and varied spread.

Allow me to tempt you with an imaginary platter of herbed French cheese spread made with cultured cashews, refreshing summer rice paper rolls stuffed with curried avocado, crunchy sweet and sour Indian bhel puri, Italian artichoke panzanella salad, or an exciting Mexican dip made from pumpkin seeds. Either for guests or yourself, these small plates will satisfy taste buds searching for big thrills.

A collection of mini-meals would not be complete without tipping a hand toward the great sandwiches of the world; from modern classics like Vietnamese bahn mi and tender seitan Greek gyros to the inspired cemita of Mexican cuisine. Jackfruit tacos, the new modern vegan classic, are so meaty-looking your carnivorous friends will marvel at your vegan culinary powers.

Thai Shredded Mango Salad

SERVES 2 TO 3

*This unexpected and refreshing combination of crisp mango, green beans, lime dressing, and chopped peanuts is many a Thai foodie's favorite introduction to tangy Thai salads. Garnish with batons of **Savory Baked Tofu** and transform this into a main course for a warm summer night.*

*For the best possible salad, make sure the unripe mango is very firm; shredding will be tricky if the mango is ripe and soft. Save riper mangos for **Avocado Mango Cashew Salad** (page 78), or use green papaya.*

1 hard, unripe mango or 1 small green
    papaya or 3 cups packed shredded
    green papaya

¼ pound raw green beans or Asian long
    beans

10 ripe red cherry or grape tomatoes

1 to 4 fresh Thai red chilies or
    ¼ to 1 teaspoon red pepper flakes

1 cup roughly chopped cilantro

3 tablespoons lime juice

4 teaspoons grated palm sugar (see page 18)
    or light brown sugar

1 tablespoon Thai thin soy sauce (page 19)
    or ½ teaspoon sea salt

2 large cloves garlic, peeled and minced

⅓ cup ground roasted peanuts or cashews

A few twists freshly ground pepper

1 recipe *Savory Baked Tofu* (page 50), sliced
    into matchsticks, or prepared baked or
    fried tofu (for an entrée salad)

1. Prepare the following vegetables and place them in a mixing bowl: Use a Y-shaped vegetable peeler (see page 30) to peel the outside of the mango or green papaya, then use a Y-shaped julienne peeler (see page 30) to slice the mango/papaya into matchsticks; take your time and flip the mango over to slice it down as close to the seed as possible (for papaya, discard the soft seeds inside). Slice green beans on an angle into long slivers no thicker than ¼ inch. Slice each cherry tomato in half. If using fresh Thai chilies, slice into the thinnest paper-thin rounds possible. Add the cilantro along with the vegetables in the bowl.

2. In a 2-cup liquid measuring cup, whisk together the lime juice, palm or brown sugar, soy sauce or salt, and garlic. Pour over vegetables, then sprinkle with chopped peanuts and ground pepper. Toss the salad and coat everything with the dressing. Mound onto a serving platter. If adding tofu, toss along with the vegetables. This salad is best consumed right away.

*Preshredded green papaya can sometimes be found where Thai groceries are sold, but Asian long beans are common in most Asian groceries. You don't need a lot of them for this recipe, and remaining green beans can be used in stir-fries, **Pad Kee Mao** (page 223), or tucked into any curry. As with all dishes with fresh chilies, use what suits you best; I love this salad very spicy, but a pinch of red pepper flakes may be all you need.*

avocado mango cashew salad

SERVES 2 TO 3

My now-defunct favorite Thai restaurant, Rice Avenue in Jackson Heights, may be gone, but their luscious fusion of ripe mango, avocado, and sweet lime dressing with a dusting of roasted rice powder lives on in this recipe. This salad tastes like summer no matter what time of year it's savored.

Dice That Mango

A thin, slightly flexible but sharp serrated knife is the best tool for slicing the soft flesh of a ripe mango. Place knife about ¾ of an inch from the stem and balance the other end of the mango on a cutting board. Cut alongside the mango while avoiding the flat wide seed of the mango that runs almost the whole length of the fruit. Using a gentle sawing motion, remove as much flesh as possible, then repeat on the other side.

Now trim around the edge of the seed to remove any remaining flesh. Returning your attention to the two mango halves, score the insides of each half into squares about ¼-inch wide, taking care not to cut through the skin. Now for the grand finale: grab the edges of the mango half and press the skin underneath to push the perfect little mango cubes outward. Peel or slice away the cubes.

2 tablespoons lime juice

1 tablespoon well-packed grated palm sugar (see page 18) or light brown sugar

¼ teaspoon salt

A big pinch of ground white pepper

1 ripe avocado, diced into ½-inch cubes

1 ripe mango, peeled and diced

1 medium-size red onion, peeled and diced into ¼-inch cubes

1 cup chopped fresh cilantro

1 tablespoon chopped fresh mint

1 small hot green chile (Thai or Serrano), finely minced (optional)

¼ cup chopped roasted cashews

1 tablespoon *Toasted Rice Powder* (page 41)

1. In a large mixing bowl whisk together lime juice, brown sugar, salt, and white pepper. Add the diced avocado and toss a few times in the dressing. Now add the mango, red onion, cilantro leaves, mint, green hot chile, and chopped roasted cashews to the bowl.

2. Use a wide rubber spatula to thoroughly stir the salad, making sure all the avocado and mango are coated with the lime dressing. Mound the salad onto a serving platter and sprinkle with roasted rice powder. Serve and eat this salad immediately!

Look for little cakes of palm sugar in Thai grocery stores. Grate a cake of palm sugar along the large holes of a box grater to use in recipes. Light brown sugar makes a good substitute when palm sugar cannot be found.

AVOCADO MANGO CASHEW SALAD

ginger-marinated cucumbers

MAKES ABOUT 2 CUPS

Cool and crisp, marinated cucumbers add a refreshing contrast to any rich Asian meal and are the traditional companion, if a new recipe can have a tradition, to the **Char Siu Seitan Bao** *(page 197)— they are a breeze to prepare while the seitan is roasting. Try using them as a topping for the* **Scrambled Tofu Breakfast Bahn Mi** *(page 109) sandwiches, too!*

Seedless English cucumbers are best in this recipe, but any variety works using the simple seed scooping method in the recipe instructions.

> ½ pound cucumbers, peeled and halved
> lengthwise
> 2 teaspoons freshly grated ginger
> 3 tablespoons rice vinegar
> 1 tablespoon sugar
> 1 heaping teaspoon kosher salt

GARNISH

> 2 scallions, green parts only, sliced as thinly
> as possible
> 1 tablespoon toasted sesame seeds

1. Use a rounded 1 teaspoon measuring spoon and scoop it down the center of the cut side of the cucumbers to remove seeds and pulp; use a ½ teaspoon measuring spoon if the cucumbers are especially small. Slice cucumber halves into thin ¼-inch slices; the slices should look like fat letter "c"s. Toss with the ginger, rice vinegar, sugar, and salt and seal in a glass or plastic container. Chill for 20 minutes before serving, occasionally shaking the container to stir around the juices.

2. To serve, spoon cucumbers on a serving dish. Garnish with sliced scallions and sesame seeds. Eat the day they're made for the best flavor and texture.

To grate ginger, peel using a vegetable peeler or by scraping with the edge of a spoon. A Microplane grater makes good finely grated ginger, or look for a specialty ginger grater tool if you're dead serious about ginger grating.

With Goji Berries: Toss in 2 tablespoons of dried goji berries (also called wolf berries) along with the cucumbers. Marinate for 30 minutes to allow the berries to plump slightly.

This fast method is great for all kinds of tender vegetables. In place of cucumbers, try using the following (or make a blend of a few vegetables and fruits).

Ginger-Marinated Daikon: Peel the daikon and slice into matchsticks.

Ginger-Marinated Japanese Salad Turnips: Peel and slice the turnips into matchsticks.

Ginger-Marinated Asian Pears: Leave the pears unpeeled, remove cores, and slice into quarters. Slice each quarter into ¼-inch slices.

Ginger-Marinated Carrots: Peel the carrots and cut into matchsticks using a knife or a mandolin (see page 30).

coconut kale summer rolls with peanut sauce

MAKES 10 FAT ROLLS

It's easy to see why summer rolls (or rice paper rolls) have such a following with Vietnamese food fans: cool veggie fillings, chewy rice wrappers, and velvety peanut dipping sauce are a winning combination. At home I make the following two variations on the traditional mellow fillings: unconventional marinated kale and crunchy pear (or bean threads or cucumber) and buttery curried mashed avocado.

Assembled rice paper rolls should be enjoyed within an hour or so of making. If you want to prepare in advance, make the dipping sauce and kale salad and store the sliced pear covered with cold water and chilled in the fridge for up to a day. For tips on rolling up a summer roll, follow the lumpia spring roll illustration on page 177.

PEANUT COCONUT DIPPING SAUCE

- ⅓ cup smooth natural peanut butter
- ⅓ cup coconut milk, regular or reduced fat
- 3 tablespoons hoisin sauce (see page 13)
- 2 tablespoons lime juice
- 2 teaspoons brown sugar
- 2 to 3 teaspoons Asian chili garlic sauce
- ½ teaspoon grated fresh ginger
- 3 tablespoons roasted chopped peanuts, for garnish

ROLLS AND FILLING

- ½ pound kale
- 3 tablespoons plus 2 teaspoons lime juice
- 2 tablespoons grated dried unsweetened coconut
- 2 teaspoons sugar or 1 teaspoon agave nectar
- 2 teaspoons grapeseed oil
- ½ teaspoon salt
- 1 large Asian pear (about ½ pound)
- 10 round 8- to 10-inch-wide rice wrappers (have a few extra just in case you have more filling or tear a few wrappers)
- 1 ounce bean thread cellophane noodles, cooked and drained according to package directions
- 10 large sprigs of cilantro
- 4 scallions, green parts only, sliced lengthwise into ¼-inch-wide strips about 5 inches long

1. Make the dipping sauce first: in a small mixing bowl whisk together all of the ingredients, except chopped peanuts. When ready to serve, scoop into a serving dish and sprinkle with chopped peanut.

2. Make the filling: strip the leaves off the kale and discard the stems. Wash, dry and stack a few leaves and roll into a tight bundle. Use a sharp knife to slice the kale into the thinnest ribbons you possibly can, ⅛-inch wide or less. In a mixing bowl combine kale, 3 tablespoons of lime juice, coconut, sugar, grapeseed oil, and salt and knead the kale with the dressing for 2 minutes until kale has reduced in bulk by half and the shreds are tender and shiny. Core the pear, slice into matchsticks no thicker than ¼ inch and toss with remaining 2 teaspoons of lime juice. Have noodles and cilantro arranged on a plate ready to use. Have the rice paper wrappers handy nearby

and fill a 12-inch pie plate (or similar dish) with 2 inches of warm water.

3. To assemble a roll, press a rice paper wrapper into the plate of warm water. After about 15 to 20 seconds it should start to become pliable but still firm enough to handle without tearing; if they soak too long they'll get too soft and may rip when handled. If you do end up tearing one, discard and soak a new wrapper for a few seconds less until you reach the perfect soaking time.

4. Remove the wrapper from water, shake off any excess water and spread onto a work surface. On the portion closest to you, mound about 3 tablespoons of the kale salad, a similar size portion of noodles, a sprig of cilantro, and a stalk of scallion. Fold over the opposite sides to overlap the filling, then firmly hold onto the filling and roll the summer roll away from you; allow a portion of the scallion to stick out of one of the ends of the roll. Repeat with remaining rolls, soaking any additional rice paper wrappers as needed. Serve immediately with dipping sauce!

Curried Avocado Summer Rolls

*A slightly more traditional filling with a twist: avocado mashed with curry powder. Serve with the Peanut Coconut Dipping Sauce. For the tofu use thin strips of **Savory Baked Tofu** (page 50) or purchased baked tofu.*

1 ripe avocado
2 teaspoons curry powder
1 tablespoon lime juice
½ teaspoon salt
10 round 8- to 10-inch-wide rice wrappers (have a few extra just in case you have more filling or tear a few wrappers)
1 ounce bean thread cellophane noodles, cooked and drained according to package directions
2 cups shredded romaine lettuce or finely shredded green cabbage
10 ½-inch-wide strips of *Savory Baked Tofu* (page 50) or purchased baked or fried tofu
10 large sprigs of cilantro
4 scallions, green parts only, sliced lengthwise into 10 ¼-inch-wide strips about 5 inches long

1. Mash the avocado with the curry powder, lime juice, and salt into a chunky paste. Assemble the remaining ingredients on a dish or cutting board and moisten the rice wrappers as directed. Fill each roll with a smear of the avocado mixture, an equal portion of noodles and romaine, a strip of tofu, a sprig of cilantro, and a slice of scallion. Fold and roll as directed for coconut kale summer rolls.

CURRIED AVOCADO SUMMER ROLLS

Ninja Carrot Ginger Dressing

MAKES 1¾ CUPS

For every Japanese restaurant in New York City there's a version of this gingery orange dressing, but Dojo's in the East Village rules them all. While my recipe isn't exactly the same (and how could it be), it will steal away your salad-loving heart like a ninja in the night.

This creamy, mayo-free dressing is best enjoyed spooned on a simple array of crisp, mild salad vegetables. Since this is a fresh dressing, it's best consumed within 2 days of preparing, but you'll find plenty of uses including spooned on steamed vegetables or veggie burgers or as a dipping sauce for baked tofu.

> 1 cup coarsely grated carrot
> ½ cup diced white onion
> 5 teaspoons grapeseed oil or flaxseed oil
> 2 tablespoons rice vinegar
> 3 cloves garlic, peeled and chopped
> 1 tablespoon minced fresh ginger
> 2 teaspoons agave nectar
> 2 teaspoons toasted sesame oil
> ¾ teaspoon salt
> 4 to 6 tablespoons water

1. In a blender pulse together all of the ingredients plus 3 tablespoons of water into a smooth sauce; depending on the strength of your blender this can take 40 seconds to 3 minutes. Then stream in 1 tablespoon of water at a time for a thin and pourable salad dressing.

2. Store dressing in a tightly covered container in the refrigerator and use within 2 days.

Miso Carrot Dressing: Use the *Ninja Carrot Ginger Dressing* recipe, omitting the salt and adding 1 heaping tablespoon light-colored miso along with the ingredients in the blender. Here are a few simple serving suggestions for this dressing:

Use it to dress thinly shredded green and red cabbage. A handful of currants or raisins sweetens this mix.

Quarter and dice 1 pound of small Japanese salad turnips. Top with the dressing, then add thinly chopped green scallions and a sprinkle of toasted sesame seeds.

Serve the dressing as a dip alongside steamed cauliflower and broccoli.

Peruvian Purple Potato Salad

SERVES 4 AS A SIDE

This purple, gently spiced twist on potato salad is inspired by Peruvian causas, a layered potato salad-like dish with avocado and olives. For a super-festive salad, try replacing half of the purple potatoes with red or yellow waxy potatoes. While causas are usually molded into shapes, I prefer to serve this salad piled into deep serving bowls.

Ají amarillo is a special South American chili pepper that gives this dish its golden color and a tropical chile flavor. While difficult to locate fresh, a convenient paste is much easier to find in Latin grocery stores or online.

1½ pounds purple potatoes

3 tablespoons ají amarillo paste

3 tablespoons olive oil

2 tablespoons lime juice

½ teaspoon sea salt, or to taste

A few twists of freshly ground pepper

4 scallions, sliced as thinly as possible

3 ripe red tomatoes, core and seeds removed and finely diced

½ cup Kalamata olives, pits removed and sliced

1 ripe avocado, diced into ½-inch chunks and tossed with 2 teaspoons lime juice

3 tablespoons finely chopped fresh cilantro or parsley

1. Peel the potatoes (or leave on the skins, just scrub thoroughly to remove any dirt), dice into 1-inch cubes, place in a 3-quart pot, and cover with 3 inches of cold water. Bring to a boil over high heat and simmer for 18 to 20 minutes or until very tender, then drain.

2. In a mixing bowl whisk together ají amarillo paste, olive oil, lime juice, salt, and pepper. Add 1 cup of cooked potato chunks and with a fork or potato masher, mash the potato into a chunky puree. Add the remaining potatoes, scallions, tomatoes, and olives. Use a rubber spatula to fold the potatoes into the dressing.

3. Mound the salad onto a serving platter or into deep bowls and arrange chunks of avocado on top. Sprinkle with cilantro and serve immediately.

orange and olive fennel salad

SERVES 4

Refreshing citrusy fennel salad blends North African and Italian flavors for a light starter for a heavy meal or as a side for any warm weather entree. You can use a mandolin (see page 30) for ultra-thin, semi-transparent fennel slices, but a sharp chef's knife and some practice will work wonders, too; work slowly and watch those fingers (same goes for using a mandolin!).

1 pound fennel (about 1 large, heavy bulb)

1 tablespoon lemon juice

2 teaspoons finely minced preserved lemon (see **Preserved Lemons, Two Ways**, page 58) or ½ teaspoon freshly grated lemon zest

1 large navel orange

½ cup sliced, pitted black Kalamata olives

½ teaspoon hot paprika

½ teaspoon sea salt

¼ teaspoon ground black pepper

2 teaspoons of olive oil for drizzling

1. Use a mandolin (see page 30) set on the thinnest setting to shave the fennel into long, nearly translucent shreds. If you're using a knife, slice the fennel in half, place cut side down on the cutting board, and carefully slice as thinly as possible. Take your time to get the best possible results. When done, place the fennel in a mixing bowl, sprinkle with lemon juice

and minced preserved lemon, and toss to coat. Peel the orange and use a chef's knife to slice it into the thinnest rounds possible.

2. Spread fennel onto a serving platter. Arrange oranges on top in a pretty circular pattern, then arrange olives on top. Sprinkle with paprika, sea salt, and black pepper and drizzle with olive oil. Or instead for a yummy, casual salad, toss in a bowl with the spices and olive oil. This salad is best enjoyed immediately after preparing.

Greek village salad with cashew faux feta (Horiatiki salad)

SERVES 4

Horiatiki salad should be simple; the season's best tomatoes, cucumbers, onions, and olives topped with feta, or in this instance creamy bits of cashews soaked in a briny marinade—no weird anchovies or extraneous lettuce leaves. Serve this salad with hunks of crusty peasant-style bread to mop up the blissful tomato-onion-olive oil juices that linger on the plate after the vegetables are gone.

CASHEW FAUX FETA

1 cup unroasted, unsalted whole cashews
2 teaspoons sea salt
3 tablespoons good-quality extra-virgin olive oil

2 tablespoons lemon juice
1 tablespoon white wine vinegar or white balsamic vinegar
2 teaspoons olive brine or more lemon juice
2 teaspoons dried oregano
1 teaspoon dried dill
1 teaspoon dried thyme
2 cloves garlic, finely minced or pressed

SALAD

1 pound ripe red tomatoes
1 large red onion, peeled
½ pound seedless cucumbers (about 1 large English cucumber)
½ cup kalamata olives, without pits
2 teaspoons dried oregano

1. Roughly chop the cashews into bite-size pieces, put in a mixing bowl, and cover with 3 inches of hot water. Stir in 1 teaspoon of salt and let stand for 2 hours or overnight; cashews should be completely soft. Drain well and use your fingers to break apart any remaining large pieces of cashews into crumbles. Combine cashews with the remaining 1 teaspoon of salt and remaining faux feta ingredients in a glass or plastic bowl, cover, and let stand at room temperature for at least 30 minutes or up to 2 hours, stirring occasionally.

2. To assemble the salad, remove the cores from the tomatoes and dice into bite-size chunks. Slice the onion in half and slice into thin half moons. Peel the cucumber, slice in half lengthwise and slice into thin half circles. Combine with the olives and cashew feta in a mixing bowl, then transfer to a large, deep salad bowl, sprinkling any remaining cashew feta juices over the salad. Sprinkle with dried oregano and serve.

Mediterranean Chopped Salad

Many of the elements of this salad are ones you'll see in salads all over the Mediterranean and Middle East. These endless combinations of diced tomatoes, cucumbers and onions are ripe for stuffing into pita or serving as part of a larger mezze spread.

1. Start with the **Greek Village Salad** recipe (page 86), leaving out the cashews and olives. Whisk together the remaining ingredients into a dressing.

2. Remove the cores and seeds from the tomatoes, peel the cucumbers (use 1 pound of cucumbers), and dice these and the onion into ¼-inch cubes. Toss with the dressing and serve immediately. Also good with the addition of 1 cup of roughly chopped flat leaf parsley.

Bittersweet Apple and Endive Salad

SERVES 4

This French-inspired endive salad of apples, parsley, and a classic shallot and mustard salad dressing is a fall favorite that's great any time of year. The glazed walnuts make this special, but toasting plain walnuts when you're pressed for time adds plenty of delicious crunch.

To serve later, prepare the walnuts and dressing. Seal each in a tightly covered container, keeping the dressing in the refrigerator until ready to use.

GLAZED WALNUTS
- 3 tablespoons sugar
- 2 tablespoons water
- ⅔ cup walnut halves
- A pinch of cayenne pepper
- ½ teaspoon sea salt

ENDIVE SALAD
- 1 pound endive (about 4 heads)
- ½ pound apples, cores removed
- ½ cup roughly chopped curly parsley
- 1 tablespoon lemon juice
- 1 teaspoon prepared Dijon mustard
- 2 tablespoons finely minced shallot
- 4 teaspoons good-quality olive oil
- 1 tablespoon red wine vinegar
- ½ teaspoon sea salt
- A few twists of freshly cracked pepper

1. Make the glazed walnuts first: in a small skillet over medium heat simmer the sugar and water until the sugar melts. Stir in the walnuts and cayenne. Stir occasionally to coat the nuts. As the sugar continues to cook, it will create a dry crust around the nuts, then as the sugar caramelizes it will darken and melt into a shiny glaze. It should take about 8 to 10 minutes for the nuts look syrupy. Immediately spread the nuts onto a lightly greased cookie sheet or silicone baking mat to cool, sprinkle with salt, and separate any large clusters.

2. Wash and pat dry the endive and slice each head in half lengthwise. Slice each half into 1-inch slices and transfer to a mixing bowl. Dice apples into ½-inch-wide pieces, place in the mixing bowl along with the chopped parsley, and toss with lemon juice.

In a small liquid measuring cup, whisk together the mustard, shallot, olive oil, vinegar, and salt. Pour over the salad, add a few twists of pepper and toss to completely cover the salad with dressing. Move to a serving bowl and scatter with candied walnuts. Serve immediately!

Removing Pomegranate Seeds Is a Slap Away!

I've experimented with many ways to remove the seeds (properly known as arils) from a fresh pomegranate, but this technique is the fastest (and loudest!).

Score a pomegranate along its equator with a sharp knife, taking care not to puncture the seeds. Use both hands to twist apart, then gently pry the outside peel slightly away from the center on both halves; don't overdo it. You're just loosening up the white pith that holds the seeds but not removing them just yet.

Hold the pomegranate half cut-side down firmly in one palm above a large mixing bowl. Grab a large wooden spoon with the other hand and proceed to firmly and rapidly slap the sides and top of the outside of the pomegranate half with the back of the spoon. Do it with conviction! Don't be afraid to be fierce! The harder you hit it, the faster the seeds will fly out of the half into the bowl without rupturing the arils too much. Repeat with the other half and pick away any white pith. The more you use this technique, the better you'll get at it and never want to waste your precious pomegranate enjoyment any other way.

kale, Preserved Lemon, and Pomegranate Salad

SERVES 4 AS A SIDE

One of my favorite ways to kale-it-up with everyone's favorite leafy green is to spike it with the Middle Eastern flavors of preserved lemon, toasted cumin, and pomegranate seeds.

> 1 pound kale
> Sea salt for sprinkling
> ½ teaspoon cumin seeds
> ½ cup finely chopped red onion
> 1 cup pomegranate arils (from about one average-size pomegranate)
> 1 generous tablespoon finely minced preserved lemon (see **Preserved Lemons, Two Ways**, page 58)
> 1 tablespoon lemon juice or preserved lemon brine
> 1 tablespoon olive oil or flax seed oil
> Sea salt, freshly ground pepper, and lemon juice to taste

1. Wash and dry kale, then tear away thick stems. Stack a few leaves on top of each other, roll into a tight tube and slice very thin, about ¼-inch wide, with a sharp knife. Place kale in a large mixing bowl and sprinkle with a little bit of sea salt, then use your hands to knead the kale for a few minutes until softened.

2. In a small skillet, toast cumin seeds over medium heat until fragrant—about 30 seconds. Pour

over kale and add onion and pomegranate arils. In a measuring cup whisk together preserved lemon, lemon juice, and olive oil. Taste mixture and season with salt, a few twists of freshly ground pepper, and lemon juice to taste. Pour over kale and use tongs to completely mix the salad. Let stand for 5 minutes before serving, or for faster, more tender kale pour on the dressing and use your hands to knead the kale for about 30 seconds or until the kale leaves are soft and tender to the bite.

sesame mung Bean sprouts

SERVES 4 AS A SIDE OR APPETIZER OR WITH BIBIMBAP

*Cool, lightly seasoned mung bean sprouts are a classic Korean side dish that's easy to prepare. These sprouts are a fresh and crunchy contrast to hot rice-based **Bibimbap** (page 308) and grilled foods, especially sweet and spicy **Korean Veggie Bulgogi** (page 249).*

> 3 quarts (12 cups) water
> 1 pound (about 3 cups) mung or soy bean sprouts
> 3 tablespoons rice vinegar
> 4 teaspoons sugar
> 1½ teaspoons sea salt
> 1 tablespoon toasted sesame seeds
> 1½ teaspoons toasted sesame oil

1. In a large soup pot bring 3 quarts of water to a rolling boil. In a large metal colander rinse bean sprouts with plenty of cold water, picking out and discarding husks along the way. Using long-handled tongs, stir sprouts into the boiling water and simmer for 2 minutes. Immediately drain the sprouts in a metal colander, then rinse with plenty of cold water to completely stop the cooking process (if the sprouts remain hot, they'll continue to cook and may become soggy). Shake the colander well to remove any excess water.

2. Place the sprouts in a mixing bowl and sprinkle with rice vinegar, sugar, salt, sesame seeds, and sesame oil. Use your hands or tongs to toss the sprouts to completely coat with the dressing. Cover and chill for 20 minutes before serving. Store tightly covered and chilled; eat within a day of preparing.

pistachio Date quinoa Salad

SERVES 4 AS AN ENTREE SALAD

Native to South America, quinoa's chewy texture and ease of preparation makes it a gluten-free and extra-nutritious stand-in for bulgur wheat. All dressed up here with Middle Eastern fruits, nuts, and spices, this is one of my favorite warm entree salads. For additional green, I love to toss it with a generous handful of baby spinach greens.

QUINOA AND SALAD

1 cup uncooked white quinoa, rinsed in cold water

1 teaspoon cumin seeds

1 teaspoon fennel seeds

1¾ cups water

½ teaspoon sea salt

1 small white onion, peeled, sliced in half, and sliced into ¼-thin half-moons

3 cups spinach leaves or tender baby salad greens, torn into bite-size pieces

½ cup chopped flat-leaf parsley

1 cup cooked chickpeas, drained and rinsed

1 cup chopped, pitted dates (medjool dates are perfect in this salad)

⅓ cup toasted pistachio nuts, coarsely chopped

4 to 6 tablespoons sumac powder (see page 10)

DRESSING

2 tablespoons extra-virgin olive oil

3 tablespoons fresh lemon juice

½ teaspoon ground coriander

½ teaspoon sea salt

Freshly ground pepper to taste

1. Pour quinoa into a 2-quart pot and toast over medium heat for 3 to 4 minutes until grains are dry and lightly toasted (you may hear a few grains popping, that's okay!). Add the cumin and fennel seeds and toast another minute, then add water and salt. Bring to a rolling boil, then stir a few times and cover the pot with a tight-fitting lid. Reduce heat to low and cook for 20 to 22 minutes or until all of the water is absorbed and grains are tender. Use a fork to fluff quinoa, cover the pot, and cool for 5 minutes.

2. While quinoa is cooking, combine the onions, spinach, parsley, chickpeas, dates, and pistachios in a mixing bowl. Prepare the dressing by whisking together all of the ingredients in a 2-cup liquid measuring cup; pour over salad ingredients, toss to coat completely, and let stand while quinoa is cooking.

3. After the quinoa has cooled slightly, transfer it to the mixing bowl and use long-handled tongs to toss the quinoa with the dressing and salad. Transfer to a large serving bowl or divide among serving plates. Sprinkle with the sumac and serve warm or at room temperature.

For easier date chopping, use a sharp knife or kitchen scissors and dip the blade frequently in cold water to prevent sticking.

Roasted Pumpkin Salad with Dukka

SERVES 4 AS AN APPETIZER

Same old hummus again? Shake things up with this delightful dip-like salad of fragrant nutty dukka (Egyptian toasted spice nut dip) and roasted squash for one of my favorite fall appetizers to serve with warm pita bread.

A small pumpkin works best, or use a large acorn or smallish butternut squash. No squash? Try the variation made with smashed steamed carrots.

PISTACHIO DATE QUINOA SALAD, PAGE 89

2 cups roasted mashed pumpkin or other
winter squash (about 3 pounds fresh
squash; see roasting directions below)

2 teaspoons lemon juice

2 teaspoons maple syrup

2 teaspoons olive oil

1 teaspoon minced preserved lemon (see
Preserved Lemons, Two Ways, page 58) or
¼ teaspoon finely grated lemon zest

¼ teaspoon ground cinnamon

¼ teaspoon sea salt

¼ teaspoon ground black pepper

GARNISH

¼ cup freshly made *Toasted Hazelnut Crunch
Dip* (page 64)

Olive oil for drizzling, about 2 teaspoons

Pita bread warmed in the oven or thin slices
of jicama for scooping

1. To roast the pumpkin or squash, slice in half, scoop out and discard the seeds, and wrap each cut side tightly with foil. Place on a large rimmed baking sheet and roast the squash at 400°F until tender and the skin is easily pierced with a fork. Remove from the oven and when cool enough to handle, scoop out the flesh into a bowl; you should have about 2 cups of roasted squash. If the roasted squash seems very watery, spread the mash into a large mesh sieve and place on top of a bowl. Drain for about 30 minutes and discard the liquid.

2. Place the squash in a mixing bowl and add lemon juice, maple syrup, olive oil, preserved lemon or lemon zest, cinnamon, salt, and pepper and use a fork to mash together. Spread in an attractive swirl into a wide, shallow serving bowl. Sprinkle with dukka and drizzle on olive oil. Serve immediately with wedges of warm pita bread or thin slices of jicama.

Carrot Salad with Dukka: Substitute 1 pound of carrots for the squash. Peel and slice the carrots into small chunks and steam in a tightly covered saucepan filled with 3 inches of water until very tender— about 15 minutes. Drain, cool, roughly mash with a fork, and season as directed above.

pumpkin seed mole dip (sikil pak)

MAKES ABOUT 2 CUPS

Raw pumpkin seeds undergo a fascinating transformation in this thick, spreadable, pale green salsa. Sikil pak is an uncommon Mexican mole sauce that goes beyond the usual tomato salsa or guacamole. Sikil pak can be further thinned with water to make a light crema for drizzling on tacos or enchiladas or served as is with tortilla chips alongside margaritas.

1 cup raw, hulled pumpkin seeds (pepitas)

3 garlic cloves, peeled and roughly chopped

1 medium-size white onion, peeled and
roughly diced

½ cup chopped fresh cilantro

¼ cup water

3 tablespoons lime juice

4 teaspoons olive oil

½ teaspoon sea salt

Tortilla chips, cherry tomatoes, and slices of
radish for dipping

1. Cover the pumpkin seeds with hot water and soak for 2 hours or overnight. Pour the seeds into a metal sieve to drain and shake well to eliminate any excess water.

2. Pour seeds into a food processor and add remaining ingredients, except for the dipping items. Pulse into a slightly gritty paste, stopping frequently to push the paste down the sides of the food processor bowl with a rubber spatula. Depending on your food processor it may take anywhere from 2 to 4 minutes, but continue to pulse until the paste has the consistency of a thick and grainy hummus. Taste the sikil pak and add a little more salt or lime juice to taste if desired. Serve at room temperature with tortilla chips, cherry tomatoes, and radishes.

Garlicky Potato Dip (Skordalia)

SERVES 4

Skordalia is a traditional Greek appetizer dip made with whipped potatoes spiked with ample fresh garlic, almonds, and olive oil. Serve at room temperature or slightly warm with warmed pocketless pita triangles or as part of **Crispy Oven-Fried Eggplant and Zucchini with Skordalia** *(page 283), of course.*

- 1 pound white, waxy potatoes, peeled and diced into 1-inch cubes
- ½ teaspoon sea salt
- 5 garlic cloves, peeled and minced
- ½ cup sliced, blanched almonds
- ⅓ cup olive oil
- 3 tablespoons fresh lemon juice
- ½ teaspoon dried oregano
- Additional olive oil, a few twists of cracked pepper, a few Kalamata olives, and dried oregano for garnish

A potato ricer is an old-fashioned gadget that operates like a giant garlic press. Potatoes pressed through its sieve become fluffy strands somewhat like cooked rice. Once gently swirled, these strands transform into the lightest, creamiest mash potatoes you've ever tasted.

1. In a large pot, cover potatoes with cold water and bring to boil, then reduce heat to medium and cook until very tender, about 15 minutes. Turn off heat and reserve ½ cup potato-cooking water, then drain the potatoes. When the potatoes are cool enough to handle but still very warm, press them through a potato ricer into a large mixing bowl. If using a potato masher, mash the potatoes until no large lumps remain. Sprinkle salt over potatoes.

2. In a food processor, pulse the garlic, almonds, and olive oil into a smooth sauce, scraping the sides of processor bowl down with a rubber spatula as needed. Add this to the mashed potatoes along with the lemon juice and oregano. Dribble in 2 tablespoons of potato water and use a large fork to thoroughly combine. The skordalia should be very thick and slightly stiff; if too thick, dribble in a tablespoon or more of potato water. Taste the skordalia and season with additional salt and lemon juice if necessary. Spread the skordalia in a thin layer in a shallow serving dish. Drizzle 2 teaspoons of olive oil on top, sprinkle cracked pepper and dried oregano, then garnish with a few olives in the center. Serve slightly warm or at room temperature.

cultured cashew spread with French Herbs

MAKES ABOUT 1½ CUPS

This spread is one of the easiest cultured vegan products you can make at home. Its dense, creamy texture and deep, tangy flavor can't be reached with just lemon juice and miso alone, and the sautéed shallots and chives are reminiscent of the luscious, French-style cheese spreads that used to grace our family holiday table when I was a kid. Serve it with baguette slices alongside crisp cornichons (teeny French pickles) and olives for an upscale treat to serve before French-inspired meals.

Avocado oil is a neutral-tasting oil that adds a buttery richness. Look for it in natural food stores. Mild virgin olive oil or grapeseed oil can be used in place of it.

Probiotic powder is most usually available in vegetarian-friendly capsules. Look for it in natural food stores, sometimes stored in the refrigerator case. To use, carefully break open 3 to 4 capsules and measure out the powder; don't worry if you use slightly more than ½ teaspoon. Look for probiotic powder that is dairy free.

1½ cups unroasted, unsalted whole cashews
4 teaspoons light miso (shiro miso) paste
½ teaspoon probiotic powder
4 teaspoons avocado oil or grapeseed oil
2 tablespoons finely minced shallots (about
    1 very large shallot)

1 tablespoon lemon juice
1 clove garlic, peeled and chopped
¼ teaspoon sea salt or to taste
3 tablespoons finely chopped chives
3 tablespoons flat-leaf parsley

1. Soak the cashews covered in 3 inches of warm water for 2 hours or overnight until completely soft and pliable. Drain the water but set aside ¼ cup of the soaking liquid. In a food processor or a Vitamix-style blender, pulse the cashews, miso, and 2 tablespoons of reserved water to form a very thick paste. Occasionally scrape the sides of the container down and pulse, making sure to eliminate any stray chunks of cashew. The mixture should resemble a thick hummus. If too thick to pulse into a paste, add 1 tablespoon of reserved water at a time and pulse the mixture again until the desired consistency is reached. Don't add too much water initially; you don't want the spread to become a loose dip. Go easy on adding the water and keep scraping and pulsing the mixture until it's as smooth as possible. Pulse in the probiotic powder.

2. Wash and then rinse a 1-pint (2-cup) wide-mouth glass jar with boiling water. Dry completely, then use a clean rubber spatula to transfer the cashew mixture to the jar. Tap the jar a few times on a countertop to release any large air bubbles. Use a rubber band to secure a double layer of clean cheesecloth over the top of the jar. Wrap the jar in a thick towel (a big, clean bath towel is fine) and place the jar in a warm and draft-free location; an oven with the pilot light or any small, warm space (a closet near a heater, for example) works well. Leave the jar undisturbed for about 10 hours. The spread should now have a sharp but pleasant smell and be a creamy beige color. It may have increased slightly in volume from having developed small gas bubbles. A slightly dark-

ened top layer may develop from contact with the air; this is normal and won't interfere with the flavor.

3. In a small skillet heat the oil over medium-low heat. Sauté the minced shallots for 4 minutes or until gently browned, then turn off the heat. Transfer the cashew mixture to the food processor or blender once more and add the lemon juice, garlic, and salt. Blend these ingredients into the spread, scraping down the mixture as needed. Taste and add more lemon juice and salt if desired. Now add the shallots, taking care to include all of the avocado oil, and add the chopped chives and parsley. Pulse only a few times to mix in the shallots and herbs. Use a rubber spatula to scoop the spread into a shallow serving bowl. Or spread into ceramic ramekins and smooth the top for a pretty, crock-style cheese and cover the top tightly with plastic wrap. Chill at least 3 hours to blend the flavors. The flavor will continue to improve as the spread mellows in the refrigerator; stored chilled, the spread will last for at least a week.

You'll need a clean jar to culture the spread. Also required are perfectly clean, dry utensils including: a food processor or high-powered blender, rubber spatula, and a 1-pint wide-mouth glass jar (former pickle jars are ideal). Rinse the insides of the jar, the food processor container, and the spatula in boiling water and let everything air dry. If you have access to a yogurt maker (look for used ones in yard sales), this is an easy and convenient setup for culturing this cashew cheese; just use the provided jars and incubate as directed in recipe.

Creamy Walnut Red Pepper Spread (Muhamarra)

MAKES ABOUT 1½ CUPS

Muhamarra is a traditional dip with fruity sparkle from pomegranate molasses (see note on page 102), smoky roasted peppers, and crunchy walnuts. It's an exciting change from hummus that stirs up the usual Middle Eastern appetizer platter. For a hint of heat I've added Aleppo pepper flakes (see page 10), but a pinch of cayenne is fine. I like to enhance the sweetness of the bell peppers with a little agave nectar, but leave it out if you prefer a less-sweet dip.

2 red bell peppers, roasted and seeds removed (roast the same as for poblanos in the **Black Bean Soup with Roasted Poblanos**, page 118) or a 12-ounce jar roasted red peppers

1 teaspoon cumin seeds

1 teaspoon coriander seeds

⅓ cup dry white breadcrumbs

⅓ cup chopped walnuts

3 cloves garlic, peeled and chopped

4 teaspoons pomegranate molasses

1½ teaspoons lemon juice

½ teaspoon agave nectar

½ teaspoon sea salt

½ teaspoon Aleppo pepper flakes or pinch cayenne pepper

2 tablespoons good quality olive oil

1. Remove and discard the seeds and skins from the peppers, then tear the peppers into 2- to 3-inch pieces. If using jarred peppers, drain and tear into small pieces. In a small skillet toast the cumin and coriander seeds, then grind into a fine powder in a clean coffee mill.

2. In a food processor pulse together breadcrumbs and walnuts into coarse crumbs. Add the peppers, ground spices, garlic, pomegranate molasses, lemon juice, agave nectar, sea salt, and red pepper flakes and pulse into a chunky paste. Stream in the olive oil 1 tablespoon at a time to smooth out the paste. Transfer the paste to a shallow serving bowl and spread with a rubber spatula into a layer about 1-inch thick. Serve at room temperature with pita or fresh vegetables, or chill the muhamarra for 30 minutes to blend the flavors.

Bhel Puri with Pomegranates and Cashews

SERVES 4 GENEROUSLY

Bhel puri is my favorite in the grand family of Indian snack foods known as chaats. Chaats are a mash-up of crunchy, salty, sweet, tangy, savory textures and flavors spiked with chutneys and fresh herbs.

This chaat is like an edible holiday of contrasting taste and texture; melting bites of potato are folded into crispy puffed rice; crunchy sev (golden fried chickpea noodles); two tangy, fresh chutneys; fresh herbs; and the luxurious addition of roasted cashews and pretty pomegranate arils. It's also great party food, or a decadent but casual weeknight meal. Bhel puri (and most chaats) must be eaten immediately after assembling as it will become soggy the longer it sits. But it's easy to prepare the chaat elements in advance and toss it all together right before serving.

CHAAT

¾ pound potatoes, peeled and diced into
    ¼-inch cubes

½ cup pomegranate arils (see page 88)

2 plum tomatoes, cored and finely diced

1 tablespoon lime juice

1 medium-size red onion, peeled and finely
    diced

1 cup roughly chopped cilantro

1¼ cups fine sev (fried chickpea noodles,
    see Sev and Indian puffed rice, page 14)

2½ cups Indian puffed rice

⅓ cup chopped roasted cashews

¼ teaspoon *Garam Masala* (page 39) or
    store-bought garam masala

DRESSING

⅓ cup *Tamarind Date Chutney* (page 59)

⅓ cup *Cilantro Chutney* (page 61)

1. In a large saucepan, cover the potatoes with 2 inches of cold water. Bring to a boil over high heat, then reduce heat to medium and cook the potatoes for 10 to 11 minutes until tender but not overly mushy. Drain the potatoes well and let cool for 10 minutes.

BHEL PURI WITH POMEGRANATES AND CASHEWS

2. In a big mixing bowl add the potatoes, pomegranate arils, tomatoes, lime juice, onion, and cilantro. In a separate bowl combine 1 cup of sev, the puffed rice, roasted cashews, and garam masala and combine to coat with the spices. The potatoes and the sev can be left alone for about 45 minutes at room temperature prior to mixing.

3. Just before serving, pour the sev and puffed rice mixture into the bowl with the potatoes. Pour both of the chutneys over everything, then use a rubber spatula or a wooden spoon to fold all of the ingredients together, making sure that everything is coated in chutney. Mound the bhel puri onto a large serving plate and sprinkle the top with the remaining ¼ cup of sev. Serve immediately and consume as soon as possible for maximum enjoyment.

If desired, assemble only half of the bhel puri, let your guests (or you) eat their fill now and then assemble the remaining half later for fresh, crunchy second helpings.

Toss together the potato, pomegranate, tomato, lime juice, onion, and cilantro and chill in a tightly covered plastic container. Pour the sev, puffed rice, cashews, and garam masala into a large zip-top bag and keep tightly sealed. Along with separate containers for the chutneys, you can then transport your bhel puri ingredients for on-the-go chaat-making.

mango and peanut millet salad

SERVES 4 AS AN ENTREE

Millet, *a fluffy grain with a crunchy texture, is one of the stars of African cuisine and excels in salads, too. This wholesome salad is a complete meal loaded with mangoes, herbs, and toasted peanuts. If you desire more color, garnish it with a handful of thinly shredded red cabbage. Serve it as a side or as an entree for lunch or bring it along to your next potluck. This salad is best consumed the day it's made.*

MILLET

1 cup uncooked millet
1 teaspoon grapeseed or other vegetable oil
1 teaspoon cumin seeds
¾ teaspoon salt
2 cups boiling water

SALAD

3 tablespoons lime juice
2 tablespoons olive oil or grapeseed oil
¼ teaspoon salt
1 small red onion, peeled and finely diced
½ teaspoon of your favorite prepared habanero hot sauce or a big pinch of cayenne pepper
1 large ripe red tomato, core removed and diced
1 ripe mango, diced (see tip on page 78)
1 cup cilantro leaves, roughly chopped

½ cup salted roasted peanuts, chopped

A handful of thinly shredded red cabbage, for garnish (optional)

1. In a large saucepan with a tight-fitting lid, sauté the millet with the vegetable oil over medium heat for 3 minutes or until millet starts to turn golden. Add the cumin seeds and sauté another minute, then add salt and boiling water. Bring the millet to a boil, stir a few times and turn heat to low. Cover and cook for 22 to 24 minutes or until all of the liquid has been absorbed and the millet is fluffy and tender. Remove lid, gently stir with a fork, and let cool for 20 minutes.

2. In a large bowl whisk together the lime juice, oil, and salt. Stir in the onion and hot sauce and set aside for 10 minutes while you prepare the other veggies, then add tomato, mango, cilantro, peanuts, and cooled millet. Use a large wooden spoon to completely coat everything with the dressing. Mound the millet into a serving bowl and serve. If using cabbage as a garnish, scatter on salad.

Artichoke and Tomato Panzanella Salad

SERVES 4 AS A GENEROUS SIDE

Warm up to a fresh taste of summer with this thrifty, Italian-style salad; a loaf of day-old bread is transformed into lemony, garlicky croutons. Airy ciabatta bread is excellent here, but any good country bread will do. The artichokes can be grilled and marinated in the dressing a day or more before assembling the salad, and the bread cubes can be toasted a day in advance (and stored in an airtight container), too.

10- to 14-ounce loaf ciabatta bread or similar crusty Italian bread, left out overnight to turn slightly stale

2 cloves garlic, peeled

1 teaspoon sea salt

2 tablespoons lemon juice

4 teaspoons olive oil

1 teaspoon crumbled dried basil

SALAD

8 ounces artichoke hearts, packed in brine and well drained. If frozen, thaw completely

2 tablespoons olive oil

3 cloves garlic, peeled and minced

½ teaspoon salt

2 tablespoons red wine vinegar

2 teaspoons dried oregano

1 teaspoon dried rosemary, crumbled

2 tablespoons capers, drained

1 pound ripe red tomatoes, cores and seeds removed, diced into 1-inch pieces

1 bunch flat-leaf parsley, roughly chopped

Freshly ground pepper to taste

1. Preheat oven to 400°F. Slice bread into ½-inch cubes. In a mortar and pestle (see page 31) mash together the garlic and salt into a paste, then add to a large mixing bowl and whisk in lemon juice, olive oil, and basil. Add the bread cubes and toss to coat with dressing, then spread the bread on a baking sheet and toast in the oven for 12 to 14 minutes until cubes are toasted. Stir the bread cubes occasionally.

2. While the bread cubes are toasting, slice the artichokes into ¼-inch pieces. Heat half of the

olive oil in a skillet over medium heat. Layer the artichokes in the hot pan and fry on one side for 2 minutes, then turn them over and fry another 2 to 3 minutes or until the edges turn golden, then remove from heat, set aside. In a mortar and pestle, mash together the garlic and salt into a paste, spoon into a large mixing bowl, add the vinegar, remaining olive oil, oregano, and rosemary and whisk until smooth. Add the artichokes, capers, tomatoes, and the parsley. When the bread cubes are done toasting, add them to the bowl along with a few twist of freshly cracked pepper. Use salad tongs to toss everything with the dressing, making sure that all of the bread cubes have been moistened. Serve immediately.

When juicy summer tomatoes are months away, use flavorful cherry tomatoes or small heirloom tomatoes.

sweet Autumn Toasted pita and kale salad

SERVES 4 TO 6 AS AN ENTREE OR STARTER

Sweet potatoes, kale, and a sweet-tart pomegranate molasses dressing twist this classic Lebanese fatoosh salad into a hearty cool-weather meal, but make the traditional variation to fill your entire year with this dish that cleverly uses up day-old pita bread. This makes a generously sized salad, ideal for potlucks.

SALAD

   1½ pounds sweet potatoes, peeled and diced into ½-inch chunks

   4 tablespoons olive oil

   1 teaspoon cumin seeds

   Sea salt for sprinkling

   3 whole wheat or white pitas, both sides separated and sliced into bite-size pieces

   1 pound kale, leaves stripped from the stems (discard stems)

   2 cups loosely packed flat-leaf parsley, coarsely chopped

   1 large red onion, peeled and finely diced

   ¼ cup sumac powder (see page 10)

DRESSING

   3 tablespoons olive oil

   3 tablespoons pomegranate molasses (see notes on pages 102 and 136)

   2 tablespoons lemon juice

   1 tablespoon agave nectar or maple syrup

   1½ teaspoons sea salt

   ½ teaspoon ground pepper

   ¼ teaspoon cayenne pepper

1. Preheat oven to 400°F. Line a baking sheet with parchment paper. Place sweet potato cubes on the baking sheet and drizzle with 2 tablespoons of the olive oil. Sprinkle with cumin seeds, a little sea salt, and toss the cubes to coat with oil. Roast for 25 to 30 minutes, stirring occasionally with a long-handled spatula or tongs to evenly brown the sweet potato. Meanwhile, toss the pieces of pita bread with the remaining 2 tablespoons oil. When the sweet potato is done, transfer to a bowl to cool. Spread pita

pieces in a single layer over the baking sheet and bake for 8 to 10 minutes until golden brown, stirring occasionally but watching carefully so that the pita pieces don't burn. Remove from oven and cool.

2. While the sweet potatoes and pita are roasting, prepare the rest of the salad. Wash, dry, and tear the kale into bite-size pieces and place in a large mixing bowl. Add parsley and onion. Stir together all of the dressing ingredients and pour over kale, then use your fingers and massage the kale for 2 minutes or until it is softened and slightly reduced in bulk. Add roasted sweet potato and pita chips and use tongs to toss together. Taste salad and if desired season with a few twists of cracked pepper and an extra drizzle of pomegranate molasses if desired.

3. To serve, mound the salad into a large serving dish and sprinkle with sumac powder. Serve immediately. Kale salad can be chilled in a tightly covered container for up to 2 days; just toss in pita chips and top with sumac powder right before serving.

Summer Tomato Fatoosh (Traditional Fatoosh Salad): Instead of kale, use romaine or any crunchy, hearty lettuce. Omit the sweet potatoes and use 1 pound of ripe red tomatoes, cores and seeds removed and diced. Peel and dice a large cucumber and add that to the salad. Proceed as directed with making the dressing, and the pita chips and assembling and garnishing the salad with sumac powder.

Look for pomegranate molasses and sumac powder in Middle Eastern groceries. Pomegranate molasses is made from the juice of pomegranates, cooked down to a sweet and sour syrup. Don't substitute regular molasses.

mexican chopped salad

SERVES 3 TO 4 AS A SIDE SALAD

Serve this crunchy chopped salad with all things Mexican or Latin American. Delicate, juicy-crisp jicama is a great foil for spicy foods, and toasted pumpkin seeds and roasted chilies add nutty texture and smoky heat.

1 pound jicama, peeled and diced into ½-inch pieces
½ pound red ripe tomatoes, core and seeds removed and diced into ½-inch pieces
1 small red onion, peeled and diced into ¼-inch pieces
2 jalapeño or serrano chile peppers, roasted (see *Black Bean Soup with Roasted Poblanos*, page 118, for roasting instructions) and minced
1 cup cilantro leaves, roughly chopped
3 tablespoons pumpkin seeds, roasted
¼ cup lime juice
1 teaspoon agave nectar
1 teaspoon dried oregano
½ teaspoon ground cumin
½ teaspoon sea salt

1. In a mixing bowl combine the jicama, tomatoes, onion, chilies, and cilantro.

2. Pulse the roasted pumpkin seeds in a clean coffee mill into a gritty powder; then in a 2-cup liquid measuring cup, whisk together with the remaining

ingredients. Pour the dressing over the vegetables and toss well. Serve the salad immediately.

3. If desired, store the undressed chopped vegetables in a tightly covered plastic container in the refrigerator for 24 hours before tossing with the dressing.

Roasted Beet Salad with Dill Vinaigrette

SERVES 4 TO 6

I was raised on an old-school Polish beet salad my aunt would prepare for special occasions: just boiled beets dressed with vinegar, dill, and a dash of salt. Now I prefer the beets roasted (it enhances their intense sweetness), tossed with a lively dill vinaigrette, and embellished with unpeeled, diced apples and toasted hazelnuts. I enjoy this as is, but if you believe a salad needs green stuff, then by all means garnish with crunchy romaine lettuce.

If you have lonely fancy fruit vinegar stranded in the pantry (raspberry, fig, cloudberry), try it in this fresh herb vinaigrette! For the prettiest presentation keep the beets separate from the apples until moments before serving.

2 pounds beets, peeled and diced into
½-inch chunks
2 tablespoons olive oil
Sea salt to taste

DILL VINAIGRETTE

2 tablespoons red wine vinegar or fruit
vinegar
4 teaspoons olive oil
4 teaspoons agave nectar
¾ teaspoon sea salt
¼ teaspoon mustard powder
¼ teaspoon ground black pepper
3 tablespoons finely chopped fresh dill

SALAD

2 large green or yellow apples
1 tablespoon lemon juice
4 cups chopped romaine or other crunchy
lettuce
2 tablespoons chopped toasted hazelnuts
or walnuts

1. Preheat oven to 400°F, toss the diced beets with the olive oil, and spread them in a single layer on a large baking sheet lined with parchment paper. Sprinkle with a little sea salt and roast, stirring the beets occasionally, for 30 to 32 minutes or until beets are tender. Remove from oven to cool for 10 minutes before assembling the rest of the salad, or if not serving immediately, cover and keep warm in the oven.

2. Whisk all of the vinaigrette ingredients together. Remove the cores from the apples, leave the skin on and dice into ½-inch cubes, then toss right away with lemon juice. Set aside 1 teaspoon of the vinaigrette and toss the remaining vinaigrette with the warm roasted beets in a mixing bowl. Arrange the salad greens in a large serving bowl and top with beets; in another mixing bowl toss together apples and reserved dressing. Scatter apples on top of beets, then sprinkle with chopped nuts. Serve immediately.

sweet and savory jackfruit carnitas tacos

MAKES 8 TO 10 TACOS, SERVING 4 WITH A SALAD

Now a living legend in the vegan culinary scene, tropical jackfruit was first featured on the menu of the now defunct Pure Luck eatery in L.A., but versions of this have lived on in vegan blogs as an exciting, alarmingly "meaty"-looking alternative to tempeh, tofu, or seitan in vegan Mexican American cuisine.

Jackfruit flesh is all texture (visually it's reminiscent of pulled pork or shredded chicken) and can be short on big flavors, so I add pineapple juice, soy sauce, chile powder, liquid smoke, and spicy chipotles in adobo sauce for a well-rounded flush of umami, sweet, and smoky flavors. If you prefer a less-sweet filling, replace the pineapple juice with water. Once simmered, gently searing the seasoned jackfruit lightly caramelizes the shreds for that authentic carnitas touch, so don't skip this step.

Two 10-ounce cans green, brined jackfruit, or 20 ounces brined frozen unripe jackfruit, thawed (see box)
2 rounded teaspoons ancho chile powder or Mexican chile powder blend
½ teaspoon ground cumin
½ teaspoon ground coriander
½ teaspoon garlic or onion powder
1 teaspoon sea salt
2 cups pineapple juice or water

Sweet and Savory Jackfruit Carnitas Tacos

¼ cup water
2 heaping tablespoons tomato paste
2 chipotles in adobo, finely chopped
4 cloves garlic, peeled and grated on a Microplane grater or pressed
2 tablespoons soy sauce
1 tablespoon lime juice
1 tablespoon molasses
2 teaspoons liquid smoke
2 bay leaves
2 tablespoons peanut or vegetable oil, plus additional oil for frying if desired

TACOS

8 to 10 corn tortillas or **Homemade Soft Corn Tortillas** (page 201)
1 recipe **Pickled Red Onions** (page 62)
Finely shredded green or red cabbage or lettuce
2 ripe tomatoes and 1 ripe avocado, diced into bite-size chunks
1 recipe **Cashew Yogurt Sauce** (page 65) for drizzling, or **Sikil Pak** dip (page 92) for dolloping

1. Place prepared jackfruit chunks (see box) in a large mixing bowl and sprinkle with chile powder, cumin, coriander, garlic powder, and salt. Use your fingers to vigorously rub the spices into the jackfruit. In a 3-quart pot whisk together the remaining ingredients. Add the jackfruit and vigorously stir to coat with the marinade, then set aside for 20 minutes or even better, cover and chill overnight.

2. When ready to cook the jackfruit, turn the burner onto high and bring the jackfruit marinade to a rapid simmer for 2 minutes, then reduce heat to low. Partially cover the pot and simmer the jackfruit for 50 to 55 minutes, occasionally stirring; there should be some sauce still left in the pot. Turn off the heat,

uncover the jackfruit and remove the bay leaves. You can now serve the jackfruit as is, or fry it up slightly to caramelize the edges for a better texture.

3. To fry the jackfruit, preheat a 10-inch cast-iron skillet over medium heat, then spread a teaspoon of vegetable oil over the bottom. Pour in 1 cup of jackfruit with sauce and sauté for 4 to 6 minutes until most of the liquid has been absorbed and the edges of the shreds are browned and slightly caramelized. Transfer to a serving dish and sauté more jackfruit as needed in small batches.

4. To assemble a taco, preheat a cast-iron skillet to high. Overlap two corn tortillas on the dry skillet and warm just enough to get the tortillas hot and flexible, about 45 seconds. Transfer tortillas and overlap slightly on a serving dish. Pile on about ⅓ cup of jackfruit carnitas and sprinkle with toppings as desired. Buen provecho!

All Jacked Up About Jackfruit

When shopping for jackfruit, for best results look for unsweetened, brined unripe jackfruit sold in cans or jars or frozen, and don't buy jackfruit packed in syrup. Brined jackfruit has been peeled and sliced into wedges and has a firm texture and a light pinkish color. The brine helps lightly pickle the jackfruit while giving it a firmer texture and a mellow flavor.

Avoid frozen green jackfruit not packed in brine; this may look like soft white pods, not pinkish wedges or slices. Once thawed it turns into a mushy, grainy mess.

To prepare canned or jarred jackfruit, first drain the jackfruit wedges and rinse with plenty of cool water. Chop the wedges into 1-inch-wide chunks, then use your fingers to pull the pieces into shreds. The more you shred the jackfruit pieces, the more carnita-like it will look. If desired, remove the seeds for a more carnitas-like look; these are also edible, so leave them if you don't mind. Grab handfuls of the pulp and squeeze out as much water as possible before marinating.

If using frozen, thaw overnight or speed up thawing by steeping the unopened jackfruit package in hot water. Squeeze out as much water as possible and separate into chunks as described for canned jackfruit above.

Harissa Carrot Salad

SERVES 4 AS A SIDE

*Moroccan-style carrot salads are spicy-sweet and quickly come together while a tagine or couscous is simmering (or the **Bisteeya** is baking, page 256). This one packs a little heat from the addition of zingy harissa. For lemony bliss, toss in 1 teaspoon of minced preserved lemon (see **Preserved Lemons, Two Ways**, page 58).*

For the prettiest salad, use a Y-shaped julienne peeler (see page 30) or a mandolin (see page 30) to slice the carrots into long matchstick shreds.

¾ pound carrots, scraped and sliced into matchsticks or shredded
¼ cup golden raisins
½ cup roughly chopped cilantro
¼ cup freshly squeezed orange juice
1 tablespoon lemon juice

2 teaspoons olive oil

1 teaspoon *Olive Oil Harissa Paste* (page 43) or ¼ teaspoon each cayenne pepper and ground cumin

1 teaspoon agave nectar

¼ teaspoon sea salt

1. Place the carrots, raisins, and cilantro in a large mixing bowl. In a liquid measuring cup whisk together the remaining ingredients and pour over the carrots. Use tongs to toss everything together and serve immediately.

chipotle tofu cemita sandwiches

MAKES 4 BIG SANDWICHES

A cemita *is tremendous example of a delicious Mexican sandwich: refried beans, avocado, tomato, onions, cilantro or papalo (a unique leafy Mexican herb) if you can find it, and much more are lovingly stuffed into a big sesame seed bun. The traditional cemita bun typically contains egg, but you can use any big, fluffy, not-too-hard sandwich buns topped with sesame seeds.*

Papalo is a tender leafy green herb with rounded leaves and an herbal, slightly cilantro flavor; wash and pat dry for use in cemitas. This herb is tricky to find outside of Mexican markets, but when you do, it's a great reason to make cemitas. Fresh cilantro sprigs are a fine substitute.

CHIPOTLE-ROASTED TOFU

1 pound extra-firm or super-firm tofu

1 cup light-colored Mexican beer (most Mexican beers are vegan)

3 tablespoons of pureed chipotles in adobo (see page 11)

2 tablespoons lime juice

2 tablespoons olive oil

2 heaping tablespoons tomato paste

3 cloves garlic, pressed or grated

¾ teaspoon salt

SANDWICHES

1 cup refried black or pinto beans, warmed (homemade or canned is fine)

Vegan mayonnaise, to taste

1 large ripe avocado, cut into thin slices

Very thin slices of red onion or *Pickled Red Onions* (see page 62)

Thin slices of ripe tomato

Thin strips of pickled jalapeño (optional)

3 cups shredded romaine lettuce or thinly shredded cabbage

2 cups of Mexican papalo herbs or sprigs of cilantro

4 large, round, sesame-seed-topped soft sandwich buns

1. Press the tofu as directed on page 22. Preheat oven to 400°F and in a 9 x 13 x 2-inch ceramic baking dish, whisk together all of the ingredients except the tofu. After the tofu is pressed, arrange it in a single layer in the marinade and poke each slice with a fork several times, then flip over. Bake for 20 minutes, flip each piece over and bake another 20 to 24 minutes or until most of the marinade has been absorbed but the tofu still looks juicy. Turn off oven but keep warm.

2. While the tofu is baking, warm the beans and prepare the other fillings. To assemble a sandwich, split and lightly toast each roll on a warm cast iron skillet. Smear the insides of the top of the roll with ¼ cup of refried beans and the bottom side with mayonnaise, then layer two slices of tofu (along with any juices from the roasting pan) on the bottom layer. Add avocado, onions, tomato, jalapeños, lettuce, and papalo. Top with remaining half of the roll, squish the sandwich down, and serve immediately.

scrambled Tofu Breakfast Bahn Mi

MAKES FOUR 8-INCH, OVERSTUFFED SANDWICHES

This hearty bahn mi *filling of golden scrambled tofu packed in a toasted baguette is too good to eat only for breakfast—it also makes a casual but incredible weeknight meal. You can always use just carrot and cilantro for garnish, but for really amazing sandwiches make the **Star Anise Daikon Pickles** (page 62)!*

½ pound white or brown mushrooms, cleaned and thinly sliced
2 tablespoons vegetable oil
¾ cup thinly sliced shallots

SCRAMBLED TOFU BREAKFAST BAHN MI

4 scallions, white and green parts divided and very thinly sliced
4 cloves garlic, peeled and minced
1 pound firm or extra-firm tofu, drained
½ cup vegetable broth
3 tablespoons soy sauce, preferably Thai thin soy sauce (see page 19)
2 tablespoons lime juice
2 teaspoons ground coriander
1 teaspoon ground white pepper
2 teaspoons Madras curry powder or *East Indian-style Curry Powder* (page 40)

SANDWICHES

Four 6- to 8-inch crusty sandwich rolls or sliced from 2 baguettes
Vegan mayonnaise
Cilantro sprigs
Thin slices of ripe tomato
Paper-thin slices of red radish or matchsticks of daikon or jicama
Asian garlic chili sauce (such as Sriracha or sambal oelek)
½ recipe *Star Anise Daikon Pickles* (optional but awesome, see page 62)

1. Heat a wok or cast-iron skillet until nearly smoking, then sauté mushrooms with 1 tablespoon of the oil until tender and browned, about 4 to 6 minutes. Remove from wok, wipe down the surface, and add remaining oil. Add the shallots and stir-fry until golden, about 4 minutes, then add the white parts of the scallion and the garlic and stir-fry for 1 minute. Crumble in the tofu, add the mushrooms, and stir-fry for 2 minutes. Whisk together vegetable broth, soy sauce, lime juice, coriander, white pepper, and curry powder and pour over tofu. Use a large wooden spoon or rubber spatula to stir-fry tofu until all of the liquid has been absorbed and tofu is golden, about

8 to 10 minutes. Tofu should be moist, but not wet. Add the green tops of the scallions, fry for another minute, and remove from the heat.

2. Slice the rolls in half and toast if desired. Spread insides with mayo and distribute the tofu mixture evenly on the sandwiches. Top each sandwich with cilantro, tomato, radish, chili sauce, and daikon pickles if using. Eat immediately, and over a plate . . . these bahn mi are messy goodness.

BBQ Seitan Bahn Mi: Substitute the BBQ Seitan from the *Sizzling Seitan Pho Noodle Soup* (page 220) for the tofu scramble. Top with the other garnishes as desired.

chile potato rolls in homemade paratha bread (kati rolls)

MAKE 4 LARGE KATI ROLLS

*Kati rolls are something like Indian burritos; a comforting street food loaded with Indian spices that's fun to eat out of your hand. A spiced potato filling is forever a popular choice, but you can vary it up with slices of leftover **Golden Tandoori Tofu** (page 268), **Cashew Yogurt Sauce** (page 65), and a few slices of tomato and red onion.*

Both the filling and the rolled, uncooked paratha can be made up to 2 days in advance (or if you can locate dairy-free paratha made without ghee from an Indian market, shortcut directly to making the

filling). Store the potato filling in a tightly covered container and stack uncooked paratha between sheets of waxed paper in a zip-top plastic bag; chill both in the refrigerator. Warm the filling before stuffing into the bread.

POTATO CASHEW FILLING

4 teaspoons vegetable oil, divided
2 tablespoons chopped unsalted cashews
½ teaspoon black mustard seeds
2 to 4 hot green chilies (Indian, Thai, or serrano), finely chopped
1 small red onion, peeled and minced
½-inch piece peeled ginger, minced
1 pound russet baking potato (about 2 medium-size potatoes), peeled, cubed, and boiled until tender
2 teaspoons Madras curry powder or *East Indian-style Curry Powder* (page 40)
3 ripe red plum tomatoes, cores and seeds removed and finely chopped
2 tablespoons lemon juice
½ teaspoon salt, or to taste
½ cup chopped cilantro
A few twists of freshly ground pepper
4 freshly made paratha breads (see *Chappati and Paratha, Whole Wheat Indian Flatbreads*, page 189) or purchased dairy-free paratha

1. In a large skillet heat 1 teaspoon of the oil over medium heat, add the cashews, and fry until lightly browned. Transfer cashews to a dish and add the remaining oil to the skillet. Add the mustard seeds and cover the pan. Once the seeds have stopped popping, stir in the chilies, onions, and ginger and sauté for 4 minutes or until the onion is translucent and soft.

2. Stir in the boiled potato and sprinkle with curry powder. Fry the potatoes until golden, mashing with a wooden spoon or a potato masher, about 4 minutes. Stir in the cashews, tomato, lemon juice, and salt. Reduce heat to low and stir mashed potatoes for about 1 minute to further incorporate spices and onions. Taste the mixture, add more salt or lemon juice if desired, and fold in cilantro and freshly cracked pepper to taste. Turn off heat and set aside.

3. To assemble a kati roll, scoop a quarter of the warm filling into the lower third of a warm paratha and roll it up like a burrito. If desired warm the whole thing, seam side down, on a grill for a minute or two. Serve immediately!

soft Red lentil Kibbe with Fresh Herbs

SERVES 4 AS AN ENTREE OR MORE AS AN APPETIZER DIP OR SPREAD

Kibbe, *a diverse family of Lebanese patties, fritters, and casseroles made with bulgur wheat can be fried or baked. This thick, scoopable red lentil kibbe is another option that's a refreshing warm-weather meal. Drizzled with a splash of good olive oil and big handful of fresh-minced herbs, it's at once warm and cool, soft and crunchy, and it stirs up jaded palates.*

Presentation is everything with this rustic dish; this soft spread looks best either shaped into slim patties wrapped in lettuce leaves or pressed into wave patterns on a pretty serving dish and scattered

*with fresh herbs. Or the patties can be chilled for days as a cold sandwich filling along with cucumber, sweet onion, sprouts, and harissa (see **harissa paste** recipes on pages 42 and 43).*

LENTIL KIBBE

 1 small red onion, peeled and chopped very fine

 1 tablespoon olive oil

 1 teaspoon ground coriander

 1 teaspoon sweet ground paprika

 ½ teaspoon ground cumin

 2 cups water for a spread, or slightly less (about 1 ¾ cups) for firmer patties

 ½ cup red lentils, rinsed and drained

 ½ teaspoon sea salt

 ½ cup fine bulgur wheat, rinsed and drained in a metal fine-mesh sieve

 2 tablespoons tomato paste

 2 tablespoons lemon juice

 ½ teaspoon cayenne pepper or *Olive Oil Harissa Paste* (page 43)

 1 teaspoon pomegranate molasses (see notes on pages 102 and 136)

 2 tablespoons chopped parsley

HERB GARNISH

 2 teaspoons extra-virgin olive oil

 1 cup chopped parsley

 4 scallions, trimmed and thinly sliced

 Freshly ground black pepper

 ¼ cup chopped fresh mint leaves

 Lemon wedges for squeezing

 Warm pita bread or romaine lettuce leaves

For best results use fine-grained (size #1) Middle Eastern bulgur wheat. Regular natural food store, bulk-bin bulgur will make the kibbe somewhat dark and chunky, but it will still taste fine.

1. In a pot with a tightly fitting lid, sauté chopped onion with olive oil over medium heat until soft and translucent, about 6 minutes. Stir in the coriander, paprika, and cumin and stir for 1 minute, then stir in water, lentils, and salt. Bring to a boil, reduce heat to a simmer, and cover tightly. Cook for 25 minutes, or until the lentils are very soft and have a creamy consistency.

2. Stir in the bulgur wheat, simmer partially covered for 10 minutes, then turn off heat. Stir in tomato paste, cover tightly and let sit for 30 minutes; bulgur should absorb excess liquid and the mixture should resemble moist thick spread. Add lemon juice, cayenne, pomegranate molasses, and 2 tablespoons of the chopped parsley; stir thoroughly and taste the mixture, adding more salt or lemon juice if desired.

3. For spread-style kibbe, spread the lentil mixture in an even layer onto the bottom of a large shallow serving bowl. Now use the back of a spoon to press rows of decorative waves on top of the kibbe. Drizzle with olive oil, top with the remaining chopped parsley, scallions, and a few twists of black pepper and mint and serve with lemon wedges. For patties chill the mixture for 1 hour, and with lightly moistened hands form ¼- to ⅓-cup scoops into thin patties. Or serve patties on top of romaine lettuce leaves, top with olive oil and herbs. To eat kibbe scoop onto warm pita bread or a lettuce leaf, squeeze a lemon wedge over and insert into mouth. Kibbelicious!

seitan Gyro Roll ups

MAKES 4 SANDWICHES

Greek-themed street food at its finest! These toothsome rolled sandwiches will satisfy serious cravings, and if you already have a batch of seitan cutlets, they can be pulled together in less than 30 minutes.

> 1 recipe *Gyro Roasted Seitan*, kept warm (page 253)
> 4 Greek-style thick pita breads (see note)
> Additional olive oil for brushing

YOGURT SAUCE
> 1½ cups plain soy yogurt (preferably unsweetened)
> ¼ cup chopped fresh dill or 1 tablespoon dried dill
> 3 cloves garlic, peeled and finely minced
> 2 teaspoons olive oil
> ½ teaspoon sea salt

GARNISHES
> Diced ripe red tomato
> Thin slices of peeled cucumber
> Thin slices of red onion

For the most authentic sandwich possible, look for thick, no-pocket pita bread. This is typical of Greek-style pita, and this sturdy pita is well suited for holding in all the heavy moist fillings of this rolled sandwich.

1. Keep the seitan warm by covering the dish with foil. In a food processor pulse together all the Yogurt Sauce ingredients until smooth and set aside.

2. Brush both sides of each pita lightly with the additional olive oil. Preheat a cast iron skillet over high heat, then grill each pita for about 1 minute on each side until the bread is soft and the surface is gently toasted. Alternatively you can heat the pita directly on a gas burner for about 8 to 10 seconds each side; watch carefully and flip the pita frequently to prevent burning.

3. To assemble a sandwich, brush one side of a pita with a little Yogurt Sauce. Fill with ½ cup seitan or more as desired. Top with tomato, cucumber, and red onion. Drizzle more yogurt sauce on top as desired, roll the pita into a thick roll-up sandwich, and eat immediately.

Try with **Cucumber Tzatziki** (page 65).

Add a few slices of **Crispy Oven-Fried Eggplant and Zucchini with Skordalia** (page 283) to the gyro along with the seitan.

Stuff a few french-fried potatoes (either purchased or homemade, see **Beer-Bathed Seitan Stew and Oven Pommes Frites**, page 156) into the sandwich along with the seitan. It sounds crazy but it's also crazy delicious!

CHAPTER 5

SOUPS

There's an ideal soup for every person on this planet; dreamy, delicate wonton dumplings floating in a gingery broth, or the creamy yet rustic flare of French-style soups or the earthy bean soups of the Mediterranean and Latin America. The more the merrier when it comes to soup; these fully loaded soups become a whole meal, such as hearty sauerkraut shchi soup from Russia, a great friend on a cold winter's night.

All of these soups benefit from time on their side. Frozen into 2-cup plastic bowls and reheated later, many of these soups make fantastic workday lunches or fast weeknight meals. For maximum enjoyment, prepare a soup on a relaxing Sunday evening for easy meals all week long; the flavors benefit from an overnight rest.

Andean Aji Bean Stew

SERVES 6 TO 8

In the Andes of Peru, a hearty bean and vegetable stew is the tastiest way to shrug off the chill mountain life. Golden South American yellow chile (ají amarillo) paste gives this soup its special hue and sweet, spicy, lingering character. For ease and speed, I've substituted some of the traditional ingredients, but this soup will be your own delicious creation.

The ají amarillo chile has slightly less heat than the jalapeño and is used in Peruvian and some Bolivian cuisine. This ají *(the South American term for chile, pronounced ah-HEE) is commonly used in the form of a paste. Latino grocers that stock South American goods should carry it, and this paste makes it easy to add its special flavor to soups, sauces and even salads (see* **Peruvian Purple Potato Salad,** *page 84). Once open, store the jar in the fridge and use the paste within 2 weeks.*

1 large yellow onion, peeled and finely diced

1 large carrot, peeled and diced into ½-inch
   pieces

1 tablespoon olive oil

6 cloves garlic, peeled and minced

½ cup white wine or vegetable broth

¼ cup ají amarillo paste or see note for
   substitution

2 teaspoons dried oregano

1 teaspoon ground sweet or smoked paprika

1 teaspoon ground cumin

5 cups vegetable broth

1 large waxy potato, scrubbed, unpeeled,
   and finely diced

1 pound winter squash, peeled and diced
   into ½-inch cubes

One 14-ounce can (2 cups cooked)
   chickpeas, drained and rinsed

One 14-ounce can (2 cups cooked) pinto
   beans or white beans, drained and rinsed

⅓ cup uncooked quinoa, rinsed and drained

One 14-ounce can diced tomatoes

1 teaspoon liquid smoke

½ cup chopped fresh cilantro

1 teaspoon salt, or to taste

A few twists of freshly ground black pepper

Instead of ají amarillo paste, removed the seeds and stems from one yellow or orange bell pepper and puree with two fresh red jalapeños or serrano chilies.

1. Heat a 4-quart soup pot over medium heat. Add the onion and carrot and dry sauté for 6 to 8 minutes or until the vegetables have reduced in bulk by half. Add the olive oil and garlic and sauté another 2 minutes. Pour in the wine, ají amarillo paste (or pureed substitution), oregano, paprika, and cumin and deglaze the pan. Simmer until about half of the liquid has been absorbed.

2. Stir in vegetable broth, then the potato, squash, chickpeas, beans, quinoa, and tomatoes. Bring to a gentle boil, stir a few times, and lower heat to medium-low; partially cover the pot and simmer for 35 minutes or until the potato and squash are very tender.

3. Scoop 2 cups of the soup into a blender. Puree until smooth and stir the puree back into the pot to help thicken the stew. You can also use an immersion blender and pulse the soup a few times, but take care not to puree everything; leave it chunky. Stir in

the liquid smoke and cilantro and season with salt and pepper to taste.

4. Turn off the heat and allow the soup to stand for 5 minutes before serving. This soup will thicken and the flavor will be deeper the next day.

zen spinach wonton soup

SERVES 4 OR MORE

This is a delicate golden broth adrift with tender wontons and baby spinach; a riff off a popular soup at NYC veggie Asian eatery Zen Palate. A light soup that's best enjoyed as a starter to a richer and more complex meal, this gingery, peppery broth is also a great remedy if you're feeling under the weather—it'll do wonders for you and your sinuses. Regardless of when it's enjoyed, the generous amount of dumplings in this soup solves the age-old problem of "do I save the dumplings for last, or eat them all immediately?"

*The key seasoning component for the broth are Sichuan peppercorns (see **Sichuan 5-Spice Powder** page 41), which are not part of the pepper family at all. Use white pepper as substitute, but if possible try it once with Sichuan peppercorns.*

For faster soup straining, tuck the ginger and peppercorns into a large paper tea filter and securely tie the top. Simmer in the broth, then squeeze and discard when done. Tea filters look like big, long, empty tea bags and can be found where tea-and coffee-making supplies are sold.

SOUP

8 cups vegetable broth, preferably "chicken" flavored vegetable broth

1 tablespoon Sichuan peppercorns or white peppercorns, gently crushed with a mortar and pestle (see page 31), or ½ teaspoon ground white pepper

2-inch piece peeled ginger, sliced into ¼-inch rounds and gently crushed with the butt end of a knife

6 scallions, green and white parts divided and finely chopped

1 tablespoon soy sauce

2 teaspoons sugar

1 teaspoon sesame oil

3 cups baby spinach leaves, firmly packed

WONTONS

½-inch piece peeled ginger, minced

2 cutlets **5-Spice Seitan** (page 51) or one 8-ounce package purchased seitan, grated or ground up (or use finely minced **Savory Baked Tofu**, page 50)

1 tablespoon soy sauce

½ teaspoon **Sichuan 5-Spice Powder** (page 41) or store-bought Chinese 5-spice powder

¼ teaspoon toasted sesame oil

26 to 28 wonton or gyoza wrappers, thawed if frozen

1. In a large 4-quart pot, combine all of the soup ingredients except for the spinach and green parts of the scallion. Bring to a gentle boil over medium-high heat, then turn down the heat to low. Partially cover and simmer for 15 minutes. Turn off the heat and let the soup stand for 5 minutes.

2. Line a large metal mesh sieve with two layers of cheesecloth and arrange over a 3-quart bowl. Strain the soup through the sieve, then lift up the cheesecloth and give it a good squeeze. Discard the cheesecloth. Return the soup to the pot, cover it, and place it back on the stove.

3. While the soup is simmering, start making the wontons. Combine all of the wonton filling ingredients plus half of the reserved, finely chopped, green tops of the scallions. Set aside the other half of the green scallions for garnishing the soup. Use 1 heaping teaspoon of filling to assemble a wonton; use the dumpling folding illustrations on page 182 as a guide. Trace the edges of the wonton or gyoza skins with water before sealing shut. Make sure to seal the dumplings as firmly as possible to prevent them from opening up during the cooking process. Place assembled dumplings on a clean, dry dinner plate.

4. When all of the dumplings are assembled, bring the soup to a gentle simmer over medium heat. Lower the dumplings, a few at a time, into the soup. Gently stir the soup; the dumplings will cook in about 2 to 2½ minutes and are done when the wrappers are firm and chewy. Stir in the spinach leaves; after a minute or two the spinach should be wilted and tender. The soup is ready to serve. Ladle the broth with spinach leaves into large, deep serving bowls. Distribute the dumplings evenly among the bowls, sprinkle with chopped green scallions and serve immediately! Store any leftover soup along with the dumplings.

Black Bean soup with Roasted poblanos and pickled Red onions

SERVES 6 TO 8

(LOW FAT, IF PICKLED RED ONIONS ONLY ARE USED FOR TOPPING)

*Black bean soups are one of the easiest of Latin American comfort foods to prepare and are almost a familiar sight now in many parts of North America as well. A black bean soup with the Mexican flavors of roasted poblano peppers, avocado, and **Pickled Red Onions** (page 62) is a wonderful twist on this staple dish of Venezuela, Cuba, and Brazil. For the Mexican chile powder, you can use either one of the commonly found blends or a single-pepper chile powder such as mellow ancho or smoky chipotle.*

1 pound dried black beans (for canned beans, see the *Faster Black Bean Soup* variation, next page)

2 teaspoons salt

6 cups water

2 bay leaves

1 pound poblano peppers (about 3 large peppers) (see note, next page)

1 large onion, diced

2 cloves garlic, minced

1 tablespoon olive oil

1 cup diced plum tomatoes

1½ teaspoons dried oregano

2 teaspoons Mexican chile powder or
    smoked paprika

1 teaspoons ground cumin

1 tablespoon lime juice

TOPPING

Pickled Red Onions (page 62)

Diced avocado

Cashew Yogurt Sauce (page 65) or
    purchased vegan sour cream

1. Spread the black beans on a tabletop and pick them over for small stones and other debris. Place in a large bowl, cover with at least 5 inches of water, and let soak for 8 hours or overnight. Drain the beans, rinse them, and place in a large soup pot along with the water, salt, and bay leaves. Cover and bring to a rolling boil over high heat, then reduce heat to low. Partially cover and simmer for 1½ to 2 hours or until beans are very tender and crush easily when pressed against the side of the pot. Remove and discard the bay leaves.

2. Meanwhile, roast the whole, unsliced poblano peppers in a cast iron pan over high heat or place directly onto gas burners or slide under a preheated broiler on a baking sheet. Use long-handled metal tongs to frequently turn peppers until the skins are blackened and charred, then immediately transfer to a tightly sealed plastic container or a large paper bag (fold the top to seal). Set aside until cool enough to handle, then peel away the charred skin (don't worry if you can't remove all of it) and discard the core and the seeds. Slice peppers into thin strips.

3. Fry the onion and garlic with the olive oil in a large pan over medium heat until the onion is translucent and soft, about 5 minutes. Add the onion and garlic, peppers, tomatoes, oregano, chile pow-

der, and cumin to the pot with the black beans and bring to a gentle boil. Reduce heat, partially cover, and cook for another 30 minutes. Turn off heat and stir in the lime juice. Let soup stand for 5 minutes before ladling servings into large bowls and top with pickled onions, diced avocado, and a drizzle of Cashew Yogurt Sauce or a dollop of vegan sour cream if that's how you roll.

Faster Black Bean Soup: Instead of dried beans, use three 14-ounce cans of black beans. Rinse and drain the beans before adding to the pot. Since the beans are already cooked there's no need to cook them separately. You'll also want to cut back on the total salt depending on how salty the canned beans are; start with 1 teaspoon and build up if necessary by tasting the soup at the end.

Fry the garlic and onions in the soup pot and add the beans along with the roasted peppers, tomatoes, spices, bay leaves and water. Simmer for 45 minutes, add salt and lime juice to taste.

Poblano chilies are large, shiny, forest-green-colored chilies that look similar to bell peppers except for their gradually tapering end. Look for fresh poblanos in markets that carry Latin American produce.

Red Lentil Dahl with Tomatoes and Curry Leaves

SERVES 4 TO 6

Indian lentil dahls are so flexible, healthy, and filling they're likely to become a favorite weeknight meal. Freeze a batch of fresh curry leaves for whenever the mood strikes, and this red lentil version becomes pantry-friendly indeed. Serve this as an introduction to an Indian feast, or enjoy it as a meal with a home-made Indian paratha or nan bread and a chutney.

    5 cups water
    2 cups dry red lentils
    1 teaspoon sea salt
    1 tablespoon vegetable oil
    4 cardamom pods or ½ teaspoon ground
        cardamom
    2 teaspoons coriander seeds
    1 teaspoon fenugreek seeds
    1 to 3 dried red Indian or Thai chilies, or
        ½ to 1 teaspoon cayenne powder
    ½ teaspoon ground cinnamon
    ½ teaspoon ground turmeric
    1 large red onion, peeled and finely diced
    6 fresh curry leaves (see page 14)
    One 14-ounce can diced tomatoes, juice
        drained and reserved
    1 tablespoon lime juice

1. In a large stockpot combine water, lentils, and salt. Bring to a boil over high heat for 1 minute, then turn heat down to low and cook partially covered. Cook for 25 minutes, stirring occasionally. The lentils should be mostly soft and starting to look a little creamy.

2. Towards the end of the 25 minutes, heat the oil in a small skillet over low heat. Crush cardamom with the side of a chef's knife and add to the oil. In a coffee mill, grind the coriander, fenugreek, chilies, cinnamon, and turmeric into a coarse powder and sprinkle into the oil. Stir and fry for about 30 seconds, then add the onion and curry leaves. Continue to fry for 1 minute or until the curry leaves start to curl. Watch carefully and don't burn the spices.

3. Pour the reserved tomato juice into the spices and simmer, stirring occasionally until the juices dissolve any crusted spices from the bottom of the pan. Pour this into the cooking lentils, then add the drained diced tomatoes. Partially cover again and simmer dahl for 10 minutes. Season with the lime juice and additional salt if desired. Serve hot with any rice or flat bread.

Yellow Split Pea Dahl: Replace red lentils with yellow split peas, increasing the initial cooking time to 35 minutes.

Presoaking the lentils helps them cook up lightning fast. Before you leave the house in the morning, combine the lentils and 5 cups of water in a soup pot. When you come home, don't drain the lentils; just move the lentils to the stove and proceed as directed. They'll cook up creamy and soft faster than you can order Indian takeout!

Masala Potato Soup

SERVES 4 TO 6

This golden soup brings to mind my favorite South Indian–inspired flavors of potatoes richly colored with turmeric, spices, and additional textures and nutrition with a touch of dahl (split, hulled peas or lentils). Depending on the dahl used, you'll get different textures and may have to adjust the cooking time slightly. Virgin coconut oil adds buttery richness to this soothing soup that needs only freshly made roti, paratha, or a green salad to make a complete meal.

For additional fiber and flavor, leave the potatoes unpeeled (but the skins clean). Be sure to also sort through the dahl to remove any grit and rinse well and drain before adding to the pot.

2 pounds waxy yellow potatoes

4 teaspoons virgin coconut or peanut oil

2 teaspoons mustard seeds

1½-inch piece peeled ginger, minced

3 green Thai chilies or hot green chile peppers, finely minced

½ cup uncooked split pigeon peas (toovar dahl), yellow split peas, mung dahl, or similar split, peeled dahl

1 large yellow onion, peeled and diced

8 to 10 fresh curry leaves (see page 14), rolled and sliced into slivers

1 tablespoon Madras curry powder (or any curry powder you like)

½ teaspoon ground turmeric

6 cups water

1½ teaspoons sea salt

4 teaspoons lime juice

1 teaspoon *Garam Masala* (page 39) or store-bought garam masala

1½ cups lightly packed cilantro leaves, roughly chopped

1. Peel and remove any blemishes from the potatoes. Cut into 1-inch-thick chunks and keep covered in cold water until ready to use.

2. In a large soup pot melt coconut oil over medium-high heat, stir in mustard seeds, and fry until seeds just begin to pop. Stir in ginger, chilies, split pigeon peas, and onion and fry, stirring occasionally, until the onion is translucent, anywhere from 6 to 8 minutes. Stir in curry leaves, curry powder, and turmeric and fry for 1 minute, then pour in the water. Increase heat to high and bring to a rolling boil, reduce heat to medium-low and partially cover. Cook for 25 minutes, stirring occasionally.

3. Drain the potato chunks, add to the broth, and increase the heat and bring to a boil again. Boil for 1 minute, decrease heat to medium-low, and simmer for 20 to 30 minutes or until potatoes are tender and dahl is tender or mushy (depending on what kind of dahl used).

4. Reduce heat to low and carefully use a potato masher to mash the potatoes into a creamy, chunky soup. Season with salt and lime juice, stir and taste; adjust with additional salt and lime juice as desired. Turn off heat and stir in the garam masala and chopped cilantro, then serve.

yellow split pea soup with chard

SERVES 6 TO 8

*A thick stew chock-full of hearty vegetables and influenced by the flavors of Ethiopian cuisine. For the truest flavor make this soup with any leftover **Spiced Buttery Oil** (page 44) from an Ethiopian cooking spree, but olive oil will work in a pinch. Like all bean soups the flavor improves the next day.*

*If you've made the **Berbere Spice Blend** (page 44), add 1 teaspoon along with the other ground spices into the peas for more zing.*

> 1 pound yellow split peas
> 6 cups water
> 1 large red onion, peeled and finely diced
> 1 tablespoon finely chopped fresh ginger
> 4 cloves garlic
> 1 ½ teaspoons sea salt
> 2 teaspoons sweet paprika
> 1½ teaspoons ground turmeric
> 1½ teaspoons ground cumin
> 1 teaspoon ground coriander
> 3 plum tomatoes, finely chopped
> 1 pound chard
> 1 tablespoon lime juice
> 4 teaspoons *Spiced Buttery Oil* (page 44) or olive oil
> 2 red chile peppers, finely chopped

1. Sort through split peas and remove any debris. Rinse and place in a large 3-quart pot and add water, onion, ginger, garlic, salt, paprika, turmeric, cumin, and coriander. Over high heat bring the water to a rolling boil, then reduce heat to medium-low. Stir a few times and cover. Cook the peas until they are tender and beginning to turn creamy, about 55 to 60 minutes.

2. Add the tomatoes. Remove the stems from the chard, finely chop the stems, and add them to the pot; cook for 15 minutes. While the stew cooks stack a few chard leaves, roll them into a tight cigar, and slice as thinly as possible into fine shreds no wider than ¼ inch. Stir half of the leaves into the stew. When the leaves have wilted, stir in the other half and cook for another 5 minutes. Stir in the lime juice.

3. Heat the *Spiced Buttery Oil* in a small skillet over medium heat and stir in the chilies. Cook until the chilies are softened, then add to the soup. Stir and taste soup and adjust seasoning by adding more salt or lime juice as needed.

white bean farro soup with chickpea parmigiana

SERVES 6 TO 8

A great big Italian-style soup with a little Tuscan flair: white kidney beans (cannelini) have a tender, creamy flavor and they're loaded with fiber. Paired with chewy farro, an ancient variety of wheat that's pearled and similar in flavor to barley, this soup is

a whole meal in a bowl. Farro stands up to a long simmer better than pasta. Don't be surprised if you're tempted to throw in a few handfuls of spinach or escarole for additional color and nutrition.

But what makes this soup really special is the addition of a quick homemade Parmesan-like topping made from chickpea flour cooked with olive oil and lemon juice. If you miss a sharp and tangy topping for Italian soups and pasta that dissolves into the hot broth (instead of sitting on top like nut-based substitutes do), you'll love how the golden crumbs of chickpea parmigiana melt into the soup to form a lovely golden sauce; the **Chickpea Parmigiana Topping** (page 67) comes together while the soup is simmering and lasts for many servings.

1 cup pearled farro wheat berries

2 tablespoons olive oil

4 cloves garlic, peeled and minced

1 large yellow onion, peeled and finely diced

2 stalks celery, finely diced

1 large carrot, peeled and finely diced

One 14-ounce can fire-roasted diced tomatoes

2 teaspoons dried thyme

1 teaspoon crumbled dried rosemary

½ teaspoon sea salt

¼ teaspoon rubbed sage powder

8 cups vegetable broth

Two 14-ounce cans cannelini (white kidney beans)

1 cup baby spinach leaves or finely chopped escarole (optional)

1 cup chopped flat leaf parsley

Few twists of freshly cracked pepper and salt to taste

1 recipe *Chickpea Parmigiana Topping* (page 67)

Additional olive oil for drizzling (optional)

1. Pour the farro into a metal mesh sieve and rinse well. In a 4-quart soup pot, preheat the olive oil over medium heat, stir in the garlic, and fry for 30 seconds. Add the onion, celery, and carrot and fry for 5 minutes or until onion is tender and translucent. Stir in the tomatoes, thyme, rosemary, salt, and sage powder and fry for 1 minute. Stir in the vegetable broth, beans, and farro. Increase the heat to high and bring to a boil for 1 minute, then reduce heat to medium-low and partially cover. Simmer the soup for 30 to 40 minutes or until the farro grains are plump and tender. Occasionally uncover and stir the soup.

2. When the farro is tender, if using spinach or escarole stir into the soup and simmer another 5 minutes. Turn off the heat, stir in the parsley and season with pepper and salt to taste. Partially cover the soup and let stand 5 minutes before serving.

3. Ladle soup into large deep serving bowls. Sprinkle top with 2 to 3 tablespoons of chickpea parmigiana and drizzle with olive oil.

French Farmhouse Asparagus Bisque

SERVES 4 TO 6

Regardless if you're in the city or the country, enjoy this creamy and earthy soup with those essentially French elements of leeks, potato and asparagus, and a touch of fresh chives. Gently mash the potatoes for a rustic potage, or puree it to silky-smooth refinement, and then use the sautéed asparagus tips for an elegant garnish.

1 pound asparagus

1 large leek (about 1 pound)

1 tablespoon plus 1 teaspoon olive oil

½ cup dry white wine

4 cups vegetable broth

1 pound white baking potato, peeled and
    diced into ½-inch-thick pieces

6 sprigs fresh thyme or ½ teaspoon dried
    thyme

½ teaspoon salt or to taste

¼ cup plain soy or coconut-based creamer

2 tablespoons finely chopped fresh chives,
    plus 1 more tablespoon for garnish

1. Wash the asparagus and trim away the bottom ½ inch from the stalks. Slice off and set aside the tips, and dice the stalks into ½-inch pieces. Trim the roots from the leek, then trim away the top 4 inches away from the green leaves at the other end. Slice the leek in half and run under cold water, gently pushing apart the leaves to rinse away any grit. When leek is clean, slice it into slices ¼ inch thick.

2. In a 3-quart soup pot heat 1 tablespoon of the oil over medium heat and sauté the leek for 3 minutes or until it begins to soften. Add the chopped asparagus stalks and sauté for 4 minutes, stir in the wine and simmer for 2 minutes. Stir in the vegetable broth, potatoes, and thyme. Increase heat to high, bring to an active simmer for 1 minute, then reduce heat to medium-low. Cover and simmer for 22 to 24 minutes until the potatoes are very tender and mash easily when pressed with a fork.

3. While the soup is cooking, over medium heat in a small skillet sauté the asparagus tips with the remaining 1 teaspoon of olive oil for 1 to 1½ minutes or until the tips are bright green and crisp tender.

French Farmhouse Asparagus Bisque, page 123

Transfer tips to a dish and sprinkle with a pinch of sea salt.

4. Turn off heat and remove the thyme sprigs if using. Add the soy or coconut-based creamer. Use either a potato masher and mash the soup to a chunky puree, or insert an immersion blender into the soup and puree into the smoothest soup possible; take your time to ensure the soup gets very smooth. Stir in the chopped chives and salt, then taste the soup and season with more salt to taste if necessary.

To serve, ladle soup into wide serving bowls and garnish each serving with a few sautéed asparagus tips and a pinch of chopped chives.

The white stem ends of older asparagus can be filled with tough fibers. Out of season asparagus thicker than ½ inch should be trimmed by at least 1 inch from the bottom stem.

Bountiful Beet and Mushroom Borscht

SERVES 6 TO 8

*There are so many versions of this classic beet soup, it's impossible to say what is authentic and what isn't. But who cares, because this huge red-purple soup is hearty and tastes great through multiple reheatings to power you through a week of lunches. Sautéed mushrooms add chewy, meaty depth; bursting with vegetables and spices and topped with silky **Sour Dilly Cream** (page 71), every bowl is a complete luscious winter meal. There's no cabbage or greens*

here, but if you crave a cabbage-full Eastern European soup, make the *Sauerkraut Mushroom Soup (Shchi)* (page 130).

I always say that soup tastes better the next day, but it's especially true here. The flavors of this borscht benefit from rest; if you can afford to set freshly made hot borscht aside for 30 minutes before eating you'll definitely notice the difference!

10 ounces cremini mushrooms, cleaned and
    stems removed
3 tablespoons vegetable oil
6 cloves garlic, peeled and minced
1 large yellow onion, peeled and finely diced
1 large carrot, peeled and finely diced
½ pound celeriac root, peeled and finely
    diced
2 tablespoons tomato paste
8 cups vegetable broth, "beef" flavored
    broth recommended
1 pound beets, peeled and shredded
1 large potato or turnip (about ½ pound),
    peeled and diced into ½-inch cubes
2 teaspoons dried thyme
2 bay leaves
2 teaspoons black peppercorns, left whole
    or lightly crushed with a mortar and
    pestle (see page 31)
1 teaspoon dried marjoram
¼ teaspoon ground cloves
½ teaspoon sea salt
2 teaspoons red wine vinegar or white wine
    vinegar
Salt to taste
½ cup finely chopped parsley
1 recipe *Sour Dilly Cream* (page 71) or 1 cup
    plain soy yogurt
Chopped fresh dill for garnish (optional)

1. Dice the mushroom caps into quarters. In a 4-quart pot heat 1 tablespoon of the oil, add the mushrooms and sauté for 6 to 8 minutes or until the mushrooms are browned and tender. Transfer the mushrooms to a bowl and set aside. Add the remaining oil and garlic, sauté for 30 seconds and stir in the onions, carrot, and celeriac root. Increase the heat to medium-high and sauté for 10 minutes or until vegetables are softened and onion is translucent. Add the tomato paste and stir for 2 minutes to coat the vegetables. If the vegetables start to stick to the bottom of the pan, pour in ½ cup of broth and simmer while stirring constantly to dissolve any browned bits.

2. Add the vegetable broth, beets, potato or turnip, thyme, bay leaves, black peppercorns, marjoram, cloves, and sea salt. Stir and bring soup to a rolling boil for 2 minutes, then reduce heat to medium-low. Stir in the sautéed mushrooms. Partially cover the pot and simmer the soup for 30 to 40 minutes, stirring occasionally. The soup is ready when all of the vegetables are very tender. Remove bay leaves and discard.

3. Turn off the heat, stir in the vinegar and parsley, and season the soup with additional salt if necessary. Partially cover the pot and let stand for 10 minutes before serving. Ladle the soup into large, deep serving bowls. Just before serving swirl 1 or 2 tablespoons of *Sour Dilly Cream* or soy yogurt into each serving. If desired scatter a tablespoon of chopped fresh dill on each serving.

Borscht with Seitan: Extra-hearty soup to warm those winter blues: dice into ½-inch cubes two cutlets seitan (try *Seitan Coriander Cutlets* or *Mushroom Seitan*, pages 49 and 54), or use 8 to 10 ounces of purchased seitan. Sauté the cubes in 2 tablespoons of oil over medium heat until the edges of the cubes are browned, about 6 to 10 minutes. Stir in the seitan along with the vinegar when the soup is done simmering.

Borscht with White Beans: White beans are a traditional variation in borscht and complement the range of sweet root vegetables nicely. Drain and rinse one 14-ounce can (or 2 cups cooked) of navy beans or white lima beans (also called butter beans) and stir into the soup the last 10 minutes of simmering. Large white lima beans are a great, toothsome addition, too.

Greek creamy Lemon Rice soup ("no" govlemano)

SERVES 4 TO 6

The zesty classic egg-lemon chicken soup gets a vegan makeover with the help of both white beans and a touch of arborio rice. Arborio is usually reserved for risottos, but in soups it expands and softens to create a creamy base. This will thicken considerably as it cools, so for a thinner soup stir in ½ to 1 cup of hot vegetable both; a high-quality vegetarian chicken-flavored broth is especially suited here.

One tester of Greek heritage said of this soup "I was worried when I became a vegan what I would do when I had a cold—this will do very nicely." This is the highest praise to which a vegan soup could aspire.

 1 small yellow onion, peeled and finely
  diced
 1 large carrot, peeled and diced very small
 4 teaspoons extra-virgin olive oil
 4 cloves garlic, minced

¼ cup dry white wine

One 14-ounce can or 2 cups cooked white
  beans (such as cannelini, my favorite for
  this soup), drained and rinsed

6 cups vegetable or vegetarian chicken-
  flavored broth

3 tablespoons arborio rice

2 bay leaves

1 teaspoon dried oregano

½ teaspoon dried dill

½ cup uncooked orzo pasta

¼ cup lemon juice

Freshly ground pepper and salt to taste

Additional dried oregano or a handful
  chopped flat-leafed parsley, for garnish

1. In a 3-quart soup pot, fry the onion and carrot in olive oil over medium-high heat until the onion is translucent and soft, about 5 minutes. Stir in garlic and fry for another 45 seconds, then pour in the white wine and bring to a simmer, stirring frequently.

2. In a mixing bowl puree the beans with 1 cup of the vegetable broth, then add to pot along with the remaining vegetable broth, arborio rice, bay leaves, oregano, dill, and orzo pasta. Increase heat to high and bring to a boil for 5 minutes. Reduce heat to low, stir a few times, and cover the pot. Cook for 30 to 35 minutes, uncovering the pot occasionally to stir and check to see if the rice is sticking. The soup is ready when the orzo is tender and the rice is meltingly soft.

3. When done, turn off the heat, stir in the lemon juice, and keep covered for 10 minutes. Remove the bay leaves and season soup to taste with ground pepper, salt, and additional lemon juice if desired. Sprinkle each serving with a little dried oregano or chopped parsley.

Like an Egyptian Lentil Soup

SERVES 6 TO 8

Lentil soup is an important staple everyone should know how to make, but there's no excuse for it to be dull. My all-time favorite go-to lentil soup is from Donna Klein's Mediterranean Vegan; *it's familiar and homey yet with the authentically Egyptian twist of abundant onions and fragrant fennel seeds roasted in olive oil, then stirred into the finished soup.*

Make a recipe enough, and it will take on your tastes: I fry the onions on the stovetop and gently caramelize, then stir in a touch of red wine vinegar to pull together the sweet, earthy flavors. For entirely different soups try this with black or red lentils instead of the common brown lentils. Brown and black will retain their little chewy shapes and red lentils will break down into a creamy, soothing broth.

2 cups dry green, brown, or black lentils

6 cups water or vegetable broth

1 bay leaf

1½ teaspoons sea salt (use ½ teaspoon if using very salty veggie broth)

1 teaspoon ground coriander

1 large carrot, peeled and diced very small

1 stalk celery, diced very small

1 yellow onion, peeled and finely diced

3 large red onions, peeled

1 tablespoon fennel seeds

2 teaspoons cumin seeds

3 tablespoons olive oil

½ teaspoon red pepper flakes (optional)

3 cloves garlic, chopped

2 teaspoons red wine vinegar

A few twists of freshly ground black pepper

1. Sort through the lentils and pick through for any debris. In a large soup pot over high heat combine lentils, water, bay leaf, salt, coriander, carrot, celery, and yellow onions. Bring to a rolling boil, stir and lower heat to medium-low. Cover and simmer lentils for 40 minutes, stirring occasionally, until lentils are soft and vegetables are tender.

2. While lentils are cooking, slice the red onions in half and slice into the thinnest half moons possible, ¼ inch thin or less. Fry the fennel and cumin seeds in the olive oil in a cast-iron skillet over medium heat until fragrant, about 1 minute, then stir in the red pepper flakes and red onions. Fry the onions for 15 to 20 minutes until they are very soft and well browned. Stir in garlic and fry for 1 minute, then turn off heat.

3. After lentils have been cooking for 40 minutes, stir in the red onion mixture. Scoop up ½ cup of liquid from the soup and stir into the skillet to rinse off any of the cooking oils and return the liquid to the soup pot. Simmer soup for 10 minutes, stirring occasionally. Turn off heat, season with red wine vinegar, pepper, and additional salt if necessary. Cover and let stand for 5 minutes before serving.

If you're not a fennel fan, reduce the fennel to 1½ teaspoons but don't leave it out entirely.

Ginger Peanut Squash Soup

SERVES 6 TO 8

*Creamy stews kissed with peanut butter and chilies are a favorite highlight of African cuisine for many; think of this lighter, laid-back version of the more traditional **Deluxe Tofu Vegetable Mafe** (page 160) full of succulent summer squash or tropical chayote squash. A scoop of cooked rice makes a simple accompaniment.*

1½ pounds zucchini or any summer squash, diced into ½-inch cubes

1 tablespoon peanut oil

1 large onion, peeled and finely chopped

2 large carrots, peeled and diced into ½-inch cubes

2 red chile peppers, minced

4 cloves garlic, peeled and minced

1-inch piece peeled ginger, minced

1 teaspoon ground coriander

4 cups vegetable broth

2 bay leaves

½ pound plum tomatoes, cores and seeds removed, diced, or one 14-ounce can diced tomatoes with juice

⅔ cup natural chunky or smooth peanut butter

1 tablespoon lime juice

½ teaspoon sea salt plus more for sprinkling

A few twists of freshly ground black pepper

A handful fresh cilantro leaves, roughly chopped

1. Sprinkle a generous pinch of salt over the zucchini, place in a large colander over the sink, and set aside to drain while you prepare the rest of the ingredients. In a large soup pot, heat peanut oil over medium heat. When the oil begins to shimmer, add the onion and sauté for 5 minutes or until softened, then add carrot and chilies. Sauté for 1 minute, then stir in garlic, ginger, and coriander and fry for 1 minute. Pour in vegetable broth, bay leaves, and tomatoes and increase heat to medium-high to bring to an active simmer.

2. Scoop peanut butter into a mixing bowl. Pour 1 cup of hot broth (avoid scooping up a bay leaf) over the peanut butter and use a wooden spoon or rubber spatula to stir it into a creamy sauce. Return the peanut butter mixture to the pot; if desired pour a little soup back into the mixing bowl to rinse any remaining peanut butter mixture from the sides and pour back into the pot once more. Shake the zucchini in the colander to release any excess water, add to the soup, and increase heat to bring mixture to an active simmer. Turn heat down to low, partially cover the pot, and cook for 15 to 20 minutes or until the zucchini is tender.

3. Stir in lime juice, salt, and black pepper; taste the mixture and adjust with more lime juice and salt if desired. Turn off the heat, cover the pot, and let sit for 5 minutes. Stir in the cilantro leaves just before serving.

sauerkraut mushroom soup (shchi)

SERVES 6 TO 8

*Sauerkraut soup? Believe it! Sauerkraut proves a robust and tangy base for this hearty, Russian-inspired, winter-cold-cutting soup that's bursting with vegetables. Paired with crusty rye bread or **Coriander Rye Muffins** (page 202), swirled with a touch of **Sour Dilly Cream** (page 71), it's a robust, soothing supper.*

There are two ingredients that are essential for a successful shchi: a rich vegetable broth and good-quality sauerkraut. Use the richest, darkest, most full-flavored broth or bouillon you can find: I use a faux-beef flavored (the Better Than Bouillon brand), and I make it slightly more concentrated than directed. In this instance bouillon cubes, powders, or pastes are preferred over boxed broth for the rich flavor they will give this soup.

For the sauerkraut, shun the lifeless canned stuff in favor of the high-quality 'kraut sold in jars or plastic bags in the refrigerated section; even better, buy it in bulk (usually stocked in big barrels) in some kosher or Eastern European markets. You'll be using some of the juice, so be sure to set some aside!

2 cups cremini mushrooms, stems removed
    and caps wiped clean
1 large leek, root and dry leafy ends
    trimmed, cleaned and finely diced
1 cup finely diced carrot
2 stalks celery, finely diced
2 tablespoons of vegetable oil
3 cloves garlic, peeled and minced
½ cup dry white wine (or vegetable broth)
2 cups diced parsnip or potato, cut into
    ½-inch cubes
6 cups vegetable broth
2 bay leaves
¼ teaspoon ground allspice
1 teaspoon caraway seeds (optional but very
    good)
2 teaspoons dried marjoram or oregano
2½ cups sauerkraut, undrained and with
    juices
½ cup sauerkraut juice (or more vegetable
    broth)
1 teaspoon ground black pepper
½ teaspoon salt, or to taste
A few twists cracked black pepper
3 tablespoons chopped parsley, for garnish
Sour Dilly Cream (optional, page 71)

1. Slice mushroom caps in half, then slice the caps into quarters to create bite-size mushroom pieces. In a 4-quart soup pot over medium-high heat, sauté the leek, carrot, and celery in vegetable oil for 6 minutes. Stir in garlic and mushrooms and sauté for another 6 to 8 minutes, or until mushrooms have reduced in size and released most of their liquid.

2. Pour in the wine and simmer for 2 minutes, then stir in parsnip, vegetable broth, bay leaves, allspice, caraway seeds (if using), marjoram, sauerkraut, sauerkraut juice, and ground black pepper.

SAUERKRAUT MUSHROOM SOUP (SHCHI)
AND CORIANDER RYE MUFFINS (PAGE 202)

Increase heat and bring to a gentle boil, then reduce heat, stir occasionally and cover.

3. Simmer the soup for 35 to 40 minutes or until the parsnips are tender. Remove the bay leaves, turn off the heat, and season with cracked black pepper and salt if necessary and garnish with parsley. Allow soup to cool 5 minutes before serving. Top each bowlful with a generous tablespoon of *Sour Dilly Cream*.

Smoky Shchi with Seitan and Cabbage: For an extra-hearty, smoky kick, add fresh cabbage, liquid smoke, and sizzling seitan! Towards the last 15 minutes of simmering the shchi, stir in 2 cups thinly sliced Savoy or green cabbage and 1 teaspoon liquid smoke. In a skillet over medium heat, fry 2 cutlets of *Coriander Seitan* (page 49) diced into ½-inch pieces with 2 tablespoons of vegetable oil until browned. Top each serving with cubes of fried seitan, then top with *Sour Dilly Cream* (page 71).

CHAPTER 6

Curries, Hearty Stews & Beans

It's easy to get passionate about intriguing curries and their kin; you always remember your first silky Thai green or red curry, Jamaican tropical vegetable curry, or golden tagine. Perhaps you're curious about Sri Lankan curries that fuse Thai, Chinese, and Indian elements into mellow, coconut-laced broths. Economical and flavorful, curries and stews can be found the world over. A beer-spiked Belgian spin on seitan stew, a posole that's all about the fresh toppings, even a pot of zesty homemade beans—be they Indian chickpeas, Egyptian favas, or Mexican pintos—can feed you all week long for pennies, but taste like a million bucks. Don't miss out on the breads, rice, and couscous recipes in this book for ideal companions to these hearty one-pot meals.

The Great Big Vegetable Couscous

SERVES 4 TO 6

Simmer this bountiful, warmly spiced, vegetable-loaded tagine for a genuine accompaniment to couscous; you'll have loads of beautifully reheatable leftovers for the whole week. A touch of chickpea flour at the end creates a lightly creamy broth that bathes the veggies in a golden glow. It's easy to shake this recipe up by swapping in different vegetables; sweet butternut squash in the winter and zucchini in the summer are my favorites.

If you have a big clay pot or very large clay tagine use it here. If not, a heavy, enameled cast-iron or stainless-steel pot is your friend in preparing this dish.

> 1 very large yellow onion, peeled, sliced in half, and sliced into ¼-inch-thin half-moons (about 2 cups of slices)
> 3 tablespoons olive oil
> 4 cloves garlic, peeled and smashed
> 1 large leek, roots trimmed and white and light green parts sliced into 1-inch-thick rings
> 1 large carrot, peeled and diced into ½-inch chunks
> 1 smallish head of cauliflower, about 1 pound
> 2 cups diced ripe red tomatoes or one 14-ounce can diced tomatoes, drained
> 2 cups chickpeas; if using canned, rinse well and drain
> 2 teaspoons ground sweet paprika
> ½ teaspoon ground turmeric
> ½ teaspoon ground black pepper
> ½ teaspoon cayenne pepper
> ½ teaspoon ground cumin
> ½ teaspoon ground ginger
> One 3-inch stick cinnamon
> 2½ cups vegetable broth
> ½ teaspoon salt
> 3 tablespoons chickpea flour
> 1 recipe *Fluffy Spiced Couscous* (page 303), prepared and kept warm

Ras-el-hanout is a special Moroccan spice blend perfect for this couscous and tagines. If you can find some, use 1 tablespoon or more in place of the ground spices. (See page 10 for more info on ras-el-hanout.)

1. In a large pot over medium-high heat fry the onions in olive oil for 5 minutes, then add the garlic, leek, and carrot and fry another 15 minutes until leeks are softened. Slice the cauliflower into quarters, remove the leaves, and cut away the thick inner stem, then slice into large chunks at least 2 inches wide. Add to the pot along with all of the remaining ingredients except for the chickpea flour and couscous, stir everything well to incorporate the spices into the broth, and bring the broth to a gentle boil. Reduce the heat to low, cover, and simmer for 20 minutes.

2. Pour the chickpea flour into a small bowl. Scoop out ½ cup of the cooking liquid from the pot and whisk it into flour to form a thick sauce. Use a rubber spatula to scrape the sauce back into the pot and gently stir to dissolve the sauce into the broth, taking

care not to mash up the cauliflower too much. Leave the pot uncovered and simmer another 10 minutes. Test the vegetables for doneness; if they're tender enough, turn off the heat. If they could use a little longer continue to simmer for another 8 to 10 minutes until the desired tenderness is reached. Turn off the heat, cover the pot once more, and let stand for at least 15 minutes or more before serving to allow the flavors to blend and the stew to cool down slightly.

To serve, spread freshly prepared couscous onto a serving dish or individual dishes. Use a slotted spoon to scoop the veggies onto the top of the couscous, then pour the sauce over the veggies and couscous and serve immediately.

With Winter Squash: Add 2 to 3 cups chunks of peeled winter squash. Make the chunks at least 1 inch wide to prevent them from falling apart during the simmer.

With Summer Squash: Slice on a diagonal 2 pounds of summer squash into 1-inch-thick pieces. Add toward the end of the simmer along with the chickpea flour mixture and simmer until tender but not completely falling apart.

With Preserved Lemon: Stir in 1 tablespoon of finely chopped preserved lemon (see *Preserved Lemons, Two Ways*, page 58).

With Saffron: Use ¼ teaspoon of saffron threads in place of the turmeric.

With Okra or Green Beans: Replace leeks with ½ pound of trimmed, small okra pods or green beans.

Ginger Tomato Chickpeas (Chole or Chana Masala)

SERVES 6 TO 8 WITH RICE OR BREAD

Tender chickpeas simmered in a richly seasoned tomato curry gravy are the Indian vegan staple bean to master. I spike them with pomegranate molasses for an unexpected tangy bite. They're excellent served with rice or any Indian bread, perhaps with a green or cabbage salad.

1 pound dried chickpeas

1 teaspoon sea salt

1½ quarts (6 cups) water

1 teaspoon fenugreek seeds

1 teaspoon cumin seeds

1½ teaspoons coriander seeds

2 tablespoons vegetable oil

1 large white onion, peeled and diced into ¼-inch pieces

4 cloves garlic, finely minced

1-inch piece peeled ginger, minced

3 hot green chile peppers (serrano, jalapeño, Thai, etc.), finely chopped

½ teaspoon ground turmeric

Two 14-ounce cans diced tomatoes, with juices

2 tablespoons pomegranate molasses (see pages 102 and 136) or pomegranate concentrate

2 bay leaves

A handful of chopped cilantro, for garnish (optional)

Homemade chickpeas from dried beans make this special; the creamy flavor and firmer texture of home-cooked beans can't be beat. But if you would rather used canned, you'll need about 6 cups of cooked chickpeas (three 14-ounce cans). Drain and rinse chickpeas and add 1½ cups of water when adding chickpeas to tomato sauce.

1. Pour the dried chickpeas onto a large dinner plate and remove any debris, then pour into a large bowl. Cover with 4 inches of cold water and soak for 8 hours or overnight. When ready to cook, drain soaking liquid and rinse chickpeas. Transfer chickpeas to a large soup pot (at least 4 quarts), add 6 cups of water and salt, then bring to a rolling boil over high heat. Reduce heat to low, partially cover, and cook until chickpeas are very tender, about 2 hours.

2. Turn off heat and cool chickpeas for 20 minutes. Set aside 1½ cups of the cooking liquid and drain away the rest. In a small skillet toast the fenugreek, cumin, and coriander seeds over medium heat for 1 to 1½ minutes until fragrant and the fenugreek seeds have darkened slightly. Empty toasted seeds into a clean coffee grinder and pulse until ground into a fine powder.

Substitutes: *If you can't find pomegranate molasses or concentrate, stir in 1 tablespoon of tomato paste plus 1 tablespoon of lime juice. Don't substitute regular molasses!*

3. In a large pot, heat the oil over medium heat, then add the onion, garlic, ginger, and chilies and fry until onions have softened, about 5 minutes. Sprinkle in turmeric and the ground spices and fry for 1 minute, then stir in diced tomatoes, pomegranate molasses, and the bay leaves. Simmer for 5 minutes, then stir in chickpeas plus the reserved chickpea cooking liquid. Bring everything to a simmer, reduce heat and let cook for 30 minutes, stirring occasionally. Turn off the heat, remove the bay leaves, and let sit covered for 5 minutes. Before serving, garnish with the cilantro.

pumpkin coconut curry

SERVES 4 ALONG WITH STEAMED RICE OR BREAD

Pumpkin, tropical spices, and coconut are an irresistible introduction to the world of Sri Lankan curries. If good quality pumpkins are in short supply, butternut and kabocha squash always make for tasty substitutes. If using kabocha you may need to cut down on the final simmer: this starchy Japanese squash cooks slightly faster than its crispier Western cousins.

3 pounds pumpkin, or butternut, or kabocha squash

⅓ cup dried shredded unsweetened coconut

1 large red onion, peeled and diced into ½-inch chunks

6 cloves garlic, peeled and minced

3 tablespoons of water

2 teaspoons coriander seeds

1 teaspoon cumin seeds

½ teaspoon ground turmeric

1 to 3 dried hot red chile peppers or ½ to 1 teaspoon red pepper flakes (see The Care and Feeding of Fresh and Dried Chile Peppers, page 12)

1¼ cups canned coconut milk, regular or reduced fat

1 cup vegetable broth

¾ teaspoon sea salt or more to taste

1 teaspoon black mustard seeds

2 tablespoons vegetable oil or coconut oil

6 fresh curry leaves (see page 14), or use frozen

Four 3-inch pieces of frozen pandan leaves (see page 18)

One 3-inch cinnamon stick

Hot basmati rice

1. Wash the pumpkin or squash, removing any dirt or debris. Use a sharp Y-shaped vegetable peeler (page 30) to scrape off the skin and remove the seeds and the stringy flesh around the seeds. Cut the pumpkin into 1-inch cubes.

2. Over a low heat in a heavy-bottomed frying pan, dry roast the coconut until golden brown, stirring frequently with a wooden spoon. Watch carefully, as the coconut will appear not to be doing anything then bam!, suddenly, roasted coconut. When the coconut is just beginning to turn a shade of light tan, pour it into a food processor. Add the onion, garlic, and the water and grind to a smooth paste, stopping to scrap the sides of the bowl frequently with a rubber spatula. In a clean coffee mill grind together coriander seeds, cumin seeds, turmeric, and chile peppers to a fine powder.

3. In a 4-cup glass measuring cup or mixing bowl combine the coconut milk with vegetable broth and salt. In a 3-quart heavy pot heat the mustard seeds in the oil over medium heat. Keep the pan covered until most of the mustard seeds finish popping. Uncover the pan and stir in the curry leaves, pandan leaves, and the ground spices. Cover the pan again and fry for 45 seconds, then uncover and stir in the onion mixture and fry for 1 minute. Add the coconut milk mixture, cubed pumpkin, and the cinnamon stick.

4. Partially cover and gently simmer for 15 to 20 minutes or until a fork easily pierces a tender chunk of pumpkin; if using kabocha squash, check around the 12-minute mark. If liquid level reduces too much add ¼ cup more broth or water, but not too much: the curry should be moist but not swimming in liquid. Remove from heat, cover, and let stand for 10 minutes. If desired remove the cinnamon stick and pandan leaves, or leave them in as (inedible but fragrant) decoration. Don't remove the curry leaves, as these are edible. Serve warm with hot basmati rice or *Sri Lankan Coconut Roti* (page 193).

Jamaican plantain and pumpkin curry

SERVES 4 TO 6

If you love vegetable curries, then a Jamaican-style curry of tropical vegetables is an essential part of your curry education. You'll identify immediately with the golden, coconut-infused broth, but digging in you'll appreciate the differences; the floral heat of tropical chilies, the warmth of allspice, and the herbal aroma of fresh thyme. And then there are the vegetables: tender green plantains, mild chayote, and melting tropical pumpkin. Serve with any Indian flatbread, boiled rice, or **Island Brown Rice and Peas** *(page 313).*

The star ingredient here is the Jamaican-style curry powder. It's not the same as a typical supermarket curry powder, but it's easy and fun to make at home. If you prefer to buy curry powder, Grace's is a commonly found Jamaican curry powder, featuring allspice and garlic, two essential elements in this spice blend.

1 pound calabaza squash (tropical pumpkin)

2 green plantains

2 chayote squash or 1 medium-size zucchini

1 leek or 3 large scallions

1 medium-size yellow onion, peeled

2 tablespoons unrefined coconut or
    vegetable oil

3 cloves garlic, peeled and minced

2 tablespoons *Jamaican Curry Powder*
    (page 40) or store-bought Jamaican curry
    powder

½ teaspoon turmeric powder

½ teaspoon ground cumin

½ teaspoon ground black pepper

2 cups vegetable broth or water

1 cup canned coconut milk, regular
    or reduced fat

1½ teaspoons sea salt, or to taste

6 sprigs fresh thyme or 1½ teaspoons dried

1 to 2 habanero or Scotch Bonnet chile
    peppers, left whole and poked with the
    tip of knife a few times (see sidebar)

1 tablespoon lime juice or more to taste

1. With a Y-shaped vegetable peeler (see page 30), peel the calabaza and then scoop and discard the pulp and seeds. Dice the calabaza into 1-inch cubes. Use a sharp paring knife to slice off the tips of the plantains on both ends, then run the tip in a straight line end to end through the skin of the plantain. Take the edge of a butter knife, slide it into the score, and use it to pry the skin off the plantains. Cut the plantains into ½-inch-thick slices on a diagonal. Slice the ends off of the chayotes, slice into quarters, and slice each quarter into ½-inch thick slices (the soft seed is edible). Trim the roots and green end off the leek, rinse the inside to remove any grit, then slice into ½-inch-thick pieces. If using scallions, remove the roots and slice into 1-inch pieces. Slice the onion in half, then dice into ½-inch chunks. Give yourself a hug, you've survived the longest part of this recipe: chopping up the veggies.

Tropical Veggies to Know

Chayote squash is also known as *mirlitons* (the French Creole name) or *christophenes*. After plantains and yuca it's a fairly a common item wherever Latin produce is sold. Chayote squash is pear-shaped, bright green, and puckered up on the "flower" end like grandma after she's removed her dentures. Chayote is a fixture in Latin American tropical and Caribbean cuisine and usually cheap. The peel and soft white pit are edible.

Calabaza squash is a type of large tropical pumpkin available year-round and typically sold plastic-wrapped and presliced into 1- to 2-pound chunks. Look for it wherever plantains are sold.

Whole **habanero** or **Scotch Bonnet chile peppers** simmered in the curry will add some heat, but if you prefer, finely mince them (chile-sensitive folks should wear gloves handling these ultra-hot chilies) and fry along with the onion. New to habaneros or Scotch Bonnet? Use only a half or a quarter of a chile (without the seeds) to start.

2. In a heavy soup pot, melt the coconut oil over medium-high heat. Stir in the onions and leeks and sauté for 5 minutes or until they start to soften. Stir in the garlic and fry another 2 minutes, then sprinkle the **Jamaican Curry Powder**, turmeric, cumin, and black pepper and sauté for 1 minute. Pour in the vegetable broth, coconut milk, and salt. Add the plantains and chayote, then poke the thyme sprigs and habanero chile peppers into the broth. Increase heat to high and bring to a gentle boil, then reduce heat to medium-low and cover.

3. Simmer for 30 minutes, occasionally removing the cover and stirring a few times. After 30 minutes stir in the pumpkin cubes, partially cover, and simmer another 20 to 25 minutes until the pumpkin is tender. Turn off heat, remove the habanero (if left whole) and thyme, and stir in the lime juice. Cover and let the curry stand for 10 minutes. Taste and adjust seasoning with more salt or lime juice if desired. Serve hot with rice or bread.

Veggie Curry with Beans: Add 2 cups of cooked, rinsed kidney, black-eyed peas or pigeon peas to this curry along with the pumpkin.

coconut Black-eyed pea curry (Lobia)

SERVES 4

Serve this thick, bean-based Punjabi preparation with other vegetable curries for an additional protein boost. Lobia is often prepared with whole milk yogurt, but coconut milk adds the soothing richness here. Lobia refers to using black-eyed peas, but any combination of beans could be used; try using a can of black-eyed peas and a can of red kidney beans for variety. Cook the lobia for longer than the recommended time in order to produce a thicker curry for scooping up with naan. Likewise, cook for a shorter time than recommended if you want a looser stew to pour on basmati rice.

For best results use high-quality organic canned beans. Good-quality organic canned beans don't need to be rinsed for this dish, just use them straight out of the can. If you must use regular supermarket nonorganic canned beans, rinse and drain them first.

> 1 large yellow onion, peeled and chopped
> 1-inch piece peeled ginger
> 3 cloves garlic, peeled
> 2 teaspoons *Garam Masala* (page 39) or
>   store-bought garam masala
> ½ teaspoon cayenne pepper
> ½ teaspoon sea salt
> ¼ teaspoon ground cardamom
> 4 teaspoons vegetable oil
> Two 14-ounce cans (4 cups) cooked
>   black-eyed peas or red kidney beans,
>   or a combination, drained and rinsed
> ⅔ cup water or vegetable broth
> 2 bay leaves
> 1 cup coconut milk, regular or reduced fat
> 2 teaspoons lime juice
> ½ cup coarsely chopped cilantro

1. In a food processor pulse together the onion, ginger, garlic, garam masala, cayenne, salt, and cardamom to form a smooth paste. Heat the oil in a wok or stainless steel skillet over medium heat until it ripples, then stir-fry the onion mixture for

2 minutes. Add the beans, water or broth, bay leaves, and coconut milk and increase heat to high, stirring occasionally.

2. Bring the mixture to an active simmer for 5 minutes, then reduce heat to medium and simmer for 20 minutes, stirring occasionally. If a thicker consistency is desired, continue to simmer the beans. Remove the bay leaves and stir in lime juice and cilantro and serve with rice or naan.

whole cashew curry

SERVES 6 TO 8

Whole tender cashews simmered with just enough coconut milk and tropical spices go into this striking, luxuriant Sri Lankan curry. The special ingredient is pandan leaf (also called bai toey, rampe, or screwpine); it adds a unique, toasted vanilla-like aroma. Frozen pandan leaves are best suited for this dish, but pandan extract is far easier to purchase online. Serve with another vegetable curry and rice or **Sri Lankan Coconut Roti** *(page 193) for a balanced meal.*

    8 ounces unroasted, unsalted whole
        cashews
    2 teaspoons coriander seeds
    1 teaspoon cumin seeds
    1 teaspoon fennel seeds
    ¼ teaspoon ground turmeric
    1 teaspoon sea salt
    2 tablespoons vegetable oil
    1 large red onion, peeled and diced into
        ¼-inch pieces

    2 fresh green chilies, sliced into ¼-inch
        pieces
    5 cloves garlic, minced
    8 fresh curry leaves (optional; see page 14
        for more on curry leaves)
    One 3-inch cinnamon stick
    3 frozen pandan leaves (see page 18),
        broken into 3-inch pieces, or 2 drops of
        pandan extract
    1¼ cups vegetable broth
    ½ cup coconut milk, regular or reduced fat
    1 tablespoon homemade tamarind paste
        (see page 14) or 1 teaspoon tamarind
        concentrate

1. Place the cashews in a mixing bowl and cover with at least 3 inches boiling water. Soak for minimum 4 hours or overnight until the cashews are soft and plump. Drain the cashews in a mesh strainer and shake a few times to get rid of any excess moisture. Transfer the cashews to a mixing bowl. In a clean coffee grinder pulse the coriander seeds, cumin seeds, fennel, and turmeric to a fine powder. Sprinkle the ground spices and the salt on the cashews. Use your hands or a rubber spatula and stir well to thoroughly coat the nuts with spices.

2. Heat the oil in a deep, 12-inch skillet or Dutch oven over medium heat. Add onion, green chilies, garlic, curry leaves, and cinnamon and fry for about 6 to 8 minutes or until onion is soft and golden brown. Add the cashews and keep stirring until coated with oil and onions. Stir in the pandan leaves and fry for 2 minutes.

3. Pour in the vegetable broth and simmer for 2 minutes. Cover, turn down the heat to low, and simmer until cashews are tender, about 8 to 10 minutes, stirring occasionally. Stir in coconut milk and tamarind, turn up heat to medium, and simmer for 2 minutes. Remove from heat, taste and season with

more salt if necessary. Transfer to a serving dish, and if desired remove the pandan leaves (I keep them in there as garnish). Serve with rice or **Sri Lankan Coconut Roti** (page 19).

Flying Massaman Curry

SERVES 4

My speedy shortcuts for this wildly popular, peanuty Thai curry reminded me of a trapeze act, but without the fancy acrobatics. Perhaps chunky peanut butter and purchased spice blends could be called cheating, but the results are authentically satisfying; small, buttery new potatoes (tiny yellow fingerling potatoes are fantastic here) cook quickly when bathed in this nutty, velvety curry.

*Given time to rest and let the flavors develop, **Flying Massaman Curry** makes amazing leftovers (if there are any).*

3 large shallots, peeled
2 cloves garlic, peeled
1 tablespoon *Garam Masala* (page 39) or store-bought garam masala
1½ teaspoons *Sichuan 5-Spice Powder* (page 41) or store-bought Chinese 5-spice powder
¾ teaspoon sea salt
½ teaspoon turmeric powder
½ teaspoon cayenne pepper, or more to taste
½-inch piece peeled ginger

1 small red onion, peeled
One recipe *Savory Baked Tofu* (page 51) or two 6-ounce packages baked or fried tofu cutlets
1 tablespoon peanut or vegetable oil
1 pound small new potatoes, sliced into chunks no thicker than ½ inch
2 cups warm vegetable broth
1 cup canned coconut milk, regular or reduced fat
⅓ cup natural, chunky-style peanut butter
½ pound broccoli florets or green beans, trimmed
½ pound (about half a pint) cherry or grape tomatoes
1 tablespoon lime juice
2 teaspoons grated palm sugar (see page 18) or dark brown sugar
A handful of chopped fresh cilantro

1. In a food processor bowl or using the chopper attachment of an immersion blender, pulse together shallots, garlic, garam masala, *Sichuan 5-Spice Powder*, sea salt, turmeric, cayenne, and ginger to form a smooth curry paste.

2. Cut the onion in half and into ½-inch-wide half-moons. Slice the tofu into cubes or triangles no thicker than ½ inch. In a large 3-quart pot with a lid, heat the oil over medium heat, stir in the curry paste with a rubber spatula or wooden spoon, and fry for 1 minute, stirring constantly. Add the onion and fry until softened, about 3 to 4 minutes. Stir in the tofu and potatoes.

3. Meanwhile heat up vegetable broth and pour half of the broth into the pot over the potatoes. Add the coconut milk, increase heat to medium-high, and bring to a gentle simmer. In a measuring cup use a fork to combine the peanut butter and the

remaining warm vegetable broth. Stir vigorously to create a creamy sauce. Whisk this into simmering curry, reduce heat to medium-low, and cover. Simmer the curry for 20 minutes or until the potatoes are very tender and can be easily pierced with a fork.

4. Stir in the broccoli, cover, and simmer for 2 minutes or until the broccoli is crisp tender but still bright green. Add the cherry tomatoes, lime juice, and palm sugar and stir. Taste curry and adjust with more lime juice or salt if desired. Simmer for 1 more minute, turn off heat, cover the curry, and let it rest for 5 minutes. Sprinkle with chopped cilantro and serve immediately with hot rice.

sri lankan red lentil curry

SERVES 4

*This coconuty, fragrant red lentil dahl is thicker than Indian-style dahl—making it ideal for scooping up with **Sri Lankan Coconut Roti** (page 193). Along with the roti (or basmati rice), a simple salad or another vegetable curry makes this a complete meal.*

2 cups red lentils

4 cups hot water

2 teaspoons sea salt

1 teaspoon cayenne pepper

1 teaspoon black peppercorns

1 teaspoon fenugreek seeds

½ teaspoon turmeric

1 tablespoon vegetable oil

1 teaspoon black mustard seeds

1 small red onion, peeled and finely chopped

1 green Thai or serrano chile pepper, finely chopped (remove seeds for a milder dahl)

6 fresh curry leaves (see page 14), or use frozen

One 3-inch cinnamon stick

2 pandan leaves (see page 18), torn into 3-inch pieces, or 1 teaspoon pandan extract

½ cup canned coconut milk, regular or reduced fat

2 plum tomatoes, cores and seeds removed and finely diced

Sri Lankan Coconut Roti (page 193) or hot basmati rice

1. In a large mixing bowl combine lentils, hot water, and salt. Set aside to soak for 30 minutes. In a clean coffee grinder add the cayenne, peppercorns, fenugreek, and turmeric and pulse into a fine powder.

2. In a small skillet add the oil and heat over medium heat. Add the mustard seeds, cover the skillet, and fry until seeds begin to pop, then reduce the heat to low. Remove the cover, stir in the ground spices, and gently fry the spices for 1 minute. Increase the heat to medium, then stir in the onion, chile, curry leaves, and cinnamon stick. Fry for 2 minutes, then stir in the pandan leaves. Turn off the heat and move the skillet to a cool burner on the stovetop.

3. Pour the lentils with the soaking water into a 3-quart pot, transfer to the stove, and bring to a boil over high heat. Do not cover the pot. Boil for 5 minutes, then reduce heat to medium and simmer for 35 to 40 minutes; the dahl should be very thick toward the end of the simmer. Stir in the fried spice

mixture, coconut milk, and diced tomatoes. Simmer uncovered for another 10 minutes, stirring occasionally. Turn off the heat and let stand for 5 minutes. Taste and add more salt if necessary. If desired, remove the cinnamon stick and pandan leaves; the curry leaves are tender and edible. Serve warm with *Sri Lankan Coconut Roti* or rice.

Jungle Curry with Seitan, Eggplant, and Zucchini

SERVES 3 TO 4

In the delightful sprawl of Thai curries, piquant jungle curry was my first love. Two interesting twists make this curry stand out: the absence of coconut milk for a lighter dish and sharp heat from brine-packed green peppercorns—if these unripe berries were allowed to ripen, they would become the familiar black and red peppercorns. Seitan (or tofu) and eggplant soak up this bracing broth for my favorite curry that puts the kibosh on winter chills or cranks up the heat during the peak of summer produce season. Like many curries, the melding of flavors overnight makes leftovers something to look forward to.

The amount of green peppercorns and hot chilies in this recipe should please spicy food aficionados, but if you prefer mild instead of wild, reduce the peppercorns to 1 tablespoon and chilies to just 1 pepper

CURRY PASTE

2 tablespoons brine-packed green peppercorns, drained and any stems removed

4 cloves garlic, peeled

3 large shallots, peeled

1-inch piece peeled ginger

1 stalk fresh lemongrass, outer leaves removed and chopped (see page 17) or 2 tablespoons prepared lemongrass

1 to 3 fresh, thin hot chile peppers such as Thai or red serrano, stems removed and sliced into ½-inch thick pieces

¾ teaspoon sea salt

VEGETABLE CURRY

1 pound Japanese eggplant or Thai apple eggplants (see page 18) if you can find them

1 small zucchini

½ pound green beans

1 tablespoon unrefined coconut or vegetable oil

8 ounces prepared seitan, cubed or torn into shreds

2¼ cups vegetable broth

1 tablespoon brown sugar

2 tablespoons fresh lime juice

4 kaffir lime leaves or the peel from 1 lime (see *Tom Yum Noodle Soup*, page 217, for lime-peeling tips)

1 cup coarsely chopped cilantro leaves

1 tablespoon Thai thin soy sauce (see page 19)

½ cup Thai basil leaves, coarsely chopped (regular basil leaves are okay)

Hot jasmine rice (page 299)

1. Make the curry paste first: in a food processor blend all the curry paste ingredients. Process until a smooth paste forms, scraping the sides of the bowl often with a rubber spatula.

2. Trim the ends of the eggplant and zucchini and slice both on a diagonal into ½ wide slices. Trim the ends of the green beans. In a heavy 2-quart pot (enameled cast iron or stainless steel is best), heat coconut oil over medium high heat. Stir in curry paste and fry for 1 minute, then add seitan and fry for another 3 minutes. If using Japanese eggplant, add it now and fry, stirring occasionally for 4 to 5 minutes until slightly softened. Add broth, stir in brown sugar, lime juice, kaffir lime leaves or lime peel, and green beans.

3. Bring mixture to a gentle boil, reduce heat, partially cover the pot and gently simmer for 10 minutes. Stir in zucchini and simmer for another 6 to 8 minutes or until zucchini is somewhat tender but still firm and bright green. If using Thai apple eggplants, tuck them into the curry 2 minutes before it's done; this will warm them slightly but let them retain their crunchy texture. Remove from heat and remove the lime leaves or lime peel. Stir in the soy sauce, cilantro, and chopped basil. Let cool for 5 minutes then serve with jasmine rice.

Look for green peppercorns packed in brine either in jars or tins; occasionally the peppercorns will still be on the stem, just pluck them off or toss an additional whole stem into the curry as it simmers. There's no substitute for the hot, herbal flavor of green peppercorns, so make sure to find these before attempting this curry.

Curry Paste, Hot or Not?

The first answer is of course, any curry paste is always in style. But Thai food fans need a less intense curry that doesn't make 'em sweat. In either case, remove the seeds from half of the chile peppers before adding to the food processor with the rest of the paste ingredients.

If you love curry but don't like heat at all, remove *all* of the seeds and white pith from inside the fresh chilies; you may be surprised how mild the results can be.

Red Curry with Kabocha and Potatoes

SERVES 2 TO 3 WITH RICE

Green curry may be the slight victor in the curry popularity contest, but red curry is too good for an honorable mention. Red here doesn't mean stop, but instead go go go to a piquant pink curry loaded with pumpkin and potato. Smoky, fruity Mexican ancho chile powder complements the red Thai chilies by enriching the color without adding much fire.

CURRY PASTE

2 teaspoons coriander seeds

1 teaspoon cumin seeds

½ teaspoon fenugreek seeds

6 to 8 fresh red Thai chilies, stems removed

½ teaspoon ground white pepper

2½ teaspoons Ancho chile powder or any mild, red Mexican chile powder

2 large shallots, peeled and chopped in half

4 cloves garlic, peeled and chopped in half

1 stalk fresh lemongrass, outer leaves removed and chopped (see page 17), or 2 tablespoons prepared lemongrass

1-inch piece peeled ginger, roughly chopped

½ teaspoon sea salt

VEGETABLE CURRY

1 tablespoon vegetable or coconut oil

½ recipe *Savory Baked Tofu* (page 50) or 8 ounces purchased baked or fried tofu, diced into 1-inch cubes

One 14-ounce can coconut milk, regular or reduced fat

1½ cups mild vegetable broth or water

4 kaffir lime leaves, fresh or frozen, or the peel from 1 organic lime, sliced into 1-inch wide pieces (see *Tom Yum Noodle Soup*, page 217, for lime-peeling tips)

1 tablespoon lime juice

4 teaspoons brown sugar

1 tablespoon of Thai thin soy sauce (see page 19), or more to taste

2 to 2½ cups peeled and diced kabocha squash (little more than ½ pound; see page 16 for info on kabocha squash)

1 large potato, peeled and diced into 1-inch cubes (about ½ pound)

1 cup thinly sliced bamboo shoots packed in brine (see note) or baby corn, drained and rinsed

½ cup lightly packed Thai basil leaves

1. Prepare the curry paste first: In a small skillet over medium heat toast the coriander, cumin seeds, and fenugreek for 1 to 2 minutes until fragrant. Grind the toasted seeds in a clean coffee mill into a fine powder, then transfer to a food processor along with the remaining paste ingredients and pulse into a smooth, thick paste. Use a rubber spatula to scrape down the sides of the processor bowl frequently.

2. In a 2-quart pot melt the coconut oil over medium heat. Add the curry paste, stir with a wooden spoon or heat-resistant rubber spatula, and stir-fry for 1 minute. Add the tofu and fry for 2 minutes, stirring to coat with the fried curry paste. Stir in the coconut milk, vegetable broth, lime leaves, lime juice, brown sugar, and soy sauce. Increase heat to medium-high, simmer for 2 minutes, then reduce heat to medium-low.

3. Add the pumpkin, potato, and bamboo shoots and simmer for another 25 to 30 minutes or until vegetables are tender. Stir in the basil leaves and simmer another minute. Taste and season with more soy sauce and lime juice if desired. Remove from heat and let stand for 5 minutes. Serve with hot rice.

Lightly brined bamboo shoots can be purchased in cans, jars, or in some Asian markets in bulk in refrigerated open bins stored in brine. They can have a strong odor; to mellow that aroma, drain and then soak the shoots (usually presliced into shreds) in cool water for 20 minutes, then drain and rinse again. Some of the odor may linger, but once cooked the flavor will dissolve into this fragrant curry.

It's Easy Being Green Curry

SERVES 2 TO 3

A nonscientific poll (conducted by your friendly cook-book author) revealed Thai green curry to be slightly in the lead for most popular curry in the Thai curry kingdom. Buttery coconut milk, fresh cilantro, and green chilies make curry fans swoon; if you stumble upon crunchy Thai apple eggplants in your travels, be sure to use them in this classic curry!

The curry paste can be made days ahead, even frozen, making this a relatively fast weeknight meal. For a reduced-fat curry, use light canned coconut milk, or use less coconut milk and increase the amount of vegetable broth.

GREEN CURRY PASTE

2 teaspoons coriander seeds

½ teaspoon cumin seeds

1 teaspoon ground white pepper

1 cup lightly packed cilantro sprigs with stems

4 to 6 Thai green hot chilies or serrano chilies, chopped

2 large shallots, peeled and chopped in half

4 cloves garlic, peeled and chopped in half

1 stalk fresh lemongrass, outer leaves removed and chopped (see page 17), or 2 tablespoons prepared lemongrass

½-inch-wide piece fresh galangal root, optional (see page 16)

1-inch piece peeled ginger, roughly chopped

½ teaspoon sea salt

VEGETABLE CURRY

2 teaspoons virgin coconut oil or vegetable oil

½ recipe *Savory Baked Tofu* (page 50), or 8 ounces purchased baked or fried tofu sliced into ¼-inch strips

One 14-ounce can coconut milk, regular or reduced fat

1½ cups mild vegetable broth or water

4 kaffir lime leaves, fresh or frozen, or the peel from 1 organic lime (see *Tom Yum Noodle Soup*, page 217, for lime-peeling tips)

1 tablespoon lime juice

2 teaspoons brown sugar

1 tablespoon of Thai thin soy sauce (see page 19), or more to taste

1 red bell pepper, seeds removed and sliced into ½-inch strips

2 small, slender zucchini or 6 Thai apple eggplants (see page 18), stems removed and sliced into quarters

½ cup lightly packed Thai basil leaves, thinly sliced

Boiled jasmine rice (page 299), for serving

1. Prepare the curry paste first: In a small skillet over medium heat toast the coriander and cumin seeds for 1 to 2 minutes until fragrant. Grind the toasted seeds in a clean coffee mill into a fine powder, then transfer to a food processor along with the remaining paste ingredients and pulse into

IT'S EASY BEING GREEN CURRY

a smooth, thick paste. Use a rubber spatula to scrape down the sides of the processor bowl frequently.

2. In a 2-quart pot melt the coconut oil over medium heat. Add the curry paste, stir with a wooden spoon or heat-resistant rubber spatula, and stir-fry for 1 minute. Add the tofu and fry for 2 minutes, stirring to coat with the fried curry paste. Stir in the coconut milk, vegetable broth, lime leaves, lime juice, brown sugar, and soy sauce. Increase heat to medium-high, simmer for 5 minutes then reduce heat to medium-low.

3. Add the red bell pepper, zucchini (but not Thai apple eggplant if using), and basil leaves and simmer for another 8 to 10 minutes or until vegetables are slightly tender but still have a little bit of firmness to them. If using Thai apple eggplants, tuck them into the curry 2 minutes before it's done; this will warm them slightly but let them retain their crunchy texture. Remove from heat, taste and season with more soy sauce and lime juice if desired, and let stand for 5 minutes. Serve with hot rice.

Tofu and Potato Adobo Stew

SERVES 4

Simmering food with abundant fresh garlic and generous helpings of soy sauce and vinegar are the trademarks dishes prepared Filipino adobo style. The resulting bold and flavorful adobo sauce will instantly win over fans of things salty, tangy and garlicky! Filipino palm sap vinegar and coconut vinegar

are mellow, traditional vinegars used for adobo that can be found in Filipino grocery stores; sometimes they're even already bundled with big bottles of Filipino soy sauce for making lots of adobo stew. But if you can't find these special vinegars, regular white vinegar (and supermarket soy sauce, too) still make delicious, bracing adobo.

> ½ pound small waxy potatoes, red or yellow skin
> 1 pound extra-firm tofu, well drained
> 1 pound Asian eggplant, ends trimmed
> 8 large cloves garlic, peeled
> 4 tablespoons peanut oil or vegetable oil
> 2 teaspoons whole black peppercorns or 1 teaspoon of ground or coarsely cracked black pepper
> ⅔ cup mild soy sauce
> ½ cup Filipino palm sap or coconut vinegar, or regular distilled white vinegar
> 1 tablespoon brown sugar
> 2 bay leaves

GARNISH
> 1 cup roughly chopped cilantro
> 2 scallions, white part removed and green ends thinly sliced
> 1 large ripe red tomato, core removed and diced into ½-inch chunks
> 1 ripe banana, peeled and sliced into ½-inch pieces

1. Scrub clean the potatoes and remove any blemishes. Dice into chunks about 1½ inches wide, place in a small pot, and cover with 2 inches of cold water. Bring to a boil and simmer for 10 minutes,

TOFU AND POTATO ADOBO STEW

until potatoes are tender but not mushy and can be easily pierced with a fork. Drain and set aside.

2. Dice the tofu into 1-inch cubes. On a diagonal, slice eggplants into ½-inch slices. With the flat edge of a kitchen knife, smash garlic into rough pieces.

3. Heat 2 tablespoons of the oil in a large heavy stainless-steel pot or enameled Dutch oven over medium-high heat. Add the sliced eggplant, fry for 5 minutes, turning the eggplant occasionally to brown both sides, then transfer to a dinner plate. Pour in another 1 tablespoon of the oil and fry the tofu cubes, gently flipping occasionally until edges are golden, then transfer to the plate with the eggplant. Pour the remaining tablespoon of oil into the pot, add the garlic and peppercorns, and stir-fry for 30 seconds, then return eggplant and tofu to the pot, and also add the potatoes. Pour the soy sauce and vinegar over the vegetables, sprinkle with the brown sugar, and tuck the bay leaves into the sauce. Bring the sauce to an active simmer, gently stir the vegetables and tofu with a wooden spoon a few times, and reduce heat to low.

4. Cover and simmer the adobo for 25 to 30 minutes. Occasionally remove the lid and stir the adobo a few times. The adobo is ready when the sauce has reduced slightly and the eggplant is dark from absorbing the sauce. Remove from the heat, partially cover, and let stand for 10 minutes. To serve, ladle vegetables and sauce into a large serving bowl, sprinkle with cilantro and scallions and top with tomato and banana. Allow guests to scoop up a helping into individual bowls and eat with rice.

Adobo with Seitan: Replace the tofu with 8 to 10 ounces of purchased seitan or half a recipe of *5-Spice Seitan* (page 51). Slice into 1-inch strips and brown the same as the tofu, then proceed as directed.

spicy saucy soft tofu (ma-po tofu)

SERVES 4

Homemade ma-po tofu, also known as "grand-mother's tofu," is a revelation; my friend Cat prepared a meatless version of her dad's recipe and it blew me away, a world away from the oily restaurant goo I knew as a newly vegetarian teen. The crunchy wood ear mushrooms add an intriguing contrast to the tender, slippery tofu bathed in a garlicky red chile sauce. Ma-po can be very spicy, so if you're sensitive to hot stuff leave out the finishing touch of Sriracha sauce. On a cold day, it's pure comfort food to be savored with boiled rice or a pile of stir-fried greens for a complete meal.

When cooking with soft tofu, it inevitably will fall apart. Using a gentle hand along with a wide wooden spatula (the kind used for stir-frying and serving rice) can prevent the fragile cubes from completely disintegrating. Mori-Nu extra-firm silken tofu makes the sturdiest ma-po tofu, but it's not essential for a delicious dish.

> ½ cup dried black wood ear mushrooms (optional; shiitakes will also work—see variation below)
>
> 3 tablespoons peanut oil or canola oil
>
> 6 cloves garlic, smashed and finely chopped
>
> ⅓ cup toban djan garlic bean sauce (see note on next page)
>
> 2 pounds soft tofu, drained and diced into 1-inch cubes

⅔ cup vegetable broth or water

2 tablespoons Chinese Shaoxing cooking wine (see page 13) or dry sherry

¼ cup water

1 teaspoon cornstarch

1 to 2 tablespoons Sriracha chili sauce or any Asian red chili sauce

½ teaspoon sea salt or to taste

4 scallions, green part only, thinly sliced

1. In a small bowl, cover the wood ear mushrooms with 1 inch of hot water. Let soak for 30 minutes, drain, and squeeze to release any excess water. Slice into ¼-inch-wide ribbons.

2. Heat the oil in a wok or deep, 12-inch stainless-steel skillet over high heat; when the oil is rippling, add the garlic and stir-fry for 30 seconds. Stir in the garlic bean sauce and fry for 1 minute. Add the tofu and the vegetable broth, stir very gently with a wide wooden spatula or spoon (try not to break up the tofu too much), and simmer for 2 minutes. Stir in the Shaoxing wine and wood ear mushrooms, cover the wok, and simmer for 3 minutes.

3. In a liquid measuring cup whisk together the ¼ cup of water and the cornstarch. Remove the lid and very gently stir in half of the cornstarch mixture. Simmer the tofu for 2 minutes, then check the consistency: it should be thickened slightly but still rather loose and similar to a stew. If the ma-po is already very thick and you want it thinner, stir in 2 to 3 tablespoons of vegetable broth or water.

If you desire a thicker ma-po tofu, stir in the remaining cornstarch mixture and simmer for another 1 to 2 minutes until further thickened. But you don't have to use all of the cornstarch mixture . . . it's not your grandma's tofu, no matter what the name says.

4. Stir in the Sriracha sauce and taste, seasoning with salt or more Sriracha if desired. Stir in the scallions and carefully ladle the tofu into a large, deep serving bowl. Serve hot with boiled rice.

Ma-Po with Shiitake Mushrooms: Omit the wood ear mushrooms. Before frying the garlic, stir-fry 1 cup of thinly sliced fresh shiitake mushroom caps with 1 tablespoon of peanut oil in the wok for 2 to 3 minutes until tender. Remove from the wok, proceed as directed, and add cooked mushrooms along with the tofu.

This is classic Sichuan food, minus the meat but flavored with toban djan garlic bean sauce (or la do ban jiang or doubanjiang or tobanjan; there are so many spellings)—a pungent, chunky, fermented bean paste loaded with chilies and garlic, hot but not sweet. There are endless varieties of the stuff and most should be vegan friendly (read those labels!). I've found that different brands, in both jars and cans, have a wide range in their levels of beany, garlic, and hot chile flavor. Try a few brands and see; in the United States the Lee Kum Lee brand sold in jars is a balanced sauce; I sometimes use two or more different brands for a well-rounded dish.

kimchi tofu stew (jigae)

SERVES 3 TO 4

"Old" kimchi (kimchi that's looking too watery or limp) is a reason to celebrate when there's fast and super-healthy jigae stew to make. All the juices that drain from the kimchi as it ages create the broth for

this veggie-loaded dish, so make extra Fast Lane Cabbage Kimchi (page 56) and get psyched for jigae later that week! I love how this stew is spicy and stimulating yet refreshingly light, a welcome break after days of indulging in rich, heavy foods.

2 cups aged kimchi, well drained (reserve juices and measure; see instructions)

½ pound Asian eggplant, flower ends trimmed

Salt for sprinkling on eggplant

8 ounces firm tofu (half a water-packed package), fried tofu, or pressed firm tofu (see page 22)

1 tablespoon vegetable oil

1 tablespoon mirin (see page 16) or sherry

4 cloves garlic, peeled and minced

2¼ cups of a mixture of reserved kimchi juice and water

2 teaspoons sugar or 1 teaspoon agave nectar

1 teaspoon gochugaru (Korean red pepper powder, see page 15), or more to taste

6 scallions, green tops only, sliced into 1-inch pieces

1 teaspoon toasted sesame oil

1. Squeeze the kimchi over a large bowl to remove as much of the juices as possible; set aside the juices in a measuring cup. If necessary, add more water for a total of 2 ¼ cups of liquid for the stew. Chop kimchi into 1-inch-wide pieces. Slice the eggplant on a 45 degree angle into ½-inch-wide slices; sprinkle slices with a pinch of salt and let soften for 10 minutes. Dice the tofu into ½-inch cubes.

2. Heat the oil in a wok or deep, 12-inch-wide stainless-steel skillet over high heat, add the eggplant, and fry 2 minutes, turning occasionally until lightly browned. Sprinkle the mirin over the eggplant, cover the wok, and steam for 30 seconds. Add the chopped kimchi and garlic and fry for 2 minutes, stirring constantly. Pour on the kimchi juice/water mixture and bring to an active simmer.

3. Stir in the tofu, sugar, red pepper powder, and scallions. Bring the mixture to a simmer once more for 2 minutes, then reduce heat to medium and simmer for 10 minutes. Remove from the heat and sprinkle with sesame oil. Let stand for 10 minutes, taste, add more red pepper powder if desired, and serve with rice.

Ful Medames with Preserved Lemon

SERVES 6 TO 8

Egyptian fava beans (ful medames) are cute little brown beans with an unmistakably pronounced, earthy flavor. They're economical, filling, and make for a comforting lunch, dinner—or breakfast (Middle Eastern, Latin American, and Indian cuisines know the power of a hearty, legume-rich start to the day). Traditionally prepared ful medames can be very simple fare, sometimes just beans, maybe a drizzle of oil or topped with tomato or onion. I like to dress a bowl of these beans with a cool, garlicky chopped salad, preserved lemon, and a healthy drizzle of **Green Tahini Sauce** *(page 63). For a filling lunch or dinner, serve with any flat bread (homemade naan, fresh pita) or couscous.*

FUL MEDAMES

1 pound small dry brown fava beans (use only Egyptian ful medames beans; don't use larger, greenish-brown fava beans)

6 cups water

2 teaspoons sea salt

1 teaspoon ground coriander

1 teaspoon ground cumin

4 cloves garlic, peeled and minced

PRESERVED LEMON AND PARSLEY TOPPING

1 tablespoon finely minced preserved lemon (see *Preserved Lemons, Two Ways*, page 58)

2 cups flat-leaf parsley, roughly chopped

3 ripe tomatoes, core and seeds removed and finely diced

4 scallions, root ends trimmed and thinly sliced

2 cloves garlic, peeled and finely chopped

3 tablespoons olive oil

SERVE WITH:

Lemon wedges for squeezing

Green Tahini Sauce (page 63) or additional olive oil for drizzling

Warm wedges of pita bread

1. Sort through the beans by pouring a cup of beans at a time onto a large dinner plate; inspect and remove any debris. Place the beans in a bowl and cover with 4 inches of cold water. Set aside to soak for 8 hours or overnight; beans will double in size.

2. When beans are done soaking, drain and rinse. Transfer beans to a 4-quart pot, add water and remaining Ful Medames ingredients, and bring to a rolling boil over high heat for 5 minutes. Reduce heat to medium-low, partially cover the pot, and simmer for 2 hours or until beans are very tender. If the liquid level of the beans appears too low during cooking, pour in 1 cup of hot water and continue to simmer. Occasionally stir the beans with a wooden spoon.

3. Scoop out 1 cup of beans and mash into a puree by either transferring beans into a mixing bowl and crushing with a potato masher or by pureeing with an immersion blender using the chopper attachment. Return the puree to the pot and simmer another 5 minutes. The ful is ready to serve as is, but the flavor will deepen greatly the next day, or even setting aside to cool for 30 minutes.

4. When ready to serve, make the topping by combining the topping ingredients in a mixing bowl and tossing to thoroughly coat with the oil and lemon. Scoop a cup of beans into a serving bowl and scatter with about ¼ cup of the parsley topping. If desired squeeze a lemon wedge on the beans and drizzle with *Green Tahini Sauce*. Use wedges of pita to scoop up beans.

Eggplant Shakshuka with Green Tahini Sauce

SERVES 3 TO 4 WITH BREAD FOR SCOOPING

Shakshuka is a rustic simmered dish of saucy peppers, onions, and tomatoes begging to be scooped up with pita or crusty bread. It's a common entree in Israeli restaurants in New York City, but variations on it are found all over the Middle East. Poached eggs are commonly added, but this veganlicious dish is

delightful with morsels of browned eggplant and enriched with a drizzle of silky tahini sauce.

½ pound eggplant, cut into 1-inch cubes

3 tablespoons extra-virgin olive oil

2 cups thinly sliced yellow onions

3 cloves garlic, peeled and minced

1 to 2 small red chile peppers, minced or
    ½ teaspoon or more red pepper flakes

1 large red bell pepper, seeds and core
    removed, sliced into ¼-inch strips

1 large yellow or orange bell pepper, seeds
    and core removed, sliced into ¼-inch
    strips

½ teaspoon cumin seeds

One 14-ounce can diced tomatoes or
    2½ cups diced ripe red tomatoes (about
    1 pound)

2 teaspoons tomato paste (optional if fresh
    tomatoes are super-ripe and juicy)

1 teaspoon agave nectar

2 bay leaves

2 teaspoons dried thyme

½ teaspoon ground coriander

½ teaspoon sea salt, plus additional for
    sprinkling on eggplant

A big pinch of saffron strands or ¼ teaspoon
    ground turmeric

A few twists freshly ground pepper

1 teaspoon freshly squeezed lemon juice or
    more to taste

GARNISH

1 recipe *Green Tahini Sauce* (page 63)

1 cup roughly chopped flat-leaf parsley

1 cup roughly chopped cilantro

Warmed thick fluffy pita bread or crusty
    peasant-style bread

If the eggplant is young and very fresh—picked that morning from the garden or farmer's market—there's no need to salt and drain it. Salt and drain eggplant when you suspect it's not at its peak (most supermarket eggplant), as this will help relieve some of the bitterness in the skin and seeds.

1. Sprinkle eggplant cubes with a pinch of kosher salt and place in a metal colander over the sink or a bowl. Allow the eggplant to soften for about 10 minutes. In a large deep 12-inch skillet over medium heat toast the cumin seeds for about 1 minute or until fragrant; remove from pan and set aside. Heat 1 tablespoon of the olive oil in the skillet, add the eggplant and fry for 6 to 8 minutes, turning frequently with a spatula until cubes are soft and the edges are golden brown. Remove from pan onto a plate and set aside.

2. Add the remaining oil to the pan and fry the onions for 5 minutes until softened and golden brown. Stir in garlic and chilies, fry for 1 minute, and add the sliced peppers. Stir, cover, and let steam for 5 minutes, then add the cumin seeds, eggplant, and the remaining ingredients and stir. Cover and simmer for 10 minutes, or until all of the vegetables are very soft and the sauce from the tomatoes is bubbling; if not cook for another 5 minutes or until the tomatoes have released all of their juices. Taste and adjust any seasoning by adding more salt and lemon juice. Turn off heat, leave covered, and let rest for 2 minutes. Remove and discard bay leaves.

3. To serve, scoop a portion of the hot shakshuka into a wide, shallow bowl. Drizzle generously with *Green Tahini Sauce* and garnish with a healthy

EGGPLANT SHAKSHUKA WITH GREEN TAHINI SAUCE, PAGE 153

handful of chopped parsley and cilantro. Serve with warm pita or crusty bread to scoop up the juicy sauces.

Shakshuka takes easily to all kinds of Middle Eastern additions:

With Preserved Lemon: Add 1 tablespoon of minced preserved lemon (see **Preserved Lemons, Two Ways**, page 58), stirred in with the eggplant.

With Chickpeas: Fold in 1 cup of cooked chickpeas or other white beans along with the tomatoes.

With Spinach: Fold a handful of washed baby spinach leaves into the sauce during the last 5 minutes of cooking time.

Beer-Bathed Seitan Stew and Oven Pommes Frites

SERVES 4

This is a vegan riff on Belgian carbonnade à la flamande, a hearty sweet and sour stew simmered in dark beer and browned onions. Brown sugar, mustard, and cider vinegar punctuate the gravy along with fresh thyme and bay leaves, and a touch of carrot adds just the right note of substance that complements the seitan and mushrooms nicely.

If possible, spring for a bottle of Belgian-style dark beer from brands such as Chimay or Leffe I've kept it local with Ommegang Abbey Ale made in upstate

New York. If using American beer, look for dark brown brews with plenty of hoppy notes. Whatever your choice, don't use stout or porter beers, as the sweet molasses flavor isn't right in this dish.

And what better companion to this carbonnade-style stew than frites (the original Belgian French fries)? These lower-fat frites bake up crisp while the stew is bubbling, ready to be served on the side or smothered in the saucy stew.

Don't be put off by the steps; once the ingredients are prepped it's just a matter of stirring and sautéing, and the frites are as good as done once in the oven. Similar to a stir-fry, have all of the ingredients for this stew chopped and measured and ready to go. This carbonnade is put together in stages and you'll want to be able to add the ingredients quickly without having to stop and measure out or chop individual ingredients.

3 *Seitan Coriander Cutlets* (page 49) or two
   8-to 10-ounce packages purchased seitan
10 ounces cremini mushrooms
3 large yellow or white onions (about
   1½ pounds)
3 tablespoons canola or grapeseed oil
3 cloves garlic, peeled and finely minced
2 teaspoons brown sugar
2 tablespoons tomato paste
¼ cup all-purpose flour
2¼ cups vegetable broth or veggie
   beef-flavored broth
1 pound turnips or carrots (about 1 large
   turnip or 2 medium-size carrots),
   peeled and diced into ½-inch cubes
6 sprigs fresh thyme or 1½ teaspoons dried
   thyme
2 bay leaves

1½ cups (one 12-ounce bottle) dark (but not stout) beer

1 heaping tablespoon prepared brown or Dijon mustard, or 2 teaspoons apple cider vinegar, or both

A few twists of freshly cracked pepper

OVEN FRITES

2 pounds baking potatoes

3 tablespoons peanut or vegetable oil

1 tablespoon apple cider vinegar

1 teaspoon dried thyme

¾ teaspoon sea salt, or to taste

1. Slice the seitan into bite-size chunks no thicker than ½ inch. Clean the mushrooms, remove the stems, and dice the caps into quarters; if some of the caps are very large, dice them into six or more pieces. Peel the onions, slice in half and slice each half into the thinnest half-moons possible, no thicker than ⅛ inch.

2. In a large 3-quart stainless-steel or enamel-lined cast-iron pot (don't use an unglazed cast iron pot), heat 1 tablespoon of the oil over medium-high heat until it ripples in the pan. Add the seitan chunks and fry for 6 to 8 minutes, stirring occasionally, until the edges are starting to brown. Use a wooden spoon or spatula to scrape off any bits of seitan that stick to the bottom. Transfer the seitan to a large mixing bowl and set aside; bits of brown seitan sticking to the bottom of the pot are normal. Pour in ¼ cup of the vegetable broth and bring to a simmer, stirring the bottom of the pot to deglaze the bits of browned seitan.

3. Add another 1 tablespoon of oil to the pot, heat until rippling and add the mushrooms. Sauté for 2 minutes, then cover and cook for another 4 minutes. Uncover and transfer to the bowl with the seitan. Heat the remaining tablespoon of oil in the

pot, add the onions, and sauté for 5 minutes or until the onions begin to soften. Stir in the garlic, brown sugar, and tomato paste to coat the onions and fry for another 6 to 10 minutes, until the onions are very soft and juicy. Sprinkle and stir in the flour a tablespoon at a time. Continue to stir occasionally and fry the onions for another 2 minutes; the mixture will look thick and pasty. Pour in the vegetable broth and stir the bottom of the pot vigorously to dissolve any browned bits into the broth. Stir in the seitan, mushrooms, turnip, thyme, and bay leaves. Bring stew to an active simmer, turn the heat down to medium-low, and pour in the beer. It will rapidly foam and then settle; stir a few times and partially cover the pot. Simmer the stew for 22 to 26 minutes, or until the turnips are very tender. Stir the carbonnade occasionally, partially replacing the lid after each time. The flour will cook the broth into a silky light gravy.

4. While the stew is simmering, prepare the oven frites. Preheat the oven to 450°F and line a large baking sheet with parchment paper. Peel the potatoes or scrub very thoroughly if you'd rather leave them on (for European-style frites I like to peel the potatoes) and slice into thin french-fry shapes no thicker than ½ inch. Place in a large mixing bowl, pour on the peanut oil, and toss thoroughly to coat the potatoes with oil. Sprinkle on the vinegar, thyme, and salt and toss to coat again. Spread the frites on the parchment paper–covered baking sheet in a single layer and bake in the preheated oven for 20 minutes. Remove from the oven, turn each frite over, and bake another 10 to 15 minutes until the edges are browned and crisp. Turn the oven off and keep the frites in the oven to stay warm.

5. When the turnips are tender, turn off the heat and remove the bay leaves and thyme sprigs. Stir in the mustard or vinegar (or both), add a few twists of black pepper, and let stand for 5 minutes to cool

slightly. Serve either with hot oven frites on the side or pour the stew on top of frites piled into wide, shallow bowls. If preferred, this carbonnade can also be served with plain boiled or mashed potatoes or wide noodles tossed with a little vegan margarine.

lebanese moussaka stew

SERVES 4

This stew is based on a lovely dish served up at one of my favorite Lebanese restaurants in Queens; the talented chef Wafa whips up a classic eggplant moussaka that's very different from the layered Greek casserole of the same name. This thick, sweet and sour eggplant stew dotted with chickpeas and sweet spices is naturally vegan. Serve with **Bulgur Wheat Mujaddara with Toasted Orzo** *(page 307) and a salad for a very hearty meal or with a side of pita or couscous; it can also be served at room temperature with pita as a saucy appetizer. Instead of traditionally frying the eggplant I prefer to roast the eggplant cubes to tender, melting softness.*

ROASTED EGGPLANT

    2 pounds purple globe eggplants

    1 teaspoon sea salt

    2 tablespoons olive oil

STEW

    2 teaspoons coriander seeds

    1 teaspoon cumin seeds

    ¼ teaspoon ground cinnamon

    1 tablespoon olive oil

    4 cloves garlic, peeled and minced

    1 large yellow onion, peeled and diced

    2 pounds ripe red tomatoes, cores and seeds removed and diced, or two 14-ounce cans diced tomatoes with juices

    ½ cup water

    One 14-ounce can chickpeas (2 cups cooked), drained and rinsed

    1 tablespoon tomato paste

    4 teaspoons pomegranate molasses (see notes on pages 102 and 136)

    ½ teaspoon sea salt

    A few twists of freshly ground pepper

    ½ cup chopped flat-leaf parsley

1. Roast the eggplant first: preheat the oven to 400°F and line a large baking sheet with parchment paper. Remove the stems from the eggplant and dice into 1-inch cubes. Sprinkle the cubes with the sea salt and toss with the olive oil. Spread in a single layer on the baking sheet (use two baking sheets if necessary) and roast for 25 minutes, stirring occasionally, until the edges of the eggplant are browned and the cubes are tender. Turn off the oven, remove the eggplant and set aside.

2. In a skillet over medium heat toast the coriander and cumin seeds for 1 to 2 minutes until fragrant. Transfer the seeds to a clean coffee mill, add the ground cinnamon and grind to a fine powder.

3. In a 2-quart pot over medium heat, preheat the olive oil and stir in the garlic. Fry for 30 seconds, then add the onion and sauté for 3 to 4 minutes or until onion is softened and translucent. Stir in the ground spices, then add the tomatoes, water, chickpeas, tomato paste, pomegranate molasses, and salt. Increase heat to high and bring to a rapid simmer for 1 minute, then reduce heat to medium-low and partially cover. Simmer for 10 minutes, stirring occasionally. Stir in the eggplant and simmer, par-

tially covered, for another 15 to 20 minutes or until the stew becomes very thick but saucy; taste and add pepper and more salt, and if desired a teaspoon more of pomegranate molasses. Turn off the heat, cover, and let stand for 5 minutes. Just before serving sprinkle with parsley. Serve warm or at room temperature.

Seitan, Almond, and Sesame Tagine

SERVES 4 SERVED WITH BREAD, COUSCOUS, OR RICE

Tagines, *slow-simmered North African stews originally made in unique clay pots made just for that purpose, are also stovetop wonders that can be easily made in any large pot or deep skillet that has a tight-fitting lid. Like a lot of traditional tagines, this hearty concoction features spices, sweet dried fruits, and nuts that are sublime paired with chewy bites of seitan. Though originating from warmer climates, the radiant flavors of this tagine will likely remind most North Americans of cool fall fare.*

Many testers loved the meaty texture dates achieve after the long simmer; for more variety use a mixture of prunes and dried apricots along with the dates. I like the flavor of a mixture of vegetable broth and water, but you can use just broth if you like it saltier.

If the stew looks a little dry during the simmer, stream in ¼ to ½ cup extra water.

⅓ cup blanched, slivered almonds

¼ cup plus 1 teaspoon olive oil

1 tablespoon sesame seeds

1 pound red onions, peeled, cut in half, and sliced into ½-inch half-moons

4 cloves garlic, peeled and smashed

2 *Seitan Coriander Cutlets* (page 49), chopped or torn into ½-inch-thick, bite-size pieces, or 10 ounces purchased seitan

½ pound carrots, scraped and cut into ½-inch pieces

½ pound root vegetables such as turnip, parsnip, or potato, peeled and cut into ½-inch chunks

One 3-inch cinnamon stick

1 teaspoon ground coriander

½ teaspoon ground turmeric

½ teaspoon ground black pepper

½ teaspoon ground cumin

¼ teaspoon cayenne pepper

1 teaspoon agave nectar

½ teaspoon sea salt

1 overflowing cup pitted mejool dates or a combination of prunes, apricots, and dates

3 cups water, vegetable broth, or a mixture of the two

1 tablespoon finely chopped preserved lemon (see *Preserved Lemons, Two Ways*, page 58) or ½ teaspoon grated fresh lemon zest

1. In a small saucepan over medium heat, toast the almonds in 1 teaspoon of the olive oil. When the almonds turn a light tan color, stir in the sesame seeds and toast for another 30 seconds. Scrape the seeds and nuts onto a plate and set aside. In a large Dutch oven over medium heat (or a clay tagine if you have one!) add the remaining olive oil and onions

and cook until soft and juicy, about 8 minutes. Stir in the garlic and seitan and fry, stirring occasionally, another 5 minutes until edges of the seitan are browned and sizzling.

2. Add carrots, turnip, cinnamon stick, coriander, turmeric, black pepper, cumin, cayenne, agave, sea salt, dates, and water and/or vegetable broth. Turn up heat and bring mixture to a bubbling simmer, then reduce heat to bring mixture to a gentle simmer. Cover and cook for 20 minutes, then stir a few times and partially cover. Simmer for another 25 to 30 minutes, stirring occasionally, until the liquid has reduced by about a third and thickened slightly. Taste the mixture and season with salt if necessary, then stir in preserved lemon and simmer for another 2 minutes.

3. Turn off heat and sprinkle with the almonds and sesame seeds. Cover again and let the mixture stand for 10 minutes. Serve by presenting the whole dish to guests and letting them spoon their own portions into bowls alongside couscous or any flat, grilled bread.

Okra Tomato Tagine: omit dried fruit, add ½ pound trimmed small okra pods plus 2 cups roughly diced tomatoes along with the carrots. For best results prepare this tagine in either a stainless-steel or clay vessel; don't use a cast-iron pot as it could produce off flavors in reaction to the tomato.

Deluxe Tofu Vegetable Mafe

SERVES 4 TO 6

Mafe, a soothing peanut stew, is a popular dish all over West Africa. Many versions feature chicken and large hunks of cabbage, but this mafe is an assortment of bite-size marinated tofu and vegetables, simmered to tender perfection in a peanut butter–laced sauce that's a little zestier with a touch of **Olive Oil Harissa Paste** (page 43) and pumped-up spices. As is, or with the additional vegetables, this deluxe veggie mafe pulls out all the stops. Serve with rice or couscous and your favorite hot sauce or **Roasted Chile Pepper Harissa Paste** (page 42). The flavor of the mafe will improve as it sits and will be even better the next day.

*Press and fry the tofu a day in advance, or use **Savory Baked Tofu** (page 50) in place of preparing the tofu. Or replace tofu with two to three cutlets of **Seitan Coriander Cutlets** (page 49), sliced into ½-inch-wide strips.*

MARINATED TOFU

    1 pound extra-firm tofu

    ¼ cup soy sauce

    2 tablespoons lemon juice

    ½ teaspoon cayenne pepper or *Olive Oil Harissa Paste* (page 43)

MAFE STEW

1 pound Asian eggplant

½ pound green cabbage (about half of one
    small, 5-inch cabbage)

3 tablespoons peanut oil

4 cloves garlic, peeled and minced

2-inch piece peeled ginger, minced

1 large yellow onion, peeled and diced into
    ½-inch pieces

1 large red bell pepper, core and seeds
    removed, diced into ½-inch pieces

2 to 4 hot red chile peppers

2 teaspoons ground coriander

1 teaspoon ground cumin

1 teaspoon finely ground black pepper

1 cup diced tomatoes or chopped fresh plum
    tomatoes

3 cups vegetable broth

⅓ generous cup natural smooth salted
    peanut butter

¼ cup tomato paste

½ teaspoon sea salt

1 tablespoon red wine vinegar

Salt and freshly ground pepper to taste

3 tablespoons chopped roasted peanuts,
    for garnish

1. Slice tofu in eight equal pieces horizontally and press for 20 minutes (see DIY Tofu Pressing, page 22, for tips). After pressing, slice each tofu piece on a diagonal so that you now have sixteen triangles. In a shallow dish combine remaining marinade ingredients. Place the tofu in the marinade and flip several times to coat each piece in marinade. Set aside while preparing the vegetables for the stew.

2. On a diagonal, slice the eggplant into ½-inch pieces and sprinkle lightly with salt (if the eggplant is fresh from the garden or farmers' market, don't bother with this step). Remove any wilted outer leaves and the thick white core from the bottom of the cabbage and slice it into 2-inch-long chunks.

3. In heavy and wide 3-quart enameled Dutch oven or steel pot, heat 1 tablespoon of the oil over medium heat. Add the tofu and fry until lightly browned on both sides, about 2 to 3 minutes, then transfer to a dish. Add another tablespoon of oil and brown the eggplant like the tofu; remove from the pot and set aside. Add the remaining oil and the garlic, ginger, onion, bell pepper, and chile peppers and fry, stirring occasionally, until very soft and golden, about 6 minutes. Sprinkle with coriander, cumin, and black pepper and fry for 1 minute, stirring the paste into the vegetables.

4. Pour in diced tomatoes and vegetable broth and bring mixture to a simmer. Return the tofu and eggplant to the pot and add the cabbage. Turn heat down to medium low, partially cover, and simmer for 10 minutes. Scoop out 1 cup of hot broth from the pot, pour into a mixing bowl, and add the peanut butter and tomato paste; use a fork to slowly stir together until smooth. Use a rubber spatula to scrape peanut butter mixture into the pot along with the sea salt. Stir well, partially cover, and simmer for another 25 to 30 minutes or until the cabbage and eggplant are very tender. Stir in the vinegar, taste, and add salt and ground pepper as desired. Cool for 5 minutes before serving.

5. To serve, use a slotted spoon to scoop up a serving of vegetables and tofu and arrange on top of cooked hot couscous or rice. Then use a ladle or a spoon to scoop up the sauce and drizzle on top of the vegetables, sprinkle with peanuts, and eat!

For a more vegetable-filled mafe, add one of the following vegetables along with the cabbage. Or omit the tofu and seitan all together and use 2 or more of these for an all-vegetable mafe.

With Okra: Add ¼ pound of small okra pods sliced in half or kept whole.

With Winter Squash: Add ½ pound of winter squash, peeled and diced into ½-inch chunks.

With Sweet Potato: Add 1 large sweet potato, peeled and diced into ½-inch chunks.

With Carrot: Add 1 large carrot, peeled and diced into ½-inch chunks.

With White Potato: Add 1 large white potato, peeled and diced into ½-inch chunks.

Pumpkin Black Bean Posole Stew

SERVES 4 TO 6

I do love easy-to-make veggie posoles: this Mexican-style soup with soft hominy corn topped with fresh veggies is effortlessly healthy with a combination of fresh produce and pantry staples. The best part is the combination of warmly spiced, brothy soup below and cool, crunchy toppings on top, such as fried tortilla chips, avocado, tomatoes, crisp cabbage, or toasted pumpkin seeds.

1 large yellow onion, peeled and diced into ½-inch pieces

2 tablespoons olive oil

6 garlic cloves, peeled and minced

6 cups vegetable broth

1½ pounds pumpkin or winter squash, peeled and seeds removed, diced into 1-inch cubes

One 16-ounce can hominy, drained and rinsed

Two 14-ounce cans black beans, drained and rinsed (or 4 cups cooked beans)

4 teaspoons chile powder, either a blend or a single Mexican chile such as ancho

2 teaspoons dried oregano

1 teaspoon ground cumin

¼ teaspoon ground cinnamon

2 bay leaves

2 tablespoons lime juice

TOPPINGS

2 large tomatoes, diced

1 ripe avocado, diced

1 small red onion, peeled and finely diced

1 jalapeño, sliced into paper-thin rounds

2 cups thinly shredded cabbage

Long strips of fried corn tortillas or chips (blue corn looks especially snappy)

1 cup roughly chopped cilantro

⅓ cup toasted pumpkin seeds

Wedges of lime for squeezing into the soup

1. In a large soup pot over medium heat fry the onion in the olive oil until soft and translucent, about 4 minutes. Stir in the garlic and fry for another 45 seconds, then add the vegetable broth, diced pumpkin, hominy, black beans, chile powder, oregano, cumin, cinnamon, and bay leaves. Increase the heat and bring the soup to a boil, stir, then reduce the heat to a low simmer and partially cover. Cook for 20 to 25 minutes until the pumpkin is tender but not completely falling apart. Turn off the heat, keep

PUMPKIN BLACK BEAN POSOLE STEW

covered, and let stand while you prepare the toppings. Remove the bay leaves before serving.

2. Before serving, stir in the lime juice and taste the soup, adding more salt if necessary. To serve, ladle the soup into deep bowls and garnish generously with the toppings, ending with the toasted pumpkin seeds. Serve with lime wedges for posole fans to squeeze into their soup!

Mexican Homemade Beans

SERVES 6 TO 8

Preparing authentic Mexican beans is incredibly simple: simmered with an onion, maybe garlic or a few spices, they are a joy to eat. This preparation of pinto or black beans is slightly elaborated with fragrant Mexican oregano and epazote, the Mexican herb famous for making beans more digestion-friendly and for adding an intriguing, earthy flavor.

*To help soften up the beans, this recipe uses an untraditional but effective technique of lightly brining the beans in salted water during the soaking process. The resulting beans are buttery, delicate, and have a silky cooking broth. Serve the beans in their freshly cooked broth or mash and refry them the next day for luscious **Mexican Homemade Refried Beans** (page 165).*

*Serve either style of bean with **Mexican Red Rice** (page 315), **Mexican Dried Chile Salsa** (page 70), and warm tortillas.*

1 pound pinto beans or black beans

3 tablespoons kosher salt

3 quarts (12 cups) cold water

BEAN SIMMER

1 large yellow onion, peeled and sliced in half

4 cloves garlic, peeled and gently crushed with the flat side of a chef's knife, but kept whole

1½ teaspoons dried Mexican oregano (regular oregano's okay if you can't find Mexican)

1 teaspoon dried epazote

1 teaspoon sea salt

8 cups water

Olive oil for drizzling (optional)

1. In large pot stir together beans, kosher salt, and water until the salt is dissolved. Set aside the beans for 8 hours or overnight to soak. When you're ready to cook the beans, drain and rinse with plenty of cold water.

2. Return the beans to the large pot and add the onion, garlic, oregano, epazote, sea salt, and water. Bring to a rolling boil over high heat for 5 minutes, then turn down the heat to medium-low. Partially cover and simmer the beans for 65 to 75 minutes or until very tender (they should crush easily when pressed into the top of your mouth with your tongue and never feel grainy), stirring occasionally.

3. When the beans are tender, remove the onion and garlic; either discard them, or reserve for refried beans. Serve warm beans with a little of their broth, drizzle with a little bit of olive oil if desired, and serve with rice and any Mexican entree.

Mexican Homemade Refried Beans

MAKES ABOUT 3½ CUPS

*There's just no comparing homemade refried beans to the unseemly stuff from a can: made with home-made cooked beans they're sublime and ridiculously budget-friendly. Honest and comforting, you'll find dozens of ways to sneak them into meals, in a sandwich like cemitas (see **Chipotle Tofu Cemita Sandwiches**, page 107), or simply scooped up with tortillas. Homemade bean broth is the secret to smooth, creamy, and flavorful beans, all the more reason to start the process from scratch.*

    1 tablespoon olive oil
    1 small yellow or white onion, peeled and
        finely diced
    1 to 3 serrano chilies or jalapeños, stems
        removed and finely minced
    3 cups *Mexican Homemade Beans*
    1 or more cups of bean broth
    ½ teaspoon ground cumin

1. In a 10-to 12-inch cast-iron skillet, heat the olive oil over medium heat. Stir in the onion and chilies (and if you reserved the onion from cooking the beans, mince it and add it here, too), fry until soft and golden, about 3 to 4 minutes. Stir in the beans, 1 cup of broth, and cumin.

2. Simmer the beans, stirring occasionally, for 3 minutes. Now while the beans continue to simmer, use a potato masher or a large wooden spoon to mash up the beans until a chunky consistency is reached. Alternatively you could also simmer the beans in a larger pot and use an immersion blender to whip the beans into a smoother, creamier paste; this is especially appropriate for black beans (pintos are best enjoyed with a little extra texture).

3. If the refried beans look a little dry during the mashing and simmering, drizzle in bean broth to keep it creamy and moist; if you're out of broth, use warm vegetable broth or water. Serve refried beans hot and store leftovers in a tightly covered container in the refrigerator. Reheat on the stovetop and use a little bean broth or water to moisten.

Saucy Berbere Lentils (Yemiser W'et)

SERVES 4 TO 6 WITH INJERA AND OTHER STEWS

*Yemiser w'et is that spicy-sweet, brick-red lentil stew that's ubiquitous to any big Ethiopian mesob (family-style spread). Lentils are easy to cook from scratch, but if you're preparing a bunch of w'et stews, why not cut yourself some slack and seek out a can of precooked organic black lentils? For best results use firm-cooking lentils such as brown or black, or use red lentils and puree for another classic variation on this w'et. Serve with another Ethiopian stew such as **Seitan Tibs Simmered in Berbere and Wine** (page 168) and **Ethiopian Savory Crepes** (page 206).*

For a faster stew, use one 14-ounce can of cooked lentils (looks for high-quality organic lentils). That's about 2 cups cooked lentils with ¼ cup of reserved cooking liquid, just in case you need to know these things.

LENTILS

1 cup dry brown or black lentils

3 cups water

1 teaspoon salt

BERBERE SAUCE

1 large red onion, peeled and finely diced

4 cloves garlic, peeled and minced

2 tablespoons *Spiced Buttery Oil* (page 44)

5 teaspoons *Berbere Spice Blend* (page 44)

2 teaspoons sweet ground paprika

½ teaspoon ground cumin

2 tablespoons tomato paste

¼ cup lentil cooking liquid or vegetable broth

3 plum tomatoes, cores removed and finely diced, or 1 cup diced canned tomatoes

Additional salt to taste

1. In a 2-quart saucepan bring lentils, water, and salt to a rolling boil. Reduce heat to low, partially cover, and cook for 25 to 30 minutes or until lentils are tender but not overly mushy. Turn off heat and set aside about ½ cup of the cooking liquid. Drain the lentils and transfer to a bowl.

2. Clean the saucepan, and over medium heat fry the onion, garlic and *Spiced Buttery Oil* together until the onion is softened and translucent, about 6 to 8 minutes. Stir in the *Berbere Spice Blend*, paprika, cumin, and tomato paste and fry, stirring occasionally, for 2 minutes. Stir in the lentil cooking liquid and simmer for 2 minutes, then stir in the lentils and tomatoes. Reduce heat to low, cover, and simmer for 20 minutes, stirring occasionally. If a thicker stew is desired simmer uncovered for another 5 to 10 minutes. If desired, season with salt, then turn off heat and cover. Let stew stand for 20 minutes before serving warm with *Ethiopian Savory Crepes* (page 206).

Red Lentil W'et: Substitute 1 cup of dried red lentils for the brown lentils, but don't precook the lentils. Once the tomato paste and spices are frying, pour in 2¼ cups of water, 1 cup of red lentils, and the tomatoes. Bring to a boil, stir and reduce heat. Cover and cook for 30 to 35 minutes or longer until the lentils have broken down and become mushy. If necessary add a little extra water during the cooking; don't add enough to make a soup. Instead the lentils should resemble a thick mash. If desired, puree the mixture with an immersion blender for a creamier w'et.

FROM TOP TO BOTTOM: CAULIFLOWER AND GREEN BEANS IN BERBERE SPICES, PAGE 288, SAUCY BERBERE LENTILS (YEMISER W'ET), PAGE 165, FLUFFY SCRAMBLED CHICKPEA "EGGS" WITH SHALLOTS (BUT'ECHA), PAGE 269, SERVED WITH ESSENTIAL, (ALMOST) INSTANT ETHIOPIAN SAVORY CREPES (INJERA STYLE), PAGE 206.

seitan tibs simmered in Berbere and wine (seitan tibs w'et)

SERVES 4

Tender little morsels of seitan simmered in roasted spices, red wine, and tomato paste is my take on the classic Ethiopian Doro W'et stew. Seitan stands in for tibs, typically meat that's bite-size, saucy, and generously seasoned. This toothsome stew is best served along with a vegetable w'et stew, collards being my favorite green to complement the dense tomato gravy. If you crave extra-hot tibs, stir in a few additional teaspoons of cayenne or a finely minced hot chile or two.

4 tablespoons *Spiced Buttery Oil* (page 44)

6 garlic cloves, minced

2 medium red onions, peeled and finely diced

1 tablespoon finely minced ginger

2 tablespoons tomato paste

2 tablespoons *Berbere Spice Blend* (page 44)

3 cutlets of *Seitan Coriander Cutlets* (page 49), or two 8-ounce packages prepared seitan, diced into ½-inch-thick, bite-size pieces

1 cup dry red wine

1 cup vegetable broth

3 ripe red tomatoes, cores removed and diced into ½-inch pieces, or 1 cup diced canned tomatoes with juices

½ teaspoon salt or to taste

1. In a deep, 12-inch stainless-steel skillet (don't use cast iron) or 3-quart pot, heat 2 tablespoons of the *Spiced Buttery Oil* over medium heat. Stir in the garlic, onions, and ginger and cook until very soft and juicy, about 6 to 8 minutes. Add the tomato paste and berbere spice and cook for another 2 minutes, stirring occasionally. Add the remaining *Spiced Buttery Oil* and seitan, stirring to coat the chunks with the seasonings. Fry the seitan for 3 minutes, stirring constantly.

2. Pour in the red wine and stir vigorously to release and dissolve any browned bits from the bottom of the pan. When the wine has reduced by about half, pour in the vegetable broth and tomatoes. Increase the heat to medium-high and bring to an active simmer for 2 minutes. Turn the heat down to medium, partially cover, and cook for 20 minutes, stirring occasionally. The deep red sauce should thicken and coat the seitan pieces; continue to cook uncovered if the sauce looks a little thin. If the stew looks too dry, stir in a little additional wine or vegetable broth. When the sauce is done, season with salt.

3. Turn off the heat, keep covered, and let stand for 10 minutes. Serve the stew warm with plenty of *Ethiopian Savory Crepes* (page 206).

CHAPTER 7

Dumplings, Breads & Pancakes

If there's something the whole world can agree on, it's that dumplings, breads, and especially pancakes are the greatest food invention. Period. Savory pancakes—from French socca to Korean kimchi jeon to tender mucver, Turkish-style zucchini pancakes—equal dinner across the planet.

If possible, I would dedicate my life to making, writing about, and eating dumplings. This chapter may be that attempt: pierogi, momos, gyoza, mandu, potstickers, spring rolls . . . I can't decide, other than they make my world go 'round. Do they make yours? You'll just have to roll up your sleeves, make some, and find out yourself.

It's true that dumplings require more effort and attention than, say, a salad or a sandwich, but there's no substitute for these plump pouches of pure comfort. Ready-made gyoza or wonton skins are helpful shortcuts for Asian dumplings, and if you love Polish pierogi like so many of us do, you must bust out the rolling pin for a batch of smooth, supple dough. More time spent with dumplings equals more happiness, and who couldn't use an extra serving of that?

Basic Dumpling Dough

MAKES ENOUGH FOR 1 RECIPE

A basic dough for soft, opaque dumplings of any nationality. Use vegetable oil when preparing Asian dumplings and margarine when making pierogi, or any Western-style dumpling.

When working with any dough, the brand of flour will influence how much water you need to add to achieve a smooth, not too sticky and not too dry dough. Depending on the level of humidity and even where the flour is sourced from you'll need to pay attention to how your dough develops. It's not rocket science; if your dough seems too sticky, sprinkle in more flour. If it's too dry, add a little water. Always have at least 1 cup of extra flour on hand for adjusting the consistency of your dough now and later for rolling it out.

> 3 cups all-purpose flour, plus at least ½ cup
>   more for rolling
> 1 teaspoon salt
> 2 tablespoons vegetable oil or melted
>   nonhydrogenated vegan margarine
> 1¼ cups warm water

1. In a mixing bowl stir together flour and salt. Form a well in the center and pour in vegetable oil or margarine and 1 cup water. Using your fingers or a wooden spoon stir together to moisten the flour. Keep stirring to form a soft dough, adding a little more water a tablespoon at a time if the dough feels too dry. When the dough starts to pull away from the sides of the bowl, use your fingers to knead and gather up the dough into a soft ball.

2. Generously flour a work surface, place the dough on the work surface, and knead for about 3 minutes until the dough is smooth and elastic and no longer excessively sticks to your fingers (sprinkle on a little extra flour if the dough starts to stick). Form the dough into a ball, tightly wrap it in plastic wrap, and let it rest for an hour before using; or store in the refrigerator overnight. Warm chilled dough on a kitchen countertop for 20 minutes prior to using.

Garlic Chive Seitan Potstickers

MAKES 30 LARGE POTSTICKERS OR ABOUT 50 GYOZA

I make these plump, Chinese-inspired potstickers when I crave a more toothsome (I'll even say meaty) dumpling and need my fill of sweet, pungent garlic chives, an inexpensive and plentiful vegetable in most Asian markets. The filling should be pungent but not overly salty, as the dumplings are served with a sesame soy sauce. Make the filling a day in advance and shortcut the prep with gyoza wrappers for piles of dumplings to seriously satisfy takeout cravings. For more potstickers later on, make double the batch and freeze half of the uncooked potstickers as directed for pierogi (page 175), don't thaw, and steam for an additional 5 to 10 minutes, making sure to dribble in another few tablespoons of water as needed.

SEITAN POTSTICKERS

1 recipe *Basic Dumpling Dough* (page 171)
or 50 gyoza wrappers (see page 15, extra
wrappers are good idea, too)

2 cutlets *5-Spice Seitan* (page 51) or about
10 ounces of store-bought seitan

1 ounce dried shiitake mushrooms

½ pound chopped Napa or savoy cabbage
leaves (about 2½ cups loosely packed
and thinly sliced)

¼ pound garlic chives or 4 scallions,
roughly chopped

2½-inch piece peeled ginger

4 cloves garlic, minced

1 teaspoon *Sichuan 5-Spice Powder* (page 41)
or store-bought Chinese 5-spice powder

2 tablespoons soy sauce

2 tablespoons cornstarch

1¼ teaspoons toasted sesame oil

2 tablespoons canola or vegetable oil for
frying

SESAME SOY DIPPING SAUCE

3 tablespoons soy sauce

1 tablespoon Chinese black vinegar (see
page 12) or rice vinegar

2 teaspoons sugar

¼ teaspoon toasted sesame oil

1 scallion, green part only, chopped very fine

Sriracha, chili garlic sauce, or Asian chili oil
if desired

1. Prepare *Basic Dumpling Dough*, keep it tightly
covered, and allow it to rest about an hour or
overnight before using; if refrigerated, warm on a
kitchen counter for 20 minutes before shaping. Roll
out and shape dumpling wrappers as directed for
Kimchi and Tofu Manju Dumplings (page 181), except
divide the dough into thirty pieces to make wrappers. Keep them covered in plastic wrap until ready
to make potstickers. If using frozen gyoza wrappers,
thaw them overnight in the refrigerator.

2. Roughly chop seitan into large chunks. Pour
enough boiling water over shiitakes to cover and
soak until tender, about 10 minutes. Drain and rinse
to remove any grit, gather mushrooms, and squeeze
to remove as much liquid as possible. Place in a food
processor along with the seitan and pulse until the
seitan is finely ground, then transfer the mixture to
a mixing bowl. In the food processor pulse together
the cabbage, garlic chives, ginger, and garlic and
pulse a few times until roughly chopped, then add to
the seitan. Add the remaining ingredients except for
the canola oil and use you hands to knead the mixture into a moist dough. Scoop back into the mixing
bowl, knead a few times and cover with plastic wrap.
Chill for 30 minutes or overnight.

3. Assemble as for *Kimchi and Tofu Manju Dumplings* (page 181), or if using gyoza wrappers, as on
page 182, placing finished dumplings on a lightly
floured surface and keeping them covered with a
kitchen towel while you work. When you're ready to
cook a big batch, preheat a deep, 12-inch stainless-
steel skillet over medium heat. Add the canola oil
and tilt the pan to completely slick the surface with
oil. Arrange the dumplings in the pan in a spiral,
working from the outside toward the center of the
pan. They can be touching but should not be too
snug. If there's not enough room, make about half
and do a second batch. Drizzle a little extra oil over
the dumplings and leave them uncovered to fry 3
minutes, then carefully pour ½ cup of water into the
pan around the dumplings. Reduce heat to low, cover
the pan and steam for 8 to 10 minutes. The potstickers are done when the water has been absorbed and
the wrappers are fully cooked and browned on the

bottom. Uncover and use a spatula to carefully lift the potstickers out of the pan, taking care not to tear them; letting them cool for a few minutes can make this a little easier.

4. In small bowl whisk together the dipping sauce ingredients, except for the Sriracha, and pour into tiny serving dishes. Serve potstickers pipping hot and pass around the dipping sauce and Sriracha!

Potato Pierogi with Fried Onions

MAKES 3 DOZEN

These tender pasta pouches stuffed with potato have travelled beyond their Polish roots into the hearts and plates of Americans everywhere. Living in NYC, I devoured a new world of pierogi stuffed with a rainbow of fillings: spinach, sauerkraut, mushrooms, sweet potato, pumpkin, even sweet prune. But as a kid, the piles and piles my aunt would craft for holiday feasts were stuffed with humble potato—basic, yes, but still the best. This recipe looks lengthy but the ingredients can be found in any grocery store, and it's simple to double or triple the batch for extra pieogi to freeze (and nobody ever complained about extra pierogi).

Note that the wheat dough needs to rest for at least an hour to let the gluten relax and to allow for smooth, supple rolling for thinner, lighter wrappers. My aunt, a master pierogi chef, likes to use a pasta rolling machine to produce perfectly smooth,

uniform dough in mass quantities for every pierogi-making event. Another family tip: your pierogi don't have to be round. Cutting squares from the rolled dough results in no trimmings for less waste. This recipe features traditional round pierogi, but if you desire square pierogi, slice squares about 3 to 4 inches wide, fill, and fold over the dough.

1 recipe **Basic Dumpling Dough** (page 171)

FRIED ONIONS

> 1 pound yellow onion, diced
>
> 3 tablespoons nonhydrogenated vegan margarine
>
> ½ teaspoon salt

POTATO FILLING

> 2 pounds yellow potato such as Yukon Gold, peeled and diced into 1-inch cubes
>
> 1¼ teaspoons salt
>
> 1½ teaspoons dried dill or 2 tablespoons fresh, finely chopped dill
>
> ¼ teaspoon ground black pepper
>
> A big pinch of ground nutmeg
>
> 3 tablespoons nutritional yeast

FOR COOKING PIEROGI

> 4 quarts (16 cups) water
>
> 2 tablespoons kosher salt
>
> 2 tablespoons vegetable oil

1. Per the basic dough instructions above, make the dough at least an hour before assembling the pierogi. Wrap the dough in plastic wrap and let it sit on the kitchen counter for an hour before rolling. Chill overnight and warm to room temperature before proceeding.

2. Meanwhile prepare the fried onions and the filling. Melt the margarine over medium heat in a cast-iron skillet and fry the onions, stirring occasionally, for 12 to 14 minutes until deep golden brown and juicy. Sprinkle with salt. Remove from heat, pour into a serving dish, and cover with plastic wrap. Boil the potatoes in 2 quarts of cold water over high heat for 20 minutes or until very tender; reserve ¼ cup of the cooking liquid, drain away the rest, and cool for 5 minutes. Using a potato masher, mash the potatoes with 2 tablespoons of cooking water and the remaining filling ingredients until creamy; taste and add more salt and pepper if desired. If the mixture seems dry add the remaining cooking liquid.

For a fluffy, creamy potato filling use a potato ricer. It's an old-fashioned kitchen gadget (but still a common find in kitchen supply stores) for pressing cooked potato through a fine sieve. The resulting tender strands of potato easily whip up into the smoothest mashed potatoes.

3. When you're ready to assemble and cook the pierogi, fill the largest pot you have with 4 quarts of water, 2 tablespoons of kosher salt, and 2 tablespoons vegetable oil and bring it to boil over high heat. Meanwhile, divide the dough into four pieces. Keep the other pieces covered with plastic wrap, and roll out the uncovered dough on a lightly floured surface into a thin circle about 10 to 12 inches wide. Use a 3-inch wide round cookie cutter to cut out circles; remove the dough scraps and cover with plastic wrap. You may reroll the dough scraps one more

Pierogi dumplings from start to finish with two fillings: Potato Onion, page 173, and Sauerkraut Mushroom, page 176

time by allowing them to rest at least 15 minutes; this allows the gluten to relax for easier dough rolling.

Stir ¼ cup of the fried onions into the potato filling for extra sweet onion zing.

4. To form a pierogi take a dough circle and scoop a level 1 tablespoon of filling into the center. Gently stretch and pull the dough over the filling to form a half-circle and firmly pinch the edges together. Very gently press down the center of the pierogi a few times to help shape a neat half-circle.

Pierogi Primer

⊛ Cooked pierogi can also be pan-fried in a little bit of margarine or oil over medium heat; fry for 4 minutes until the filling is hot and the outside is crisp in spots and golden.

⊛ If you're serving a big portion of pierogi at a potluck, an easy way to do so is to layer the boiled dumplings in a casserole dish and drizzle a little melted margarine between each layer. Or you can also toss the pierogi with the onion mixture before packing into the casserole dish. Cover the casserole with foil and keep warm in the oven until ready to serve.

⊛ Freezing pierogi (and dumplings and spring rolls) is a great reason to make an extra batch or two. Lay a single layer of pierogi on a cookie sheet covered with parchment paper and freeze solid, then pack in tightly sealed zip-top bags. When you're ready to cook them, don't defrost; stir frozen pierogi into boiling salted water and cook until tender and the filling is hot.

Take care to pinch the edges together tightly to seal or the pierogi may fall apart during the boil. Continue to shape more pierogi, laying them on a lightly floured surface; avoid overlapping them or they may stick together. Carefully drop pierogi into the boiling water, no more than six at a time, and cook for 3 to 4 minutes. Lightly oil a casserole dish. Cooked pierogi will float to the top; if they stick to the bottom carefully nudge them free with a spoon. Use a slotted spoon to lift pierogi into the casserole dish; cover to keep pierogi warm as you cook the rest.

5. Serve warm pierogi topped with fried onions and a side of applesauce, *Sour Dilly Cream* (page 71), or vegan sour cream. While not traditional, I love to serve them with a tiny dish of prepared horseradish (easily found in Western European grocery stores).

With Celeriac: I love the sweet flavor and bouncy texture celeriac lends to mashed potato. Replace ½ pound of potato with peeled, diced celeriac and boil with the diced potato.

With Spinach and Dill: Spinach and potato double team in this irresistible pierogi filling. Steam 4 cups spinach leaves for 4 minutes and set aside to cool, then firmly squeeze to remove as much water as possible. Finely chop the spinach and stir into the potato filling along with ½ cup finely chopped fresh dill.

With Roasted Garlic and Horseradish: Sneak in 3 tablespoons mashed roasted garlic and 1 tablespoon prepared white horseradish into the potato filling for zesty, piquant potato pierogi.

Sauerkraut Mushroom Pierogi: Another fantastic savory filling! For best flavor avoid canned sauerkraut and use the fresher, refrigerated kraut sold in jars or plastic bags. For a true pierogi feast, double

the dough and make a batch of this filling along with the potato filling.

> 2 cups drained sauerkraut
> 8 ounces white mushrooms, wiped clean and finely diced
> 1 tablespoon vegetable oil
> 1 small yellow onion, finely diced
> 2 cloves garlic
> ¾ teaspoon ground black pepper

Squeeze the sauerkraut and remove any excess moisture. Sauté the mushrooms in the oil along with the onions over medium-high heat until browned and reduced in bulk, about 10 minutes. Stir in the garlic and cook for 1 minute, then fold in the sauerkraut and pepper. Turn off the heat and let the mixture cool to room temperature before filling pierogi.

watercress coconut lumpia spring rolls

MAKES 18 SPRING ROLLS

If there's a homemade spring roll to attempt, it's Filipino lumpia. Lumpia are chock-full of flavor and texture beyond the standard spring roll, from ingredients such as potato, watercress, and coconut, plus the outside skins are crispy and delectable baked (but they can be fried, too). The zesty vinegar soy garlic dipping sauce just makes lumpia more irresistable. Lumpia can be frozen before baking and baked

up in some distant future in need of lumpia (and it does). And of course, you can pan fry lumpia, too.

Look for egg-free spring roll wrappers in the freezer section of Asian markets. The Spring Home TYJ Spring Roll Pastry brand is a vegan-friendly brand imported from Singapore that's plentiful in Filipino and Asian markets here in NYC. Experiment with various wrapper sizes for meal-and appetizer-size lumpia!

LUMPIA

⅓ cup dried grated coconut

3 tablespoons vegetable oil

1 large carrot, peeled and grated

2 cups shredded Napa or other green cabbage

3 cups coarsely chopped watercress

1 large yellow onion, peeled and diced

6 cloves garlic, peeled and minced

½ pound potatoes, peeled and grated

1 teaspoon salt

½ teaspoon freshly ground black pepper

2 teaspoons light-colored vinegar such as coconut, sugar cane, or distilled

18 (plus a few extra) 5-to 6-inch square vegan spring roll pastry wrappers

Cooking oil spray

LUMPIA DIPPING SAUCE

¼ cup soy sauce (not tamari)

1 tablespoon white vinegar or coconut or palm sap vinegar

1 tablespoon agave nectar

1 clove garlic, grated or pressed

¼ teaspoon ground black pepper

1. Preheat oven to 425°F and line a baking sheet with parchment paper. In a dry wok over medium heat toast the coconut until golden, about 3 minutes, then transfer to a large mixing bowl. Heat half of the oil in the wok and sauté the carrot and cabbage until wilted and softened, about 4 minutes; add the watercress and sauté another 2 minutes, then move everything into the bowl with the coconut. Add the remaining oil and sauté onion and garlic until translucent, about 4 to 5 minutes, then add potato and sauté another 3 minutes. Turn off heat and transfer the onion mixture to the mixing bowl, add salt, pepper and vinegar, and mix thoroughly. Taste the mixture and season with more salt and pepper if needed.

2. To assemble a lumpia, place a spring roll wrapper on a clean work surface. Scoop ¼ cup of filling, then spread it over the bottom third of the spring roll wrapper, leaving 1 inch clear around the edges. Fold the left and right edges of the wrapper over the filling. Now fold the bottom edge over the filling. Continue to roll the lumpia to meet the top edge of the wrapper. Wet the tips of your finger in water and seal the edge; it should look like a tiny burrito. Place seam side down onto a baking sheet and repeat with remaining filling and wrappers (see illustration).

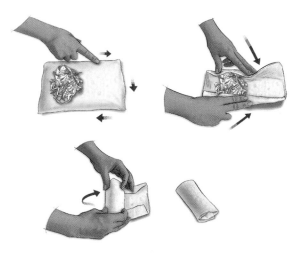

3. Generously spray lumpia with cooking oil spray and bake for 20 minutes. Remove from the oven, flip each lumpia over, spray with oil, and bake another 8 to 10 minutes until the wrappers are crisp and golden. While the lumpia bake prepare the dipping sauce by combining all the ingredients and pouring into serving dish. Serve hot lumpia rolls immediately with dipping sauce.

4. To pan-fry lumpia, heat a tablespoon of oil in a deep 12-inch skillet over medium-high heat. Place 3 to 4 rolls seam side down into the pan and cook for 2 minutes before turning the rolls occasionally to brown all sides. Add more oil when needed to prevent sticking. If desired lay hot lumpia on paper towels to drain a little before serving.

5. To freeze lumpia, lay unbaked in a single layer on a baking sheet and freeze solid before storing in zip-top plastic bags. Don't thaw, just bake directly in a 425°F preheated oven on parchment-lined baking sheets as directed.

creamy and crunchy Edamame gyoza

MAKES ABOUT 34 GYOZA

Gyoza are the new wontons of our time. Veggie gyoza are standard fare in Japanese restaurants and on trendy takeout menus. Yet homemade gyoza using frozen gyoza wrappers are fast enough for a weeknight, a thousand times tastier, and even fun to make. This delicate edamame filling has a surprising crunch from daikon, and the pale green color glows through the translucent wrappers; steaming is the healthy way to cook gyoza, but try a quick sauté in a wok with a few blasts of cooking spray for fast, golden dumplings. Yuzu lemon juice, though not cheap, is a nice addition to the minimalist dipping sauce, but regular lemon juice is fine as well.

2 quarts (8 cups) water
12-ounce bag frozen shelled edamame
    soybeans
4 cloves garlic, peeled and minced
1-inch piece peeled ginger, finely minced
4 scallions, green and white parts separated
    and finely chopped
2 tablespoons mirin (see page 16)
¾ teaspoon sea salt
1 teaspoon toasted sesame oil
½ cup minced daikon (peel the daikon first,
    then mince)
Oil cooking spray or oil if frying gyoza
Large lettuce leaves to cover the bottom of
    the steamer if steaming gyoza
34 purchased frozen gyoza wrappers (plus a
    few extra just in case), defrosted at room
    temperature

DIPPING SAUCE

3 tablespoons soy sauce
4 teaspoons lemon juice
2 teaspoons mirin
1 teaspoon agave nectar or 2 teaspoons
    sugar
A sprinkle of toasted sesame seeds

1. In a large pot bring 2 quarts of water to a rapid boil and stir in a teaspoon of salt and the frozen edamame. Cook for about 5 minutes or until beans are very soft, then drain.

2. In a food processor puree the edamame with the garlic, ginger, white tops of scallions, mirin, sea salt, and sesame oil into a grainy paste. Add the green tops of scallions and daikon but pulse only a few times; the mixture will be chunky. Taste and add more salt and sesame oil if desired.

3. To assemble a gyoza, unwrap the wrappers and keep them covered with a clean, damp kitchen towel. Place a wrapper on a cutting board and just barely dampen the edges with a fingertip dipped in water. Scoop a generous rounded tablespoon of filling into a wrapper, fold the edges over and firmly crimp down the edges. Repeat with remaining filling and wrappers. To steam, layer a steaming basket with lettuce leaves or parchment paper and steam for 3 to 4 minutes until wrappers are translucent and filling is hot.

4. For pan-fried gyoza, heat a wok or skillet over medium high-heat and generously spray with cooking spray. Fry several gyoza at a time for about 2 minutes on each side, flipping and spraying with cooking spray if necessary until firm and the sides are golden brown.

5. While the gyoza are cooking make the dipping sauce by whisking together all of the ingredients and pouring into a serving dish. Serve hot gyoza immediately with dipping sauce!

shanghai kale dumplings in sesame sauce

SERVES 2 DUMPLING FIENDS OR 4 AS AN APPETIZER

Sweet, succulent Chinese kale (gai lan or kai lan) *is great stir-fried but is also fantastic featured in tender dumplings smothered with spicy sweet sesame sauce. These dumplings are piquant comfort food, so set aside the takeout menu, make a batch, and see for yourself. And don't skip out on the toppings of black vinegar, chile sauce, scallions, and soy sauce: these ingredients together are a classic Chinese combination that make dumplings and noodles irresistible.*

Square, wheat starch–based "Shanghai-style" wonton wrappers are ideal for these dumplings and occasionally can be found made without eggs in Chinese grocery stores in the refrigerator case. If you see them in Asian markets grab a pack if only to make these as soon as possible. However, typically egg-free and easier-to-find gyoza wrappers work great, too.

Authentic-tasting Chinese-style sesame sauce is made with Chinese sesame paste and not Middle Eastern tahini. This brown, earthy, and slightly gritty paste is essential for an authentic sauce. For this recipe use the greyish-brown paste instead of black sesame paste. But if you can't make the trip to an Asian grocery to locate sesame paste, you have my permission to use tahini as a fallback, just because I really want to you make these excellent dumplings!

1 pound Chinese kale (gai lan) or leafy green kale

4 teaspoons peanut oil

1 cup finely minced purchased fried tofu or *Savory Baked Tofu* (about ½ recipe; see page 50)

4 scallions, root ends trimmed and thinly sliced

½ teaspoon grated ginger

½ teaspoon *Sichuan 5-Spice Powder* (page 41) or store-bought Chinese 5-spice powder

1 teaspoon salt

2 tablespoons Chinese (Shaoxing) cooking wine (see page 13)

2 teaspoons vegetable oil

2 teaspoons kosher salt

About 26 to 30 three-inch-square eggless wonton wrappers or gyoza wrappers

3 quarts (12 cups) water

SESAME SAUCE

¼ cup brown Chinese sesame paste (see page 12) or sesame tahini

1 heaping tablespoon smooth, salted natural peanut butter

3 tablespoons soy sauce

2 tablespoons rice vinegar or Chinese black vinegar (see page 12)

4 teaspoons dark brown sugar

2 cloves garlic, peeled and grated or pressed

1 teaspoon toasted sesame oil

½ teaspoon freshly grated ginger

2 to 4 tablespoons hot black tea or hot water

TOPPINGS

3 scallions, green tops only, finely chopped

1 tablespoon Chinese black vinegar

2 tablespoon soy sauce

1 tablespoon toasted sesame seeds

Asian-style smooth red chili sauce like Sriracha

1. Prepare the filling first. Chop 1 inch of tough stems from the bottom of the Chinese kale, then tear away the stems from the leaves. Chop the stems into pieces ¼ inch wide or smaller, then roll up the leaves and slice into very thin shreds less than ¼ inch wide. Heat the peanut oil in a wok over high heat, add the chopped stems and cook for 2 minutes; then add the leaves and cook another 2 to 3 minutes to reduce the mixture. Fold in the tofu and scallions, sprinkle with the ginger, 5-spice powder, and salt and fry another minute. Sprinkle on the cooking wine and continue to fry and stir the mixture until it's cooked down to about 2 cups of filling. Transfer the filling into a bowl to cool.

2. Make the sesame sauce: in a mixing bowl stir together all of the ingredients except for the hot tea to form a thick paste. Now dribble in the hot tea a tablespoon at a time to reach a consistency like a thick salad dressing. The sauce will look lighter as more liquid is added; continue to add more liquid for an even thinner sauce. The sauce also thickens as it sits; loosen it up with a little hot water if the sauce is made hours before serving. For the smoothest sauce, pulse in a blender.

3. When ready to make the dumplings, bring a large stockpot with 3 quarts of water to a boil; add 2 teaspoons each of salt and vegetable oil to the water. To shape a dumpling, place a wonton wrapper on a cutting board, dip a finger in cold water, and trace the edges of the wrapper with water. Place one level tablespoon of filling in the center, and fold over two opposite corners to form a triangle. Press down firmly to seal the edges (this is important!), then with the remaining opposite edges bend them

towards each other and press the tips together to form an almost tortellini-like shape (see illustration of folded dumpling on page 182). Place the finished dumpling on a piece of parchment paper and finish assembling the rest.

4. Carefully lower four or five dumplings at a time into the boiling water; dumplings will cook in 3 to 4 minutes and the skins will look slightly translucent when done. Use a long-handled mesh skimmer to carefully scoop one dumpling at a time, shake off the drops of excess water, and lower into a wide, shallow serving bowl or several smaller ones. Continue with remaining dumplings.

5. To serve, generously spoon sesame sauce over the hot dumplings. Then drizzle with desired amount of chili sauce, a handful of scallions, a tablespoon or more of black vinegar, a scattering of soy sauce, and a sprinkle of sesame seeds. Serve immediately.

kimchi and tofu manju dumplings

MAKES ABOUT 26 DUMPLINGS, SERVING 4 TO 6

Plump, chewy, Korean-style manju dumplings are the delicious reason to make extra **Fast Lane Cabbage Kimchi** *(page 56); the older the kimchi, the better the filling will taste. This recipe makes plenty, enough for crispy, pan-fried dumplings the next day. Complete this dumpling meal with seasoned spinach and mung sprout sides (use the toppings for* **Bibimbap***, page 308), and don't skip the tangy vinegar dipping sauce!*

Shortcut these dumplings with egg-free wonton or gyoza wrappers; thaw the wrappers completely before using. Dip your finger in water to seal the edges of the wrappers before pinching them together. Gyoza wrapper dumplings can also be directly pan-fried without the need for the additional boiling step.

1 recipe **Basic Dumpling Dough** (page 171) or about 30 round gyoza wrappers, thawed if frozen
1 tablespoon vegetable oil
2 teaspoons kosher salt

KIMCHI FILLING
2 tablespoons vegetable oil
4 cloves garlic, chopped
1 cup chopped finely chopped scallions, both green and white parts
½ pound firm tofu, crumbled
2 generous cups **Fast Lane Cabbage Kimchi** (preferably a few days old) or store-bought, drained (reserve the liquid in case the filling is dry) and chopped very fine
¼ teaspoon roasted sesame oil
Soy sauce (optional)

DIPPING SAUCE
¼ cup soy sauce
1 tablespoon rice vinegar
1 tablespoon agave nectar
½ teaspoon toasted sesame seeds
1 tablespoon finely chopped scallion

1. Before anything else, prepare a batch of **Basic Dumpling Dough**, wrap it tightly in well-floured plastic wrap, and let it sit at room temperature for about an hour to allow the gluten to relax. If using frozen gyoza wrappers, make sure they are completely thawed.

2. Meanwhile prepare the filling: heat the vegetable oil in a wok or 12-inch skillet and sauté the garlic for 30 seconds. Stir in the scallions, fry for 1 minute, and add the tofu, kimchi, and sesame oil. Continue to mix and fry the filling for another 3 to 4 minutes until well blended and juicy looking. Taste the mixture; it should be slightly crunchy from the kimchi and not too dry; add a little kimchi juice to moisten, or sprinkle with a dash of soy sauce if it needs more salt. Remove from the wok and cool the filling.

3. Prepare the dipping sauce by whisking together all of the ingredients and pouring into small serving dishes.

4. If using **Basic Dumpling Dough:** on a lightly floured surface divide the dumpling dough in half and wrap up one of the halves. Roll the dough into a rope about 13 inches long, and with a sharp knife slice into 13 pieces. Shape each piece into a flat circle, and with a floured rolling pin or dowel roll each piece into a disk about 3½ to 4 inches wide; flip the circle over often and lightly dust with flour to prevent sticking. Lay the disks on a large sheet of parchment paper and take care not to overlap them.

5. To assemble a dumpling, place a dough circle or gyoza wrapper on a lightly floured work surface. Scoop a rounded tablespoon of filling into the center of a dough circle. Grab one of the edges of the circle and pull it over the filling to form a half-circle. Firmly pinch the edges of the dough together; this prevents the dumplings from opening up during the boiling process (see illustration for dumpling shaping). Repeat with the remaining dough and filling, and do the same with the other batch of dough. Halfway though shaping the dumplings, fill a 3-quart pot half full of water and bring to a gentle boil over medium-high heat. Add a tablespoon of oil and 2 teaspoons of kosher salt to the water and have handy a long-handled mesh skimmer and a large, deep serving dish.

6. Gently lower the dumplings into the boiling water; don't cook more than 4 dumplings at a time to prevent any sticking together. Boiled dumplings cook fast; about 3 to 4 minutes. Dumplings are done when the wrappers look slightly translucent and they float to the top. Gently scoop up dumplings with a skimmer. Transfer to the serving dish and serve with dipping sauce.

7. To pan-fry precooked dumplings, heat a small amount of oil in a skillet over medium heat; cooking spray works well for fast and greaseless fried dumplings. Cook until they are hot inside and the edges are golden. If you're using gyoza wrappers you can skip the boiling step and pan-fry them directly for slightly longer, about 2½ to 3 minutes per dumpling.

Afghan Pumpkin Ravioli with Spicy Tomato Sauce

SERVES 4 TO 5 AS AN APPETIZER OR 4 AS AN ENTREE WITH A SALAD

Delicate Afghan-style dumplings (mantu) served with a spicy tomato sauce and a cool yogurt sauce may remind you a little of ravioli, especially for fans of the squash-filled variety. This recipe uses gyoza wrappers (or use egg-free wonton wrappers if you got 'em) as a shortcut, and canned pumpkin speeds up these aromatic dumplings. Served alone, they are a great appetizer or a main course along with a crisp cucumber and cabbage salad. They require a few extra steps, but the enticing combination of pumpkin, spiced tomato sauce, and garlicky yogurt will repay you with sheer deliciousness.

*Cooks with extra time may want to try these dumplings with **Cashew Yogurt Sauce** (page 65), but busy sorts should use the sauce included in this recipe.*

Prepare the sauces and filling a day before shaping and boiling the dumplings. The dumplings should be boiled immediately after assembling, so set aside about an hour for cooking the dumplings the first time you make them.

PUMPKIN MANTU DUMPLINGS

- 2 teaspoons coriander seeds
- 1 teaspoon cumin seeds
- ½ teaspoon powdered ginger
- 1 tablespoon olive oil
- 1 small yellow onion, peeled and minced
- 4 cloves garlic, peeled and minced
- 2 cups canned pumpkin puree or homemade roasted, mashed pumpkin
- 1 tablespoon brown sugar
- ¼ teaspoon ground black pepper
- ½ teaspoon sea salt
- 3 tablespoons fine dry breadcrumbs

- 36 square or round 3-inch vegan gyoza wrappers (if frozen, thaw completely in the refrigerator the day before)
- 1 tablespoon kosher salt
- 1 tablespoon vegetable oil
- 3 quarts (12 cups) water

SPICY TOMATO SAUCE

- 2 teaspoons fennel seeds
- 1 teaspoon coriander seeds
- ½ teaspoon cayenne pepper
- 1 tablespoon olive oil
- 1 small yellow onion, peeled and minced
- 3 cloves garlic, peeled and minced
- One 14-ounce can (2 cups) diced tomatoes with juice
- ½ teaspoon sea salt

GARLIC YOGURT SAUCE

- One 6-ounce container (¾ cup) plain soy or coconut yogurt, preferably unsweetened
- 2 cloves garlic, peeled
- ½ teaspoon sea salt

GARNISH

- 1 cup chopped cilantro
- 2 tablespoons chopped mint
- 2 tablespoons finely chopped walnuts (optional)

1. Prepare the filling first: heat the coriander and cumin seeds in a dry skillet over medium heat for 1 to 2 minutes, until toasted and fragrant. Immediately transfer to a clean coffee mill add the ginger, and grind to a fine powder. Preheat the olive oil in a large, stainless-steel skillet over medium-high heat, add the onion, and fry for 4 minutes or until softened and translucent, then add the garlic and fry for 45 seconds. Stir in the pumpkin, ground toasted spices, brown sugar, black pepper, and salt and cook for 1 minute, then stir in breadcrumbs and cook for 1 minute, stirring constantly until slightly thickened. Remove the filling from the heat, scoop into a bowl, and refrigerate for 20 minutes while preparing the sauces. Clean the skillet.

2. For the tomato sauce, toast the fennel and coriander seeds in a skillet over medium heat for 1 to 2 minutes. Transfer to a clean coffee mill add the cayenne, and pulse until fine. Preheat the olive oil in a large, stainless-steel skillet over medium-high heat, add the onion and fry for 4 minutes or until softened and translucent, then add the garlic and fry for 45 seconds. Stir in the tomatoes with their juices, the ground spices, and salt and bring to a simmer. Stir and cook for 2 to 3 minutes or until sauce has thickened slightly. Turn off heat and cover; before serving gently warm the sauce. Next, make the yogurt sauce: pulse all of the ingredients in a blender until smooth. Keep yogurt sauce chilled in the refrigerator until ready to use.

3. In a large soup pot combine the kosher salt and vegetable oil with the 3 quarts of water and bring to a boil. While the water is boiling, assemble the dumplings: prepare a clean work surface and a small cup of cold water. Place about 2 rounded teaspoons of filling into the center of a gyoza wrapper. Moisten a fingertip with water and trace along the edges of the wonton wrapper. Fold in half, press the opposite edges together and firmly pinch the edges

together to seal. See illustration for folded dumpling (page 182). Edges not properly sealed may open up during the boiling process. Place uncooked dumplings on a plastic wrap, taking care they don't touch or they may stick together.

4. Use a large slotted spoon and gently lower 4 to 5 dumplings at a time into the boiling water. Cook for 2 to 3 minutes; when done the dumplings will float to the top and the wrappers will look translucent. Use the slotted spoon or a long-handled mesh skimmer and gently transfer cooked dumplings to a lightly oiled dish. Keep covered until ready to serve.

5. When ready to serve, ladle a few spoonfuls of warmed tomato sauce onto a shallow serving bowl or individual appetizer plates. Arrange dumplings on top of the sauce, then spoon more tomato sauce over dumplings. Drizzle on the yogurt sauce, then scatter chopped herbs and the walnuts, if using, on top. Serve immediately, with a green salad and flatbread to scoop up the sauces from the plate.

Momo Dumplings with Spicy Sesame Tomato Sambal and Cabbage Slaw

MAKES 25 TO 30 DUMPLINGS

Momos are the dumplings of Tibetan and Nepalese cuisine; there are infinite kinds of fillings including veggie variations that feature whatever vegetable is handy. These homemade gems are my spin on a former hole-in-the-wall Tibetan dumpling house

in Queens; instead of watery cabbage, this filling is bursting with leafy greens and golden turmeric tofu, balanced by ample fenugreek and caramelized red onions. You could make these momos with large round gyoza wrappers, but the homemade dumpling dough makes mouthwatering, big and chewy dumplings.

Serve momos with a tangy sambal chile sesame sauce and a simple and refreshing cabbage slaw (see ingredients list). Leftover steamed momos can be gently pan fried to crisp the edges.

1 recipe *Basic Dumpling Dough* (page 171) or 30 to 35 large round gyoza wrappers, thawed if frozen
1 recipe *Cabbage Slaw* (recipe follows)
1 recipe *Spicy Sesame Tomato Sambal* (page 72)

FILLING

4 cups firmly packed, finely chopped kale, Chinese broccoli, collard greens, or mustard greens
2½ teaspoons fenugreek seeds
2 teaspoons coriander
1 teaspoon cumin seeds
1 teaspoon ground turmeric
2 to 4 small green chilies, finely minced
1 tablespoon finely minced garlic
1 tablespoon minced ginger
2 tablespoons vegetable oil
2 large red onions, peeled and finely minced
½ pound soft tofu, drained and crumbled
1 teaspoon sea salt, or more to taste
1 large carrot, peeled and diced into ¼-inch cubes
1 cup cilantro leaves, finely chopped
Lettuce or cabbage leaves to line the steamer basket

1. Gently steam the kale in a large pot filled with 2 inches of boiling water; cover and steam until the greens are bright green and tender, about 4 minutes. Remove from the heat, drain, and when cool enough to handle squeeze out any excess water. Set aside.

2. Toast the fenugreek, coriander, and cumin seeds in a skillet over medium heat for 1 to 2 minutes or until fragrant. Pour seeds into a clean coffee mill, add turmeric, and grind into a fine powder. Over medium heat in a deep, 12-inch-wide skillet fry the chilies, garlic, and ginger in the vegetable oil for 2 minutes over low heat, then stir in the diced red onion and carrot. Cook this mixture, stirring occasionally, until the onions are golden brown and lightly caramelized, about 10 minutes. Add the tofu, ground spices, and salt and increase heat to medium. Continue to stir-fry for 3 minutes. Stir in the cooked greens and fry for 1 minute. Stir in cilantro and turn off heat; taste the filling, and stir in more salt if desired. Transfer the filling to a mixing bowl to cool.

3. While the filling is cooking, prepare your steaming set up, be it a bamboo steamer or electric steamer or a trivet positioned above boiling water; the most important thing is that the dumplings never touch the water during steaming. Line the steaming baskets with lettuce or cabbage leaves.

3. To prepare the dumpling wrappers, divide the dumpling dough and keep the unused portion wrapped in plastic wrap until ready to use. On a generously floured surface, roll and shape the dough into a thick rope about 15 inches long. Use a ruler to mark and slice off pieces about 1 inch thick and keep the pieces covered with plastic wrap or a damp, clean kitchen towel. Use a rolling pin to roll out each piece into a circle at least 3 inches wide; keep your work surface well dusted with flour and flip the dumpling wrapper frequently to prevent sticking and ensure an evenly round circle. If using gyoza wrappers, keep

them covered with a damp clean kitchen towel to prevent them from drying out.

4. If your momos are made with dumpling dough, shape them like bao buns; see the illustration on page 199 for shaping technique. These will be smaller than bao and won't puff up as big, due to the fact the dumpling wrappers use an unyeasted dough. But they'll be delicious and authentic all the same. Scoop a rounded 1 tablespoon of filling into the center of a dough circle and cradle the soon-to-be-momo in one hand. With your other hand pinch the dough from the edge of the circle and pull it away from the center; do it again right next to your first pinch, then pinch the two points together bending the dough toward the filling. Repeat this grab, pinch, and bend technique, taking care to pinch all of the ends together. Work around the entire circle this way until you have something that resembles a pleated pouch of dough. Now twist the peak firmly to seal the top. Don't worry if the momo doesn't look perfect; steaming will firm the dough and keep the filling in place. Repeat with the remaining portion of dough to shape another fifteen momos for a total of thirty.

If using gyoza wrappers instead, fold into half-moons as instructed for gyoza on page 179.

5. Place the assembled momos on top of the lettuce leaves in the steaming basket, positioning them at least ½ inch apart as they will expand during steaming. Steam each batch for 10 minutes and take care moving freshly steamed momos as they are somewhat delicate. For best results steam uncooked momos as soon as possible, working in small batches of rolling, filling, assembling, and steaming. Serve hot momos with **Spicy Sesame Tomato Sambal** and **Cabbage Slaw**.

6. To fry steamed momos, gently sauté with a little vegetable oil over medium heat in a wok or cast-iron skillet until edges are crisped and browned. If using gyoza wrappers, there's no need to boil—they can be directly pan fried after assembling. Serve hot momos as directed in step 5.

To finely chop collard greens or kale, remove thick stems, stack a few leaves and roll into tight bundles. Slice into ribbons as thin as possible, then chop the still-rolled ribbons several times.

cabbage slaw

MAKES ABOUT 4 CUPS

Crunchy cabbage salad is a refreshing side paired with spicy cuisine and perfect with warm, chewy momos. This comes together quickly while the dumplings steam.

> 4 cups finely shredded green or red cabbage or savoy cabbage
> 1 cup roughly chopped cilantro leaves
> 1 large carrot, peeled and grated
> 2 tablespoons rice vinegar
> ½-inch piece peeled ginger, minced
> 4 teaspoons sugar
> 1½ teaspoons sea salt
> 1 teaspoon toasted sesame oil
> ½ teaspoon ground turmeric
> ½ teaspoon ground black pepper

1. In a large mixing bowl, combine the cabbage, cilantro, and carrot. In a small cup whisk together the remaining ingredients and pour over the cabbage. Toss the cabbage with the dressing or use your hands to massage the vinegar into the cabbage for a few minutes. Serve immediately, or store in a tightly covered container in the fridge for up to two days.

Gluten-Free Kimchi Pancakes (kimchijeon)

MAKES UP TO 3 THICK, 10-INCH PANCAKES

Jeon *refers to a wide-ranging family of pancake-like Korean dishes, and anywhere in the world there's a pancake you can count me in. My favorite jeon is loaded with kimchi, and my version also also happens to be gluten free; the combination of rice flour and cornstarch creates a springy pancake that hugs the juiciness of the kimchi and scallions. As with many dishes using kimchi, the older your kimchi the better; the abundant juices contribute to the moisture in the batter and infuse it with more fiery savory flavor. While kimchijeon is typically served as an appetizer, there's no reason you can't make a whole meal of it served with* **Sesame Wow Greens** *(page 279).*

> 2 cups *Fast Lane Cabbage Kimchi* (page 56) or store-bought kimchi, drained of juices (reserve it) and chopped into 1-inch pieces
>
> 1 cup mixture of kimchi juice and water (use whatever amount of drained juice is reserved from the kimchi, the rest should be water)
>
> 2 teaspoons vegetable oil
>
> 4 scallions, root ends trimmed and finely chopped
>
> 3 cloves garlic, minced
>
> 1½ teaspoons toasted sesame oil
>
> 1 teaspoon gochugaru (Korean red pepper powder, see page 15)

> ¾ cup white rice flour
>
> ½ cup cornstarch
>
> ½ teaspoon sea salt
>
> 3 tablespoons vegetable oil for frying
>
> Additional cooking oil spray
>
> Dipping sauce from *Kimchi and Tofu Manju Dumplings* (page 181)

For easier flipping make lots of small 3- to 5-inch individual pancakes instead of 3 big pancakes. Heat any leftover pancakes on a lightly oiled skillet to revive the crisp edges.

1. Preheat a 10-inch cast-iron skillet over medium heat for at least 6 minutes. In a large bowl combine kimchi, kimchi juice/water mixture, oil, scallions, garlic, sesame oil, and red pepper powder. Pour in the rice flour, cornstarch, and salt. Stir to form a thick, chunky batter.

2. Pour 1 tablespoon of the oil in the skillet, then tilt the skillet to spread around the oil. Spread a third of the batter over the griddle, using the back of a spoon to evenly distribute the kimchi chunks throughout. Fry for 5 to 7 minutes, occasionally shifting the pan to evenly brown the pancake. It's ready to flip when the edges appear dry and bubbles have form all over the top. If the pancake begins to stick, use a little more oil on the next pancake or spray the pan with additional cooking spray.

3. Slide a thin spatula underneath the pancake to loosen the bottom and check the color; it should be golden brown and firm. Using a large wide spatula, carefully but quickly flip the pancake; if it's too difficult, try sliding the pancake onto a plate first, then flipping it over into the skillet. Cook for 2 to 3 minutes until the other side is golden. Loosen the pancake with a spatula, then slide it onto a dinner plate, slice into wedges and serve with the dipping sauce.

chappati and paratha, whole wheat indian flatbreads

MAKES 4 LARGE FLATBREADS ABOUT 8 INCHES IN DIAMETER

Fresh, hot Indian flatbreads can made in a flash while a curry is bubbling; they're faster to make than rice, and the chewy texture and shape is perfect for scooping up soupy curries. Look for finely milled whole grain atta *flour in Indian groceries for authentic-tasting breads, or use a mix of whole wheat white flour and all-purpose flour for a readily made substitute.*

Chappati is traditionally a lean bread, but it can be enhanced it with a little oil or melted margarine. Paratha, however, is a rich and flaky flatbread, sometimes stuffed with tempting fillings. You can even double a batch of this dough and make a little of both.

GLUTEN-FREE KIMCHI PANCAKES (KIMCHIJEON), PAGE 187

CHAPPATI AND PARATHA DOUGH

- 1¼ cup chappati (atta) flour or ¾ cup whole wheat white flour and ½ cup all-purpose flour
- ¾ teaspoon salt
- ⅔ cup warm water
- 2 to 4 tablespoons melted nonhydrogenated vegan margarine or mild-tasting vegetable oil, plus additional oil for brushing paratha
- Additional flour for dusting

1. In a bowl stir together flour and salt, then pour in warm water and oil. If you're making chappati, you can either skip the oil altogether or add up to 2 tablespoons for additional richness. For paratha, add all 4 tablespoons oil. Use a wooden spoon or rubber spatula to stir everything together to form a soft dough; if the dough is too dry, dribble in extra warm water 1 tablespoon at a time; if too wet, sprinkle in a little extra flour. Now use your hands to knead the dough until smooth; this can be done in the bowl or on a lightly floured surface. Divide the dough into four balls and remove from the bowl and pour a teaspoon of vegetable oil into the bowl. Place the dough balls in the bowl, roll to coat with oil and cover with plastic wrap. Set aside in a warm place to rest for at least 30 minutes.

2. When you're ready to roll out chappati or paratha, start heating a large cast-iron skillet or griddle over medium-high heat. Have nearby a large, clean kitchen towel. Or if you have a tortilla warmer, that's even better!

For chappati: Lightly dust your work surface with flour and roll a piece of dough into a very thin circle about 10 inches wide. To help roll a neat circle, rotate the dough with every stroke of the rolling pin and occasionally flip over. Sprinkle the circle with a little additional flour if it starts to stick to the rolling pin. Cook bread on an ungreased 12-inch cast-iron skillet heated over high heat, cooking on each side until bubbles begin to form in the dough and the edges appear dry. Wrap hot chappati in a large, clean kitchen towel to keep soft and warm; this is essential as chappati will harden as they cool.

For basic paratha: After rolling the dough into a circle, brush with a little oil or melted margarine, roll into a tight tube, and roll the tube into a tight snail-like spiral. Roll the spiral flat, roll again into a 10-inch circle, and brush with oil. Roll once more into a coil, roll again into a 9- to 10-inch circle, brush one side with oil, and drop the bread oil side down into a 10-inch cast-iron skillet preheated over high heat. Cook bread until large bubbles begin and the edges appear dry; brush the top with a little oil. Flip only once; a few dark marks on the dough is fine, even desirable. Wrap hot paratha in a large, clean kitchen towel to keep it soft and warm.

sweet potato–stuffed paratha

MAKES FOUR 7-INCH PARATHA

Paratha are wonderful, but stuffed with tender veggie fillings they're an enticing light meal or filling snack. They're a little more work than plain paratha but are wonderful reheated for hearty weekday breakfasts, brilliant brunch bread, or nibbled as a light lunch Indian-style, paired with any chutney, Indian store-bought savory pickles, and a side of soy yogurt.

PARATHA

1 recipe *Chappati and Paratha* dough (page 189)
3 tablespoons of melted nonhydrogenated vegan margarine or vegetable oil

FILLING

¾ pound sweet potato (about one 6-inch sweet potato)
2 tablespoons grated dried coconut
1 tablespoon peanut or canola oil
1 teaspoon black mustard seeds
6 fresh curry leaves (see page 14), or use frozen
2 cloves garlic, minced
1 teaspoon ground cumin
½ teaspoon ground turmeric
½ teaspoon sea salt
Lime juice as needed

1. Prepare the dough as directed for *paratha* (on this page, column one) up until rolling the dough into circles for the last time and stack them between sheets of waxed paper. Try to make the paratha as round and close to 8 inches in diameter as possible. Cover with plastic wrap or a damp clean kitchen towel and keep covered until ready to use.

2. To make the filling, peel and boil the sweet potato in 4 inches of water in a tightly covered saucepan over high heat until it's tender and can easily be pierced with a fork, about 15 minutes. Drain and let cool, then use a fork to mash it into coarse chunks.

3. In a large skillet over low heat toast the coconut, stirring frequently with a wooden spoon or rubber spatula until light golden brown. Quickly trans-

fer the coconut to a dish and set aside. Heat the oil in skillet and add the mustard seeds and curry leaves. When the seeds pop, stir in the garlic, sprinkle with the spices, and add the mashed sweet potato and coconut. Sauté for 1 minute, turn off the heat, and sprinkle with salt and lime juice as desired and mash the mixture. Remove the pan from the stove and cool the filling for 10 minutes. Scoop the mixture into four portions about ⅓ cup each and form into patties 1 inch thick; snack on any remaining filling.

4. Heat a cast-iron skillet or griddle over medium heat and have nearby the oil and a pastry brush. Arrange a paratha on a lightly floured surface. To assemble, place one sweet potato patty in the center of an unbaked paratha. Fold a corner of the dough towards the center of the patty, then fold another corner overlapping the previous fold (see illustration). Repeat until your have about five or six overlapping folds and pinch the center together; the folded dough should look a little like a hexagon-shaped pinwheel (it's much simpler to make than it sounds). Gently flip over and use a rolling pin and gently roll the paratha once or twice and flatten it to about ½ inch thick and 7 inches wide; roll carefully to prevent the filling breaking out (some filling showing through the dough is okay). If rolling feels too risky, try flattening with your palms.

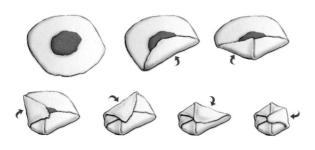

5. Brush the surface of the hot skillet with a little oil and place the paratha seam side down. Brush the top with oil and cook on each side for about 4 to 5 minutes until dark brown spots form on each side. Serve hot paratha immediately or wrap in clean kitchen towels to keep warm. Serve with a chutney, Indian pickle (spicy mango pickles are perfect), and side of plain soy yogurt for dipping. Paratha are best eaten the day they are made but can be stored in the fridge for 3 days and reheated on a skillet.

If you've ever eaten in an Indian restaurant you'll see there are many variations on paratha. Have fun and make some of your own! Replace the sweet potato with the following:

Cauliflower-Stuffed Paratha: Use 1½ cups finely chopped, steamed cauliflower.

Potato Pea Cashew–Stuffed Paratha: Use the Potato Pea Cashew Filling from the *Filo Samosas* (page 209).

Banana-Stuffed Paratha

MAKES 4 STUFFED FLATBREADS ABOUT 8 INCHES IN DIAMETER

Get ready for repeated requests for these tender paratha overflowing with gooey, gently spiced warm bananas. Make these for special weekend breakfasts or a wholesome and filling snack served with hot almond milk cocoa spiked with cinnamon and cloves.

Warning: The melty banana filling fresh off the griddle will be extremely hot! When serving to kids or anyone who doesn't enjoy burning their mouth, use a sharp, serrated knife to slice paratha into quarters and cool about a minute prior to serving.

PARATHA

> 1 recipe *Chappati and Paratha* dough (page 189)
>
> 3 tablespoons of melted nonhydrogenated vegan margarine or vegetable oil

FILLING

> 2 cups sliced ripe banana
>
> 1 teaspoon lemon juice
>
> 2 tablespoons dark brown sugar
>
> ¼ teaspoon ground cardamom
>
> ¼ teaspoon ground cinnamon
>
> A big pinch of ground nutmeg
>
> A pinch of salt

1. Prepare the dough as directed for paratha (page 190, column one) up until rolling the dough into circles for the last time and stack them between sheets of waxed paper. Try to make the paratha as round and close to 8 inches in diameter as possible. Cover with plastic wrap or a damp clean kitchen towel and keep covered until ready to use.

2. When you're ready to stuff the paratha, preheat a 10-inch largest cast-iron skillet or griddle over medium-high heat. Have nearby a large, clean kitchen towel, a pastry brush, and the melted margarine or oil. Prepare the banana filling: in a mixing bowl gently stir together the banana slices and lemon juice, then sprinkle in the brown sugar, spices, and salt.

3. Scoop a quarter of the banana filling into the center of a paratha dough circle. Fold as directed for **Sweet Potato–Stuffed Paratha** on page 190 (and see illustration on page 191); fold a corner of the dough towards the center of the filling, then fold another corner overlapping the previous fold. Repeat until your have about five or six overlapping folds and pinch the center together; the folded dough should look like a hexagon-shaped pinwheel (it's much simpler to make than it sounds). Gently flip over and use a rolling pin and gently roll the paratha once or twice and flatten it to about ½ inch thick and 7 inches wide; roll carefully to prevent the filling breaking out (some filling showing through the dough is okay). If rolling is too difficult, try flattening with your palms.

4. Gently place a paratha seam side down onto a well-oiled hot griddle and brush the top with melted margarine or oil. Cook for 2 to 3 minutes until the underside is lightly browned. Flip and continue to bake on the other sides; a few dark marks on the paratha is fine, even desirable. A little bit of the moist filling may leak out of the sides, that's okay. Use a wide spatula and transfer the very hot paratha to the kitchen towel and wrap to keep warm. Repeat the shaping and baking for the remaining paratha.

spinach coriander Roti

MAKES 8 LARGE ROTI FLATBREADS

*In this unusual twist on Indian roti flatbread, I've infused the dough with convenient frozen spinach for a deep green, tender bread that's a vegetable-rich addition to any West or East Indian meal. Great with any curry or soup but especially good with red lentil stews like **Red Lentil Dahl with Tomatoes and Curry Leaves** (page 120).*

1 pound frozen chopped (not cut-leaf)
  spinach

½ teaspoon ground coriander

½ teaspoon ground cumin

¼ teaspoon cayenne pepper

2 cups chapatti flour (whole-grain durum
  wheat flour), plus additional for rolling

1½ teaspoons salt

2 tablespoons vegetable oil, divided

¾ to 1 cup warm water

1. In large wire mesh strainer or colander rinse the frozen spinach with warm water until thawed. Squeeze the spinach with all your might to remove as much water as possible: you'll have a little over 1 cup of spinach when done.

2. In a mixing bowl combine ground coriander, cumin, cayenne, chapatti flour, salt, 1 tablespoon of the oil, and the squeezed spinach. Work the mixture with your fingers to evenly distribute the ingredients, breaking up any large chunks of spinach to form a crumbly mixture. Pour in ¾ cup warm water and use your hands mix to form a soft dough; if necessary work in additional water 1 tablespoon at a time. Knead the dough for an additional 2 minutes, pour in the remaining tablespoon of oil, and roll dough in the bowl to evenly coat with oil. Let stand for 10 minutes.

3. Heat a large cast-iron skillet over medium-high heat. Divide dough into eight equal pieces and roll into balls. Lightly flour a large, clean work surface, place a dough ball in the center, and sprinkle with flour. Use a rolling pin to roll dough as thin as possible and into a round circle about 8 to 10 inches wide. For best results frequently rotate and flip over the circle, roll with one or two long strokes and rotate again; this will help shape the circle evenly.

4. Cook roti on the ungreased hot skillet for 4 to 5 minutes. The cooking roti will begin to puff up in places and look dry around the edges. Use a bent spatula to flip over the roti and cook on the other side for another 1 to 2 minutes. Dark brown spots on the roti are fine, even desirable.

5. Line a large bowl with a clean kitchen towel; flip the hot, cooked roti into the towel and fold over the towel edges to keep the roti moist and warm. Continue to roll, cook, and cover with towels the hot roti. Wrap any uneaten roti tightly in plastic wrap and reheat on a grill or directly over a gas burner (hold the bread with long-handled metal tongs).

Sri Lankan Coconut Roti

MAKES 8 ROTI FLATBREADS

A thick yet delicate roti with buttery, natural sweetness from loads of (almost) fresh coconut. Frozen grated coconut (see page 14) is convenient and almost as good as grating fresh coconuts yourself; look for it in the freezer section of Indian and Southeast Asian markets. Consider making a double batch for now to serve with spicy curries, then tomorrow toasted for breakfast and schmeared with orange marmalade and vegan butter.

2 cups grated frozen coconut, thawed at
  room temperature and firmly packed

1¾ cups unbleached all-purpose flour

2 tablespoons plus 1 teaspoon vegetable oil

1 teaspoon baking powder

1 teaspoon sea salt

½ cup or more warm water

1. In a large mixing bowl combine coconut, flour, 2 tablespoons vegetable oil, baking powder, and salt. Use your fingers to rub the ingredients thoroughly together until crumbly. Slowly work in a little of the warm water at a time to form a soft dough. Pay close attention to the consistency; once the dough begins to feel sticky, stop adding more water. Knead in the bowl for 2 to 3 minutes, press into a ball and drizzle on the remaining oil. Roll the dough in bowl to completely coat with oil, cover the top of the bowl with a large, clean kitchen towel, and set aside for 20 minutes.

2. Divide dough into eight pieces, roll into balls, and flatten with your fingers. Press and pat the dough between your palms to flatten the dough to about ¼ inch thickness, repeat with remaining dough. If desired lightly oil hands to prevent any sticking. You can also try rolling out the roti between sheets of plastic wrap, but these roti should not be too thin (unlike Indian chappati bread). While shaping the roti, preheat a cast-iron skillet over medium-high heat. Have nearby a large bowl covered with a large, clean kitchen towel; we'll use this to wrap up the hot roti and keep it warm and soft. The skillet is ready when a few drops of water sprinkled on the surface sizzle immediately.

3. Place a roti on the skillet and cook on each side for about 2 to 2 ½ minutes. The surface of the roti should feel firm to the touch but never hard, with a few dark brown spots on each side. Transfer hot roti to the bowl covered with the kitchen towel and wrap within the towel; always keep roti covered or it will get hard. Cook the remaining roti and stack the hot roti on top of each other. Serve immediately and store any leftovers in a tightly covered container. To reheat, warm on a preheated skillet; if you make the roti small enough, try toasting them in a toaster on low setting for breakfast!

yogurt naan griddle Bread

MAKES 8 LARGE NAAN FLATBREADS

Naan, that Indian restaurant flatbread rock-star loved by foodies everywhere, can be made with excellent results at home baked on an ungreased cast-iron griddle or skillet, no special tandoori oven required. Tightly wrap and freeze leftover naan; to reheat, let naan defrost on the kitchen counter for 5 minutes then throw on a hot griddle again to toast piping hot.

These naan were an overwhelming tester favorite; if you're going to make just one bread from this book, make it these!

Replace half the flour with white whole wheat flour for wholesome naan.

¾ cup warm water
1 tablespoon sugar
¼-ounce package active dry yeast
¾ cup plain soy or coconut yogurt
3 tablespoons mild vegetable oil
1¾ teaspoons salt
3½ to 4 cups bread flour, plus additional for kneading
3 tablespoons nonhydrogenated vegan margarine, melted

1. Pour warm water into a large mixing bowl, stir in the sugar, and then sprinkle with yeast. Set aside for 10 minutes to proof the yeast; the mixture

YOGURT NAAN GRIDDLE BREAD

will look frothy. Use a wooden spoon to stir in the soy yogurt, 2 tablespoons of the vegetable oil, and the salt. Shake in a little at a time of the 3½ cups of flour and stir into soft dough. If the dough is tacky, stir in another ½ cup of flour a tablespoon at a time until the dough is no longer sticky.

2. Lightly flour a large work surface and knead the dough until smooth, about 3 minutes. Clean the mixing bowl, pour in the remaining tablespoon of oil, and add the dough; roll the dough in the oil to completely coat the surface. Cover the bowl with plastic wrap and place in a warm, draft-free place for an hour; as the dough rises, it should double in size. Punch down the dough and lightly flour the work surface again. If adding additional ingredients (see the variations that follow), stretch out the dough to about an inch thickness, sprinkle on the garlic, onions, or herbs, and fold the dough several times to work in these ingredients. Divide the dough into eight pieces and place on a lightly floured baking sheet. Cover with plastic wrap and set aside in a warm place for a second rise, about 20 to 30 minutes or until pieces are doubled in size.

3. When ready to cook naan, heat a cast-iron griddle, skillet, or grill pan over high heat. Flour that work surface one more time and lightly flour a piece of naan dough. Use a rolling pin or dowel to roll into the thinnest circle possible, at least ¼ inch. Lower the naan onto the griddle, brush with margarine, and sprinkle with dried herbs or seeds if using and cook for 2 to 4 minutes; the naan will puff up as it bakes and form a few large bubbles. Check the underside of the naan; when golden, turn it over and cook for another 2 to 2½ minutes. Wrap hot naan in a large, clean kitchen towel and repeat cooking process with remaining dough, stacking and wrapping together to keep hot and soft.

Serve naan hot, if desired cutting in quarters to scoop up curries.

Plain naan are good, but flavored naan are excellent. If you can't decide which one, why not make a few different kinds? Since the flavorings are added to the dough during in the second kneading or simply pressed into the top, divide the dough into as many flavors as your naan-shaped heart desires.

Knead into the naan dough one of the following:
Garlic Naan: 3 tablespoons minced garlic
Red Onion Naan: ½ cup finely chopped red onion
Scallion Naan: ½ cup finely chopped scallions, green part only
Mint or Cilantro Naan: ¼ cup finely chopped mint or cilantro

Press onto the top of each naan before cooking:
Rosemary Naan: 1 tablespoon of dried rosemary per naan
Cumin Seed Naan: 1 teaspoon cumin seeds per naan
Black Cumin Seed Naan: ½ teaspoon kalonji (black cumin) seeds per naan. Look for kalonji seeds where Indian spices are sold, also called nigella seeds.

Prepare naan dough and store in the refrigerator for a day to slow the rising. 1 hour before baking, remove from the refrigerator and divide into pieces.

Middle Eastern za'atar Flatbread

I love using this naan dough as a hack on zesty Middle Eastern flatbreads topped with nutty za'atar. Made with thyme, sesame, and sumac, za'atar is a richly aromatic Middle Eastern spice blend used to flavor bread. Look for big bags of this gritty green powder in Middle Eastern groceries.

Right before the naan is done baking, brush the bubbling top with olive oil (instead of melted margarine) and sprinkle 2 or 3 tablespoons of za'atar per naan; don't be shy, this spice should thickly coat the top of the bread. Use a spoon or fingertips to press the spices into the top of the bread, then continue cooking as directed. Slice hot za'atar flatbread into 2-inch-wide strips and serve hot.

steamed BBQ seitan buns (char siu seitan bao)

MAKE 12 HUGE BAO

Fluffy steamed Chinese buns are a great outlet for crafty cooks; it's fun to shape the soft yeasted dough into peaky bao that steam up tender and comforting. Saucy faux-pork bao are the flagship dish of any vegetarian dim sum house worth their dumplings (with three veggie dim sum houses in NYC, I'm an expert at eating veggie bao). Even if your first batch doesn't look picture-perfect, they'll taste as delectable as any from a leisurely dim sum brunch.

If you love steamed bao as much as I hope you will, try stuffing them with the fillings from other dumplings in this chapter: momo, lumpias, leftover Ma-Po tofu, or even just chopped sautéed cabbage, mushrooms, and tofu with plenty of ginger and a touch of soy sauce.

3 cutlets of *5-Spice Seitan* (page 51), baked instead of steamed
⅓ cup dark agave nectar
¼ cup hoisin sauce (see page 13)

¼ cup Chinese Shaoxing cooking wine (see page 13) or mirin (see page 16)
¼ cup Chinese vegetarian stir-fry sauce (see page 13)
3 tablespoons vegetable oil
2 tablespoons soy sauce
1½ teaspoons *Sichuan 5-Spice Powder* (page 41) or store-bought Chinese 5-spice powder
2 teaspoons cornstarch
1 recipe *Fluffy Bao Dough* (recipe follows)

Prepare the filling up to 24 hours in advance.

1. Preheat the oven to 375°F and lightly oil a 9 x 13-inch ceramic baking dish. Cut twelve 3-inch-wide squares out of parchment paper and set aside for now. Dice the seitan into ¼-inch pieces and transfer them to the baking dish. Whisk together the remaining ingredients, except for the cornstarch and fluffy bao dough. Pour half of the marinade over the seitan and combine. Bake for 24 to 28 minutes, stirring the seitan occasionally, until the marinade is sticky and bubbling and the seitan is browned. Remove from the oven and set aside for 5 minutes.

2. In a large saucepan, whisk together the remaining marinade with the cornstarch. Stir in the roasted seitan, then over medium heat cook the mixture, stirring constantly, until the sauce has thickened, about 3 to 5 minutes. Remove from heat and set aside to cool for 20 minutes.

3. Meanwhile, knead the dough a few times, then slice in half with a sharp knife. Keep one half covered with plastic wrap. The dough should be soft but not sticky; lightly flour your work surface only if the dough starts to stick during the shaping process. Use your palms to roll the dough into a tube about 12 inches long and slice into six pieces. Press a piece of dough into a circle with your finger about 4 ½ to 5

inches wide or use a rolling pin to shape into a circle. For best results I use a combination of both, starting with my fingers and finishing with a wooden dowel to get an even circle about ¼ inch thick. Repeat with remaining dough. Set up your steamer and get it fired up and ready to steam. The bao must not touch the water during the steaming process.

4. Assemble a bao! First, see illustration below for bao-shaping tips. Now place a dough circle in your nondominant hand and place a heaping 2 tablespoons of filling in the center. With your other hand take a generous pinch of dough from the edge of the circle and pull it away from the center; do it again right next to your first pinch, then pinch the two points together bending the dough toward the filling. Repeat this grab, pinch, and bend technique, taking care to pinch all of the ends together to form a big fat point. The bao should resemble a pleated, peaked pouch of dough. Grab the peak and firmly twist to seal the top of the bao. Don't sweat it if your bao are not completely air-tight: bao take plenty of practice to look perfect, but even your first attempts will taste great. Place each completed bao on a square of parchment paper.

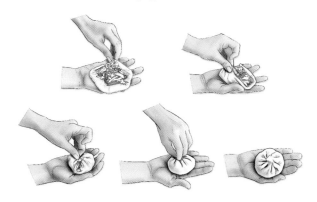

STEAMED BBQ SEITAN BUNS (CHAR SIU SEITAN BAO), PAGE 197

5. Bao expand during steaming to almost double the size, so space bao at least 2 inches apart in the steamer. For a 10-inch diameter steamer, that's about 3 to 4 bao per batch to allow the buns to expand without mashing into one another. Steam each batch of bao for 14 to 16 minutes; cooked bao will feel firm yet puffy and will spring back when poked. Serve bao warm with plenty of hot, steamy Chinese black or jasmine green tea!

Fluffy Bao Dough

MAKES ENOUGH FOR 12 LARGE BAO

Bao needn't be complicated; this dough is kneaded in minutes and steams up light, tender, and with a hint of sweetness just right for savory fillings. I like the creamy color unbleached flour lends, but for bright white buns like those seen at dim sum houses, use the bleached stuff. Giving the dough ample time to rest helps the gluten unwind and makes your job of shaping and rolling the buns easier: if the dough becomes too tight during shaping, set aside to rest 5 minutes between batches.

1.2-ounce packet instant dry yeast
1 cup lukewarm water
3 cups unbleached all-purpose flour
2 tablespoons sugar
1 ½ teaspoons baking powder
½ teaspoon salt
3 tablespoons plus 1 teaspoon canola oil
    or mild vegetable oil

1. Sprinkle the instant dry yeast over the warm water in a measuring cup; set aside for 3 to 4 minutes as yeast begins to foam. In a mixing bowl stir together the flour, sugar, baking powder, and salt and form a well in the center. Pour in the yeast mixture, add the 3 tablespoons oil and with a rubber spatula or wooden spoon stir together to form a soft dough; then use your hands to gather the dough into a ball and knead until it's no longer sticky, about 2 to 3 minutes. If necessary, add a teaspoon of flour at a time until the dough does not stick to the sides of the bowl. The dough should be moist and just barely tacky but leave the sides of the bowl clean.

2. Turn the dough onto a large, clean work surface and continue to knead for about 2 minutes or until very smooth; the dough should not require any flour to keep it from sticking to the surface, but if necessary sprinkle the work surface with flour until this smooth dough is reached. Pour the remaining teaspoon of oil into the mixing bowl, add the dough, and roll the ball in the oil to coat. Use plastic wrap to tightly cover the bowl, top with a kitchen towel to keep out any drafts, and let rest in a warm place for about an hour.

3. Punch down the dough, transfer it to the work surface, and slice it in half. Roll one-half into the desired length, cut into pieces, and roll into balls as directed for the recipe. Repeat with other half, cover the dough balls with plastic wrap and the kitchen towel and let rest for 10 minutes before shaping into bao.

4. Bao dough, tightly wrapped and chilled, can be stored up to 24 hours in advance. Let warm on the counter for 30 minutes prior to shaping.

Turkish Zucchini Pancakes (Mucver)

SERVES 4 TO 6

Mucver, *savory Turkish-style zucchini pancakes are a relaxed dinner that answers that eternal summer question, "How do we eat all this zucchini, before it eats us?"*

Serve these hearty vegetable entree pancakes with cool **Cashew Yogurt Sauce** *(page 65),* **Roasted Chile Pepper Harissa Paste** *(page 42), and a ripe tomato salad. Small young zucchini are always preferable to huge overgrown squash; fewer seeds, less water, and more flavorful flesh for tastier pancakes.*

1½ pounds young tender zucchini
1 teaspoon kosher salt
1 cup chopped fresh dill
4 scallions, root ends trimmed and finely chopped
½ cup chopped flat-leaf parsley
1 small carrot, finely grated
1 small white onion, peeled and finely chopped
¾ cup unsweetened plain soy milk
2 tablespoons olive oil
1 tablespoon lemon juice
⅔ cup unbleached all-purpose flour
¼ cup chickpea flour
2 teaspoons cornstarch
1 teaspoon baking powder

¼ teaspoon sea salt

A few twists of freshly ground pepper

Olive oil spray for frying

1. Wash and grate the zucchini with the large holes of a box grater or use a food processor with a shredder disk. Place the zucchini in bowl, sprinkle with kosher salt, and set aside for 30 minutes; drain any excess liquid. Heap zucchini into the center of a clean, smooth kitchen towel or in the center of a triple layer of large, strong paper towels and gather into a bundle. Hold the bundle over the sink and firmly squeeze to extract as much liquid as possible. Return the zucchini to the mixing bowl.

2. Stir into zucchini shreds dill, scallions, parsley, carrot, onion, soy milk, olive oil, and lemon juice. Form a well in the center and sift in the flour, chickpea flour, cornstarch, baking powder, sea salt, and pepper and stir just enough to combine and moisten the ingredients, but don't overmix to prevent tough pancakes. Heat a 10-inch cast-iron skillet or griddle over medium heat; the skillet is ready when a few drops of water flicked onto the surface sizzle. Spray surface generously with olive oil cooking spray.

3. Drop ⅓ cup of batter onto the skillet and use the back of a measuring cup or spoon to spread the batter about ¼ inch thick; add one or two more pancakes depending on the size of the skillet, taking care not to crowd the skillet. While the pancakes are cooking, rotate the skillet a few times to evenly distribute the heat under the pan; cook the pancakes until the edges look dry and some bubbles try to push through the center of the pancake, about 3½ to 4½ minutes. Use a wide spatula to carefully flip each pancake over and cook another 2 minutes on the other side until pancakes are golden brown.

4. Slide pancakes onto serving dishes and serve with **Cashew Yogurt Sauce** and harissa. If you're serving all of the pancakes at the same time, stack them onto a large plate and keep warm in a 200°F oven; cover the pancakes with foil if not serving within 45 minutes. Pancakes can be made a day ahead and reheated on a skillet.

Homemade soft corn tortillas

MAKES TWELVE 5-INCH TORTILLAS

In my book about vegan Latin cuisine, Viva Vegan!, I said that if you can lift a bag of masa harina, you can make soft and toasty homemade corn tortillas in minutes. It's still true today, so don't delay and make some already! They're a world apart from store-bought tortillas, and masa harina is easy to use even for beginner chefs. Mexican masa harina is essential for making tortillas; regular American cornmeal won't work.

Use either an inexpensive aluminum tortilla press or just a rolling pin to shape tortillas. They cook even faster than any flatbread, making a breakfast of warm tortillas possible on busy weekday mornings. Tacos are elevated to gourmet fare with homemade tortillas, and even humble rice and beans get a boost of excitement when partnered with 'em.

1½ cups white or yellow Mexican masa harina

1¼ cups warm water

¼ teaspoon salt

1. In a mixing bowl combine masa harina, water, and salt. If the dough feels a little dry, stream in a little more water; if too moist, sift in a tablespoon or two of masa harina. Knead dough for 2 minutes or until smooth.

2. Separate dough into twelve equal pieces and roll into smooth balls. Cover dough balls with a damp, clean kitchen towel. Heat a cast-iron skillet or griddle over medium-high heat. Do not oil the skillet. The pan is ready when a few drops of water flicked onto its surface sizzle on contact.

3. If using a tortilla press, line both the bottom and top plates with plastic wrap. If using a rolling pin, fold a 14-inch piece of waxed paper in half. To shape a tortilla with a press, put a ball of dough in the center of the bottom plate, then press down with the top plate. Gently squeeze together the handles to press the tortilla into a thin circle less than ⅛ inch thick, and slowly, carefully peel the tortilla off of the plastic wrap and drop immediately into the preheated skillet. If using a rolling pin, roll the dough between the folded waxed paper into a circle less than an ⅛ inch thick, rotating the tortilla a few degrees during the rolling process to help shape an even circle, then transfer to the hot skillet to bake.

4. Cook tortillas on each side for about 30 to 40 seconds, flipping once, or until surface of tortilla feels firm but not overly dry; watch carefully and don't overcook the tortillas. Wrap hot tortillas in a clean kitchen towel; corn tortillas toughen as they cool, so it's imperative you keep them warm. Cook the remaining dough balls, then stack the hot tortillas on top of one another and keep them well covered.

5. Serve hot tortillas immediately. If the tortillas cool, reheat by warming in the pan for 20 to 30 seconds. Store leftovers tightly wrapped in the fridge.

coriander rye muffins

MAKES 12 MUFFINS

There's a traditional Russian sourdough rye bread with an intriguing name, borodinsky, *that I grew to love when I once lived in south Brooklyn. The tiny Russian bakery would run out of these much demanded, earthy loaves fast: sturdy, rich, and subtly sweet,* borodinsky *tickles the tongue with a dash of whole toasted coriander seeds.*

Sometimes I want that borodinsky, but I can't wait for a yeasted bread or the Q train ride to Brooklyn. These sleek muffins are my borodinsky quick fix: lightly sweetened, dense, and moist with rye flour, and baked while a hearty soup is simmering. These are not dessert muffins (but are a wholesome breakfast)—they're destined for greatness alongside a cabbage, beet, or other northern European soup.

3 tablespoons coriander seeds
1¼ cups plain unsweetened soy or almond milk
4 teaspoons apple cider vinegar
3 tablespoons ground flax seed
1¼ cups rye flour
¾ cups whole wheat flour or white whole wheat flour
1 tablespoon cocoa powder
2½ teaspoons baking powder
½ teaspoon baking soda
¾ teaspoon salt
¼ cup canola oil
⅓ cup molasses

1. Preheat oven to 350°F and generously grease a 12-cup muffin pan. In a small skillet over low heat toast the coriander seeds for 1 ½ minutes. Set aside 1 tablespoon of coriander seeds for a topping, then pour the remainder into a large mixing bowl.

2. In a 2-cup liquid measuring cup whisk together the soy milk, vinegar, and flax seed and set aside for 2 minutes. Meanwhile in the mixing bowl with the coriander seeds stir together rye flour, whole wheat flour, cocoa powder, baking powder, baking soda, and salt, then form a well in the center. Return to the soy milk mixture and whisk in the oil and the molasses, then pour into the center of the dry ingredients.

3. Use a rubber spatula to stir together only just enough to moisten the dry ingredients, then divide the batter among the 12 muffin cups (an ice cream scooper works great for this). Sprinkle the tops of the muffins with reserved coriander seeds. Bake for 26 to 32 minutes or until a toothpick inserted into the center of a muffin comes out clean (a few moist crumbs are okay). Remove from the oven and let cool for 10 minutes, then remove the muffins from the pan and move them to a cooling rack to complete cooling.

With Raisins or Prunes: Stir ½ cup dark raisins or finely chopped prunes into the batter.

your International House of Dinner crepes

MAKES EIGHT 9-TO 10-INCH CREPES

If you can make pancakes, you can certainly make crepes! Crepes stuffed with a saucy filling scream elegant dinner but are also relaxed weeknight meals or brunches. With some planning, any of the sautés and stews in this book are candidates for fun, savory crepes (see variations below). Make the crepes on a Sunday afternoon, wrap them tightly, and they'll keep in the fridge all week long for spontaneous dinners or simply snacking with a smear of almond butter or jam.

> 1 ½ cups plain soy milk or almond milk
> ½ cup water
> ¾ cup all-purpose flour
> ⅓ cup chickpea flour
> 1 tablespoon cornstarch
> 2 teaspoons olive oil
> ½ teaspoon salt
> Cooking oil spray or vegetable oil for cooking the crepes
> Softened nonhydrogenated vegan margarine, for more buttery flavor (optional)

1. In a blender, pulse together all of the ingredients except the cooking oil spray/vegetable oil/margarine into a smooth, thin batter. Pour into a plastic container, cover and chill in the refrigerator for at least an hour or overnight.

2. When ready to bake, give the batter a good stir or shake. Preheat a 9-to 10-inch crepe pan or well-seasoned cast-iron skillet to medium-high heat. The skillet is ready when a few drops of water flicked onto the pan sizzle immediately. Generously spray the insides of the pan with plenty of cooking oil spray. For additional buttery flavor dab a silicon pastry brush into softened margarine and brush along the bottom and sides of pan.

3. Ladle ⅓ cup of batter into a 9-inch pan and up to ½ cup of batter for a 10-inch pan. Pour the batter into the center of the pan. As the batter starts to sizzle immediately tilt the pan in a circular motion to help spread a thin layer of batter to the edges of your pan. Use your wrist to tilt the pan and if there's still some batter left, continue to tilt the pan as the last of the batter spreads and sets. Your first crepe won't be the best, but as you continue to bake them they'll look better and you'll cook them faster.

4. Bake the crepe until the top looks dry and the edges appear firm, about 1½ to 2½ minutes. Gently run the spatula along the edges and underneath the crepe to loosen it. Peek under the crepe; it should be golden with a few light brown spots. If not, release it back into the pan and let it bake another minute. When ready, carefully flip the crepe over and cook on the other side for 30 seconds. Slide the crepe onto a regular-sized dinner plate. Brush a little more margarine or spray oil onto the pan and bake another crepe; if crepes start to stick, give another spray of nonstick cooking spray. If bits of batter collect on the pan or the pan seems too oily, quickly swirl the crumpled paper towel across the surface to remove crumbs. For even cooking of the crepes, occasionally rotate the pan on the stovetop to help redistribute the heat.

5. Stack baked crepes on top of each other. If not serving immediately, cover the entire batch with plastic wrap and store it in the refrigerator. To reheat a cold crepe, warm on a preheated pan for 1 to 2 minutes until hot.

A UNITED NATION UNDER (AND INSIDE) CREPES

Crepes bring the world together, or at least make a good encasing for the following. Use a rounded ⅓ cup as a general guide for filling 1 crepe:

Red Wine–Braised Leeks and Mushroom Crepes (page 265): spoon extra wine sauce on top of crepes.

Gyro Roasted Seitan Crepes (page 253): drizzle with *Cucumber Tzatziki* (page 66).

Beer-Bathed Seitan Crepes (page 156, without the frites): spoon extra sauce on top of the crepes.

Lebanese Eggplant Moussaka Stew Crepes (page 204): drizzle with *Green Tahini Sauce* (page 63).

Potato Cashew Crepes (use filling from the *Chile Potato Rolls in Homemade Paratha Bread*, page 110): top with *Cilantro Chutney* (page 61).

very Nice chickpea crepes (French socca)

MAKES 4 TO 5 LARGE CREPES ABOUT 11 INCHES WIDE

American chef in Paris David Lebovitz, while not vegan, knows his socca: a sleek-pan roasted chickpea crepe that's effortlessly vegan and a delightful snack, a specialty in Nice and typically served with a crisp glass of rosé wine. This recipe is an adaptation of his excellent recipe: it's delicate and delicious with a sprinkle of sea salt, olive oil and a twist of black pepper. Or enliven it with onions, olive, or flecks of sundried tomatoes (see variations below). Eating these thin, crisp socca is like nibbling on hummus in cracker form, and if this isn't enough to win your vegan affections, then I don't know what is.

Socca are baked in the oven, unlike most crepes. As you'll be working with very high temperatures and a heavy pan, it's important to have all of your ingredients (batter, flavorings, etc.) easily accessible and right near the oven. This will go a long way toward a a less-stressful socca-making experience.

> 1 cup chickpea flour
> 1 cup plus 2 tablespoons of water
> 2 tablespoons olive oil
> ½ teaspoon each dried thyme, marjoram, and rosemary or 1 tablespoon of any Herbes de Provence blend
> ½ teaspoon sea salt
> Olive oil for brushing the pan
> Sea salt and freshly cracked pepper

A super-hot oven makes good socca, but a pre-heated broiler makes even better socca. Preheat the oven broiler on high for at least 5 minutes to get really hot. Place the pan with socca batter directly under the broiler flame and watch it carefully. Broil each socca for 2 to 2½ minutes. Take note on exactly how long it takes to bake the socca and have slightly charred, crisp edges. Cooking socca this way is super-fast, but to prevent any sad burned socca, no wandering away from the oven while broiling!

1. Pulse in a blender the chickpea flour, water, olive oil, dried herbs or herb blend, and salt to form a thin batter. Pour into a container, cover, and let stand at room temperature for an hour.

2. When ready to prepare, move an oven rack to the top section of the oven (or position it closest to where the heating element in the oven is located) and preheat the oven to 475°F. Place an ungreased 10-to 12-inch cast-iron pan in the top part of the oven to preheat. When the oven has reached 475°F (about 20 minutes for an average home oven), stir the batter, remove the pan from the oven and brush the insides generously with olive oil. Pour about ¼ cup of batter in the pan and swirl to coat the bottom with a thin layer of batter. Use more batter for the next crepe if it doesn't quite cover the pan, and stir the batter before pouring each crepe.

3. Bake the socca for 3 to 5 minutes on the top rack of the oven. The socca is done when dry on the edges and with dark brown spots on top. Remove from the oven immediately and use a bent metal spatula to gently pry the socca from the pan. Slide the socca onto a cutting board.

4. To serve, slice the socca into wedges. Drizzle with a teaspoon of olive oil and sprinkle with salt and a twist of black pepper. Serve hot, making fresh socca while nibbling on the previous batch.

While socca is often simply seasoned, a dash of Herbes de Provence dried herb blend is an elegant addition. Look for these Provence-style herb blends that often feature thyme, marjoram, rosemary, and even lavender among many other herbs.

Crepe Conquest!

Making good crepes is like being in a band; more practice means better crepes and increased crepe confidence. Also helpful: use the right pan. My favorite pan is a well-seasoned carbon steel crepe pan. Unlike standard cast-iron skillets, carbon steel is lighter and easier to tilt when spreading the batter inside the pan. A seasoned cast-iron skillet comes close second; requiring more muscle to tilt, this skillet transforms ordinary crepe baking into an iron-man workout. Third is a nonstick pan, but these still require a generous amount of cooking oil spray and margarine for best results (unlike a well-seasoned carbon steel or cast-iron pan). Inexperienced crepe makers should avoid stainless-steel pans for baking crepes; you'll have to use *a lot* of oil to prevent sticking.

Whatever pan you use, preheating it before adding the batter will help prevent sticking, so preheat it for at least 5 minutes.

Other helpful things: a silicon basting brush (that can withstand contact with a hot pan), nonstick cooking spray, a crumpled paper towel for wiping the crepe pan or skillet, and a long, thin, bent spatula (like the kind used to frost cakes) for releasing crepes from the pan.

Onion Socca: Peel 1 small red onion and slice into rounds as thin as possible, ⅛th inch or less. Scatter a few slices of onion on top of the socca before baking.

Tomato, Olive, and Garlic Socca: Stir 2 tablespoons each of diced, pitted Kalamata olives, sun-dried tomatoes and 2 cloves of minced garlic into the socca batter. Stir each time before ladling into the pan.

Indian Socca: Chickpea flour crepes are a natural fit in Indian cuisine. Stir in one or more of the following into the batter: ½ teaspoon of ground cumin, coriander, garam masala, or curry powder. Scatter a tablespoon of chopped cilantro on each baked, hot socca.

Ethiopian Savory Crepes (injera style)

MAKES EIGHT 10-INCH CREPES

Presenting my hack of injera, a crepe-like bread that's a must alongside Ethiopian dishes. These mild, chewy crepes are by no means authentic, but they go perfectly with any Ethiopian recipe and are the ideal eating utensils for scooping up sauces. Teff flour is authentic to real injera and can be found in many health food stores, but more common buckwheat flour adds a similar earthy color and flavor to this easy, homemade injera substitute.

Serve injera as a "plate" (but on top of a real dinner plate) with dollops of different stews on top or rolled up and served on the side with a selection of stews. Or folded into quarters like a kerchief, the method is still the same: tear off a piece of injera crepe and use it to pinch or scoop up morsels of food. For general tips on making crepes, read **Crepe Conquest!** on the previous page before cooking the injera.

Injera are baked on one side only, don't flip over. Occasionally check the bottom of a cooked injera to make sure you're not over-browning it; the underside of the injera should be relatively pale. If they're getting too brown, turn down the heat slightly. If injera stick to the bottom of the skillet, use more nonstick spray. I've had the most success with a well-seasoned, evenly heated cast-iron skillet.

> 2 cups warm water
> ½ teaspoon active yeast
> 1 tablespoon apple cider vinegar
> ½ cup unbleached all-purpose flour
> ¼ cup teff flour or buckwheat flour
> ½ teaspoon sea salt
> ⅛ teaspoon baking soda
> Vegetable oil for cooking the crepes

1. Pour 2 cups of warm water into a mixing bowl and sprinkle with the active yeast; set aside for 10 minutes or until it looks foamy. Stir in the vinegar, then sift in the remaining ingredients except oil. Vigorously whisk into a smooth batter, cover with plastic wrap, and set aside for 1 hour in a warm location.

2. Preheat a 9-to 10-inch seasoned cast-iron or nonstick skillet over medium-high heat for 5 minutes. Have nearby a large dinner plate and a spatula.

3. Lightly spray the skillet with nonstick cooking spray before baking each injera. The skillet should be hot, and a drop of water flicked onto the surface should sizzle immediately on contact. Whisk the batter each time before baking an injera.

4. For each injera use a generous ¼ cup per crepe for a 9-inch pan, or about ⅓ cup for a 10-inch pan. Start pouring the batter on the outside of the hot griddle about half an inch from the inside and work in a spiral toward the center. Tilt the pan to run batter over any holes in the crepe, and immediately cover the top of the pan with the loose-fitting lid. Bake the injera for 2 to 3 minutes; the injera is done when the top is no longer shiny or wet and feels firm to the touch. Use a bent spatula or your fingers to pick up the injera and transfer it to a plate. Cover immediately with a clean kitchen towel or plastic wrap.

5. Stack injera on top of each other. Keep them covered with a towel to keep them moist and soft. Injera taste best when allowed to cool slightly and can be eaten room temperature or slightly warm. To reheat injera wrap in moist paper towels and microwave for 25 to 30 seconds or until soft and pliable.

Golden coconut crepes (vietnamese Banh xeo)

MAKES SIX 9-INCH PANCAKES

My *vegan international house of pancakes would feature these lovelies in 10-foot neon letters. Bahn xeo are neon-yellow coconut milk crepes with savory fillings baked into the batter, then folded like an omelet. Onions and bean sprouts are the standard fare that take well to additions; my favorites are*

baby spinach, fresh mushrooms, and seasoned tofu. Pouring sweet and sour **Mock Nuoc Cham** sauce (page 67) over a sizzling hot crepe is pure bliss.

The batter makes a lot of crepes, so it's easy to keep leftover batter and filling in the refrigerator for midweek banh xeo breaks.

CREPE BATTER

½ cup cornstarch

1½ cups rice flour

1 cup water

One 14-ounce can coconut milk, regular or reduced fat

1 teaspoon turmeric powder

1 teaspoon ground coriander

½ teaspoon ground white pepper

¾ teaspoon sea salt

FILLING

2 cups white button mushrooms, cleaned and sliced ½ inch thick

8 ounces purchased or *Savory Baked Tofu* (page 50), sliced into matchsticks

2 tablespoons soy sauce or Thai thin soy sauce (see page 19)

2 tablespoons lime juice

2 teaspoons brown sugar

2 fresh Thai or serrano chilies, sliced into paper-thin circles

2 large shallots, peeled and sliced paper thin

½ teaspoon ground coriander

¼ teaspoon ground white pepper

1 large yellow onion, peeled, cut in half, and sliced into ¼-inch-thin half-moons

3 cups baby spinach, washed, patted dry, and torn into bite-size pieces

2 cups mung bean sprouts, rinsed and drained

¼ cup peanut oil or vegetable or nonstick cooking spray

GARNISHES

12 large, clean red leaf or romaine lettuce leaves

Handful of chopped cilantro

Mock Nuoc Cham (page 67)

Your favorite Asian chili garlic sauce

Hoisin sauce

1. In a blender jar pulse together all of the batter ingredients until smooth and chill the batter for 30 minutes.

2. In a large mixing bowl toss together the mushrooms, tofu, soy sauce, lime juice, brown sugar, chilies, shallots, coriander, and pepper; keep this bowl of filling near the stovetop as you work. Arrange slices of onion, spinach, and sprouts on a dish near your work space. Heat a 9-to 10-inch cast-iron skillet or crepe pan over high heat for 6 minutes, then drizzle in 2 teaspoons of the oil or spray pan with nonstick cooking spray.

3. Whisk the batter and ladle ⅓ cup to ½ cup into the hot pan, swirling the pan to cover the bottom with batter. For each crepe, scatter about 2 to 3 tablespoons of marinated mushrooms and tofu on top of the cooking crepe, then scatter with about 2 tablespoons of sliced onions, ¼ cup of sprouts and ¼ cup of spinach leaves, then cook for 1 minute.

4. Reduce heat to a low flame, place a large lid on top of the pan and cook covered for 3 to 5 minutes. The crepe is done when edges are dry and bottom is brown and crisp: use a thin spatula to separate the crepe from the pan and take a peak underneath to check doneness. If it needs another minute, cook the crepe with the pan uncovered.

5. Using the spatula fold the crepe in half like an omelet, flip it over, and cook 30 to 45 seconds. Slide the crepe onto a plate, scatter a little chopped cilantro on top and serve immediately. To eat, tear pieces of hot crepe, wrap in a lettuce leaf and dip into nuoc cham sauce, chili sauce, and/or hoisin sauce.

Filo Samosas

MAKES 14 OR MORE BAKED SAMOSAS

Samosas, *potato-pea-stuffed Indian savory pastries, are perhaps the most popular of Indian street food morsels, but when dining at home I like to sidestep the heavy, greasy fried shell for something lighter. Enter flakey filo dough to the rescue! Baking is a mess-free alternative to frying, and while these crisp triangles may look Mediterranean, the golden filling is all Indian. It's possible to cut down on the fat further and use cooking oil spray on the filo. Serve hot with* **Tamarind Date Chutney** *(page 59),* **Cilantro Chutney** *(page 61), or both!*

Ten 14 x 18-inch sheets filo dough
(preferably #10 thicker "country-style" filo), thawed if frozen
Cooking oil spray or vegetable oil (about ⅓ cup)

POTATO PEA CASHEW FILLING
2 pounds russet potatoes, peeled and diced into 1-inch pieces
2 tablespoons vegetable oil

1 teaspoon black mustard seeds
½-inch piece peeled ginger, minced
2 to 4 hot green chilies (Thai or serrano), finely chopped (remove seeds for a milder filling)
¼ cup chopped cashews
1 yellow onion, peeled and finely chopped
1 tablespoon *Garam Masala* (page 39) or store-bought garam masala
½ teaspoon ground turmeric
1 teaspoon salt or to taste
1 cup frozen green peas
2 tablespoons lime juice
½ cup chopped cilantro
A few twists of freshly ground pepper to taste

1. Prepare the filling first: place the potatoes in a large saucepan, cover with 3 inches of cold water, and bring to a boil over medium-high heat. Boil the potato for 15 minutes or until tender. Reserve 1 cup of the cooking liquid, drain the rest, and set the potatoes aside.

2. Preheat the vegetable oil in a wok or deep, 12-inch skillet heat over medium heat. Add the mustard seeds, cover the wok, and when the seeds finish popping, stir in the chilies and ginger. Stir-fry for 1 minute, then add the cashews and fry another minute, then add the onion and stir-fry for 3 to 4 minutes or until the onion is soft. Add the cooked potato, garam masala, turmeric, salt, and about ½ cup of reserved cooking liquid. With a wooden spoon, mash the potato into the frying onions and spices, stirring and mashing the potato until the mixture is golden and the filling resembles chunky, moist mashed potatoes. If the potato mixture seems overly dry, dribble in a little extra reserved cooking water. Stir in the peas, lime juice, and cilantro. Taste

the mixture and season with freshly ground pepper and more salt and lime juice if needed. Remove from heat, transfer filling to mixing bowl and set aside to cool enough to handle.

3. Follow the filo-handling instructions for baklava on page 329, then cut the filo sheets lengthwise into three long strips about 4½ inches wide by 18 inches long. Keep covered with plastic wrap until ready to assemble the samosas.

4. When ready to assemble samosas preheat oven to 375°F. Line baking sheets with parchment paper. To assemble a samosa, lay a strip of filo with the short end near you and brush or spray the entire length with oil. Scoop about ¼ cup of filling on the end of the strip closest to you, then fold the filo away from you into a triangle. Continue to fold the filo up and away until the entire thing is folded into a triangle (see page 254). Spray or brush the top of the triangle with oil, then carefully transfer to the baking sheet. Continue to assemble samosas; you may have some extra filo dough left over.

5. Bake the samosas for 28 to 30 minutes or until filo is golden and edges begin to brown, then serve hot with chutney. To reheat, wrap in foil and bake at 350°F for 8 to 10 minutes. Store leftovers chilled in a tightly covered container.

Beans and Rice corn-crusted Empanadas

MAKES ABOUT 20 SMALL EMPANADAS

These plump little-corn crusted pastries are typical of the empanadas of Venezuela or Colombia. The crust is made with masarepa flour, a kind of specially prepared corn flour used in Venezuela and Colombia; look for this where Latin American groceries are sold. White or yellow masarepa flour works fine; look for bags of masarepa flour labeled "for arepas" and know you're buying the right product.

*The easiest way to fill these little empanadas is to use a combination of rice and beans (especially leftovers!); you can also shake things up by adding a recipe of **Chorizo Tempeh Crumbles** (page 52). Serve these with **Indian Cilantro Chutney** (page 61), which is very similar to South American–style cilantro salsas, or your favorite hot sauce.*

While frying creates the most flavorful, tender crust, these can also be baked with good results.

This recipe uses masarepa flour, a precooked corn flour that's used in Venezuelan and Colombian recipes that's different from Mexican masa harina flour. It can be found in either white or yellow varieties, has a mild flavor, and cannot be substituted with either Mexican masa harina or regular corn meal. Goya sells their own repackaged brand that's commonly found in American grocery stores.

2 cups white or yellow masarepa corn flour

½ teaspoon salt

2¼ cups of warm water

½ recipe of *Colombian Coconut Lentil Rice* (page 314) or *Island Brown Rice and Peas* (page 313), chilled

Vegetable oil for deep-frying

1. Prepare the dough first: in a large bowl combine masarepa flour and salt. Form a well in the center of the flour and pour in the warm water. Use your hands to mix the water into the flour to form a soft dough, then knead with your fingers, eliminating any hard lumps. If dough feels a little too dry or stiff, work in a tablespoon of warm water at a time. The arepa dough should have the consistency of firm mashed potatoes. Cover the bowl with plastic wrap until you're ready to assemble the empanadas.

2. When you're ready to prepare the empanadas, pour about 2½ inches of oil into a 10-inch-wide heavy pot with walls at least 4 inches high; a cast-iron Dutch oven is the best possible pot to deep-fry anything in. Preheat the oil for at least 8 minutes over medium-high heat. The oil is ready when a little ball of dough immediately sizzles when lowered into the oil.

3. While oil is heating, assemble the empanadas: spread a large piece of plastic wrap onto a work surface; only plastic wrap can effectively keep the dough from sticking. Have nearby a rolling pin and a small bowl 4 inches in diameter.

4. Take a piece of dough about 2 inches wide, roll it into a ball, and place it on the plastic wrap. Fold the plastic wrap over the dough and press down with your palm to flatten it slightly. Use the rolling pin to roll the dough into a circle ¼ inch thick. Scoop a heaping tablespoon of filling in the center of the circle. Now, holding onto the plastic under the dough, fold it over the filling to create a half-moon shape.

5. Get ready to be amazed: take the bowl or mug and press down on top of the semi-circle, lining up the edge of the bowl with the outer curve of the half moon. Firmly press down into the dough; this does the double duty of sealing the empanada tightly *and* trimming away the excess dough, all at the same time! Lift up the bowl and you'll see a perfectly shaped half-moon pocket. Carefully remove the plastic wrap. Peel away the excess dough and knead the scraps into the remaining dough.

6. Carefully lower the empanada directly into the hot oil and fry for 2½ to 3 minutes per side, or until the empanada is golden and firm. Use a metal mesh skimmer to transfer empanadas to a dinner plate lined with crumpled brown paper or paper towels to drain. Continue to shape and fry empanadas, but don't fry more than four at a time to prevent overcrowding the pot and cooling down the oil (too-cool frying oil may make the empanadas soft and greasy). Serve empanadas with *Cilantro Chutney* (page 61), but take care biting into a piping-hot empanada!

7. To bake empanadas, preheat the oven to 425°F and line a baking sheet with parchment paper. Place empanadas on the baking sheet, brush or spray with a little oil, and bake for 25 to 30 minutes until the crust is firm and the edges are golden. Flip the empanadas over halfway through baking.

Also look for masarepa flour where Venezuelan, Colombian or Caribbean groceries are sold. The package should mention "for arepas" and be a product of either Colombia or Venezuela.

Chorizo R&B Empanadas: Stir in 1 recipe of *Chorizo Tempeh Crumbles* (page 52) into any of the rice and beans fillings.

jamaican curry seitan patties

MAKES ABOUT SIXTEEN 4-TO 6-INCH PASTRIES

When I first moved to Brooklyn and was introduced to Christie's Jamaican Patties in Park Slope, I made great friends with their excellent veggie patties. As great as they are, I imagined how excellent a vegan version of their famous beef patty could be. Years later, this patty brimming with shredded seitan, a little bit of potato, and lots of spice satisfies that longing. These sunny yellow pastry pockets are to be savored with your favorite Scotch Bonnet hot sauce and a tropical fruit smoothie any time of year for a warm breezy island feeling.

DOUGH

2 cups all-purpose flour, plus more for rolling
1 cup whole wheat flour
1 teaspoon turmeric powder
¼ teaspoon baking powder
1½ teaspoons salt
10 tablespoons chilled nonhydrogenated shortening
¾ cup or more cold water (drop a few ice cubes in the water to keep it very cold)

SEITAN FILLING

½ pound white potatoes, peeled and diced into ½-inch cubes
3 cutlets of *Seitan Coriander Cutlets* (page 49), or two 8-ounce packages store-bought seitan (or enough for 2½ cups when ground)
3 tablespoons vegetable oil
1 large yellow onion, peeled and finely diced
½ cup finely chopped shallots
1 or more hot chile peppers, finely minced, or ½ teaspoon or more cayenne pepper
4 teaspoons *Jamaican Curry Powder* (page 40), or store-bought
2 teaspoons dried thyme
½ teaspoon ground cumin
¼ teaspoon ground allspice
1 teaspoon sea salt
⅔ cup vegetable broth
Ground black pepper
¼ cup plain soy or almond milk for brushing patties

To ensure your dough stays tender, handle it as little as possible to avoid overdeveloping the gluten in the flour. Press (don't knead) together the dough after you moisten it and use as few rolling pin strokes as possible when rolling out the dough. I find that making a few long strokes, instead of several shorter ones, when rolling out the dough helps prevent the dough from getting tough.

1. Prepare the pastry first, if desired up to a week before making the patties. In a food processor pulse together both the flours, turmeric, baking powder, and salt. Pulse in the shortening a few tablespoons at a time until the mixture looks sandy. Stream in the cold water, pulsing until the dough pulls away from the sides of the processor; you don't

JAMAICAN CURRY SEITAN PATTIES

have to use all of the water. Transfer the dough to a work surface, divide in two, and pat into discs about 1 inch thick. Wrap in plastic and chill for 2 hours or overnight.

Also it's helpful to keep the dough as cold as possible when working with it. If your kitchen is very warm, work the dough in batches and keep any unused portions chilled until you're ready to use it. You can store for up to a week in the refrigerator. Or roll and cut out the dough circles, stack them between pieces of waxed paper, and keep them chilled for up to 2 weeks. The filling can be made 2 days in advance and chilled until ready to use.

2. To shape the pastry, roll a chilled dough disk on a floured surface into a circle less than ¼ inch thick. Use a 4-to 6-inch bowl as a guide to cut out circles; stack the circles between small sheets of waxed paper. Gather the scraps and reroll once more to cut out as many circles as possible. Keep the pastry tightly wrapped and chilled until ready to use.

3. For the filling, place the potatoes in a large saucepan, cover with 3 inches of cold water, and bring to a boil over medium-high heat. Cook the potatoes for 10 minutes or until tender, drain, and set aside. In a food processor grind the seitan into fine crumbles.

4. Heat the vegetable oil in a deep, 12-inch skillet heat over medium heat. Stir in onion, shallots, and chile and fry until onions are soft and juicy, about 4 minutes. Stir in the ground seitan, fry for 2 minutes then sprinkle with the curry powder, thyme, cumin, allspice and sea salt and fry for another minute. Add the potatoes, then pour the vegetable broth over the seitan. Simmer and stir constantly for 2 minutes until the liquid has been absorbed but the seitan is still moist and no remaining browned bits are on the bottom of the pan. Remove from the heat, let cool for a few minutes, and taste mixture, adding salt

and black pepper to taste if necessary. Set aside until cool enough to comfortably handle. When ready to assemble patties preheat oven to 375°F. Line baking sheets with parchment paper. Have handy the chilled pastry circles, soy milk, and a pastry brush.

5. To assemble a patty, take a pastry circle, gently stretch it slightly outwards by its edges, and lightly brush with soy milk. Scoop a generous ¼ cup of filling, adjusting the amount of filling depending on how many circles you've rolled. Place filling into the center of the circle and leave about ¼ inch of space along the edge of the dough. It's important to make sure filling doesn't spill over; the wet filling can make crimping the edges a little tricky. Fold the pastry over the filling to create a half-moon shape. Press down to seal the edges, then press the tines of a fork into the edges of the patty to secure the seal. Carefully transfer to the baking sheet, brush with plenty of soy milk, and make more patties.

6. Bake the patties for 28 to 32 minutes or until the crust is golden and edges are lightly browned. Filling will be extremely hot out of the oven, so if possible cool for 5 minutes before serving. To reheat wrap in foil and bake at 350°F for 8 to 10 minutes. Store leftovers tightly wrapped and refrigerated.

CHAPTER 8

Asian Noodles to Mediterranean Pasta

I could write something about thanking Marco Polo for getting his butt to China and discovering pasta, but besides not being accurate (in regards to the history of pasta, that is), this chapter has a healthy sampling of Asian noodles that are both authentic and radically veganized: bountiful noodle soups such as pho and silky sesame ramen, or the outrageously popular Thai noodle stir-fries of Pad Kee Mao or Pad See Ew. There are essential Mediterranean pasta dishes, too, including my favorite application of pesto with potatoes (modest in oil, big in taste) and the creamy-topped, cinnamon-scented centerpiece of your next dinner party, a vegan spin on pastichio, Greece's answer to the ever popular dish lasagna.

curry noodle soup with oyster mushrooms (curry laksa)

MAKES 4 REALLY BIG SERVINGS OR 6 SMALLER ONES

Re-laksa, this veggieful version of curry laksa, *the famous Malaysian rice noodle soup with a lush, fiery coconut curry broth, can be tailored to your tastes: make it rich or light, spicy or mellow. All versions of this soup should include a generous topping of fresh herbs and crunchy sprouts (or slivered daikon or shredded cabbage.)*

Laksa should have some heat, but reduce the amount of cayenne pepper and chilies according to your tastes. The chile-pepper phobic should start with one; chile fanatics, go for the whole amount. For best results, have all the ingredients chopped and ready to go before frying the curry paste. Alternately, reduced-fat coconut milk and extra chilies make for a spicy light broth that's exactly what you need when recovering from a winter cold.

If you're interested in trying out brown rice noodles, this soup is the ideal springboard.

For a very smooth curry paste, add 1 to 2 tablespoons of coconut milk to the paste and pulse as smooth as possible. The turmeric in this curry paste may lightly stain the bowl of your food processor, so if you live or die by the good looks of your food processor, hold off on adding the turmeric until the frying of the paste in the soup pot. For a faster

soup, prepare the curry paste in advance and store in a tightly covered container in the refrigerator for up to 3 days.

LAKSA CURRY PASTE

- 2 teaspoons coriander seeds
- 2 teaspoons fennel seeds
- 1 teaspoon cayenne pepper or 6 or more dried red Thai chilies (or use ¼ teaspoon cayenne or 2 chilies for less spicy soup)
- 2 teaspoons turmeric
- 4 large shallots, peeled and roughly chopped
- 2 stalks fresh lemongrass (see page 17) or ¼ cup prepared lemongrass
- 4 cloves garlic, peeled
- 3 tablespoons chopped unroasted cashews
- 1½-inch piece peeled ginger, chopped
- ½ inch fresh galangal root (see page 16), peeled and chopped (optional but very good)
- 2 to 6 fresh Thai chilies or green chile peppers
- 1 teaspoon salt

NOODLES AND SOUP

- One 10-ounce package rice noodles
- 2 tablespoons vegetable oil
- 10 ounces oyster mushrooms, ends trimmed and sliced into ½-inch-wide pieces
- One 14-ounce can coconut milk, regular or reduced fat
- 5 cups vegetable or vegetarian chicken-flavored broth
- ½ teaspoon salt or to taste (use less if the broth is very salty)
- One 6- to 8-ounce package fried tofu puffs (found in the refrigerated section of

many Asian markets), cut into 1-inch pieces

4 cups roughly chopped spinach or bok choy

3 cups bean sprouts or thinly sliced Napa cabbage

1½ cups roughly chopped cilantro leaves

¼ cup roughly chopped mint leaves

1. Make the curry paste first: in a small skillet over medium heat toast the coriander, fennel seeds, and dried red Thai chilies (if using) until fragrant. Pour in a spice grinder, add the turmeric, and pulse until finely ground. In a food processor pulse this spice mixture along with the rest of the curry paste ingredients into a smooth paste, stopping to scrape the sides of the food processor bowl often.

2. Boil the rice noodles according to package directions, drain and rinse well with cold water. Set aside to drain. In a 3-quart soup pot heat the oil over medium-low heat, add the curry paste and fry, stirring frequently for 3 minutes. Add the mushrooms, stir to coat with curry and fry for 2 minutes. Stir in the coconut milk, vegetable broth, and salt. Increase heat to medium, partially cover, and simmer for 20 minutes.

3. While soup is simmering distribute noodles into 4 large, deep, 1-quart serving bowls (or 6 smaller but deep bowls). Arrange the tofu puffs on top of the noodles. Three minutes before the soup is done, stir the spinach into the broth and cook until wilted but still bright green. Ladle the hot soup on top of the noodles and evenly distribute mushrooms, greens, and broth among the bowls. Top each soup with sprouts, cilantro, and mint and serve immediately with big spoons and chopsticks!

Extra-Creamy Curry Laksa: I love customizing this soup as needed, such as adding a touch of creamed coconut for a luxurious broth. Creamed coconut sold in blocks is hard when cold but becomes

Galangal & Rau Ram

These two Southeast Asian ingredients are somewhat difficult to find, but if you do stumble upon them use them in this soup:

Galangal looks similar to ginger and has its own pungent, aromatic character. Use 1 to 2 teaspoons of chopped fresh galangal in the curry paste.

Rau ram/rau rahm, also called Vietnamese coriander, is sometimes used in laksa. Try it by adding 3 tablespoons of the finely chopped herb to the curry paste.

soft when warmed. Look for creamed coconut that's 100 percent pure coconut without any dairy added. To prepare creamed coconut, place ¼ to ⅓ cup of creamed coconut in a mixing bowl and pour on ½ cup of hot curry broth. Stir to emulsify the creamed coconut into a smooth sauce, then stir back into the soup before adding the greens and tofu puffs.

tom yum noodle soup

SERVES 4

Tom yum soup, *that crazy popular hot and sour Thai soup, is refreshingly simple to make with a combination of authentic Thai ingredients plus a few substitutions. It may not taste like your favorite restaurant's tom yum, but it will satisfy cravings. Or it might even be better! The light broth is bursting with abundant lime, fresh chilies, lemongrass with a*

touch of sweetness; add some Pad Thai rice noodles and this transforms into a whole meal. Tom yum is a wonderful soup to master, easy to make, low-calorie, and a friend to stuffy sinuses in need of relief from mid-winter chills.

The amount of fresh hot red chilies in this soup is entirely up to you. Chile pepper champions, go for the maximum amount. A hot food novice, start with 1 chile and before adding the tomatoes taste first, then add more if that's not enough.

Use a small, thin-skinned organic lime for this soup if you can't find kaffir lime leaves. Easiest way to peel a lime: slice into quarters and use your fingers to separate the peel from the pulp. Squeeze the remaining lime pulp juice into the broth.

2 quarts (8 cups) water

4 ounces Pad Thai rice sticks (half of an 8-ounce package)

1 stalk fresh lemongrass (see page 17) or 3 tablespoons prepared lemongrass

2 large shallots, peeled and sliced into ¼-inch rings

4 cloves garlic, minced

2 tablespoons peanut or vegetable oil

6 cups vegetable broth, preferably vegetarian chicken flavored

1½-inch piece peeled ginger, sliced into matchsticks

2 to 6 fresh red hot chilies (serrano or Thai), stems removed and sliced into paper-thin slices

4 kaffir lime leaves or the peel from 1 lime, cut into 1-inch-wide strips

4 dried shiitake mushrooms

2 tablespoons brown sugar

2 tablespoons Thai thin soy sauce (see page 19)

2 cups (about 4 ounces) thinly sliced fresh mushrooms

½ pound ripe red tomatoes, stems removed and diced into 1-inch pieces

¼ cup lime juice

8 baby corn (from jar or canned), sliced in half lengthwise

4 ounces fried tofu or ½ recipe *Savory Baked Tofu* (page 50), sliced into ½-inch-thin strips (optional)

1 cup fresh cilantro leaves

1. Boil 2 quarts of water in a large pot, then stir in the noodles and simmer 4 minutes. Drain, rinse with cold water and transfer the noodles to a bowl. Cover them with 1 inch of cold water and set aside. If using a whole, fresh stalk of lemongrass see page 17 for tips on preparing lemongrass (not necessary if using minced prepared lemongrass).

2. In a large 3-quart soup pot sauté the shallot and garlic in the oil over medium heat until softened, about 4 minutes. Add the broth, then the lemongrass, ginger, chilies, lime leaves, shiitake mushrooms, brown sugar, and soy sauce. Increase heat and bring mixture to an active simmer, then reduce the heat. Add the mushrooms. Partially cover the pot and simmer for 20 minutes, stirring occasionally. Remove the lime leaves (or lime peel) and any large stalks of lemongrass if you used a whole stalk.

3. Stir in tomatoes, lime juice, baby corn, and tofu if using and simmer, partially covered, for 10 minutes. Taste the soup and add a dash of lime juice or a teaspoon of brown sugar to taste for a sweeter or tangier broth. Turn off the heat, then divide the noodles among four large, 1-quart serving bowls. Ladle the soup over the noodles, making sure to include tomatoes, tofu, and corn in each serving. Garnish each serving with cilantro and serve immediately.

Tom yum soup: Without the noodles, this soup is a classic starter for a Thai feast or just a comforting broth when you're recovering from a cold.

Fresh wheat Noodles in Miso Broth

SERVES 4 GENEROUSLY

This steaming sesame miso noodle bowl is inspired by Korean-style udon noodle soups loaded with silky tofu, tender spinach, and chewy noodles. It has a healthy balance of protein, greens, and vegetables and is a satisfying one-bowl weeknight meal. Fresh noodles shine here, but be sure to read the label carefully to avoid noodles made with eggs (see page 13), or use dried udon noodles.

To slice a block of delicate silken tofu, drain the package then slide onto a cutting board. Run a very sharp knife through the block a few times vertically and horizontally to create cubes. Don't separate the cubes just yet; instead, use a wide spatula to lift the entire block and slide the whole thing directly into the soup.

NOODLES

> 3 quarts (12 cups) cold water
> 3 tablespoons kosher salt
> 1 pound fresh udon noodles or 10 ounces dried udon noodles
> 2 teaspoons toasted sesame oil

BROTH

> 6 large dried shiitake mushrooms
> 1 large yellow onion, peeled and sliced into half-moons
> 1 tablespoon vegetable oil
> 4 cloves garlic, finely chopped
> 4 scallions, white and green sections divided and finely chopped
> 6 cups water
> One 4-inch strip dried kombu seaweed
> 1 pound silken tofu, drained and sliced into 1-inch cubes (see note for slicing tips)
> 3 tablespoons soy sauce
> 1 teaspoon gochugaru (Korean red pepper powder, see page 15)
> ⅔ cup light miso paste (shiro miso)
> 1 tablespoon toasted sesame oil
> 3 cups fresh spinach leaves, loosely packed
> 2 tablespoons toasted sesame seeds

1. In a large soup pot bring water and salt to a rolling boil; slide in the fresh wheat noodles, and cook for 5 to 7 minutes or until tender but still firm (al dente). Drain and rinse well with cold water, then toss with sesame oil. In a mixing bowl cover dried shiitake mushrooms with 2 cups of boiling water and let stand for 20 minutes or until tender. Remove mushrooms, discard any hard stems, and slice into very thin strips. Strain the mushroom-soaking liquid through a colander double-lined with cheese-cloth to remove any grit and set aside.

2. Fry the sliced onion and oil in the large soup pot for 4 minutes or until soft and translucent. Add garlic and white parts of scallions and fry for another minute, then pour in the 6 cups of water and reserved mushroom-soaking liquid. Add the kombu strip, increase heat to high, and bring soup to a boil. Reduce heat to low and bring the soup to gentle simmer, then stir in sliced mushrooms, tofu,

soy sauce, and red pepper powder. Cover and simmer for 5 minutes.

3. Scoop the miso into a mixing bowl and add 1 cup of hot broth. Use a rubber spatula to stir the broth into the miso to form a creamy smooth paste, then stir the miso mixture back into the soup. Add the toasted sesame oil and spinach leaves and simmer until the spinach is wilted and tender, another 2 minutes. Turn off the heat and keep the soup covered. Discard the kombu strip before serving.

4. Divide the noodles into large, deep serving bowls. Ladle the soup on top of the noodles, making sure to distribute the tofu, spinach, mushrooms, and lots of broth in each bowl. Sprinkle with sesame seeds and the chopped green tops of the scallions. Serve right away with chopsticks and big soup spoons.

sizzling seitan pho noodle soup

MAKES 4 HUGE SERVINGS

Eating pho, that famous Vietnamese noodle soup, is about making choices: sip a spoonful of aromatic star anise–infused broth, grab a rice noodle with chopsticks, nibble on spicy Asian basil, or chomp on sizzling seitan or crisp veggies. Thanks to these enticing choices eating pho may feel like mediation, but this brief-yet-meaningful relationship is worth every second.

Making pho is best done in stages: prepare the broth the day before, marinate the seitan overnight and assemble the noodles and garnishes right before eating. With everything done in advance, just heat the broth and ladle over the rest for one-bowl weeknight meals.

Chinese black vinegar is an inexpensive, sweet and sour dark vinegar that adds unique depth to this broth. It's similar in character to balsamic vinegar, which can be substituted for Chinese black vinegar in this case.

PHO BROTH

½ teaspoon whole cloves (about 6)

4 star anise pods

1 heaping tablespoon coriander seeds

Three 3-inch cinnamon sticks

1 teaspoon black or mixed whole peppercorns

2-inch piece peeled ginger, cut into ¼-inch slices

1 large red onion, sliced into ½-inch-thick rings

1 tablespoon vegetable oil

3 quarts (12 cups) water

8 large dried shiitake mushrooms

2 stalks fresh lemongrass, well bruised (see page 17)

3 tablespoons dark brown sugar

2 heaping tablespoons tomato paste

1½ teaspoons sea salt

½ cup soy sauce

3 tablespoons dark balsamic vinegar or Chinese black vinegar (see page 12)

SOUP

1 recipe marinated, grilled seitan from *Grilled Seitan Noodle Salad* (page 234), kept warm, or one 8-ounce package fried tofu puffs or thinly sliced *Savory Baked Tofu* (page 50)

1 pound baby bok choy sliced into ¼-inch-wide pieces, or washed, baby spinach leaves

1 large carrot or small daikon (about ½ pound), sliced into matchsticks or *Star Anise Daikon Pickles* (page 62)

1 large package rice noodles, either Pad Thai style or vermicelli, cooked, drained, and rinsed with cold water (see *Tom Yum Noodle Soup*, page 217, for guidelines)

TOPPINGS (DIVIDE EVENLY BETWEEN 4 SERVINGS)

4 cups fresh mung or soy bean sprouts

1½ cups cilantro springs

4 big sprigs Thai basil

4 sprigs mint

4 big fat lime wedges

¼ cup fried shallots, homemade (see sidebar for instructions) or purchased

Asian hot chili sauce as desired

1. In a cast-iron skillet or stainless-steel skillet over medium heat, toast the cloves, anise, coriander, cinnamon sticks, and peppercorns until fragrant, about 2 minutes; transfer toasted spices to a bowl and set aside. Fry ginger, onion, and vegetable oil over high heat for 8 to 10 minutes, stirring occasionally until the edges of the onion and ginger are seared a dark blackish brown. Transfer the onion and ginger to the bowl with the spices. While the onions are searing, fill a large soup pot with the 3 quarts of water and turn heat to high.

2. Once the onions have been removed from the skillet, scoop out 2 cups of water from the soup pot and pour them into the cast-iron skillet. Swirl it around to pick up any remaining roasted onion juices and then return the water back to broth pot.

3. Add the toasted spices, browned onions, and ginger to the soup pot, then add the shiitake mushrooms, lemongrass, brown sugar, tomato paste, and salt. Cover the pot and bring to a boil, then reduce heat to low and simmer for 45 minutes, stir occasionally. Turn off the heat and cool for 20 minutes, and then strain out the vegetables using a colander lined with cheesecloth. Make sure to press down on the vegetables to remove as much liquid as possible. Gather up the cheesecloth, twist into a bundle and squeeze like crazy to remove all of those flavorful juices; discard the bundle. Return the strained broth to the stove and stir in the soy sauce and vinegar. Bring to a simmer over medium heat, reduce heat to low, and cover to keep warm while preparing everything else for the soup. Taste the broth and adjust

Fried Shallots

A sweet and fatty garnish for noodle soups: heat 2 tablespoons of peanut or vegetable oil in a cast-iron skillet over medium-high heat. Stir in ½ cup of very thinly sliced shallot rings; slice the shallots no thicker than ⅛ of an inch. Stir frequently and fry until the shallots are a deep golden brown, but be careful not to burn. Transfer to a paper towel–lined plate to drain and cool and sprinkle with a little bit of salt. Store fried shallots in a tightly covered container in the fridge. It's also possible to find crunchy, already fried shallots in Asian groceries.

seasonings with additional soy sauce, salt, and vinegar if desired.

4. While the broth is heating, prepare the seitan as directed for the **Grilled Seitan Noodle Salad** (page 234), cover, and keep warm. Now is also a great time to prepare the noodles according to package directions; after cooking the noodles, drain and rinse with cold water and set aside. Arrange the herbs and other toppings on a large serving dish. Make the fried shallots if using.

5. To assemble a pho, bring the pho broth to a steaming simmer over medium-high heat, stirring occasionally. Divide the noodles into the biggest, deepest serving bowls you own; I strongly recommend using 2-cup bowls at a minimum. Use about 1 heaping cup of noodles per serving. Arrange the sliced bok choy on top of noodles and ladle on enough hot broth to cover most of the bok choy. Arrange slices of seitan on top of noodles and serve; the super-hot broth will lightly blanch the veggies, but take care when sipping it! Heap as much bean sprouts, cilantro, mint, and basil as desired onto each serving of pho and scatter with a few shreds of pickled daikon and a sprinkle of fried shallots, if using. Squeeze a lime wedge over everything and serve. Eat with chopsticks and a really big soup spoon, adding chili sauce as needed.

Tofu Pho: Substitute seitan with purchased fried tofu cutlets or puffs from the chilled section of any Asian market. Slice tofu into ½-inch-thick pieces and layer on top of noodles before pouring on the hot broth.

Sizzling Seitan Pho Noodle Soup, page 220

Pad Kee Mao (Spicy Drunken Noodles)

SERVES 2 TO 3

There are many colorful stories about the origins of this addictive, fiery Thai noodle dish, but the strangest one may be about the wife who was so fed up with her drunken husband she turned to revenge via loading up his favorite noodles with fistfuls of hot chile peppers. Seems like her plan backfired, because the heady mixture of savory sauces and fiery chilies made him (and countless fans after) swoon and ask for seconds. Your homemade spin on this takeout favorite need not be punishingly hot to be just as good.

*Like her sister recipe, **Pad See Ew** (page 230), Pad Kee Mao is best made with genuine Thai soy sauces. One bottle of each Thai sauce will last for dozens of noodle dishes, making spontaneous Thai-style noodles an easy weekday meal treat. Chinese- or Japanese-style sauces don't have the correct flavors; your dish may be good, but it won't taste like Thai food. Thai thin soy sauce (light amber color, thin consistency, and strong, salty taste) does the job of standing in for fish sauce. Golden Mountain sauce is a special Thai seasoning sauce with a consistency and flavor slightly like Worcestershire sauce; it's vegan, with complex flavors that soy sauce alone can't cover. Thai black soy sauce and sweet soy sauce are thick and sweet sauces with molasses-like notes; both have their own unique character, but in a pinch are interchangeable. But for the most authentic tasting dish, use both!*

Authentic Thai vegetables are much more challenging to find than the sauces, but a little cabbage, carrot, or even a few florets of broccoli or a handful of snow peas are fine.

Regarding the rice noodles, you have license to use whatever you can find. Many Thai restaurants use slippery, chewy, wide fresh rice noodles. These noodles are delicious and will make the most authentic-tasting dish but can be difficult to find. If you can't find sliced, fresh flat rice noodles at Thai markets, investigate Chinese markets for bags of soft fresh rice ho fun noodles: huge rice noodles that resemble a floppy kitchen towel folded into a squishy bundle. Regular Pad Thai rice sticks, if not authentic, are an easy-to-find substitute.

If you can't use fresh ho fun noodles immediately, they can be refrigerated but will be stiff after being chilled a few hours (but they can keep for weeks, so it's worth stashing an extra bag in the fridge for future stir-fries). To refresh ho fun noodles, steam them for 4 to 8 minutes until soft and pliable enough to unfold; the older the noodle, the more steaming required. Gently unfold this super noodle (if it rips a little don't worry), and slice or tear into pieces. Don't worry if they're not pretty, they'll taste like dynamite in noodle stir-fries. Keep the fresh noodles covered with a moist paper towel until ready to stir-fry.

DRUNKEN NOODLE SAUCE

2 tablespoons Chinese vegetarian stir-fry sauce (see page 13)

2 tablespoons Thai thin soy sauce (see page 19)

4 teaspoons brown sugar or palm sugar

1 tablespoon Thai Golden Mountain sauce (see page 18)

2 tablespoons Thai black soy sauce or Thai sweet soy sauce (see page 19), or 1 tablespoon of each sauce

2 teaspoons rice vinegar

2 teaspoons lime juice

2 to 3 teaspoons Asian chili garlic sauce or hot red pepper flakes

NOODLES AND VEGETABLES

12 ounces Thai fresh flat rice noodles or Chinese fresh ho fun noodles

3 tablespoons peanut, canola, or grapeseed oil

5 cloves garlic, roughly chopped

3 to 4 red or green hot chile peppers (Thai, Indian, or serrano), sliced into paper-thin rings

One 8-ounce package fried tofu or 1 recipe *Savory Baked Tofu* (page 50), sliced into ¼-inch thin strips

3 cups shredded Napa or savoy cabbage

1 carrot, sliced into matchsticks

3 scallions, both green and white parts, thinly sliced

½ cup lightly packed Thai basil leaves

½ cup lightly packed cilantro leaves

Lime wedges for squeezing over noodles

1. If the rice noodles are very fresh and soft, you don't need to cook them; just tear into bite sized pieces if needed and proceed to the stir-fry. If already sliced, gently separate the noodles and set aside, or refold the ho fun several times into a wide tube and slice into wide, 2-to 3-inch strips. If the noodles have been refrigerated and are hard, set up a bamboo or metal steamer over boiling water. Steam the Thai noodles or the whole, unsliced ho fun until soft (4 to 8 minutes), then turn off the heat and keep covered.

PAD KEE MAO (SPICY DRUNKEN NOODLES), PAGE 223

If using ho fun, when the noodle is cool enough to handle, either slice into strips or tear into pieces 2 to 3 inches wide with your fingers. Keep covered until ready to use.

2. In a liquid measuring cup whisk together the vegetarian stir-fry sauce, Thai thin soy sauce, brown sugar, Golden Mountain sauce, black or sweet soy sauce, rice vinegar, lime juice, and chili sauce. Chop the vegetables and arrange all of the ingredients within easy reach of the stove for the stir-fry.

3. Preheat a wok or large skillet over high heat, then pour in 1 tablespoon of the oil. When the oil is rippling, stir in the garlic and chilies, stir-fry for 1 minute, then add the tofu and fry another 2 to 3 minutes until the tofu browns on the edges. Transfer the tofu to a dinner plate. Add another tablespoon of oil and add the carrot, cabbage, and white part of scallions and fry for 2 minutes until slightly softened. Transfer to the plate with the tofu.

4. Add the remaining tablespoon of oil, add the noodles, and stir-fry for 1 minute. If the noodles start to stick, dribble in a teaspoon or two of water; whenever sticking starts to happen add a little water but don't add too much or the noodles will become mushy. Now drizzle on half of the sauce, stir-fry for 2 minutes and return the tofu, cabbage, carrot, green parts of scallions, and the remaining sauce. Stir in the basil leaves and cilantro. Continue to stir-fry for another 1 to 2 minutes or until most of the liquid has been absorbed, everything is coated in sauce and the noodles are gently seared in some places. Transfer immediately to serving plates and squeeze lime wedges over noodles before devouring.

Add any of the following to the stir-fry before adding the noodles:

With Green Peppercorns: Stir in 2 to 3 teaspoons of fresh green peppercorns along with the chilies.

With Shallots: Slice a large shallot into paper-thin slices and fry along with the garlic and chilies until golden.

With Snow Peas, Baby Corn, or Broccoli: Add a handful of snow peas, baby corn or thinly sliced broccoli along with the cabbage

Without Noodles: Or omit the noodles entirely and double the amount of vegetables for a spicy all-vegetable Thai stir-fry

Pad Kee Mao with Pad Thai Rice Sticks: Prepare an 8-ounce package of Pad Thai rice sticks as directed for ***Pad Thai with Avocado and Spicy Greens*** (page 233), keeping them stored in water until ready to use. Drain and use as directed for fresh rice noodles.

Ramen Noodles in Soymilk Sesame Broth

MAKES 4 LARGE SERVINGS

Japanese ramen noodle soups loaded with exciting toppings are more popular than ever in the United States and too much fun to be off-limits to vegans. A delicious vegan ramen needs a flavorful broth with substance, and this opaque, velvety, cream-colored broth mimics the traditional cloudy tonkotsu-style broth with a gently simmered blend of unsweetened soy milk, shiro miso, nutty sesame tahini, and seared sweet vegetables. After the noodles, the topping

choice is extremely flexible (see suggestions below), but together they make this a complex yet balanced meal in a bowl.

If you can't find suitable vegan ramen noodles, udon noodles or wholesome buckwheat soba noodles are a delectable substitute. For the unsweetened soymilk, use a brand with minimal ingredients for the broth; I like Edensoy Unsweetened Plain soymilk (it has only 2 ingredients, soybeans and water). The choice of toppings is ultimately up to you, but corn, finely chopped scallions, and dollop of something spicy are absolutely essential.

BROTH

- 1 tablespoon vegetable oil
- 1 large yellow onion, skin left on and sliced into ½-inch-thick circles
- 2-inch piece unpeeled ginger, sliced into ½-inch slices
- 10 cloves garlic, peeled and minced
- 6 scallions, white and green parts separated
- 1 large leek, both white and green part, cut into 1-inch pieces
- 10 dried shiitake mushrooms
- 8 cups water
- 4 cups (1-quart box) unsweetened plain soy milk
- 1 ½ teaspoons sea salt, or to taste
- 2 tablespoons white miso paste, such as shiro miso
- 3 heaping tablespoons smooth, light-colored sesame tahini
- 1 tablespoon mirin (see page 16)

NOODLES AND RAMEN TOPPINGS

- 10 ounces uncooked ramen noodles, udon noodles, or buckwheat soba noodles
- ½ pound baby bok choy, washed and sliced into ½-inch-thick slices
- 2 cups corn kernels, fresh or frozen (if frozen thawed at room temperature)
- 1 pound silken soft tofu, drained
- 4 tablespoons pickled ginger slices, sliced into thinnest shreds possible
- 1 sheet toasted nori seaweed
- Wasabi paste, La-Yu Japanese hot chile oil, or Sriracha, as desired

1. In a 10-inch cast-iron skillet, preheat the oil over high heat, then lay the onion slices cut side down and squeeze the ginger and garlic cloves in between the slices. Sear these vegetables, flipping occasionally, until the outsides are nearly blackened. Transfer to a 4-quart soup pot and add the white parts of the scallions, leek, shiitakes, and water. Over high heat bring to a rolling boil, then reduce the heat to low and cover. Simmer for 45 minutes. Uncover the pot and stir in the soy milk, return the cover and continue to simmer for 45 minutes. At this point if you're not in any particular hurry, you can allow the broth to simmer on low for another 30 minutes to deepen the flavor, but it's okay to stop simmering it now, too. Remove the heat and set the broth aside to cool, at least 30 minutes.

2. When the broth is just cool enough to handle, strain it through a colander lined with a double layer of cheesecloth. Gather the cheesecloth into a bundle and firmly squeeze any remaining liquid into the broth; discard the vegetables. Return the broth to the soup pot and warm over medium heat and stir in the salt. Place miso and tahini in a mixing bowl, add 2 cups of warm broth, and use a spoon to combine everything until creamy. Transfer the miso mixture to the soup pot and add the mirin. Stir well and taste the mixture; season with more salt if desired. Turn heat to low and keep the broth covered. If you're not serving the ramen in the next 30 minutes, remove

from heat, cool and store the broth in sealed plastic containers and reheat thoroughly before serving.

3. While the broth is simmering, prepare the noodles as directed on the package, rinse with plenty of cold water until they don't stick together, and set aside. In a large saucepan bring 3 cups of water to a rolling boil; add the bok choy and blanch for 1 minute; remove the bok choy with tongs, rinse with cold water and set aside. Place the corn in a colander and pour the remaining boiling water over the corn to blanch it; rinse the corn with cold water, drain and set aside. Slice the tofu as directed for **Fresh Wheat Noodles in Miso Broth** (page 219) and set aside. Chop the green tops of the scallions as finely as possible (about ⅛ inch wide) and set aside. Use kitchen scissors to cut the nori sheet into 3 x ½-inch strips, and store in a dry container. If desired prepare all of these toppings up to a day in advance, store in their own individual containers in the fridge until it's time to serve the ramen.

4. Scoop the miso mixture into a mixing bowl and stir in 1 cup of hot broth. Use a rubber spatula to stir the broth into the miso mixture to form a smooth sauce and stir this back into the broth. Turn off the heat and cover the soup pot to keep warm. If reheating the broth, don't boil, just bring to a steamy simmer over medium heat.

5. Divide the noodles into very large, deep soup bowls (they should be able to hold 3 cups of liquid comfortably). On top of the noodles, place three separate little piles of corn, tofu cubes, and bok choy. Gently ladle hot broth on top of the noodles. Scatter on top of each serving some chopped green scallion, 1 tablespoon sliced pickled ginger, and a quarter of the nori seaweed strips. Serve with chopsticks and big soup spoons and pass around the wasabi paste or hot chile oil.

TOPPING VARIATIONS

The range of toppings for ramen is limitless. Some of my favorite options include:

⊖ Rescue the most tender shiitakes from the broth vegetables before straining and slice into very thin strips

⊖ Lightly fermented bamboo strips (menma) are a delicate, sweet, and chewy. Look for these in Japanese markets in the refrigerator section.

⊖ Diced, roasted, or boiled bite-size pieces of kabocha squash

⊖ Crunchy sweet enoki mushrooms. Eat them raw scattered on top of the soup.

⊖ A handful of baby spinach leaves with a sprinkle of sesame seeds. Place this on the noodles, then ladle hot broth over the leaves to wilt them slightly.

Double Mushroom Glass Noodles (Jap Chae)

SERVES 6

Shimmering, chewy Korean jap chae *stir-fried noodles are fun to prepare and make great potluck food. Though slippery, these semi-transparent noodles drink up the garlicky soy sauce marinade clinging to the sautéed veggies and tofu. A lightly seasoned Korean-style veggie or a cabbage salad tossed with sesame dressing completes this veggie-loaded dish.*

Grey, translucent dried Korean sweet potato noodles are often very long and need to be trimmed into easier-to-eat lengths; after the cooked noodles have

been drained and tossed with sesame oil, use clean kitchen scissors to cut noodles into pieces about 10 inches long. Some brands of noodles come already pretrimmed into easy-to-cook lengths.

NOODLES

One 12-ounce package Korean sweet potato glass noodles (dang myeon noodles)

1 tablespoon toasted sesame oil

3 quarts (12 cups) water

GARLIC SOY SAUCE

½ cup soy sauce

6 cloves garlic, minced

3 tablespoons brown sugar

4 teaspoons toasted sesame oil

2 teaspoons gochuchang (Korean red pepper powder, see page 15), red pepper flakes, or 2 fresh red hot chilies, minced

VEGGIES AND STIR-FRY

6 large dried shiitake mushrooms, soaked in boiling water until soft

¼ cup dried black cloud ear mushrooms, soaked in boiling water until soft

1 pound baby bok choy, well washed to remove any grit

3 tablespoons canola or peanut oil

1 large white onion, peeled, halved and sliced into thin half-moons

1 large carrot, peeled and sliced into matchsticks

4 scallions, root ends trimmed and sliced into 1-inch pieces

2 tablespoons toasted sesame seeds

Additional toasted sesame seeds for garnish (optional)

1. Prepare the noodles first. In a large soup pot bring to a rolling boil over high heat 3 quarts of water. If the noodles are uncut and very long, use clean kitchen scissors to cut noodles into smaller lengths, about 10 inches long. Add noodles and cook for 4 to 5 minutes until al dente; don't overcook the noodles. Drain in a colander, rinse with plenty of cold water, and drain again. Pour noodles into a mixing bowl and toss with the sesame oil.

2. In a measuring cup mix together the garlic soy sauce ingredients. Drain the mushrooms, discard the liquid, and slice into strips about ¼ inch thin. Separate the bok choy leaves from the stalks and set aside. Slice the stalks into ¼-inch-wide diagonal pieces.

3. Over high heat preheat a wok or 12-inch stainless-steel pan. When the wok is almost smoking hot, add the oil, onions, and carrots and stir-fry for 2 minutes. Stir in the mushroom strips and fry for another 2 minutes, then add the bok choy stems. Fry for another 2 minutes, then add the drained noodles, bok choy leaves, scallions, and sesame seeds and pour on the garlic soy sauce. Continue to cook and stir until the noodles are hot and the bok choy leaves have wilted slightly, about another 2 to 3 minutes. Remove from heat, sprinkle with sesame seeds if desired, and serve immediately.

Jap chae loves additions such as:

With Tofu: Add ½ recipe *Savory Baked Tofu* (page 50) or 8 ounces of packaged fried tofu sliced into matchsticks; add along with the mushrooms.

With Spinach: Replace the bok choy with baby spinach or any Asian leafy green.

With Bell Pepper or Cabbage: Add 1 to 2 cups of very thinly sliced red bell peppers or shredded Napa or savoy cabbage; stir-fry with the mushrooms.

pad see ew (sweet soy sauce pan-fried noodles)

SERVES 2 TO 3

Thai noodle dishes involve delicious choices, such as between Pad Thai or Pad Kee Mao; but often I settle upon Pad See Ew, a sweet and savory dish of chewy noodles and crisp Chinese broccoli. With the right Thai soy sauces and a little luck in finding fresh rice noodles, you can create something as tempting and spot-on as your favorite Thai restaurant. Scoring authentic Thai ingredients makes all the difference, and a bottle or two of these special soy sauces will last through dozens of excellent noodle dishes. Large Chinese supermarkets often carry the entire range of Thai sauces, so stock up while you're there! Once open, store Thai sauces in the refrigerator to maintain the best flavor.

*For details on finding and using Thai sweet soy sauce, black soy sauce, light soy sauce, and fresh rice noodles, go to the **Pad Kee Mao (Spicy Drunken Noodles)** recipe on page 223.*

> 12 ounces Thai fresh flat rice noodles or Chinese fresh ho fun noodles
>
> 3 tablespoons peanut, canola or grapeseed oil
>
> 1 pound Chinese broccoli (yu choy or gai lan), thick stems chopped away from leafy tops
>
> 5 cloves garlic, roughly chopped

> 8-ounce package fried tofu or 1 recipe *Savory Baked Tofu* (page 50), sliced into ¼-inch-thin slices
>
> 3 scallions, green and white parts separated and thinly sliced
>
> About ½ teaspoon ground white pepper for sprinkling

PAD SEE EW SAUCE

> 3 tablespoons Thai sweet soy sauce (see page 19)
>
> 2 tablespoons Thai thin soy sauce (see page 19)
>
> 2 tablespoons Thai black soy sauce (see page 19)
>
> 2 teaspoons brown sugar or grated palm sugar (see page 18)
>
> 2 teaspoons rice vinegar

For best results divide the ingredients in half (or enough for each portion) and stir-fry one batch of Pad See Ew at a time. This will ensure everything is cooked evenly, quickly. And your end results really will taste better.

1. If your rice noodles are very fresh and still soft, you don't need to cook them. If already sliced, gently separate the noodles and set aside, or refold the ho fun several times into a wide tube and slice into wide, 2- to 3-inch strips. If the noodles have been refrigerated and are hard, set up a bamboo or metal steamer over boiling water. Steam the Thai noodles or the whole, unsliced ho fun until soft (4 to 8 minutes), then turn off the heat and keep covered. If using ho fun, when the noodle is cool enough to handle, either slice into strips or tear into pieces 2 to 3 inches wide with your fingers. Keep covered until ready to use.

2. In a liquid measuring cup whisk together the sweet soy sauce, Thai thin soy sauce, black soy sauce, brown sugar, and rice vinegar. Chop the vegetables and tofu and arrange all of the ingredients within easy reach of the stove for the stir-fry.

3. Preheat a wok or large skillet over high heat, then pour in 1 tablespoon of the oil. When the oil is rippling, stir in the Chinese broccoli stems and stir-fry for 2 minutes or until bright green. Stir in the leafy tops and fry only until they just start to wilt, about 1 minute, and then transfer to a plate. Add another tablespoon of oil, add the garlic, and fry for 30 seconds. Add the sliced tofu and white parts of scallions and fry another 2 to 3 minutes until the tofu browns on the edges. Transfer the tofu to the plate with the broccoli.

4. Add the remaining tablespoon of oil. Add the green tops of scallions and the noodles, and stir-fry for 1 minute. If the noodles start to stick, dribble in a teaspoon or two of water; whenever sticking starts to happen add a little water. But don't add too much or the noodles will become mushy. Now drizzle on half of the sauce, stir-fry for 2 minutes, and add the broccoli and tofu and the remaining sauce. Continue to stir-fry for another 1 to 2 minutes or until most of the liquid has been absorbed, everything is coated in sauce, and the noodles are seared in spots. Transfer immediately to serving plates. Sprinkle the tops of each serving with a dusting of ground white pepper and eat right away!

With Watercress or Bok Choy: Use watercress, bok choy or any other Asian leafy green in place of Chinese broccoli.

Pad See Ew with Pad Thai Rice Sticks: If you can't find fresh rice noodles, substitute Pad Thai noodles as directed for *Pad Kee Mao with Pad Thai Rice Sticks* (page 226).

Takeout Stir-Fry Noodles with Mushrooms and Greens

SERVES 2 TO 3

Put down the phone and take out the wok: presenting Chinese takeout-style noodles, much less greasy and rippling with chewy mushrooms and sharp greens. A good recipe to sharpen your stir-fry skills with (a wok makes this a great deal easier and more authentic tasting, too), and once you get the hang of working with noodles, greens, and sauces it's easy to add almost any vegetable, seitan, or tofu for endless variations on this dish.

Look for eggless pulled fresh wheat noodles (in the refrigerator case , see page 13), vegetarian stir-fry sauce (sometimes called vegetarian oyster sauce), and fresh shiitakes at reasonable prices in large, well-stocked Chinese markets. For a more intense mushroom flavor use dried shiitake mushrooms as described in the variations below.

For best results divide the ingredients in half (or enough for each portion) and stir-fry one batch of noodles at a time. This will ensure everything is cooked evenly and quickly, and your end results really will taste better. In the case of this recipe, return the star anise to the pan with each batch of noodles.

3 quarts (12 cups) water

1 tablespoon kosher salt

1 pound fresh thick wheat Asian noodles

½ pound fresh shiitake mushrooms

1 pound Asian greens such as yu choy,
    gai lan, or baby or adult bok choy

6 teaspoons peanut oil or canola oil

4 cloves garlic, peeled and minced

1 large shallot, finely minced

1 star anise

3 tablespoons soy sauce

2 tablespoons Chinese Shaoxing cooking
    wine (see page 13)

1 tablespoon vegetarian stir-fry sauce (see
    page 13)

4 scallions, green tops only, sliced into
    2-inch pieces

1. Fill a large, 4-quart pot with 3 quarts of water and bring to a rolling boil. Add 1 tablespoon of kosher salt to the cooking water and add noodles. Cook according to package directions—this shouldn't be long for fresh noodles, about 4 to 5 minutes. Drain immediately and rinse with plenty of cold water to keep noodles from sticking together and set aside to drain of excess water.

2. Remove thick stems from shiitakes and slice tops into 1-inch-wide pieces, if necessary for large mushrooms. Remove tough ends from yu choy (or whatever green you're using), wash and dry greens, and slice into pieces no longer than 3 inches and no wider than ½ inch.

3. In a wok or large, deep, 12-inch skillet heat 2 teaspoons of the oil and add the mushrooms. Sprinkle with a pinch of salt, stir and cover the wok for 2 minutes to sweat the mushrooms. Remove cover and cook until most of the water has evaporated, move mushrooms to a dinner plate, and set aside.

Heat another 2 teaspoons oil in pan, add greens and sprinkle with another pinch of salt. Sauté until bright green, 2 to 3 minutes. Transfer greens to the plate with the mushrooms.

4. Add the remaining 2 teaspoons of oil, add the minced garlic, shallot, and star anise and fry for 30 seconds. Add drained the noodles and fry for 3 to 4 minutes until hot, then pour in soy sauce, rice wine, and vegetarian stir-fry sauce and fry another 2 minutes. Add cooked mushrooms, greens, and scallions and combine until everything is evenly heated. Remove the star anise and serve immediately.

With Seitan: Stir-fry separately 1 to 2 cutlets of *5-Spice Seitan* (page 51), sliced into ¼-inch-thick strips until lightly browned. Add to the noodles along with the cooked greens.

With Tofu: Add *Savory Baked Tofu* (page 50) or any purchased baked or fried tofu, sliced into ¼-inch-thick strips along with the greens.

With Hot Chili Sauce: Stir in 2 teaspoons hot chili sauce along with soy sauce and rice wine.

With Dried Shiitakes: Soak in hot water the contents of a 3-ounce package of whole dried shiitake mushrooms for an hour or overnight until mushrooms are plump. Remove tough stems from mushrooms, shake off excess water, and slice into ¼-inch slices.

Pad Thai with Avocado and Spicy Greens

MAKES 2 TO 3 SERVINGS

(GLUTEN FREE, IF MADE WITH GLUTEN-FREE SOY SAUCE)

How you prepare Pad Thai, that insanely popular Thai noodle takeout classic, is just as important as what's in it. Pad Thai is stir-fry and those rules still apply; a great big pan (a wok can't be beat), high heat, cook fast, veggies cut the same size, and never crowd the pan. For best results divide the ingredients among servings and cook each serving one batch at a time. Ninety percent of the work for stir-fries is preparing everything before cooking, making Pad Thai an ideal dish for chopping all the elements on the weekend for fast dinners through the work week.

You'll need additional counter space, preferably near your stove, for the chopped vegetables, bowl of noodles, the sauce, and serving dish.

NOODLES AND VEGETABLES

8 ounces Thai rice stick noodles
1 recipe *Savory Baked Tofu* (page 50) or 8 ounces purchased fried or baked tofu, diced into ½-inch cubes
4 cups torn arugula, watercress, radish greens, or finely shredded kale
4 cloves garlic, minced
4 large shallots, thinly sliced

4 scallions, trimmed, white and green parts separated and sliced into ½-inch pieces
6 tablespoons peanut oil or vegetable oil

PAD THAI SAUCE

⅓ cup light brown sugar or grated palm sugar (see page 18; for a less sweet sauce, use 3 tablespoons or less)
¼ cup lime juice
3 tablespoons soy sauce or Thai thin soy sauce (see page 19)
3 tablespoons all-natural ketchup
1 teaspoon light-colored miso
1 tablespoon tamarind paste (see page 14) or 2 teaspoons tamarind concentrate
½ teaspoon ground coriander
1 finely minced red chile pepper or 2 teaspoons hot chili sauce, or to taste

TOPPINGS

3 cups mung bean sprouts
1 ripe avocado, diced into ½-inch cubes and tossed with 2 teaspoons of lime juice
1 cup chopped cilantro leaves, loosely packed
⅔ cup coarsely ground roasted, unsalted peanuts
Lime wedges for squeezing

Store the chopped veggies and tofu in separate containers or bags, along with a tightly closed container of the sauce, chilled in the refrigerator for up to 3 days. Pulse the peanuts in a food processor to a coarse consistency (but don't make peanut butter!), and store tightly sealed in a small plastic container.

1. In a large bowl cover noodles with 4 inches of hot water and soak for 20 minutes. Arrange in separate piles on plates or bowls near your cooking area the tofu, greens, garlic, shallots, white part of scallions, and green parts of scallions. In a 2-cup liquid measuring cup whisk together all of the sauce ingredients and keep that nearby the stove, too.

2. Rinse the bean sprouts in cold water and drain. Arrange the avocado, cilantro leaves, and ground peanuts on a separate serving dish for garnishing the finished Pad Thai.

3. Going forward, you'll be cooking one serving of Pad Thai at a time. It will take only minutes to do so, and your noodles will come out much better than if you just cooked the whole thing in one big batch. Make all the ingredients ready to go and near the preheated wok. Drain the Pad Thai noodles and keep them handy in a bowl near, you guessed it, the wok. Pour the oil into a small cup and keep a teaspoon in the oil; you'll add extra oil in stages during the stir-fry as needed.

4. Heat a wok or deep, 12-inch stainless-steel skillet over high heat until nearly smoking then add 2 teaspoons of oil. Add a quarter of the greens and green scallion tops. Use long-handled metal tongs and stir-fry for 2 minutes or until the greens are wilted, then transfer to a plate. Add 3 teaspoons of oil to the wok and toss in a quarter of the garlic, sliced white scallion, and shallots and stir-fry for 2½ minutes or until shallots are softened. Add a quarter of the tofu, stir-fry for 2 minutes or until edges start to brown. Now add 2 teaspoons of oil to the wok and a quarter of the noodles, stir a few times, and add the cooked greens. Use tongs to toss the greens with the noodles and tofu, then pour in a quarter of the Pad Thai sauce. Continue to toss and stir-fry the noodles for 3 to 5 minutes; when crusty bits of noodles begin to form on the edges of the pan, the Pad Thai is ready. If some of the noodles stick to the surface of the wok,

scrape them off with your tongs and keep stirring. Those crusty noodle bits add chewy texture to the dish, but if they stick too much drizzle in another teaspoon of oil.

5. Mound hot Pad Thai onto one serving dish and top with sprouts, cilantro, ground peanuts, and diced avocado as desired. Squeeze a big lime wedge over everything and eat immediately!

Grilled Seitan Noodle Salad (Seitan Bo Bun)

SERVES 3 TO 4

Grilled hot seitan, warm chewy rice noodles, crunchy peanuts, and fresh herbs makes this Vietnamese dish a party in a bowl. Salad looks aside, this is a satisfying and filling entree that will please even carnivorous friends. There are several components to this dish, but many can be prepared in advance. For best results make the seitan a day in advance to achieve the best texture. Almost all of the work is in prepping the salad vegetables; the seitan grills in minutes and the sauce can be made up to a week in advance. Even better, make a double batch for yummy bahn mi sandwiches later (page 109).

1 recipe prepared **5-Spice Seitan** (page 51),
chilled for 1 hour or overnight
Peanut or vegetable oil for grilling seitan

MARINADE
3 tablespoons sugar
3 tablespoons lime juice

2 tablespoons soy sauce

2 large shallots, peeled and finely minced

4 cloves garlic, grated on a Microplane grater

1 stalk lemongrass, finely chopped (see page 17), or 3 tablespoons prepared lemongrass

2 scallions, root ends trimmed and thinly sliced

1 tablespoon peanut or vegetable oil

NOODLES AND SALAD

½ pound rice vermicelli noodles (try brown noodles for a wholesome dish)

1 cup finely chopped roasted, unsalted peanuts

2 cups mung bean sprouts

3 cups shredded leafy green lettuce such as romaine or Boston

1 large cucumber, peeled and diced into ½-inch pieces

1 large carrot, peeled and sliced into matchsticks

2 scallions, root ends trimmed and thinly sliced

1 cup cilantro leaves, torn into bite-size pieces

½ cup Thai basil leaves, torn into bite-size pieces

½ cup mint leaves, torn into bite-size pieces

1 recipe *Mock Nuoc Cham* sauce (page 67)

1. Marinate the seitan first: combine all of the marinade ingredients in a large glass container with a fork or wire whisk. Slice the cold seitan on a diagonal into thin slices about ¼ inch wide. Layer in the marinade and cover the container tightly. Marinate 1 hour or even better, overnight, occasionally stirring or shaking the container.

2. In a large, 4-quart pot bring 8 cups of water to a rolling boil. Slide in the noodles and stir for one minute, then turn off the heat and let the noodles soak for 20 minutes. Drain and rinse with cold water and store in a colander until ready to serve. Noodles can be made a day in advance and stored in the fridge in a tightly covered container; just rinse with cold water and drain before using. Chop the salad toppings and have them ready to go before grilling the seitan.

3. Heat a cast-iron pan or cast-iron grill pan over high heat and brush generously with peanut oil. When the oil is rippling, add a layer of marinated seitan, taking care not to overlap the pieces. Brush with a little of the marinade during grilling and use long-handled metal tongs to flip the seitan over after about 2 minutes. Grill on the other side for another 2 to 2½ minutes until the edges are golden and the seitan looks juicy; do not overcook or the seitan will dry out. Move to a dish arranged on top of the stove range to keep the previously grilled seitan warm while grilling the remaining seitan.

4. To serve, divide the noodles among four large, 1-quart serving bowls. Top with the grilled seitan then scatter on top an equal amount of bean sprouts, shredded lettuce, cucumber, carrot, scallions, cilantro, basil, and mint. Sprinkle generously with ground peanuts. Serve immediately and pass around the *Mock Nuoc Cham* sauce!

Bo Bun with Spring Rolls: A fun variation (and extremely popular Vietnamese dish) on noodle salads would be to replace the grilled seitan with crunchy spring rolls. Not traditional but more delicious that plain spring rolls, make *Watercress Coconut Lumpia Spring Rolls* (page 176), slice while hot into bite-sized pieces, arrange on top of the noodles, vegetable toppings, and peanuts, and serve with *Mock Nuoc Cham* sauce (page 67).

classic sesame noodles with marinated cucumbers

SERVES 3 TO 4

Everybody loves sesame noodles; make some tonight and make more friends who agree with you on this important matter. My recipe is inspired by the noodles served at New York's Chinatown House of Vegetarian restuarant: a pile of soft wheat noodles tucked under a mound of nutty sesame sauce, topped by a huge drift of shredded iceberg lettuce. Yep, you read that right; iceberg lettuce (or finely shredded green cabbage) is redeemed with these noodles as a cool foil to the rich sauce. I prefer to not mix the sauce or vegetables into the noodles and leave that to my dinner guests, but you can toss the noodles with the sauce and vegetables. It's a love fest of peanut noodle goodness any way you serve it.

NOODLES AND CUCUMBERS

- 3 quarts (12 cups) water
- 1 tablespoon kosher salt
- 1 pound fresh thick Asian wheat noodles (Japanese buckwheat soba noodles are a hearty, nutritious substitute)
- 1 teaspoon sesame oil

GRILLED SEITAN NOODLE SALAD (SEITAN BO BUN), PAGE 234

- 1 recipe *Ginger-Marinated Cucumbers* (page 80) or 1 large seedless cucumber (about ½ pound)
- 2 cups thinly sliced iceberg lettuce or savoy cabbage
- 2 tablespoons toasted sesame seeds

SESAME PEANUT SAUCE

- ¼ cup Chinese brown sesame paste (see *Shanghai Kale Dumplings in Sesame Sauce*, page 179) or sesame tahini
- 2 heaping tablespoons smooth, salted natural peanut butter
- 3 tablespoons soy sauce
- 2 tablespoons rice vinegar or Chinese black vinegar (see page 12)
- 4 teaspoons dark brown sugar
- 2 cloves garlic, peeled, grated, or pressed
- 1 teaspoon toasted sesame oil
- ½ teaspoon freshly grated ginger
- 3 to 4 tablespoons hot black tea or hot water

The noodles, sauce, and cucumbers can all be prepared a day in advance and chilled until serving time. If you do have extra time, warm the noodles on the kitchen counter for 20 minutes prior to serving. You can also skip marinating the cucumbers entirely if you want to fast forward a step.

1. Fill a large, 4-quart pot with 3 quarts of water and bring to a rolling boil. Add 1 tablespoon of kosher salt to the cooking water and add noodles. Cook according to package directions, which shouldn't be very long for fresh noodles, about 4 to 5 minutes. (If using Japanese soba noodles, cook noodles according to package directions.) Drain immediately in a large metal colander and rinse with plenty of cold water to keep noodles from sticking together. Shake the noodles in the colander a few times to get rid of

any excess water. Toss the noodles with the sesame oil and set aside.

2. If you're not marinating the cucumbers, prepare the cucumber as follows: use a vegetable peeler to scrape off the cucumber skin and slice it in half lengthwise. Use a rounded 1 teaspoon measuring spoon and scrape it down the center of the cut side of the cucumbers to scoop out the seeds and pulp; use a smaller measuring spoon if the cucumbers are especially small. Slice cucumber halves into ¼-inch slices; the slices should look like fat letter "c"s.

3. For the peanut sauce: in a mixing bowl stir together all of the ingredients except for the hot tea to form a thick paste. Now dribble in the hot tea a tablespoon at a time to reach a consistency like a thick salad dressing. The sauce will get lighter the more liquid you add; if desired add more liquid than listed for a thinner sauce. The sauce will also thicken as it sits, so you may want to loosen it up with a little hot water if making more than 30 minutes before serving. For a really smooth sauce, pulse in a blender.

4. Serve the noodles family style and pile the noodles into a large shallow serving bowl. Dollop the sesame sauce on top of the noodles, then top with the cucumbers, scatter the lettuce on top, and sprinkle with sesame seeds. Each diner will use chopsticks or a big spoon to scoop a serving of noodles, sauce, and vegetables onto her plate and stir everything together.

Greek Eggplant Lasagna (Pastichio "vegani")

MAKES A LARGE CASSEROLE SERVING 6 TO 8

Pastichio *is the Greek answer to lasagna: a tomato-kissed filling is sandwiched between two layers of chewy, tube-shaped pasta, then topped with a creamy bechamel-like sauce and baked to golden brown perfection. Pastichio is Greek holiday or party food, great for sharing or hoarding the tasty leftovers all to yourself. This "vegani" version is bursting with mushrooms, roasted eggplant, and a luscious, creamy cashew topping.*

The pasta traditionally for pastichio is a long, smooth, hollow, tube-shaped pasta. This Greek pasta may be tricky to locate outside of specialty markets; look for the Misko brand and grab a bag of "Macaroni #2." Beyond that, Italian bucatini-style pasta is a close second, with smoothly textured penne tubes at third place.

Like the original pastichio, this dish is prepared in stages and best reserved for weekends or a luxurious evening in the kitchen; but if you like to unwind after a workday in the kitchen (you know who you are), this project is for you. Comforting, filling pastichio is best served with a simple green salad.

SILKEN ALMOST-BECHAMEL TOPPING
    1 cup unroasted, unsalted cashews
    1 pound silken tofu, drained
    2 cloves garlic, peeled and chopped
    2 teaspoons cornstarch
    1 teaspoon garlic powder
    1 teaspoon sea salt

2 tablespoons lemon juice

¼ teaspoon ground nutmeg, plus additional nutmeg for sprinkling

MUSHROOM FILLING

10 ounces brown (cremini) mushrooms

1 large onion, peeled and finely minced

1 tablespoon olive oil

3 cloves garlic, peeled and minced

½ cup dry red wine

1 pound roma tomatoes, cores and seeds removed, diced fine, or two 14-ounce cans diced tomatoes

1 bay leaf

2 teaspoons dried oregano

1 teaspoon dried thyme

¼ teaspoon ground cinnamon

1 teaspoon sea salt (use ½ teaspoon if using canned tomatoes)

A few twists of freshly cracked pepper

PASTA

1 pound uncooked Greek tube-shaped pasta, Italian bucatini, or smooth penne pasta

3 quarts (12 cups) water

3 tablespoons kosher salt

4 tablespoons nonhydrogenated vegan margarine

3 tablespoons all-purpose flour

1 cup plain soy milk

3 tablespoons nutritional yeast

1 tablespoon lemon juice

¼ teaspoon sea salt

1 tablespoon cornstarch

Olive oil to grease pan

1. Prepare the topping first: cover the cashews with hot water and soak for 1 hour or overnight until soft and plump and then drain away the water. Puree the cashews with the remaining topping ingredients in a blender or food processor until creamy, scraping the sides of the blender jar occasionally with a rubber spatula. Depending on how powerful the blender is this may take 1 to 4 minutes. Set topping aside while you prepare the other ingredients.

2. To make the filling, remove the stems from the mushrooms and dice the caps into small, ½-inch pieces. In a 12-inch stainless-steel skillet over medium heat, fry the onion in the olive oil for 4 minutes or until soft, then stir in the garlic and fry for 30 seconds. Stir in the mushrooms and cook for 6 minutes, stirring occasionally until the mushrooms have reduced in bulk and most of their liquid has been absorbed. Pour in the red wine and add the tomatoes, bay leaf, oregano, thyme, cinnamon, and salt; cover and simmer for 10 minutes. Uncover and remove and discard the bay leaf. Cook for 2 minutes and taste the filling; add more salt if desired and a few twists of freshly cracked black pepper. Turn off the heat and set aside.

3. While the mushroom mixture cooks, boil 3 quarts of water and stir in 3 tablespoons of kosher salt. Stir in the pasta and cook according to package directions to an al dente consistency (firm and tender to the bite but not mushy), about 7 to 9 minutes. Drain in a large colander and rinse with plenty of cold water, then set the colander above the sink or a large bowl and drain while making the sauce.

4. Preheat the oven the 375°F and generously rub the insides of a 9 x 13 x 2-inch metal or ceramic lasagna pan with olive oil. In the pot you cooked the pasta in, melt the margarine over medium heat, then sprinkle in the flour. Cook the flour roux mixture until it's bubbling and a pale golden color, about 4 to 6 minutes; stir constantly. Whisk in half of the

soy milk and continue 1 to 2 minutes until the sauce thickens, then turn off the heat. Stir in the nutritional yeast, lemon juice, and salt. In a cup whisk together the remaining half of the soy milk with the cornstarch and whisk into the sauce until smooth. Add the drained pasta and stir vigorously to coat every piece with the sauce.

5. Firmly press two-thirds of the pasta evenly on the bottom of the lasagna pan, then top with the mushroom filling. Spread the remaining pasta over the mushrooms. The pasta will not completely cover the filling; don't worry, you'll be covering everything with the cashew topping. Use a rubber spatula and spread the cashew topping over the pasta completely to the edges of the pan. Sprinkle the top with a big pinch of grated nutmeg and bake uncovered for 26 to 28 minutes or until the top feels somewhat firm. Now heat the oven broiler on high and broil the pastichio for 3 to 4 minutes or until browned in spots—that authentic Greek casserole touch!

6. Let the pastichio cool for 10 minutes, then slice it into big squares with a thin sharp knife and use a bent spatula to lift out individual servings. Pastichio is the ideal dish to prepare the day before serving; to reheat cover with foil and bake at 350°F for 20 to 25 minutes or until the center is hot.

Mushroom Eggplant Pastichio: Roasted eggplant in the mushroom filling is doubly delicious and I'll admit this is an extra step in all already involved process. But if you love eggplant, you must try this!

A slice of Greek Eggplant Lasagna, Pastichio "Vegani," page 238, and a helping of Greek Village Salad with Cashew Faux Feta (horiatiki salad), page 86

Between making the topping and preparing the filling, preheat the oven to 375°F and line a large baking sheet with parchment paper.

Remove the stems from 1½ pounds of purple globe eggplant and dice it into 1-inch cubes. Toss the eggplant with 3 tablespoons of olive oil, sprinkle with a little sea salt, and roast it for 25 minutes, stirring occasionally until the edges of the eggplant are browned and the cubes have softened. Turn off the oven, remove the eggplant, and let cool.

Stir the roasted eggplant into the mushroom filling after the final simmer, stirring thoroughly to coat the eggplant with the sauce.

Fusilli with Almost-Sicilian Arugula Pesto, Potatoes, and Peas

SERVES 3 TO 4

Pesto, peas, and potatoes do a delicious dance in this traditional, earthy pasta. The kicky dark green pesto borrows a few elements (almonds and a touch of chile pepper) from Sicilian pesto to enhance the dish with Northern Italian sensibilities.

Fresh basil leaves can be very gritty; it's easiest to cover them with cold water and soak the leaves for 10 minutes, occasionally swishing around the leaves to release any sand. Remove the leaves and shake any water drops off.

PESTO

- 1 green chile pepper, jalapeño or serrano
- 2 cloves garlic, peeled
- 1 cup basil leaves, washed and firmly packed
- 1 cup small, young arugula leaves, washed, spun dry, and firmly packed
- ½ teaspoon salt
- 3 tablespoons or more extra-virgin olive oil (see note for leaner pesto)
- 2 ripe roma tomatoes, seeds removed
- ½ cup sliced, blanched almonds

PASTA AND VEGETABLES

- ½ pound potatoes, peeled and diced into ½-inch cubes
- 10 ounces fusilli or penne pasta
- 4 quarts (16 cups) water
- 1 tablespoon kosher salt
- 2 cups frozen peas (preferably petit pois) or ½ pound fresh green beans, ends trimmed and sliced into 2-inch pieces
- Freshly cracked pepper
- *Chickpea Parmigiana Topping* (page 67) for sprinkling (optional)

1. Prepare the pesto first: in a food processor pulse all of the ingredients except for the nuts into a thick, smooth paste. Add the nuts and pulse them into the pesto; a slightly gritty texture is best. Taste the pesto and add more salt if necessary.

2. Cook the potatoes and pasta: fill a large pot with 4 quarts of cold water and add the potatoes. Bring to a rolling boil over high heat, then reduce the heat to low and boil the potatoes for 10 minutes or until they are tender but not mushy.

3. Stir the salt into the water, then add the pasta. Cook the pasta until almost al dente, about 8 minutes (always check the package of the pasta you're using for the exact times). Stir in the peas and cook for another 2 minutes, then drain but set aside about ¼ cup of cooking water. Return the pasta and vegetables to the pot.

4. Add the pesto to the pot, plus a few twists of black pepper, and 2 tablespoons of pasta cooking water and stir well with a wooden spoon to coat everything with the pesto. To serve, mound the pasta into a large pasta serving bowl or into individual bowls. If desired, pass around a small bowl of *Chickpea Parmigiana Topping* (page 67) for sprinkling on top.

Roasted Gnocchi with Roasted Tomato Caper Sauce

SERVES 3 TO 4

Roasting gnocchi—*little potato pasta dumplings—makes them bouncy and gives them a chewy crust that transforms ordinary store-bought gnocchi into toothsome fare. Pair it up with a puttanesca-style oven-roasted tomato-caper-olive–chile pepper sauce and relax away from the stove, the oven's got it.*

ROASTED TOMATO CAPER SAUCE

2 pounds plum tomatoes, cores and seeds removed

3 tablespoons olive oil

2 teaspoons dried oregano

1 teaspoon dried rosemary, crumbled

1 teaspoon dried thyme

A pinch of sea salt

3 garlic cloves, sliced into thin slivers

2 tablespoons capers

½ cup sliced green olives

1 teaspoon red pepper flakes

2 teaspoons red wine or balsamic vinegar

1 tablespoon chopped fresh basil leaves

Freshly cracked black pepper

ROASTED GNOCCHI

One 17-ounce package eggless potato gnocchi

3 quarts (12 cups) water

1 tablespoon of kosher salt

1 tablespoon olive oil

You don't have to roast the gnocchi to enjoy the roasted sauce; or try it on your favorite pasta. I recommend purchased gnocchi (my favorite are the usually egg-free gnocchi that come in shelf stable packages) for this recipe as a time-saver.

1. Arrange a rack in the center of the oven, then arrange a second rack underneath it near the bottom of the oven. Preheat oven to 375°F and generously spray with cooking spray (preferably olive oil spray) a 9 x 13 x 2-inch metal or ceramic baking dish. Slice the tomatoes in quarters, then slice each piece in half and add to the pan. Rub the tomatoes with olive oil, oregano, rosemary, thyme, and salt. Stir in the garlic, capers, olives, and red pepper flakes.

2. Place the pan on the center rack of the oven for 35 to 40 minutes, stirring the contents of the pan occasionally; tomatoes will be soft and very juicy. Remove from the oven and stir in the vinegar, basil leaves, and a few twists of black pepper. Cover the pan with foil to keep warm if the gnocchi is not finished roasting

3. While the sauce is roasting, boil the gnocchi in 3 quarts of water salted with 1 tablespoon of kosher salt. Stir gnocchi into the boiling water and cook for 2 minutes; the dumplings will rise to the top. Drain and rinse with cold water, then drain well again and toss with olive oil. Spray a baking sheet with nonstick cooking spray or cover with a sheet of parchment paper. Spread gnocchi in a single layer on the baking sheet.

4. During the last 20 minutes of roasting the tomato sauce, move the gnocchi to the bottom rack of the oven and roast for 10 minutes. Remove from the oven, use a spatula to flip each piece, and bake another 10 minutes until gnocchi is golden and slightly crusty on the outside. To serve, transfer the roasted gnocchi to a serving dish. Spoon roasted sauce on top and mangia!

CHAPTER 9

Hearty entrees

I apologize in advance for the diversity of deliciousness in this chapter. Panko-crusted tempeh katsu cutlets (baked, not fried!), crisp and creamy filo pies, spicy Ethiopian seitan stews, garlicky Korean barbequed mushrooms, leeks sweetly braised in red wine with a touch of French country cooking . . . it was difficult to label all of these outrageously good entrees made on top and insideof your oven under one banner. So for now we'll call this dinner. Let's eat!

sesame panko tempeh cutlets (tempeh *katsu*)

SERVES 2 REALLY HUNGRY TONKATSU FANS OR 3 WITH RICE AND SALAD

Marinated tempeh is jacketed Japanese-style in panko crumbs (katsu-style) and sesame, then baked crisp and golden; served with BBQ-like homemade tonkatsu sauce and cool shredded cabbage it's both refreshing and comforting. The tempeh can be marinated for a day or two in advance and the tonaktsu sauce made up to a week in advance for this katsu for dinner on busy weeknights.

MARINATED TEMPEH

> 8-ounce rectangular cake of tempeh
> 3 tablespoons soy sauce
> 1 tablespoon mirin (see page 16)
> 3 cloves garlic, peeled and grated on a
>   Microplane grater
> ½ teaspoon finely grated fresh ginger
>   (see page 80 for fresh ginger tips)

COATING

> ⅓ cup plain, unsweetened soy milk
> 1 tablespoon lemon juice
> 2 tablespoons cornstarch or tapioca flour
> 6 tablespoons all-purpose flour
> 1 cup panko bread crumbs
> 2 tablespoons white sesame seeds
> 2 tablespoons peanut or canola oil
> Cooking oil spray

GARNISH

> 3 cups finely shredded green cabbage
> 2 scallions, sliced very thin
> Lemon wedges
> 1 recipe prepared *Tonkatsu Sauce* (page 70)
> Hot boiled short-grain white rice, brown
>   rice, or soba noodles cooked according to
>   package directions

No cooking spray? Dip a pastry brush into oil, hover the ends of the brush no less than 3 inches above, and gently flick oil over the surface as needed.

1. Slice tempeh cake in half into two squares, then slice each piece horizontally for a total of four thin squares of tempeh. In a small pot bring about 2 cups of cold water to a rolling boil; gently slide the tempeh in and cook for 5 minutes. While that's going on, in a shallow baking dish whisk together the marinade ingredients. Remove the tempeh from the water with long-handled tongs, shake free any excess water, and slide it into marinade. Let it stand for at least 20 minutes (or overnight), turning the tempeh occasionally to absorb as much marinade as possible.

2. Preheat oven to 420°F and line a baking sheet with parchment paper. In a pie plate use a fork to whisk together soy milk, lemon juice, cornstarch, and 2 tablespoons of the flour. Pour the panko crumbs and sesame seeds into a large shallow bowl or large dinner plate, then drizzle the oil over the crumbs; use your fingers to mix together. Form a panko-crusting assembly line with the panko closest to the baking sheet, then the soy milk batter, and lastly the tempeh.

SESAME PANKO TEMPEH CUTLETS (TEMPEH KATSU)

3. For each cutlet, gently lift from the pan and shake off any remaining marinade. Place tempeh on a cutting board, then, to help absorb some of the surface moisture, sprinkle a little of the remaining flour over each side of the tempeh. Now use one hand to dip the tempeh into the soy milk batter; flip it over to coat both sides with batter. Drop the tempeh into the panko crumbs, and with your other hand (the one not used to touch the soy milk batter), pile crumbs over the tempeh and carefully press in as much panko as possible all over the surface of the cutlet. Gently transfer it to the baking sheet and spray generously with cooking spray. Repeat with remaining cutlets and bake for 15 minutes, then use a spatula to gently flip over the cutlets. Bake another 8 to 10 minutes until the crumbs are golden.

4. To serve, use a spatula to slide a tempeh cutlet onto a cutting board. With a sharp, heavy knife use a single downward motion (don't saw back and forth, you'll mess up the coating) and slice cutlets into ½-inch-wide slices. Slide the spatula under the sliced cutlet and slide onto a serving dish; arrange a mound of fluffy shredded cabbage next to the cutlet and sprinkle with scallions. Serve with a lemon wedge and a condiment dish of warm *Tonkatsu Sauce*. For a more substantial meal, serve with boiled short-grain rice (page 299).

How to eat tempeh tonkatsu? Squeeze the lemon wedge over the tempeh; use chopsticks to dip a tempeh strip into the sauce, and occasionally nibble on cabbage strands to refresh the palate.

sensei tofu hijiki burgers

MAKES 8 BURGERS

Dojo's restaurant in the heart of NYC's East Village must pump out hundreds of hearty fried hijiki-flecked tofu burgers a week, feeding hungry college students or those who like to live like students for decades. Still some of the best tofu slung in town if you ask me. Baked (or even lightly pan-fried) these are lighter and protein packed and should be served with a generous helping of **Ninja Carrot Ginger Dressing** *(page 84), a crisp salad, and short-grain brown rice. For a near-authentic at-home experience, drizzle the patties with* **Tonkatsu Sauce** *(page 70) before serving.*

Dried hijiki seaweed resembles fine black filaments that expand into plump shreds when soaked in water. A little goes a long way; a 2-ounce package of dried hijiki will stretch through four or more batches of these tofu burgers.

TOFU PATTIES

　　1 pound firm tofu, drained

　　2 tablespoons dried hijiki seaweed

　　2 tablespoons sesame seeds, pulsed into a fine powder in a coffee grinder

　　3 cloves garlic, peeled then grated or pressed

　　2 tablespoons soy sauce

　　2 teaspoons toasted sesame oil

　　2 scallions, root ends trimmed and thinly sliced

　　⅓ cup panko bread crumbs

COATING

   ¾ cup panko bread crumbs
   1 tablespoon vegetable oil
   Vegetable oil or vegetable oil spray

1. Crumble the tofu into a large metal colander. Arrange the colander over the sink or on top of a bowl. Cover the tofu with plastic wrap or a paper towel, then place a few heavy items in the colander (cans or a bag of onions works well). Set the tofu aside for about 20 minutes to drain. Meanwhile in a small bowl cover the hijiki with hot water and soak for about 5 minutes; the seaweed is ready when the hijiki strands are plump and soft. If you're baking the burgers, preheat the oven to 375°F and line a baking sheet with parchment paper.

2. After about 20 minutes, remove the weights and paper towel from the tofu. Gather the tofu in your hands and give it one final squeeze to eliminate any extra moisture, then transfer it to a mixing bowl. Drain the seaweed and press it on top of a metal sieve to remove excess moisture, then add to the tofu. Add the sesame seeds, garlic, soy sauce, toasted sesame oil, scallions, and ⅓ cup of panko bread crumbs to the tofu. Use your hands to thoroughly knead these ingredients into the tofu to create a soft dough. Divide the dough into eight pieces and shape them into eight round burger patties about ½ inch thick; place them on a dish or cutting board.

3. On a large dinner plate, sprinkle the remaining ¾ cup of panko breadcrumbs. Drizzle the 1 tablespoon of oil over the crumbs, then use your fingers to toss the breadcrumbs and work the oil into the crumbs. Gently dredge both sides of a tofu burger in the crumbs, pushing up some crumbs and pressing them along the sides of the burger. If baking the burgers, transfer to the baking sheet and repeat with remaining burgers. Generously spray tops of burgers with cooking oil spray and bake for 15 minutes,

remove from the oven and use a spatula to carefully flip each burger over. Spray tops with cooking oil spray, return to the oven, and bake another 15 minutes or until panko crumbs are golden. Remove from the oven and serve immediately with salad, **Ninja Carrot Ginger Dressing** (page 84) and boiled or steamed short-grain rice if desired.

4. To fry the burgers, preheat a cast-iron skillet over medium high heat for 5 minutes. Don't add the 1 tablespoon of oil to the breadcrumbs used for dredging the burgers; just cover them with plain unoiled crumbs. Pour a thin layer of oil over the surface of the pan and fry two to three burgers at a time, about 3 to 4 minutes per side until the panko is golden. Use a spatula to gently flip the burgers; they can be fragile when hot.

Korean Veggie Bulgogi (sweet soy BBQ)

SERVES 4 HUNGRY BBQ FANS, OR 6 WITH EXTRA SIDES OR APPETIZERS

(NOT INCLUDING MARINATING TIME)

From Seoul to Queens, Korean-style BBQ is a cooking event. Gathered around a table, scooping up sweet and savory grilled morsels and wrapping them up in cool lettuce leaves and garlicky sauces—it's a party for friends, family, and frenemies.

A great vegan version of Korean bulgogi can be enjoyed at home starring pressed tofu, thinly sliced homemade seitan, and an assortment of tender

mushrooms. King mushrooms (also called elf mushrooms) have fat, succulent stems that are my favorite on the grill and a common find in Asian groceries.

Indoor grilling with a cast-iron pan works just fine, but if you have the opportunity to grill outdoors then go Korean bulgogi; it might be tough BBQing any other way.

Marinate the ingredients up to 24 hours in advance; the longer the tofu sits in the marinade, the more flavor it drinks up.

MIXED GRILL

1 pound extra-firm tofu
10 ounces seitan or ½ recipe of *5-Spice Seitan* (page 51) or 8 to 10 ounces tempeh
10 ounces fresh shiitake mushrooms, large portobello mushrooms (2 to 3 caps), oyster mushrooms, or king mushrooms
10 garlic cloves, peeled

MARINADE

⅔ cup soy sauce
⅓ cup dark brown sugar, packed
½ cup finely grated apple, pear, or Asian pear (unpeeled)
3 tablespoons mirin (see page 16)
2 tablespoons vegetable oil
4 cloves garlic, finely grated
4 scallions, trimmed and finely chopped
2 tablespoons toasted sesame seeds
1 teaspoon toasted sesame oil
Several twists of freshly ground black pepper
½ cup or more peanut oil or high-heat canola oil for grilling

To grate the fruit for the marinade, use the finest holes on a box grater. This will create a pulpy fruit mush, excellent for juicy marinades.

ACCOMPANIMENTS

Boiled white or short-grain brown rice
10 to 15 large leaves of leafy green lettuce such as Boston or romaine, washed and dried
Korean garlic soybean paste (see page 15)
Fast Lane Cabbage Kimchi (page 56) or store-bought

1. Press tofu as directed for *Savory Baked Tofu* (page 50). If using steamed seitan, use a very sharp chef's knife and slice lengthwise as thin as possible, no thicker than ¼ inch; if using purchased seitan drain and slice into bite-size pieces. For the tempeh, slice each cake in half lengthwise, slice in half and then slice each square into triangles; steam for 8 minutes. For the mushrooms, slice portobello mushrooms into ½-inch-thick strips; separate oyster mushrooms into single mushrooms; keep shiitake mushrooms whole and remove any hard stems. Brush away any dirt from mushrooms with a damp kitchen towel. Keep garlic cloves whole and if grilling outside skewer the garlic cloves together on a bamboo or metal skewer to prevent them from falling into the fire.

2. In a large mixing bowl whisk together the marinade ingredients. Marinate the food either separately in its own dish and distribute the marinade evenly, or put everything, except the tempeh, together in a big mixing bowl. For the tempeh, marinate it in its own dish to prevent it from crumbling. Set aside for at least 1 hour, or tightly cover and refrigerate overnight. Occasionally stir to redistribute the marinade.

3. When it's time to grill, cook the rice and keep warm. Wash, spin dry the lettuce leaves, seal in a zip-top plastic bag and keep chilled until ready to serve. Scoop the garlic soybean paste into serving dishes. Now fire up the grill or over high heat, preheat a cast-iron grill pan and have ready long-handled metal tongs, peanut oil, and a heat-resistant basting brush. Grill the food in a single layer over high heat, taking care to oil the pan whenever the food starts to stick. The tofu will take the longest, about 2 to 3 minutes per side for a golden brown crust; after that the tempeh around 2 minutes per side. When grilling the seitan and mushrooms, watch carefully and don't overcook, about 1 to 1½ minutes per side to prevent drying out. Grill the garlic cloves until they are tender and golden, about 3 to 4 minutes.

4. Arrange grilled food on a serving platter and let guests assemble their own wraps using a lettuce leaf, a smear of garlic soybean paste, a few spoonfuls of rice if desired, and a piece of grilled tofu, tempeh, seitan, or mushroom and include a chunk of grilled garlic. Nibble on kimchi, drink a beer, and have a good time!

Barbequed seitan strips (char siu seitan)

SERVES 4 AS AN ENTREE WITH RICE, 6 OR MORE AS AN APPETIZER

Recipe testers adored these strips of seitan roasted in sticky char siu *sauce, reminiscent of the Chinese barbequed ribs of their childhood. Make this when a craving for old-fashioned Chinese takeout strikes; these strips are unapologetically meaty and toothsome. And if you have the prepared seitan already, most of the cooking time is done in the oven, leaving time for a quick veggie stir-fry.*

*There are two ways to roast these; less time for juicy, saucy seitan for the traditional accompaniment of **Ginger-Marinated Cucumbers** (page 80), sautéed greens, and boiled short-grain rice (page 299). Or a longer roast for shiny and crispy edges tinged a deep mahogany (your new favorite appetizer).*

1 recipe (4 cutlets) of *5-Spice Seitan* (page 51), completely cooled (preferably overnight)

MARINADE

⅓ cup dark agave nectar

3 tablespoons hoisin sauce (see page 13)

3 tablespoons peanut or grapeseed oil

3 tablespoons Chinese Shaoxing cooking wine (see page 13) or dry sherry

3 tablespoons vegetarian stir-fry sauce (see page 13)

2 tablespoons soy sauce

1½ teaspoons *Sichuan 5-Spice Powder* (page 41) or store-bought Chinese 5-spice powder

2 scallions, green part only, thinly sliced

1 tablespoon toasted sesame seeds

1. Slice each seitan cutlet into ½-inch-wide strips. Whisk all of the marinade ingredients in a large measuring cup.

2. Spread seitan slices in a ceramic 9 x 13 x 2-inch dish or two smaller ceramic baking dishes. Pour the marinade over the seitan and with tongs toss to thoroughly coat each piece with marinade. Marinate at room temperature for 1 hour, stirring seitan strips

occasionally. The last 20 minutes of marinating the seitan, preheat oven to 400°F.

3. For saucier seitan for eating over rice, roast for 20 to 25 minutes or until seitan is sizzling but there is still some thick sauce under the strips. Use long-handled tongs to frequently stir the seitan strips during the roasting process. Serve hot, garnished with sliced scallions and sesame seeds.

4. For chewier, sticky seitan with a glossy sheen and crisped edges, roast for 30 to 35 minutes. Use long-handled tongs to frequently stir the strips during the roasting process. Most of the sauce should be absorbed and what little is left is sticky. Turn on the broiler to high and broil for 2 minutes, until edges of the seitan are just starting to brown. Immediately remove from broiler; cool 5 minutes before serving. Slice into bite-size pieces if desired. Sprinkle strips with sliced scallions and sesame seeds and serve hot.

Gyro Roasted Seitan

SERVES 4 ALONG WITH SIDES OR IN A PITA

Seitan gets the gyro makeover, oven roasted in a bracing marinade of olive oil, lemon juice, oregano, and plenty of garlic. Use these as a building block for authentic-tasting gyro sandwiches (page 112) or a complete Mediterranean meal with **Lemon Garlic Potatoes** *(page 285),* **Lemony Dill Rice** *(page 304),*

BARBEQUED SEITAN STRIPS (CHAR SIU SEITAN), PAGE 251

and **Greek Village Salad with Cashew Faux Feta** *(page 86).*

> ¼ cup lemon juice
> ⅓ cup vegetable broth or white wine
> 3 tablespoons olive oil
> 6 cloves garlic, peeled and minced
> 1½ teaspoons dried oregano
> ½ teaspoon ground cumin
> ¼ teaspoon sea salt
> 2 cutlets of **Lemon and Olive Chickpea Seitan** (page 54), any of the **Seitan Coriander Cutlets** variations (page 49), or 10 ounces commercially prepared seitan

1. Preheat oven to 400°F. In a 9 x 13 x 2-inch ceramic or glass baking dish, whisk together all the ingredients except the seitan.

2. Slice the seitan into strips ¼ inch wide. Add to marinade and flip strips several times to coat completely. Set aside to marinate while oven is preheating.

3. Roast the seitan for 25 minutes, turning the strips frequently with long-handled tongs. Remove from oven and serve immediately.

This Is Sparta! Spinach Pie

MAKES ONE 9 X 14-INCH PIE

My first attempts at Greek spinach pie can be found in the pages of Isa Moskowitz's classic Vegan with a Vengeance. *That recipe still rocks, but since then I've been won over by the versatility of soaked, blended cashews to help produce a creamy mouth-feel for the perfect vegan "cheesy" filling. Sometimes I like to mix up the spinach filling by replacing half with sweet, crunchy chard. Just be sure to mince the stems as finely as possible before sautéing with the spinach.*

This style of spinach pie is the easiest method of assembly, where the filling is inserted between two layered sheets of filo (or phyllo) dough to create one large pie. More labor intensive but rewarding, single-serving pies in two shapes are a delight to look at and eat: either the classic triangle shape or the lovely coiled "snail" bun (see illustrations), a favorite you'll see in many bakery windows in Athens and Sparta. Serve any shape of this pie with a crisp tomato, cucumber, and crunchy lettuce salad dressed with abundant lemon and olive oil for a fresh and filling entree.

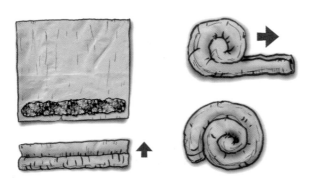

FILLING

> 1 cup whole unroasted, unsalted cashews
> 6 cloves garlic, peeled
> ¼ cup nutritional yeast
> 1 teaspoon sea salt
> 4 tablespoons lemon juice
> 2 tablespoons olive oil
> 2½ teaspoons light-colored (shiro) miso
> 1 pound soft tofu (not silken), drained and gently squeezed to remove extra water
> 2 pounds fresh spinach
> 1 cup roughly chopped fresh dill
> 6 scallions, root ends trimmed and finely chopped
> ½ teaspoon ground black pepper

FILO

> 8 tablespoons (½ cup or 1 stick) of nonhydrogenated vegan margarine, melted
> ½ cup olive oil
> 1 pound of frozen filo dough, approximately twenty 13 x 18-inch sheets, completely thawed (you will have some leftover sheets)

1. First, prepare the filling: place cashews in a bowl and cover with 2 inches of boiling water. Set aside for 1 hour or overnight; cashews are ready to use when plump and soft. Drain the cashews and pour them into a food processor. Add the garlic, nutritional yeast, sea salt, lemon juice, olive oil, and miso and pulse into a thick paste, scraping down the sides of the food processor frequently with a rubber spatula. In a separate mixing bowl crumble the tofu, then add the cashew mixture (no need to mix together yet) and set aside.

2. Wash and dry the spinach and remove thick stems. Stack a few leaves, roll them into a tight

cigar, and chop the leaves and stems as finely as possible. In a large, deep skillet heat the olive oil over medium heat and add the spinach. Stir frequently and cook spinach until wilted and soft, 4 to 5 minutes. Remove from the heat and let cool completely.

3. Grab a handful of cooked spinach and with both hands firmly squeeze to remove as much liquid as possible; do this over another mixing bowl or the sink for less mess. Add the squeezed spinach to the tofu mixture and repeat with remaining spinach. Add the dill, scallions, black pepper, and spinach to the tofu mixture and mix thoroughly. Taste the mixture and add more lemon juice or salt as desired for a tangier or saltier filling.

4. Preheat the oven to 400°F. In large cup, combine the melted margarine and olive oil. Use this mixture to generously brush the insides of a 9 x 13 x 2-inch ceramic or metal baking pan. Prepare

Filo Finagling (Working With, Not Against Filo)

→ Create plenty of work space. You'll need enough room on the kitchen counter or a tabletop to fit side-by-side the filo dough, the pan you're baking it in, plus bowls for the filling and oil-margarine mixture.

→ Filo dough must be protected against drying out. The easiest way is to sandwich the stack of dough sheets between plastic wrap and then top the plastic wrap with a clean kitchen towel. Always keep unused filo covered.

→ To prepare the filo dough for use, gently remove completely thawed filo from the package and carefully unroll. Work quickly and with a very sharp knife trim the filo to fit the insides of the pan. Layer the trimmed sheets on top of each other, and return to keeping them covered until ready to use.

→ To oil a sheet of filo, pull back the kitchen towel and carefully transfer a trimmed sheet into the bottom of a well-oiled baking pan. Immediately cover up the remaining filo sheets, then use a pastry brush dipped in the oil or an oil-margarine mixture to sprinkle plenty of oil over the filo. Then use long, gentle brush strokes to completely spread the oil over the dough, dipping the brush into the oil if the dough looks dry.

→ Repeat by adding another sheet from the stack (quickly covering up the stack after removing a sheet to keep them moist), arrange this sheet on top of the oiled sheet and brush with oil. Repeat as needed.

→ Avoid touching filo with wet fingers or placing filo dough on a wet counter top; sheets will stick together and make a mess. To guard against any unwanted moisture on the work surface, sprinkle your filo work surface with all-purpose flour. This is especially helpful when making individual filo pies. If the edges of a stack of filo sheets do stick together, use the tip of a sharp knife to separate them while still damp and sprinkle with a little bit of flour. Once more, remember to cover up the dough to keep it from drying out!

→ Gently roll and tightly wrap any unused filo dough. Once thawed, it should not be frozen again, but it can be kept in the refrigerator for up to 2 weeks.

the filo dough for use as directed in "Filo Finagling" (on the previous page), slicing the sheets in half (or whatever size necessary) to fit inside the pan. Arrange a sheet of trimmed filo into the bottom of the pan.

5. Using a pastry brush, lightly brush this sheet of filo with the oil-margarine mixture, top with another sheet, and repeat until you have ten layers total. Spread half of the filling evenly over the filo. Repeat another layering of filo brushed with the oil for eight sheets total, then spread the other half of filling over this layer. Top the filling with a final layer of ten sheets of dough and gently press the pie down. Using a thin, sharp serrated knife and pressing down on sections of the pie to keep it from moving around too much, cut the pie all the way through to the bottom into diamonds or squares about 4 inches wide. Bake the pie for 20 minutes, then remove from the oven. Pour the leftover oil mixture evenly over the top and bake for 24 to 26 minutes or until the top is a very light golden brown and lightly puffed. Remove the pie from the oven and let stand for 10 minutes before serving. Run the knife through the sliced sections once more to loosen the slices before lifting out of the pan.

For Single-Serving Triangles or Spirals

Brush a 13 x 18-inch sheet of filo with the margarine-oil mixture. Spread it with ¼ cup of filling as shown on the previous page and fold as illustrated. Brush the top of each pie with more margarine-oil mixture and bake for 30 to 35 minutes as directed for the filo pie or until golden brown.

Moroccan Vegetable Filo Pie (Bisteeya)

SERVES 6 TO 8

Bisteeya *(or bastilla or pastilla) is a glorious show-off entree pastry, a large pie made of layers of filo and toasted almonds encasing a creamy, aromatic filling that's both savory and a little bit sweet. Traditionally it's baked in enormous pans, but for our purposes a springform pan does a great job at containing the pie for a cozy dinner for six. Bisteeya is classically stuffed with pigeon and eggs, but this pie is filled with the internationally accepted vegan substitute for the darling bird and egg binder: cauliflower, chickpeas, and silken almond milk sauce. A touch of saffron gives the filling a golden glow and the top is dusted with an unexpected flourish of powdered sugar and cinnamon for a play on sweet and savory flavors (the sugar topping is traditional, so give it a try and enjoy this unusual combination).*

Make this bisteeya when you have a few hours set aside. It's also possible to spread the construction of the ingredients over a few days and enlist a friend to help with the preparation of the filling and layering of the filo. The assembled pie can be chilled for 4 hours prior to baking, helpful because bisteeya is best relished warm out of the oven. Pair this with a spicy **Harissa Carrot Salad** *(page 106) to complement your work of filo art.*

Follow the filo-handling advice for the spinach pie on the previous page.

SILKEN ALMOND MILK SAUCE

1 cup plain almond milk

6 ounces firm silken tofu (½ box of Mori-Nu shelf-stable tofu)

2 tablespoons cornstarch

2 tablespoons lemon juice

SAFFRON VEGETABLES

1 large yellow onion, peeled and finely diced

2 tablespoons olive oil

6 cloves garlic, peeled and minced

1½-inch piece peeled ginger, minced

2½ cups finely diced cauliflower

One 14-ounce can chickpeas (2 cups cooked), drained and rinsed

1 cup vegetable broth

1½ teaspoons salt

1 tablespoon of baharat spice blend (purchased or homemade, page 43) or a combination of 1 teaspoon ground cinnamon, 1 teaspoon ground black pepper, 1 teaspoon ground ginger, and ½ teaspoon cayenne pepper

A big pinch of saffron threads, crumbled

¼ cup fine dry bread crumbs, plus a little extra if needed

⅓ cup finely chopped flat-leaf parsley

⅓ cup finely chopped fresh cilantro

GROUND ALMONDS

1⅔ cups blanched, sliced almonds

3 tablespoons powdered sugar

FILO DOUGH AND TOPPING

Eight 13 x 18-inch sheets of filo dough, thawed

8 tablespoons nonhydrogenated vegan margarine, melted

6 tablespoons olive oil

2 tablespoons powdered sugar

1 teaspoon ground cinnamon

1. Make the Silken Almond Milk Sauce first: pulse the almond milk, tofu, cornstarch, and lemon juice in a blender until smooth and set aside.

2. Now sauté the vegetables: in a deep, 12-inch skillet over medium heat sauté together the onion and olive oil until the onion is tender and translucent, about 4 minutes. Stir in the garlic and ginger, sauté for 1 minute, then stir in the cauliflower. Sauté for 4 minutes, then stir in the chickpeas, vegetable broth, salt, baharat spice blend, and saffron. Increase heat to medium heat and bring to an active simmer. Simmer, partially covered for 5 minutes. Uncover the pan and continue to simmer for another 4 minutes or until most of the vegetable broth has been absorbed.

3. Stir in the silken almond sauce. Continue to stir and cook the mixture for 3 to 4 minutes or until the sauce has thickened slightly. Sprinkle in the breadcrumbs, parsley, and cilantro and fold into the filling. The filling should have the consistency of a soft stuffing and not be too wet. If the filling is very wet, sprinkle in 2 to 3 additional tablespoons of breadcrumbs. Turn off the heat and transfer the skillet to a cold burner to cool off.

4. Make the ground almonds: in a small skillet over medium heat, toast the almonds until pale golden brown, about 4 to 6 minutes; remove the pan from the heat, and cool for 5 minutes. Set aside 2 tablespoons of sliced almonds for topping the bisteeya. Transfer the remaining almonds to a food processor, add the powdered sugar, and pulse into coarse crumbs.

5. Get ready to put together the bisteeya! Preheat the oven to 350°F and have nearby a 9½-inch

springform pan and small baking sheet to put underneath the pan. Combine the margarine with the olive oil and grab a pastry brush. Prepare the filo dough as instructed for spinach pie on page 255, but don't trim the filo to the round shape of the springform pan. Instead, trim the sheets to large, 13 x 9-inch rectangles (the size of about half of an average-size filo sheet). Make sure to keep the filo covered at all times to prevent drying out.

6. Assemble the bisteeya: brush the insides of the springform pan lightly with the margarine mixture. Lay a sheet of filo in the center of the pan and press the long ends up the sides of the pan, overhanging the edges over the edge of the pan. Brush the top with a little margarine mixture. Now take another filo sheet, turn it 90 degrees, and lay it perpendicular to the sheet underneath it; press the longs ends up the sides of the pan and overhang the edges over the edge of the pan. Brush with margarine, then repeat layering the filo pastry, turning each new layer 90 degrees until the entire insides of the pan have filo encasing them. Use ten trimmed sheets of filo dough to line the pan. If at any point you run out of margarine while brushing the filo, melt a little extra or continue brushing with just olive oil.

7. Sprinkle half of the almond mixture in the bottom of the pan on top of the filo. Scoop the filling on top of the almonds, spreading it all the way to the edges. Sprinkle the remaining half of the almond mixture on top of the filling.

8. Layer another six sheets of filo on top of the filling, turning each sheet another 90 degrees before adding another sheet. Brush each layer with a little margarine. Now fold the overhanging edges

of filo toward the center of the pie; this doesn't have to look neat, as this will eventually become the bottom of the pie that nobody will see. Brush with any remaining margarine, and place the pan on top of the baking sheet. Bake for 45 to 55 minutes or until the filo is golden brown and crisp.

9. Remove pie from the oven and let stand for 10 minutes. Place a large serving dish on top of the pie, slide an oven mitt underneath the pan and flip it over onto the serving dish. Remove the ring and the bottom from the springform pan. Dust the top of the pie with powdered sugar, then cinnamon, then lastly scatter the reserved 2 tablespoons of toasted almonds on top. To serve, slice the hot pie with a sharp serrated knife.

Roasted Tomatoes and Peppers Stuffed with Dill Rice (Yemista)

SERVES 6 AS AN ENTREE, MORE AS A STARTER

This succulent homestyle Greek specialty of stuffed and roasted tomatoes and bell peppers is often vegan and served as a meatless entree, as the savory herb-flecked stuffing is substantial. Most any summer vegetable can be made into yemista, including surplus zucchini from the garden along with the most popular choice for yemista, large, ripe red tomatoes.

This recipe is versatile: it's a beautiful entree to serve at elegant dinners or can be prepared with smaller vegetables for engaging appetizers along-

MOROCCAN VEGETABLE FILO PIE (BISTEEYA), PAGE 256

side a salad or **Lemon Garlic Potatoes** (page 285). Yemista are delicious served hot or at room temperature, so if you're going to bother turning on the oven in the summer, go ahead and double or triple this recipe.

Have an extra tomato or pepper handy; depending on the size of the vegetables, the filling is generous and can be stretched far.

3 pounds ripe red tomatoes (about 6 to 8 large tomatoes)

1 pound green or red bell peppers (3 to 4 average-size peppers) or young zucchini or eggplant no thicker than 3 inches wide

¼ cup extra-virgin olive oil

1 large white onion, peeled and finely diced

6 cloves garlic, peeled and minced

1 cup uncooked long-grain white rice

1 cup vegetable broth

1 large carrot, peeled and finely grated

⅓ cup chopped fresh dill

2 tablespoons finely chopped fresh mint

1½ teaspoons dried oregano

½ teaspoon salt or more to taste

Freshly ground pepper

¼ cup chopped walnuts

Additional olive oil for drizzling, about 1 teaspoon per stuffed vegetable

1. Preheat oven to 425°F. Lightly oil or spray with cooking spray a 9 x 11 x 3-inch metal or ceramic baking dish. Even better, try fitting your tomatoes and peppers into baking dishes first and see if they'll all stand side by side; if there's not enough room, use additional baking dishes to fit all of the vegetables. The vegetables need to be supported so they can stand up in the dish.

2. Wash the tomatoes and peppers. Carefully cut the tops off the tomatoes and peppers, creating a lid about ½ inch thick, and set aside. Remove the core from the peppers and discard seeds. Use a spoon and gently hollow out the tomatoes, leaving a ¼-inch-thick wall, and set aside the pulp. If using zucchini or eggplant, create the lid by slicing off the top third of the vegetable lengthwise; use a tablespoon to hollow out the center and set aside the pulp. Lightly sprinkle the insides of the tomato, peppers, and zucchini, if using, with sea salt. Turn the vegetables upside down on top of paper towels to absorb any juices draining from the insides.

3. Finely chop or squish the tomato pulp into a thick liquid. If you're using zucchini, dice the hollowed-out pulp as fine as possible, then combine with the tomato pulp. Measure the pulp. You want about 1½ cups of juicy pulp; if you have any more than that discard it, if you have any less add extra vegetable broth or white wine to reach 1 ½ cups total.

4. Heat ¼ cup of the olive oil in a large saucepan over medium heat. Add the onions and garlic and fry for 2 minutes, then stir in rice and fry for another 2 minutes. Add the vegetable broth, stir, cover and simmer for 12 minutes to partially cook the rice. Most of the liquid will be absorbed by the rice, but the grains will be hard in the center and the rice should be wet. Turn off the heat and uncover.

5. In a large bowl combine the rice mixture with the 1½ cups of tomato pulp, grated carrot, dill, mint, oregano, salt, pepper, and walnuts. Taste the filling and add more salt if necessary. Shake the hollowed-out tomatoes and vegetables to remove any excess liquid. Stand upright in the baking dish and fill each vegetable only ¾ of the way with rice mixture. It's important not to completely fill the vegetables as the rice will continue to expand during baking and may burst through the delicate skins of the tomatoes.

6. Top the tomatoes and vegetables with their respective "lids." Drizzle the tops of the vegetables with olive oil and sprinkle with a little more salt.

Carefully pour ½ cup of water around only the sides of the vegetables in the pan. Cover the top of the pan tightly with foil. Bake for 30 minutes, remove the foil, continue to bake for another 20 to 30 minutes or until tops of tomatoes are browned, the rice filling is tender, and most of the water around the sides of the vegetables has evaporated. If the water level in the pans gets very low before the baking is done, carefully pour in another ½ cup of hot water around the vegetables. Serve yemista hot or at room temperature.

Baked Punky Pumpkin Kibbe

SERVES 4 TO 6

If you recall that I adore kibbe (see page 111 for an entirely different take on this Lebanese classic), you won't be surprised if I say this also is my favorite recipe. Filled with pumpkin, sweet spices, caramelized onions, and walnuts, this baked style of kibbe is a riff off an exquisite dish offered at The Middle East restaurant in Cambridge, Massachusetts, which is one hell of a Lebanese restaurant and punk rock venue rolled into one big pita. If you're not sure what to expect, imagine a golden pumpkin vegetable loaf fragrant with mellow autumn spices; serve with cool **Cashew Yogurt Sauce** *(page 65), a big dollop of* **Roasted Chile Pepper Harissa Paste** *(page 42), and a* **Mediterranean Chopped Salad** *(page 87).*

ONION WALNUT FILLING

> 1 pound red onions, peeled and finely diced
> 2 tablespoons olive oil
> ⅔ cup finely chopped walnuts
> ½ teaspoon ground cinnamon
> ½ teaspoon ground cumin
> ½ teaspoon sea salt
> A pinch of ground cloves

KIBBE DOUGH

> 2½ cups fine-grained bulgur wheat
>   (No. 1 bulgur)
> 2 pounds sugar pumpkin, peeled and seeds
>   removed
> 2 large yellow onions (about ½ pound),
>   peeled and coarsely chopped
> 3 tablespoons olive oil
> ¼ cup finely chopped parsley
> 2 teaspoons dried oregano
> 1½ teaspoons ground cinnamon
> 1¼ teaspoons sea salt
> 1½ teaspoons ground coriander
> ¾ teaspoon ground black pepper
> ½ teaspoon ground mace or nutmeg
> ¼ teaspoon cayenne pepper
> Additional olive oil for brushing (about
>   2 tablespoons)

For best results, use fine, peeled bulgur from a Middle Eastern market for a delicate, tender kibbe; the chunky, dark "hippy" stuff from bulk natural food store bins will make a coarser loaf.

1. Pour bulgur into a large, very fine gauge metal mesh strainer and rinse with cool water. If the holes in your strainer are too big (as the bulgur is a very fine grain this may happen), line your strainer with damp paper towels before adding the bulgur.

Place the strainer on top of bowl to drain any excess moisture.

2. Make the filling: in a large, 12-inch skillet over medium heat, fry the onion with the olive oil and sauté until soft and golden brown, about 14 to 16 minutes. Stir in walnuts, cinnamon, cumin, salt, and ground cloves and fry for another 2 minutes. Turn off the heat and set aside to cool.

3. Make the kibbe dough: fit the food processor with a shredding disc and feed a few chunks of pumpkin at a time into the processor until all of it is finely shredded; if the processor bowl starts to get too full, transfer some of the pumpkin to a mixing bowl. Now, feed the onion through the processor to grind it into a pulp. The dough will be juicy, but that's okay! Empty any remaining pumpkin, onion and their juices into the mixing bowl and stir in the soaked bulgur, olive oil, parsley, oregano, cinnamon, salt, coriander, mace, cayenne, and pepper and mix thoroughly with your hands. One more time, working in two to three batches, run the pumpkin mixture through the food processor to creat a thick, evenly ground paste. Taste the kibbe paste and add more salt if necessary.

4. Preheat oven to 375°F. Brush a deep 9 x 13 x 2-inch (or similar size) ceramic or glass baking dish with plenty of olive oil. Use your hands to pat half of the kibbe paste into a thin layer at the bottom of the dish, smoothing out the surface to make it as even as possible. Spread the filling over the kibbe dough layer all the way to the edges, then top with remaining kibbe dough and pat out evenly to the edges of the pan. Use a sharp knife dipped in water to score the top with a

BAKED PUNKY PUMPKIN KIBBE, PAGE 261, WITH A DOLLOP OF CASHEW YOGURT SAUCE, PAGE 65, ROASTED CHILE PEPPER HARISSA PASTE, PAGE 42, AND MEDITERRANEAN CHOPPED SALAD, PAGE 87

diamond pattern (make the diamonds about 1 inch wide), cutting no deeper than ¼ inch into the kibbe crust. Brush with plenty of olive oil and bake for 35 to 40 minutes or until the top is golden and firm. If desired broil on high for 2 to 3 minutes to deepen the color of the crust. Let the kibbe stand for 5 minutes before slicing; the cooling allows it to firm up, making it easier to lift out of the pan with a bent spatula.

Ella's Buck wild Stuffed cabbage with sunflower cream Tomato Sauce

SERVES 6 TO 8

Ella Nemcova, the Regal Vegan queen of creamy vegan pâté (get her faux gras at theregalvegan.com), lends us this recipe for Eastern European soul food. In her words: "This recipe is pretty intensive but well worth it. It is a traditional Russian/Eastern European dish . . . it's apparent to everyone that this took some time and love to make. This recipe makes enough for a party—each head of cabbage has some 18 (or so) leaves so you can make a big batch."

Blanching the cabbage leaves (to soften them up for rolling) is essential; it makes leaf removal tear (as in both torn leaves and crying) free and it's easier than it sounds. Use a long-handled fork (a BBQ prong is ideal) and take your time. Or if you do have the time, wrap the cabbage in plastic wrap and freeze overnight. Then move the cabbage to the refrigerator to thaw: as the cabbage warms up, you'll be able to peel off the softened leaves. This is a project that takes over 2 days, so you may just prefer the fast track of just blanching the cabbage instead.

CABBAGE ROLLS

   1½ cups buckwheat groats (kasha)
   1 cup short-grain white rice (sushi rice is
      fine)
   1 large green cabbage, about 2½ pounds
   1 tablespoon good-quality olive oil
   1 large yellow onion, peeled and finely diced
   2 pounds white or brown mushrooms,
      brushed clean and chopped into ¼-inch
      pieces
   1 large carrot, peeled and grated
   1 cup chopped walnuts
   2 cloves garlic, peeled and minced
   1 tablespoon smoked salt or 1 tablespoon
      kosher salt plus 2 teaspoons liquid smoke
   1 tablespoon nutritional yeast
   2 teaspoons dried thyme
   Freshly cracked pepper and salt to taste

   Sunflower Tomato Cream Sauce (recipe
      follows)

1. Cook the grains for the filling first: bring 3 cups of water to boil over high heat. Add the buckwheat, cover the pot, and reduce the heat to low. Cover and cook for 6 minutes, then dump contents of the pot into a large bowl. Now pour in 1 ½ cups of water into the same cooking pot and bring to a boil over high heat, add the rice, cover the pot and reduce heat to medium. Cook for 15 minutes until the rice has absorbed the water, turn off the heat, and set aside to cool for 10 minutes. Transfer the rice to the bowl with the buckwheat. Preheat the oven to 350°F.

2. Now prepare the cabbage leaves: fill a 4-quart pot about two-thirds of the way with water and bring to a rolling boil over high heat. Use a sharp paring knife to cut the core out of the cabbage. Insert a long-handled fork into the hollowed out core of the cabbage; make sure it's securely speared inside the cabbage (this will help you to stabilize the cabbage while peeling off the leaves), then lower the cabbage into the boiling water. After a few minutes, use another fork to pierce a leaf and lift it away from the cabbage; use the large fork you speared it with to maneuver the cabbage head in the pot to make this easier. Transfer the peeled cabbage leaf to a plate. Continue to remove as many cabbage leaves as possible; you want to have at least eighteen large cabbage leaves. You can continue to peel off leaves for smaller rolls, or remove the remaining cabbage and save it for making soup (such as *Sauerkraut Mushroom Soup*, page 130).

3. Preheat a deep, 12-inch skillet, then add the olive oil. Add the onion and sauté until translucent, about 4 minutes. Add the mushrooms and sauté until they release their juices and then reabsorb them. Once the mushrooms are dark in color and completely soft, add them to the bowl with the grains. Add the rest of the stuffing ingredients, adding salt and pepper last to taste, and mix thoroughly.

4. Prepare the *Sunflower Tomato Cream Sauce*. While the sauce is simmering, begin assembling the cabbage rolls. Place a blanched cabbage leaf on a work surface in front of you. If the seam of the leaf is too large, slam it down on your cutting board with the side of a knife to flatten. Next, place two heaping tablespoons of stuffing on the bottom third of the leaf; feel free to adjust the amount of filling for the size of the leaf. Roll the leaf over the stuffing and spread it out in the leaf into a log shape. Roll the sides of the leaf over this part like the sides of an envelope, then roll the whole thing up like a burrito (or lumpia, page 177). Place the roll seam side down on a plate and continue until all the rolls are done.

5. Assemble the cabbage roll casserole: ladle about one-third of the tomato cream sauce into the bottom of a ceramic 9 x 13 x 3-inch lasagna-type pan. Arrange the cabbage rolls, seam side down, in a single layer of neat rows in the pan. It's okay to squeeze the rolls into the pan. Cover the rolls with another one-third of the sauce and cover the top of the pan tightly with foil. Bake for 30 minutes. Serve hot with the remaining third of the sauce, gently warmed and passed around in a serving dish.

Sunflower Cream Tomato Sauce

6 tablespoons sunflower seeds

4 rounded tablespoons arrowroot, cornstarch, or kuzu powder

4¼ cups water

6 tablespoons tamari

4 heaping tablespoons tomato paste

½ teaspoon ground black pepper

½ teaspoon sea salt

1. Grind sunflower seeds in clean coffee grinder or food processor into very fine crumbs. In a small bowl whisk together the arrowroot and ¼ cup of the water to create a thick slurry.

2. In a 3-quart pot over high heat, bring the remaining 4 cups of water to a rapid simmer. Use a wire whisk to stir in the ground sunflower seeds and the arrowroot slurry. Add the tamari and tomato paste and stir constantly until the sauce has thickened, about 6 to 8 minutes. Whisk in the black pepper and salt, taste the sauce, and season with more salt and pepper as desired.

Red Wine–Braised Leeks and Mushrooms

SERVES 4 WITH POTATOES OR WHITE BEAN AND CELERIAC PUREE, PAGE 294

*Braising leeks, mushrooms and seitan in red wine with a French technique is both romantic and rustic. The juices from the vegetables, infused with the wine and a touch of vegan buttery spread creates a light, luscious sauce. Serve up this elegant entree with pasta or potatoes or on a bed of delicate **Luscious White Bean and Celery Root Puree** (page 294) and enjoy an extra helping of ooos and ahhs.*

1 pound leeks, preferably thinner leeks no wider than 2 inches in diameter

10 ounces cremini mushrooms, brushed clean and tough ends of stems sliced off

3 tablespoons of olive oil

2 cups dry red wine

1 teaspoon dried marjoram

½ teaspoon salt, plus additional for sprinkling

4 sprigs fresh thyme or ½ teaspoon dried thyme

2 tablespoons nonhydrogenated vegan margarine

A few twists of freshly ground pepper

1. Trim away most of the green stalks on the leeks, leaving about an inch near the white part. Slice away the tip of root end, and slice each leek in half lengthwise. Firmly hold the leek so that it doesn't fall

apart, and rinse under cool running water to remove any grit or dirt. Place leeks on a cutting board and slice each piece into sections about 2½ inches long, hold the pieces together to prevent the leaves from separating too much. If the leeks fall apart while cooking don't worry, but for the prettiest presentation try to keep them together.

2. Slice the mushrooms into quarters (see page 5 for illustration). Over medium-high heat, sear the mushrooms in 1 tablespoon of the olive oil. Fry the mushrooms, stirring occasionally, until both sides are browned and mushrooms look juicy, about 4 minutes. Remove from the pan and transfer to an oven-proof dish. Sprinkle the mushrooms with a pinch of sea salt, cover with foil, and put in an oven set at 250°F to to keep warm.

3. Heat the remaining olive oil and place the leeks cut side down in the oil. Brown the leeks for 2 to 3 minutes, carefully lifting them up to check and see if the undersides are seared and the edges of the leaves are browned. Pour in the wine, sprinkle with marjoram and salt, and tuck the thyme sprigs into the wine. Increase the heat and bring the wine to an active simmer and cover the pan. Reduce the heat to low and simmer for 10 minutes.

4. If serving on top of white bean puree, potatoes, or pasta, mound individual servings (about 1 cup) of hot puree in serving dishes. Divide the mushrooms on top of the servings of puree. Uncover the pan and using tongs, carefully lift the leeks and arrange on top of mushrooms. Increase the heat to medium-high and bring the juices in the pan to a rapid simmer for 2 minutes, stirring occasionally. Reduce the heat to low and swirl the margarine into the juices. Use a wire whisk to continuously stir the sauce until smooth and lightly thickened. Drizzle a little bit of the sauce over each serving of leeks and mushrooms and serve immediately.

Just Leeks in Red Wine: These braised leeks make an intriguing starter or side dish on their own, served warm or room temperature. Leave out the mushrooms entirely and proceed as above. Especially nice prepared with baby leeks or ones fresh from the farm.

Braised Seitan and Leeks: Make this dish even heartier with seitan! Slice two cutlets of homemade seitan (use the Herbes de Provence variation on page 206) or purchased seitan into ½-inch-thick strips. Brown the strips in 2 tablespoons olive oil over medium heat, turning the pieces several times to brown the slices evenly. Transfer the seitan to a dish and keep warm in the oven along with the mushrooms. Prepare the leeks and mushrooms as directed above. Arrange the seitan on top of the white bean puree or potatoes, top with mushrooms (you can even leave them out and use just seitan) and braised leeks, and drizzle with sauce.

spicy black-eyed pea cakes

MAKES 12 SMALL PATTIES

*Borrowing flavors from Senegal, these spicy little black-eyed pea patties can be fried with a minimal amount of oil, but are just as tasty baked. Serve with **Cilantro Chutney** (page 61; this Indian chutney works with most anything!), your favorite hot sauce, and **Mango and Peanut Millet Salad** (page 98).*

The heat of these little cakes will vary depending on the brand of hot sauce used. Standard American cayenne pepper–based sauces will make moderately spicy cakes, while habanero sauces will result in much hotter, bolder patties.

One 14-ounce can black-eyed peas (2 cups cooked), drained and rinsed

2 tablespoons vegetable oil

1 small yellow onion, minced

4 scallions, root ends trimmed and thinly sliced

4 cloves garlic, peeled and minced

1 to 2 hot green chile peppers (serrano or Thai), minced

1 tablespoon lemon juice

½ teaspoon sea salt

1 tablespoon prepared hot sauce

2 tablespoons chickpea flour

2 tablespoons vital wheat gluten flour (see page 52)

½ cup dry breadcrumbs

2 ripe roma tomatoes (roma tomatoes are firmer, ideal for these patties)

2 tablespoons vegetable oil for brushing tops of patties (or vegetable oil cooking spray)

1. If baking the patties, preheat oven to 400°F. Line a baking sheet with parchment paper and use a brush dipped in oil to brush twelve circles about 2 inches wide, about 1 inch apart (or use cooking oil spray to spray out twelve circles).

2. In a mixing bowl use a potato masher or large fork to mash together peas and oil into a chunky paste. Mash in onion, scallions, garlic, chile pepper, lemon juice, salt, and hot sauce until blended. Sprinkle in the chickpea flour and gluten flour and knead with your hands into a thick dough, then knead in the breadcrumbs. Remove the core and seeds from the tomatoes. Finely dice the tomatoes, gather in

your hands, and squeeze over a sink to remove any excess liquid. Mix into the bean dough.

3. Use a large ice cream scoop to scoop balls of bean mixture onto the baking sheet, or use your hands and grab about ¼ cup of dough. Use your hand to flatten each ball to about ¾ inch thick, then brush the tops generously with oil. Bake for 20 minutes and remove from the oven. Carefully flip over the patties, brush other side with oil, and bake another 10 to 15 minutes or until the top is golden. Remove from oven and if desired brush the hot patties with a little more oil. Serve hot!

4. To pan fry patties, preheat a cast-iron skillet over medium heat. Coat the bottom of the pan with a thin layer of vegetable oil and fry three to four patties at a time. Add a little more oil to the bottom of the pan after each batch of patties. Drain the patties on a plate lined with a few paper towels and eat hot.

preserved Lemon Braised Tempeh with green olives

SERVES 2 TO 3

Juicy tempeh is drenched with the classic Moroccan flavors of preserved lemons and green olives in this easy stovetop tagine. The olives are usually left whole for the prettiest presentation, but sliced, pitted olives may be easier to eat. Get your preserved lemons started especially for this dish, or use the fast-track freezer preserved lemons (page 58) for a slightly more spontaneous tagine.

*This briny, tangy dish is best served with **Fluffy Spiced Couscous** (page 303) or **Freekeh and Millet Pilaf** (page 306) and **Harissa Carrot Salad** (page 106).*

8 to 10 ounces tempeh

2 teaspoons soy sauce

2 tablespoons olive oil

2 cups thinly sliced yellow onion half-moons

4 cloves garlic, peeled and smashed

1½ cups vegetable broth

⅔ cup orange juice

1 teaspoon preserved lemon liquid (see **Preserved Lemons, Two Ways**, page 58) or lemon juice

1 teaspoon ground sweet or hot paprika

1 teaspoon ground ginger

¼ teaspoon ground coriander

¼ teaspoon ground black pepper

¼ teaspoon ground cinnamon

¼ teaspoon ground turmeric

1 large carrot or small turnip, peeled and sliced into ½-inch chunks

1 preserved lemon (see **Preserved Lemons, Two Ways**, page 58)

1 cup green olives without pits, picholine or Sicilian or manzanilla

½ cup chopped flat-leaf parsley

¼ cup chopped cilantro

1. Slice the tempeh cake in half lengthwise, then slice into four rectangles. Slice each rectangle diagonally into triangles, spread on a plate, and sprinkle with soy sauce. In a deep, 12-inch skillet over medium heat sauté the tempeh in 1 tablespoon of the oil, flipping each piece occasionally using long-handled tongs or a spatula until the tempeh is golden brown. Remove from the heat and transfer the tempeh back onto a plate.

2. Add the remaining oil to the pan and fry onions until golden and slightly caramelized, about 10 minutes. Add the garlic and sauté for 1 more minute, then add vegetable broth, orange juice, preserved lemon liquid, all of the ground spices, and the carrot. Increase the heat and bring to a boil, then tuck tempeh slices into the sauce to cover. Partially cover the pan and simmer for 10 minutes. While that is going on remove and discard (or return to the lemon jar) the pulp from the preserved lemon, and slice the peel into slivers as thin as possible.

3. After 10 minutes uncover the tempeh and gently stir in the preserved lemon peel. Increase heat to bring sauce to a rapid simmer and cook for another 5 minutes uncovered, then turn off the heat. Stir in the olives, parsley, and cilantro. Cover and let stand for 2 minutes. On a serving dish arrange the couscous in a large mound, then use a slotted spoon to ladle the tempeh and vegetables over the couscous. Now pour on the sauce from the skillet over the tempeh and serve immediately.

Golden Tandoori Tofu

SERVES 2 TO 3

No need for a clay tandoori in your kitchen to work tandoori-style magic with tofu; the pores of pressed tofu greedily drink up this nearly traditional, bold soy-yogurt masala marinade. The tofu then bakes in an ordinary oven and takes on a golden, richly

spiced crust. Great with any Indian rice, paratha, and a green salad.

Marinate the tofu for up to 2 days in the fridge or make double the batch for a few dinners of tandoori tofu through the week.

TOFU SLICES

> 1 pound extra firm tofu, drained
>
> 2 tablespoons soy sauce

MARINADE

> 1½ cups plain soy yogurt
>
> 2 tablespoons vegetable oil
>
> 3 tablespoons tomato paste
>
> 4 cloves garlic, peeled and grated on a Microplane
>
> 3 tablespoons lime juice
>
> 2 teaspoons ground coriander
>
> 1 teaspoon ground turmeric
>
> 1 teaspoon ground cumin
>
> ½ teaspoon ground cinnamon
>
> ½ teaspoon cayenne pepper, or more to taste
>
> ¾ teaspoon salt
>
> 1 small red onion, peeled and sliced into ½-inch-thick slices

1. Slice and press tofu as directed on page 22. When tofu is finished pressing, pat it dry with a paper towel and sprinkle each side with soy sauce.

2. Preheat oven to 400°F. In a ceramic or glass 9 x 13 x 2-inch baking dish, combine the marinade ingredients; toss the onions in the marinade and then push them to one side of the pan. Place tofu into marinade in a single layer and flip a few times to coat each side. Bake for 20 minutes, remove from oven, and flip each piece of tofu. Bake for an additional 20 to 25 minutes or until most of the marinade

has crusted the top of the tofu with a golden brown. Serve immediately with the roasted onion bits and spoon any remaining sauce from the pan on top of the tofu.

Tandoori Seitan: Substitute 2 *Seitan Coriander Cutlets* (page 49), sliced into ½-inch wide strips, for the tofu. Instead of turning it over halfway through roasting, occasionally move the seitan and onions around in the pan with long-handled tongs. Total roasting time should be around 28 to 30 minutes or until the seitan strips look juicy and most of the marinade has been absorbed into the seitan. Take care not to overcook the seitan or it may become dry.

Fluffy Scrambled Chickpea "Eggs" with Shallots (But'echa)

SERVES 4 TO 6 WITH INJERA

Prepare this easy and protein-rich dish and you'll understand why sometimes it's referred to as "false eggs." When cooled and crumbled, the cooked chickpea flour mash, seasoned with spiced oil, chilies, and olive oil, transforms into moist, buttery-looking chunks that eerily resemble scrambled eggs. This recipe has a sharp, lemony tang, but go ahead and adjust the amount of lemon to taste. Although but'echa is very dense and filling on its own, it's best served with a vegetable w'et stew and Ethiopian Injera (page 206) for a balanced, exciting spread.

1 cup chickpea flour

2 tablespoons *Spiced Buttery Oil* (page 44)

2 large shallots, finely minced

2 green hot chilies (jalapeños, serranos, or Italian hot peppers), seeds removed and minced

1⅔ cups warm water

¾ teaspoon sea salt

3 tablespoons lemon juice

2 teaspoons extra-virgin olive oil

1. Pour the chickpea flour into a large, 2-quart saucepan and toast for 1½ to 2 minutes over medium-low heat, stirring constantly. The flour will smell toasted and darken slightly; transfer to a bowl. Add the *Spiced Buttery Oil*, shallots, and chilies to the pan and stir-fry until the shallots just beginning to soften, about 2 minutes. Transfer the vegetables to a small dish. Add the water, salt, and lemon juice to the pan and increase heat to medium.

2. Add the chickpea flour back to the pan, stirring in a few tablespoons at a time. Stir constantly with a wire whisk to incorporate the flour into the water; some small lumps are okay. Continue to cook and stir the mixture until it becomes too thick to stir with a wire whisk (about the consistency of very thick muffin batter), about 4 to 6 minutes. Set aside the whisk and switch to a wooden spoon or even better, a heat-resistant silicone spatula. Stir constantly and cook the mixture for another 4 to 6 minutes; the dough will become very thick and stiff and pull away from the sides of the pan when stirred. The dough is done when a thin film forms on the sides and bottom of the pan and the dough pulls away from the sides. It will have a consistency similar to very thick polenta. Stir in the chilies and shallots. Taste mixture and season with more salt if desired.

3. Remove from heat and spread a layer about an inch thick onto a large dinner plate. Cool at room temperature for 10 minutes, or until the mixture feels firm to the touch. Drizzle top with olive oil. Drag a fork through the dough to break up the but'echa into crumbly, fluffy pieces, mashing the oil into the crumbles. Serve at room temperature or chill (where it will continue to firm up) and serve cold with *Injera* (page 206) and a w'et stew.

Yassa Lemon Mustard Tofu

SERVES 3 TO 4

Lemon and mustard is the exciting flavor team-up in the West African dish known as yassa. Chewy baked tofu excels smothered in this zesty sauce along with a scattering of deeply roasted carrots and onions. Enjoy this hearty fare alongside any rice or millet dish.

1 pound extra-firm tofu, sliced and pressed (or see above if you're rather let the oven do the work)

2 large carrots, peeled and cut into diagonal slices ½ inch thick

¼ cup soy sauce

⅓ cup lemon juice

3 tablespoons lime juice

3 tablespoons minced garlic

2 tablespoons peanut or vegetable oil

¼ cup prepared Dijon mustard

1 small hot chile pepper, minced

2 cups thinly sliced yellow onions

1. Press the tofu as directed for *Savory Baked Tofu* (page 50). Place the carrots in a large saucepan, add ½ cup of water, and bring to a boil; steam the carrots for 5 minutes, drain, and set aside. When your tofu is ready to proceed, preheat the oven to 400°F and lightly spray a 9 x 13 x 2-inch ceramic dish with cooking spray. Slice each piece of pressed tofu into a triangle for a total of sixteen triangles.

2. Pour the soy sauce, lemon juice, lime juice, garlic, peanut oil, mustard, and chile pepper into the baking dish and whisk together. Add the sliced onions and carrots and stir to coat them in marinade, then shove them aside and layer the tofu into the pan. Press the tofu into the marinade then flip the slices over to coat the other side. Spread the onions and carrots on top of the tofu and bake for 20 minutes. Remove the pan and use a narrow spatula to carefully flip the tofu slices over, moving the onions and carrots over the top of the tofu. Bake another 25 to 30 minutes or until the tofu and carrots are golden brown. Serve immediately.

Seitan Yassa: Substitute 2 *Seitan Coriander Cutlets* (page 49), sliced into ½-inch-wide strips, for the tofu. Instead of turning it over half way through roasting, occasionally move the seitan and veggies around in the pan with long-handled tongs. Total roasting time will probably be around 30 minutes; take care not to over cook the seitan or it may become dry.

Jerk-Roasted Seitan Strips

SERVES 4 ALONG WITH RICE OR BREAD

*Roasting seitan strips in piquant, sweetly aromatic Jamaican jerk sauce blended from fresh vegetables is as natural and easy-going as an island breeze. Great with extra-firm tofu, too, or use both seitan and tofu for an exciting "mixed" jerk grill. Serve with **Island Brown Rice and Peas** (page 313).*

4 *Seitan Coriander Cutlets* (page 49), sliced into ½-inch strips

FRESH JERK SAUCE

1 large yellow onion, peeled and chopped

2 scallions, root ends trimmed and chopped

4 cloves garlic

1 Scotch Bonnet chile pepper (or half a chile for the chile-challenged)

2 tablespoons soy sauce

2 tablespoons brown sugar

2 tablespoons lime juice

½-inch piece peeled ginger

2 teaspoons dried thyme

1½ teaspoons ground allspice

½ teaspoon sea salt

½ teaspoon ground black pepper

2 tablespoons peanut oil

¼ cup pineapple juice or water

1. Preheat oven to 400°F. Generously rub with peanut oil a 9 x 13 x 2-inch ceramic or glass baking dish and add the seitan strips.

2. In a blender or food processor pulse all of the fresh jerk sauce ingredients as smooth as possible. Add to the pan and toss with the seitan strips; massage the sauce into the strips.

3. Roast the seitan for 25 to 30 minutes, turning the strips frequently with long-handled tongs; strips are ready when golden brown and slightly saucy. Remove from the oven and serve immediately, spooning any remaining sauce from the pan onto the strips.

If you're not a fan of super-hot Scotch Bonnet chilies, use a milder hot chile such as serrano or jalapeño.

Jerk Tofu: Press firm or extra-firm tofu as directed on page 22 and slice into thin ¼-inch slices. Gently toss with sauce and roast at 400°F for 20 minutes, then gently flip over the tofu. Roast another 15 to 18 minutes or until sauce is thick and bubbling and tofu is golden brown.

Mostly Mediterranean Eggplant Parmigiana

SERVES 4 WITH A SALAD AND BREAD

Lighten up, eggplant parmigiana! My take on this classic vegetable entree embraces its Sicilian origins along with an added dash of Mediterranean spice, forgoing the heavy breadcrumb crust of American casseroles for bare slices roasted with olive oil for a lighter, juicier, and naturally gluten-free dish in fewer steps.

*Food historians debate over word "parma" here, suggesting that it may not refer to the well-known cheese or Italian city but be derived from an old Persian word for wooden shutters . . . because the strips of eggplant look like layered wooden planks? Persian spices echo its possible ancestry: the sauce is enhanced with **Persian 7-Spice Blend** (page 43) and fruity Aleppo red pepper (page 10), and the casserole is smothered with the creamy topping from the Greek pastichio casserole (page 238). If you have a little bit of extra **Chickpea Parmigiana Topping** (page 67, or from **White Bean Farro Soup**, page 122), sprinkle on top before baking for a charming, rustic casserole.*

If possible, allow this casserole to cool for at least 20 minutes before slicing. The flavors further develop from after a generous cooling, and the once-boiling hot sauce won't burn your dainty mouth. Serve with a green salad and fresh, crusty peasant-style bread.

MOSTLY MEDITERRANEAN EGGPLANT PARMIGIANA

EGGPLANT

    3 pounds purple globe eggplant

    Salt for sprinkling

    Olive oil cooking spray or olive oil for
        brushing

SAUCE

    1 tablespoon olive oil

    4 cloves garlic, peeled

    Two 14-ounce cans plain tomato sauce

    2 teaspoons dried oregano or dried mixed
        Italian herb seasoning

    2 tablespoons chopped fresh basil leaves or
        1 teaspoon dried basil

    ¾ teaspoon *Persian 7 Spice Blend* (page 43)
        or ¼ teaspoon each ground cinnamon,
        coriander, and cumin

    1 teaspoon Aleppo pepper flakes (page 10)
        or red pepper flakes

    ½ teaspoon sea salt

    1 recipe *Silken Almost-Bechamel Topping*
        from *Greek Eggplant Lasagna (Pastichio*
        "Vegani") (page 238)

    ½ cup *Chickpea Parmigiana Topping*
        (page 67, optional)

1. Preheat oven to 425°F and line two large baking sheets with parchment paper. Wash the eggplants, remove flower ends, and slice lengthwise into ¼-inch-thick strips. Layer in a large metal colander, occasionally sprinkling slices with a pinch of salt. Position the colander over the sink or a bowl and set aside for 20 minutes. When the oven is ready, transfer the eggplant to the baking sheets and arrange in a single layer. Spray or brush both sides lightly with olive oil. Roast the eggplant for 12 to 14 minutes on each side or until the flesh is tender and lightly browned. Use a spatula to flip each piece over once. Transfer the eggplant to a plate and repeat with any remaining eggplant.

2. While the eggplant is roasting, prepare the sauce: in a 2-quart saucepan, preheat the olive oil over medium heat then stir in the garlic and fry for 30 seconds. Stir in the remaining ingredients and simmer sauce for 15 minutes, then turn off heat and set aside. In a blender or food processor pulse together the ingredients for the béchamel sauce into a smooth sauce.

3. To assemble the casserole, spoon ¼ cup of tomato sauce on the bottom of a 9 x 14 x 3-inch or slightly smaller ceramic baking dish. Layer half of the eggplant (overlapping slices as needed), then top with remaining tomato sauce. If you're using the *Chickpea Parmigiana Topping*, sprinkle half of that over the sauce. Layer on the remaining eggplant and spread remaining tomato sauce on top. Spread the *Silken Almost-Bechamel Topping* over the casserole all the way to the edges of the pan; it's okay if some of the tomato sauce swirls into the cashew topping. If desired sprinkle with remaining *Chickpea Parmigiana Topping* and a generous pinch of dried oregano or basil. Bake for 45 minutes; the creamy topping should be golden and the tomato sauce bubbling. Set casserole aside to cool for 15 minutes before serving. Use a sharp, serrated knife to slice and a wide bent spatula to lift up servings.

Shortcut this dish with a 25-ounce jar of your favorite prepared all-natural tomato basil pasta sauce. Whisk the **Persian 7-Spice Blend** *and the Aleppo pepper into the unheated sauce before spreading in the casserole.*

CHAPTER 10

Robust Vegetable Entrees & Sides

Vegetables are not be thrown to the side (dish). From **Roasted Eggplant Masala (Baingan Barta)** (page 277) to crunchy **Daikon Edamame Lettuce Wraps** (page 286), these recipes feature vegetables as the major player of light, nourishing meals.

Certainly there side dish ideas here, too; take your pick from nutty **Sesame Wow Greens** (page 279), zesty **Lemon Garlic Potatoes** (page 285), creamy **Luscious White Bean and Celery Root Puree** (page 294), and many more. Even better, make the ultimate fusion meal by pairing together two or more sides with a rice dish from chapter 11 and a salsa or chutney from chapter 3. Sides go front and center when they're as delicious and globally inspired as these.

shredded cabbage with toasted mustard seeds

SERVES 4 AS A SIDE

A nice change of pace from mushy, overcooked cabbage, this twist on an Indian-style cabbage dish is fresh and lively. Featuring finely shredded green cabbage tossed with a warm turmeric dressing, it's a fast and inexpensive side vegetable to complement not only Indian entrees but Middle Eastern or African dishes.

1 pound green cabbage (half a smallish head of cabbage)

1 to 3 green hot chile peppers (serrano or Thai chilies), finely minced

1 small red onion, peeled and finely diced

1½ teaspoons sea salt

2 tablespoons grapeseed oil

2 teaspoons black mustard seeds

1 teaspoon ground coriander

1½ teaspoons ground turmeric

3 tablespoons red wine vinegar

4 teaspoons agave nectar

A few twists of freshly cracked pepper

½ cup roasted whole cashews, coarsely chopped

1. Remove any wilted leaves from outside of cabbage, slice in half, then in quarters, and remove core. Using a mandolin (see page 30) or a sharp chef's knife, slice the cabbage as thin as possible into fine shreds, no thicker than ⅛ inch. Place the cabbage, chilies, and red onion in a large mixing bowl and sprinkle with the sea salt; toss the shreds with your hands and set aside for 10 minutes. Occasionally stir the cabbage.

2. Heat the oil in a small skillet heat over medium-high heat; add mustard seeds, cover the skillet, and cook until seeds pop. Turn the heat down to low, stir in the coriander and turmeric, and fry for 30 seconds. Turn off the heat and stir in the vinegar (stand back, as this will sizzle and pop at first), agave nectar, and a few twists of ground pepper.

3. Pour the dressing over the cabbage mixture, sprinkle in the cashews, and use tongs to toss; continue to mix the cabbage until the shreds are tinted yellow. Taste and add more salt or vinegar if desired. Serve immediately.

Indian fried green tomatoes

SERVES 4 AS AN APPETIZER OR SIDE

Fried green tomatoes are an American specialty, a luscious end to the surplus of unripe produce from the garden at the end of summer. Hard unripe tomatoes won't turn to mush when pan-fried, unlike ripe red ones. Spicy fried vegetables dipped in chickpea batter are an Indian favorite, so put the two together for spicy fried green tomato goodness!

*Serve these hot with a squeeze of fresh lemon juice, **Tomato Dill Apple Raita** (page 66) or any Indian chutney.*

BREADCRUMB COATING

1 teaspoon black mustard seeds

⅔ cup fine breadcrumbs

½ teaspoon salt

¼ teaspoon ground cumin

¼ teaspoon cayenne pepper

CHICKPEA BATTER

½ cup plain soy milk (sweetened is fine
   to use)

1 tablespoon lemon juice

1 tablespoon chickpea flour

½ teaspoon ground turmeric

A pinch of salt

TOMATO SLICES

1½ pounds green tomatoes (about
   4 medium-size tomatoes)

Salt

5 tablespoons chickpea flour

2 teaspoons peanut oil or vegetable oil for
   frying, plus additional as needed; for a
   special treat, fry in coconut oil

*You may also use hard red tomatoes in place of
green, but don't use them if they're even slightly
soft; they'll fall apart during cooking.*

1. Preheat a dry skillet or wok over medium-high heat, then add the mustard seeds, cover the pan, and cook until they begin to pop. Immediately pour the seeds onto a large dinner plate, add the remaining breadcrumb coating ingredients, and stir.

2. In pie plate or wide, shallow bowl whisk together the chickpea batter ingredients. Remove the cores from the tomatoes and slice them into ¼-inch-thick rounds. Spread in a single layer on a separate plate and sprinkle with a little salt. Pour the 5 tablespoons of chickpea flour into a small dish near the tomato slices.

3. Preheat a cast-iron skillet over medium high heat, then spread about 2 teaspoons of oil over the surface. You'll now create a tomato-coating process in this order: use *only* one hand to dip both sides of a tomato slice into the dish of chickpea flour (shake away any excess flour). Next dip the slice into the chickpea batter and shake away extra batter. Last, drop the slice into the plate of breadcrumbs.

4. Now use your opposite hand (the one not touching the batter), and sprinkle some of the breadcrumb mixture over the top of the slice. Flip over and press more crumbs onto the top of the slice. Transfer the slice to the hot pan. Fry 3 to 3½ minutes per side, or until the crumb coating is golden brown; use a spatula to flip only once and occasionally move around the pan to help cook evenly. Add more oil if the slices look dry or are not browning evenly. Continue to fry the remaining slices in several batches, but don't overcrowd the pan. Serve the tomato slices hot with raita or chutney.

Roasted Eggplant Masala (Baingan Barta)

SERVES 4

Roasted eggplant weaves its silky spell in this classic Punjabi eggplant curry. Eggplant is roasted (or grilled) and folded with chilies, tomatoes, and abundant spices for a tender, juicy vegetable curry. A favorite served with soy yogurt raita and naan.

2½ pounds Asian or globe eggplant, whole and unpeeled

2 tablespoons coconut oil or canola oil

1 teaspoon black mustard seeds

4 cloves garlic, minced

1 large onion, peeled and chopped

2 to 3 green hot chile peppers, seeds removed (if desired), and minced

1½ teaspoons ground coriander

1 teaspoon ground cumin

½ teaspoon ground turmeric

1 cup chopped tomatoes or 2 large plum tomatoes, cored and finely diced

¾ teaspoon sea salt

½ teaspoon amchur powder (see note on page 281) or 1 tablespoon lime juice

¼ cup roughly chopped fresh cilantro

Slim Asian eggplants cut down the roasting time, but this dish is just as good with rounded purple globe eggplant. Green or red Thai chile peppers are best, followed by long hot Italian peppers and then jalapeños; they're all different, so use the chile pepper that appeals to you the most (or is easiest to find).

1. Preheat oven to 425°F and line a large baking sheet with parchment paper. Poke eggplants all over with a fork, place on the baking sheet, and roast for 20 to 30 minutes (or more, depending on the size of the eggplant) until the skin is heavily wrinkled and the eggplant can be easily pierced with a knife. Remove from the oven and cut a slit down each eggplant to allow some of the steam to escape. When cool enough to handle, spread eggplant open and use a large metal spoon to scoop out all of the flesh. Heap it on a cutting board and roughly chop. Discard the skins.

2. Heat the oil in a wok or stainless-steel skillet over high heat until it ripples and sprinkle in the mustard seeds. Cover the pan as soon as the seeds pop. When the popping almost stops, uncover the skillet, stir in the garlic, and stir-fry for 15 seconds. Stir in the onions and chilies and fry for 3 minutes or until the onions are softened, then stir in the coriander, cumin, and turmeric and stir-fry for 30 seconds.

3. Add the eggplant, tomatoes, and salt. Reduce heat to medium-high and simmer for 6 to 8 minutes, stirring occasionally; the eggplant should look juicy and bubbling. Stir in the amchur or lime juice, taste, and adjust seasoning with more salt, or even more amchur powder, or lime juice. Turn off heat and cool for 5 minutes, then transfer to a wide, deep serving bowl. Garnish with cilantro and serve with bread or rice.

Thrill to Grilll

Got an outside grill? Then make amazing, smoky baingan barta! Place the whole eggplants directly on the grill, then turn occasionally and roast until the skins are charred and the eggplants are very soft. If eggplants are very fresh, once cool enough to touch, it may be easier to peel away the roasted skins. If not, slice open and scoop out the insides.

sesame wow greens (a spin on oshitashi)

SERVES 2 TO 4 AS A SIDE OR APPETIZER

Oshitashi usually is prepared with spinach in Korean and Japanese cuisine, but this method is delicious with young, tender collard greens, chard, or everybody's favorite green stuff, kale. And of course spinach is a reliable favorite, and excellent mixed with any greens for this dish.

This is a great side with roasted tofu or tempeh, or a light meal served with noodles with sesame sauce (page 179, and use either udon or soba) or as a starter for any Asian entree as a fresh and nutty green side veggie. It's best enjoyed immediately after it's made.

> 2 pounds greens such as spinach, kale, or collard greens (see special directions for chard at the end)
>
> 3 tablespoons white sesame seeds
>
> 2 tablespoons soy sauce or tamari
>
> 2 teaspoons agave nectar
>
> 2 teaspoons rice vinegar
>
> A pinch of Japanese red pepper or gochugaru (Korean red pepper powder, see page 15)
>
> Additional sesame seeds for garnish

1. If using collard greens or kale, tear away thick stems and discard. Stack 2 to 3 leaves, roll as tightly as possible into a cigar, and holding your chef's knife firmly, slice into the thinnest ribbons possible; each ribbon should be no thicker than ¼ inch. Wash greens in a large bowl, drain but don't completely shake excess liquid away (you want the greens to be a little wet).

2. In a skillet lightly toast sesame seeds over medium heat until light tan; transfer to a dish to cool and grind seeds to a course powder in a clean coffee mill or pound with a mortar and pestle (see page 31).

3. In a large stainless steel skillet add collards or kale and ¼ cup of water; if using spinach use only 2 tablespoons water. Cover and bring water to a simmer over medium heat; cook until the greens are bright green and tender, about 6 to 8 minutes for collards and kale, 2 to 3 minutes for spinach. If the greens stick to the bottom of the pan during the steaming, add a few tablespoons more water. Use long-handled tongs to transfer cooked greens to a large dinner plate to cool. When greens are cool enough to handle, grab a handful and over the sink or a bowl squeeze out as much water as possible. Repeat with remaining greens, then add the squeezed greens to a mixing bowl.

4. Pour the ground sesame, soy sauce, agave nectar, vinegar, and red pepper over the greens and mix thoroughly with your fingers. Gather about ¼ cup of greens and press into a ball. Shape remaining greens and arrange balls on a serving dish. Sprinkle with additional sesame seeds.

Sesame Chard: Use very fresh rainbow or yellow chard with thin stems; remove the stems and stack the leaves. Roll leaves into a tight cigar and shred with a sharp knife. Chop the stems into tiny bite-size pieces, no thicker than ¼ inch, and set aside. Steam, cool and squeeze the leaves as directed for the greens, add the dressing and form into balls. Toss the diced stems with a teaspoon each of rice vinegar and soy sauce. Sprinkle the diced stems on top of the balls as a crunchy garnish.

okra masala (Bindi Bhaji)

SERVES 4

Okra haters, prepare to be wooed. While normally I flag okra dishes for okra lovers only, many testers served this to okra skeptics (including themselves) with smashing results! This single-vegetable Indian curry is easy to love, loaded with garam masala and a touch of fresh tomato. A complete meal with any Indian bread or rice, bindi bhaji reheats beautifully. For best results use the freshest okra you can find; pods should be firm and the tips snap off easily.

Tangy, bracing amchur powder is Indian dried powdered green mango, seek it out where Indian spices are sold. Substitute with lime juice or use both to boost the juicy, dense okra.

1 pound fresh okra pods

2 tablespoons vegetable oil

1 teaspoon black mustard seeds

3 cloves garlic, peeled and finely chopped

1 large yellow onion, peeled and finely chopped

2 teaspoons *Garam Masala* (page 39) or store-bought garam masala

1 teaspoon ground turmeric

½ teaspoon ground cinnamon

½ teaspoon cayenne pepper (optional for a less spicy dish)

1 teaspoon sea salt

2 to 4 tablespoons vegetable broth or water

1 cup diced tomatoes or 2 plum tomatoes, cores and seeds removed and finely diced

1 teaspoon amchur powder or 1 tablespoon lime juice

Additional *Garam Masala* for sprinkling

1. Trim and discard any stems from the okra. Slice the okra into ½-inch-thick pieces. Heat the oil in a wok or large stainless-steel skillet over high heat, add the mustard seeds, cover the wok, and give it a gentle shake a few times. Once the seeds pop, uncover the pan and immediately stir in the garlic and fry for 10 seconds. Add the onion and sauté for 2 to 3 minutes until soft, then stir in the okra and fry for 2 minutes.

2. Sprinkle the garam masala, turmeric, cinnamon, cayenne, and salt over the okra and stir-fry for 2 minutes. Pour in 2 tablespoons of vegetable broth and cover the wok. Turn the heat down slightly to medium-high. With the wok covered, cook the okra for 12 to 14 minutes, occasionally uncovering and stirring the okra.

3. Occasionally during the cooking, check to see if the vegetables are sticking to the bottom of the wok; if so, add a tablespoon of water and stir. Cook the okra until it's tender and some of the natural sliminess has reduced slightly. Uncover, stir in the tomatoes and the amchur powder or lime juice (or use both for extra-tangy okra), and fry for 2 more minutes, stirring frequently. Taste and season the okra with more amchur or lemon juice if desired. Remove from heat, sprinkle with a big pinch of garam masala, and serve with bread or rice.

OKRA MASALA (BINDI BHAJI)

crispy oven-fried eggplant and zucchini with skordalia

SERVES 4

*Crunchy fried zucchini and eggplant slices served with **Garlicky Potato Dip (Skordalia)** (page 93) are enjoyed throughout the Mediterranean. It's a wonderful summer appetizer or light meal that highlights peak summer produce. At home instead of deep frying, bake up a lighter treat with herbed panko crumbs (and the secret ingredient, vegan mayonnaise . . . nobody will guess!).*

> 1 pound eggplant, preferably Asian
>   eggplants no wider than 2 inches
> 1 pound young zucchini, preferably no
>   wider than 2 inches
> About 1½ teaspoons sea salt
> ½ cup vegan mayonnaise
> 1½ cups plain panko bread crumbs
> 2½ teaspoons dried oregano
> 1 teaspoon dried rosemary, crumbled
> 1 teaspoon dried thyme, crumbled
> Olive oil cooking spray

CRISPY OVEN-FRIED EGGPLANT AND ZUCCHINI
WITH SKORDALIA

1. Preheat the oven to 425°F and cover two large baking sheets with parchment paper. Slice the eggplant and zucchini on a diagonal into ¼-inch slices and lightly sprinkle with salt. Arrange on layers of paper towels and set aside for 30 minutes to drain, then blot off any excess moisture released from the vegetables. In a shallow bowl, beat vegan mayonnaise with a fork until smooth. In a small baking dish, combine panko crumbs, oregano, rosemary, and thyme.

2. Take a slice of eggplant or zucchini and coat both sides with a thin layer of mayonnaise; the easiest way is to dip it in mayo and scrape off any excess on the side of the dish. Dredge each slice generously with herbed panko, and then place in a single layer on baking sheets. Spray generously with olive oil and bake for 10 minutes, then flip each piece over, spray with more oil, and bake for an additional 8 to 10 minutes until panko coating is golden and crisp. Move to a serving platter and serve immediately with *Skordalia*.

crisp stir-fry greens with veggie oyster sauce

SERVES 4

Bright, tender-but-still-crisp greens complete any Asian meal. The vegetarian oyster sauce is more commonly called vegetarian stir-fry sauce, but I like the romance of the name for this dish (see page 13). This technique is great for Chinese broccoli, but try it with any cooking green. And don't forget sweet, yummy

pea shoots in addition to your favorite greens. Technique is essential for this recipe: a wok is ideal here, as is dividing the leafy tops from the thicker stalks.

Use this recipe for a quick green leafy side veggie or when it's time to clean out the veggie bin. This is also a good recipe to test drive any mystery cooking green found at the Asian grocery store.

1½ to 2 pounds of baby bok choy, Chinese broccoli, Chinese mustard greens, Napa cabbage, collards, kale, pea shoot greens, or a combination of 2 or more

2 tablespoons peanut oil or high-heat canola oil

3 cloves garlic, roughly chopped

3 tablespoons vegetable broth or water

A pinch of salt (optional)

3 tablespoons vegetarian stir-fry (vegetarian oyster) sauce

½ teaspoon toasted sesame oil

1. Wash and spin dry the greens. Trim away any dried ends of stems or wilted leaves. Separate thick stems (½ inch thick or wider) from leaves. If using bok choy or cabbage, slice off the bottom root end. If using leafy greens like bok choy or Chinese broccoli, chop leaves away from stems. If using kale or collards (remove and discard stems) or cabbage, stack and roll leaves and slice into ½-inch-wide ribbons.

2. Preheat a wok over high heat and swirl in the oil; when the oil ripples it's ready to use.

3. If using greens with thick, hard stems, add the stems first and the garlic and stir-fry for 2 minutes. Add the leaves, vegetable broth, and the salt and stir-fry 1 minute. Cover the wok and let steam 1 to 3 minutes or until leaves are wilted and stems are crisp-tender. Use long-handled tongs to lift the greens from the wok and arrange on a serving dish.

Stir the vegetarian stir-fry sauce into the remaining bubbling juices in the wok (if there absolutely are none, add 2 tablespoons of broth or water) and bring to a simmer. Pour over the vegetables and serve.

4. If using cabbage or leafy greens without stems, fry the garlic for 15 seconds and then add handfuls of the chopped greens, stirring constantly, until all of the greens are in the wok and just beginning to wilt. Add the vegetable broth and salt and stir-fry 1 minute. Cover and steam for 2 to 4 minutes or until greens are tender but still crisp. Use long-handled tongs to lift the greens from the wok and arrange on a serving dish. Add the stir-fry sauce as directed above and pour on top of vegetables.

5. Just before serving, sprinkle the toasted sesame oil over greens.

Western broccoli is thicker than other leafy greens, so it's best to stir-fry this on its own. Remove stalks from the head, peel the stalks with a vegetable peeler and slice into ¼-inch-thick batons. Slice the florets into pieces no thicker than ½ inch. Sauté the stems first for 2 minutes, then add the florets and proceed as directed below. Broccoli will take about 2 to 4 minutes longer to cook than most leafy greens.

There are endless ways to change up this stir-fry; a few simple and good ones include adding one of the following to the stir fry just before adding the green's stems:

⊙ ½ teaspoon red pepper flakes

⊙ 1 whole star anise (remove before serving)

⊙ ½-inch piece peeled ginger, sliced into thin slivers

Roasted cauliflower with mint

SERVES 2 TO 3

Fear frying but love luscious fried Middle Eastern cauliflower? Try this fusion of oven "steaming" and roasting for succulent slices of cauliflower with delightfully browned edges. Pass around as an appetizer or serve it over a rice dish for a complete entree. Switch up the seasonings with a little curry powder or garam masala and this cauliflower is a great addition to any Indian meal.

> 1 large head of cauliflower
> 3 tablespoons of olive oil
> 1½ teaspoons kosher salt
> ½ teaspoon ground cumin
> A few twists of black pepper
> 2 tablespoons finely chopped fresh mint
> Lemon wedges

To make sure your oven is very hot for roasting the cauliflower, use an oven thermometer to correctly gauge the temperature of your oven.

1. Preheat the oven to 425°F and line a large baking sheet with parchment paper. Tear off two pieces of foil large enough to cover and crimp over the baking sheet. Remove the leaves and stem from the cauliflower and slice in half; cut the thick stem out of the cauliflower but take care to keep the halves in one piece. Slice each half into wedges about ½ inch thick. Arrange the slices on the baking sheet and drizzle with half of the oil and sprinkle with half of the salt and cumin. Rub the oil and seasonings into the cauliflower, then flip over each piece. Drizzle with oil, sprinkle with remaining salt and cumin and rub into the cauliflower. Cover the entire pan tightly with foil and bake for 12 minutes.

2. Remove the sheet from the oven and remove the foil. Return to the oven and roast for 6 to 8 minutes or until the edges are browned, remove from the oven and use a spatula or tongs to carefully flip over each wedge. Roast for another 6 to 8 minutes or until the cauliflower is golden and the edges are golden brown. Remove from the oven, sprinkle with pepper, and transfer cauliflower to a serving dish. Sprinkle with the mint and serve hot or at room temperature with wedges of lemon for squeezing over the cauliflower.

Roasted Indian Curried Cauliflower: Replace cumin with 1 teaspoon of Madras-style curry powder or *Garam Masala* (page 39). If desired replace the mint with fresh cilantro leaves.

Lemon garlic potatoes

SERVES 4 AS A SIDE, 6 AS AN APPETIZER

Super lemony, saucy and sublimely garlicky roasted potatoes is a beloved Greek specialty, and simple enough to become your new go-to potato side with greens and a protein entree. Large starchy baking potatoes, without the peel, are typically used, but unpeeled red potatoes or Yukon Gold are also delicious and make this dish even easier to prepare.

2½ pounds russet baking potatoes or any
   thin-skinned potatoes, yellow or red
2 cups vegetable broth
8 cloves garlic, finely chopped
¼ cup good-quality olive oil
½ cup lemon juice (bottled is fine)
1 heaping tablespoon dried oregano
1 teaspoon dried thyme
1 teaspoon sea salt
2 bay leaves
A handful of chopped parsley
Additional dried oregano for sprinkling
A few twists freshly cracked pepper

1. Preheat the oven to 425°F and get ready a deep, 9 x 14 x 2-inch baking dish and enough foil to tightly cover the top of the dish. Scrub the potatoes very thoroughly and remove any eyes, stringy roots, or blemishes. If using baking potatoes, peel, slice in half, and slice each half lengthwise into thick, 2-inch-wide wedges. If using waxy potatoes, don't peel and slice into 1-inch-thick pieces.

2. In the baking dish whisk together the vegetable broth, garlic, olive oil, lemon juice, oregano, thyme, and salt. Add the potatoes and the bay leaves. Stir to coat potatoes and cover the top of the dish tightly with foil.

3. Bake for 30 minutes, then remove foil and stir again; potatoes should be tender, if not, cover and roast another 4 to 8 minutes. Then uncover the potatoes and bake for 10 to 12 minutes, occasionally stirring the potatoes. The potatoes are ready when the edges are golden and the sauce is bubbling. There will be sauce surrounding the potatoes; if desired continue to roast the potatoes for a drier dish, or serve the potatoes with the sauce spooned on top. Remove from the oven and let cool 5 minutes, then sprinkle with parsley, oregano, and pepper before serving.

Daikon Edamame Lettuce Wraps

SERVES 4 AS AN APPETIZER, 2 FOR AN ENTREE

I'll never forget my first lettuce wrap. In a bustling, family-style Chinese restaurant in the breezy Chinatown of Honolulu and peeking out from a dozen other dishes was a sizzling jumble of bite-size veggies unexpectedly served with a stack of lettuce leaves. The frantic reaching (and elbowing) for the biggest leaf or a scoop of crunchy filling soon revealed a thrill ride of cool, hot, crunchy, and salty mouthfuls worth fighting over.

This is a lighter version with far less oil but big on fresh herbs, ginger, garlic, edamame, chewy tofu, and your choice of toasted walnuts or peanuts.

FILLING
   1 tablespoon peanut or grapeseed oil
   3 cloves garlic, peeled and minced
   1-inch piece peeled ginger, minced
   ½ pound daikon or Japanese salad turnip,
      chopped fine (¼-inch cubes)
   1 cup frozen, shelled edamame
   2 scallions, ends trimmed and thinly sliced
   ½ recipe *Savory Baked Tofu* (page 50) or
      4 ounces purchased baked or fried tofu,
      finely diced (about 1 cup diced)
   1 tablespoon soy sauce
   1 teaspoon *Sichuan 5-Spice Powder* (page 41)
      or store-bought Chinese 5-spice powder

2 tablespoons finely chopped fresh cilantro

⅔ cup toasted walnuts or roasted unsalted peanuts, coarsely chopped

GARNISH

10 or more large lettuce leaves, washed, dried, and kept chilled until ready to serve

¼ cup (or more to taste) hoisin sauce (see page 13)

Sriracha hot sauce or any Asian hot sauce to taste

1. Preheat a wok or large skillet over high heat and add oil. When the oil starts to ripple, add the garlic and ginger and fry for 45 seconds. Add the daikon and stir-fry for 3 minutes until soft and lightly browned. Stir in the edamame and fry for another 2 minutes. Stir in the sliced scallions and pressed tofu. Sprinkle with soy sauce and 5-spice powder and stir-fry for 3 minutes.

2. Turn off the heat and stir in the cilantro and toasted walnuts or peanuts. Mound the stir-fry into a serving bowl. Stack the lettuce leaves on a separate serving plate, and spoon the hoisin sauce and Sriracha into a small condiment dish.

3. To eat, take a lettuce leaf and spoon two or more tablespoons of hot vegetable filling into the center. Dab a little hoisin sauce and Sriracha on top of the filling. Fold the bottom of the leaf toward the filling, then overlap the sides (like a tiny burrito) and eat immediately.

Try a variety of lettuce leaves for these wraps. Iceberg is a favorite, but I love seasonal favorites like butter, Bibb, and red romaine for their color and tender texture.

Roasted Broccoli with Sage

SERVES 3 TO 4

Roasting broccoli adds a new dimension to this everyday vegetable; it intensifies the sweetness in the stalks, while gently crisping the edges of the florets. Perfectly roasted broccoli is achieved by thoroughly massaging the olive oil into the florets and stalks; this prevents dry, tough broccoli and keeps in the juices. The addition of lemon and sage dress it up for Mediterranean meals, or as a light veggie entree with pasta or potatoes.

2 pounds broccoli

3 tablespoons olive oil

1½ teaspoons rubbed sage or 6 fresh sage leaves, sliced into thin shreds

1 teaspoon sea salt

2 tablespoons lemon juice

A few twists of freshly cracked black pepper

1. Preheat oven to 375°F and line a large baking sheet with parchment paper. Slice the broccoli florets away from the stem, and slice in half any big florets (wider than 3 inches). Trim off the dry bottom edge of the broccoli stem, and use a vegetable peeler to remove the tough outer peel of the stem. Slice the stem into ½-inch-wide french-fry sticks.

2. Line a baking sheet with parchment paper and pile the florets and stems in the center. Pour the olive oil over the broccoli, then sprinkle with sage and salt. Now use your fingers to thoroughly rub the oil into the broccoli florets and stems, making sure

to evenly coat the stems and get some oil in between the crevices of the florets.

3. Spread the broccoli in a single layer on the baking sheet and roast for 20 to 26 minutes, turning broccoli occasionally with long-handled tongs. Broccoli stems should be tender and the flower buds gently browned. Watch carefully and don't let the broccoli burn, or the tops of the florets may dry out and become bitter. Remove the baking pan from the oven, sprinkle the broccoli with lemon juice and black pepper, and toss thoroughly. Serve hot or at room temperature.

cauliflower and green Beans in Berbere sauce

SERVES 4 TO 6

*These spicy, saucy vegetables are a hearty side served with **but'echa** (chickpea scrambled "eggs," see page 269). For a well-rounded meal with **injera-style crepes** (page 206) serve with easy **Saucy Berbere Lentils (Yemiser W'et)** (page 165) to satisfy Ethiopian food cravings.*

I like to make two versions of this flexible vegetable dish for a big spread of three or more Ethiopian dishes, one with collards, the other often with cauliflower, potatoes, or carrots.

> 1 large yellow or red onion, diced
> 2 cloves garlic, minced
> 1 tablespoon minced ginger
> 4 teaspoons *Spiced Buttery Oil* (page 44)

¼ cup white wine or vegetable broth
2 teaspoons *Berbere Spice Blend* (page 44)
1 teaspoon sweet or hot ground paprika
1 cup vegetable broth or water
3 ripe red tomatoes, cored and diced into ½-inch pieces, or 1 cup diced canned tomatoes (optional)
¾ teaspoon salt, or to taste
2 tablespoons lemon juice

USE ONE OR A COMBINATION OF THESE VEGETABLES:

> 1 pound collard greens, stems removed and sliced into ¼-inch-wide ribbons
> 1½ pounds potatoes, peeled and diced into ½-inch cubes
> 3 to 4 cups diced cauliflower
> 1 pound green beans, trimmed into 2-inch pieces
> 1 pound carrots, peeled and sliced into diagonal ½-inch pieces

1. If you're preparing collard greens, precook them by either steaming until bright green and tender, about 8 minutes, or cook in a pot over medium-high heat filled with 4 inches of water until tender, about 12 to 14 minutes. Drain the greens and shake out the excess water. If using potatoes, place in a large pot and cover with 3 inches of cold water. Bring to a boil over high heat, reduce heat to medium, and simmer for 10 to 14 minutes until tender, then drain. Don't precook the other vegetables.

2. In a deep, 12-inch stainless-steel skillet over medium heat, fry the onion, garlic, ginger, and *Spiced Buttery Oil* together until the onion is softened and translucent, about 6 to 8 minutes. Add the wine or vegetable broth, bring to simmer, and stir. Simmer for 2 minutes, then stir in your choice of vegetables.

3. Sprinkle the **Berbere Spice Blend** and paprika over the vegetables and fry, stirring occasionally, for 2 minutes. Stir in the water or vegetable broth, tomatoes if using, and salt. Simmer for 3 minutes. Cover, reduce heat to low, and simmer for 4 to 8 minutes or until the vegetables are just starting to turn tender; you may want to simmer longer for collards. Remove the cover and simmer another 2 to 4 minutes to reduce most (but not all; this should be a little juicy) of the liquid and finish cooking the vegetables until completely tender. When done, turn off heat and sprinkle with lemon juice. Serve with warm with *Ethiopian Savory Crepes* (page 206) or couscous.

YU-XIANG EGGPLANT (SICHUAN SPICY EGGPLANT)

SERVES 4 ALONGSIDE RICE OR NOODLES

My friend Cat shares this recipe for her dad's famous Sichuan-style eggplant; the meltingly tender eggplant on fire with spicy Chinese garlic bean paste—also known as chili bean sauce or toban djan. The Lee Kum Kee brand has a nice balance of bean, chili and garlic (see page 13 for more on toban djan garlic bean sauce) and a common find in most Chinese grocery stores in America. Serve with plenty of steaming white rice to soak up the fiery sauces. Slim Asian eggplants are essential to this dish, as the skin on each slice keeps the individual eggplant pieces from falling apart during the cooking. If the eggplant is old, you may need to salt and drain them (page 154).

4 large, firm Asian eggplants, preferably no wider than 2 inches in diameter (about 2½ pounds of eggplant)

3 tablespoons peanut oil or canola oil

2 to 3 tablespoons toban djan sauce (increase for a hotter dish!)

8 garlic cloves, peeled and minced

2 tablespoons soy sauce

3 tablespoons rice vinegar

2 teaspoons light brown sugar

¼ cup water

2 teaspoons cornstarch

6 green onions, green part only, sliced into 1-inch pieces

1. Remove stems from tops of eggplants. Cut each eggplant into a section 2½ to 3 inches long, then slice each section in half lengthwise. Now slice each section into three pieces lengthwise. Repeat with remaining eggplant. Each eggplant slice should look like a short, plump stick with a little bit of purple skin on one side.

2. In a wok heat 2 tablespoons of the oil over medium-high heat until it's shimmering. Add the eggplant, stirring briskly with long-handled metal tongs or a long-handled metal spatula. Continue to cook for about 5 to 6 minutes or until slightly tender. Transfer the eggplant to a dinner plate and set aside.

3. Add the remaining 1 tablespoon of oil to the wok. When oil is rippling, add the toban djan bean sauce and garlic and cook for 30 seconds, then stir in the eggplant. In a measuring cup stir together soy sauce, rice vinegar, and sugar. Pour this over the eggplant. Stir-fry the eggplant for 3 minutes, cover the wok, and cook for 4 to 6 minutes. Check the eggplant; pour in 2 to 4 tablespoons of water and stir-fry for another 1 to 2 minutes. The eggplant should be soft and tender; if not, cover and continue to cook for

another few minutes, stirring the eggplant occasionally and making sure it doesn't burn or dry out (add more water if necessary).

4. In the measuring cup you used to mix the soy sauce, stir together the water and cornstarch. Drizzle half over the eggplant and stir into the juices; the idea is to cook the starch mixture until the eggplant sauce is thickened to a desired consistency. If you want a thicker sauce (or just more sauce), keep drizzling in the cornstarch mixture while stirring constantly. You don't have to use the entire mixture; Cat said it was okay by her dad!

5. When the eggplant sauce is as thick as desired, turn off heat and stir in the chopped green onions. Transfer the eggplant to a serving dish and eat immediately with cooked rice or noodles.

crispy plantains with East Meets West chocolate mole dip

SERVES 4 TO 6 AS AN APPETIZER OR SNACK

Crunchy, twice-fried green plantain slices (tostones) are great sprinkled with salt and lime juice, but special when served with this piquant and intense chocolate mole sauce. Chocolate-based mole sauce can be notoriously complex, but this fast hack uses a secret ingredient: Indian garam masala as a fast substitute for the sweet spices that infuse this classic Mexican mole.

For lighter tostones, you can bake the chips after the first fry. The resulting slice won't be as tender but will have absorbed less oil. Tostones taste best served piping hot, so to save time make the mole a day or two in advance and warm up just prior to frying the plantains.

Peanut, canola, or vegetable oil for deep-frying
4 to 6 dark green plantains (about 1 plantain per person)
Salt as needed

East Meets West Chocolate Mole Dip
   (page 291)

1. Pour the frying oil into a large, heavy pot (cast iron is best) and preheat over medium-high heat for at least 5 minutes. You'll need 2 inches of oil for the plantain slices to float in the oil to ensure even cooking. Prepare a large plate covered with paper towels or crumpled brown paper for draining hot tostones. The oil is hot enough when a piece of raw plantain immediately bubbles on contact. Very hot (but never smoking) oil will help the tostones fry without soaking up a lot of oil.

2. Slice the tips off both ends of the plantains and run a sharp paring knife through the skin from one end of the plantain to the other. If the skin seems very hard, run another cut on the other side of the plantain. Use your thumb or the edge of a butter knife to pry off the skin, working it under the peel. If any tiny bits of peel remain slice them off.

3. On a 45-degree diagonal, slice plantain into 1½-inch-thick pieces. Lower the slices into the hot oil and fry for 4 to 5 minutes, flipping once. Don't overcrowd the pot (this lowers the temperature of the oil and will result in soggy tostones). Use a slotted

spoon or mesh skimmer to transfer the tostones to the paper towel–lined plates and drain for 2 minutes.

4. When fried slices have cooled down but are still warm, flatten to a thickness of about ⅜ of an inch or slightly thicker. See note for suggested methods. Use metal tongs to return plantains to the oil. Fry for another 3 to 4 minutes, turning once, until golden and crisp along the edges. Return to paper to drain again. Sprinkle hot tostones with salt and serve immediately with mole dip.

Half-Baked Tostones: While the oil is preheating, preheat the oven to 425°F and line a baking sheet with parchment paper. Spread the once-fried plantains on the baking sheet and bake for 10 minutes, flip over each piece, and bake another 10 minutes or until the edges are golden. Serve hot with mole dip.

Tostone Tips

Use very green, firm plantains for the tostones.

There are countless methods for crushing plantains for their second frying. Soup cans, coffee cans, tortilla presses, even a rolling pin can be used. There's a special paddle-shaped device called a *tostonera* that creates perfectly shaped tostones. They range from (cheap) unfinished wood to (pricey) bamboo or plastic.

Use gentle but even pressure for successful plantain crushing, and take care not to completely crush or it will fall apart.

East Meets West Chocolate Mole Dip

MAKES 2 CUPS

Traditional mole sauce, as wonderful as it is, can be epic to make. After a little bit of soul-searching, it seemed obvious that garam masala's blend of cumin and sweet spices, along with semi-sweet chocolate chips and fire-roasted canned diced tomatoes, can provide the basis for an intense and delicious chocolate mole hack. This thick mole is designed for dipping, but it can be thinned by swirling in 1 to 2 cups of hot vegetable broth for drizzling over steamed carrots, sweet pumpkin, or sautéed zucchini and fresh corn.

½ cup sliced almonds
1 small yellow onion, peeled and diced
2 cloves garlic, peeled and minced
1 tablespoon peanut oil
One 14-ounce can fire-roasted diced
    tomatoes, preferably one with green
    chilies
2 tablespoons chile powder (either ancho or
    a blend of Mexican chile powders, mild
    or hot depending on your taste)
1½ teaspoons *Garam Masala* (page 39)
    or store-bought garam masala
½ cup semi-sweet chocolate chips
½ teaspoon salt
2 teaspoons lime juice

1. In a small skillet over medium heat, toast the sliced almonds until golden and fragrant, about 2½ to 3 minutes. Pour the almonds into a clean coffee grinder and grind into coarse crumbs.

2. In a 3-quart pot over medium heat, sauté the onion and garlic in the peanut oil until the onion is soft and golden, about 5 minutes. Stir in the tomatoes, chile powder, and garam masala and bring to a rapid simmer. Simmer for 5 minutes, then stir in the ground almonds, chocolate chips, and salt. Stir until the chips have melted, then simmer another 2 minutes. Remove from the heat and cool for 5 minutes.

3. Add the lime juice, then puree the sauce in a blender or use an immersion blender to puree it in the pot until very smooth. The sauce should be thick; taste the sauce and add more salt or lime juice as needed. Pour into a serving dish and serve with warm tostones.

Jeff's Lazy Sunday Stuffed Artichokes

SERVES 4 TO 6

Jeff Blanchard of vegan late-night munchies hotspot Food Swings in Williamsburg, Brooklyn, contributes this Italian specialty of fresh summer artichokes loaded with garlicky, olive oil–laced bread crumbs. And what better way to spend a leisurely Sunday afternoon than making batches of these beauties?

When he says ¼ cup of chopped garlic, he really means it, so don't skimp and measure out your garlic (but it's okay to chop a boatload of garlic in a food processor; save the rest for any of these recipes). Jeff recommends making extra artichokes to snack on all week long; go crazy when artichokes have their peak flavor during the cool spring growing season.

Jeff's tip: Use smaller, younger artichokes (under 3½ inches); young artichokes are sweeter and the soft leaves are easier to stuff.

> 16 ounces of plain, fine bread crumbs
> (about 4½ cups)
> ¼ cup minced garlic
> 5 teaspoons dried oregano
> 1 tablespoon dried thyme
> ⅓ cup freshly chopped flat-leaf parsley
> 2 tablespoons salt
> 1 tablespoon ground black pepper
> 1 large lemon, sliced in half
> 1 cup good-quality olive oil
> 5 to 6 fresh artichokes

1. Preheat a 12-inch frying pan over medium heat, then pour in the bread crumbs. Add the garlic, oregano, thyme, parsley, salt, and pepper. Stir and toast the crumbs and garlic for 10 minutes or until toasted a golden brown. Squeeze half of the lemon into the crumbs, then stir in the olive oil. Continue to stir for another minute, then remove from heat. During the entire process be sure to watch the crumbs carefully to prevent any burning.

2. Prepare the artichokes for stuffing: slice off the bottom stems, then cut off the top 1 inch or so (depending on the size of the 'choke, cut off more on larger ones) to create a nice flat surface. Now open the artichoke and use a metal spoon to scoop out the center of the artichoke. Try to remove all the little hairs in the bottom inside of the artichoke, so dig deep with a spoon and scoop it all out.

3. Now stuff the artichokes with the bread crumbs. Use your fingers or a small spoon and pack as much as possible (a teaspoon to a tablespoon, depending on the size of the leaf) into the spaces between each leaf, then firmly stuff a good portion of crumbs into the center of each artichoke. After you

stuff the artichokes, place them standing upright in a round pot 10 to 12 inches wide. Use the smallest pan that can fit all of the artichokes so they can fit in tightly; you don't want them falling over while baking. Fill the pot with only enough water to reach about an inch from the edge of the artichoke where the stuffed leaves start.

4. Slice the remaining half of the lemon into paper-thin slices and make enough slices for each artichoke (4 to 6 slices). Take a slice of fresh lemon and place on top of each artichoke. Bring the water in the pot to a rapid simmer over high heat, then reduce to low and partially cover. Simmer the artichokes for 45 minutes, then turn off the heat and let stand for 30 minutes to cool. Serve at room temperature.

Braised Greens with Lemon and Olive Oil

SERVES 4 AS A SIDE

Juicy braised greens with lemon and olive oil are a hearty side ready in minutes for any Mediterranean meal. You could use just one green, but a blend of leafy greens makes the most rewarding dish. Try chicory or escarole greens as a base (they're so very Greek and Italian in character), then throw in a handful of spinach, chard (without the stems), those long leaves of late-season arugula, and even dandelion (use only organic, harvested dandelion . . . not the stuff from the neighbor's lawn). Use only tender

greens here and save the harder greens like kale and collards for other recipes.

*For a Spanish dish, make the variation with chard or spinach and toss in raisins and pine nuts. This is a tasty tapa or sweet veggie side for **Artichoke Skillet Paella with Chorizo Tempeh Crumbles** (page 316).*

> 2-pound mix of tender cooking greens such as escarole, chicory, curly endive, large arugula leaves, or dandelion
> 4 cloves garlic, peeled and minced
> 3 tablespoons olive oil
> 1 teaspoon sea salt
> 3 tablespoons white wine or vegetable broth
> 3 tablespoons lemon juice
> A few twists of freshly cracked black pepper
> 2 to 3 lemon wedges

1. Remove any tough stems and thick stem bases from the greens. Chop the leaves and stems into 2-inch pieces, move them to a big mixing bowl or salad spinner, and cover completely with cold water. Let the greens soak for 5 minutes, swishing them around occasionally to remove any grit, and drain them well. Shake away any excess water.

2. In a deep, 12-inch skillet fry the garlic in olive oil over medium heat for about 1 minute, then add handfuls of greens. Stir to reduce bulk of greens, adding more greens until everything is in the pan. Sprinkle with salt and cook until greens are reduced in bulk and juicy looking but still bright green; this can take 4 minutes or up to 8 minutes. Then stir in the white wine or broth and lemon juice, simmer for 2 minutes, and remove from the heat.

3. To serve, use tongs to lift greens out of the skillet and into a shallow serving dish. Pour the

pan juices over the greens, add a few twists of black pepper, and serve with lemon wedges for spontaneous squeezing. Greens can be served either piping hot or warm.

Spinach or Chard with Pine Nuts: Use spinach, chard, or a combination of the two. Stir in ⅔ cup of dark raisins along with the wine and lemon juice. Once plated, sprinkle the top with ¼ cup of pine nuts, lightly toasted in another pan over medium heat until golden. Serve with lemon wedges.

Luscious White Bean and Celery Root Puree

SERVES 4

*White bean purees are a soothing bed for braised foods in French cuisine; here they are enriched with the ugly yet tasty celeriac root, a wholesome substitute for mashed potatoes. Topped with vegetables braised in red wine like **Red Wine–Braised Leeks and Mushrooms** (page 265), this puree is a pillow for a romantic, rustic mid-winter meal. Or try it as a lush foundation for toothsome **Beer-Bathed Seitan Stew** (page 156).*

Celeriac root is covered with stringy roots and knotty nubs; use a paring knife to remove the particularly twisted root ends that harbor sand and grit.

1 tablespoon olive oil

3 cloves garlic, peeled and minced

2 shallots, peeled and minced

⅓ cup dry white wine

1½ pounds celeriac root, peeled and diced into ½-inch chunks

½ cup vegetable broth

4 sprigs fresh thyme or ½ teaspoon dried thyme

One 14-ounce can (2 cups) cannellini (white kidney) or navy beans, drained and rinsed

½ teaspoon sea salt

1 teaspoon lemon juice

1. In a large, heavy 3-quart saucepan heat the olive oil over medium heat. Stir in the garlic and fry for 30 seconds until fragrant, then stir in the shallots and fry 2½ to 3 minutes until softened. Pour in the white wine and bring to an active simmer for 1 minute, stirring a few times to deglaze the pan. Add the celeriac root, vegetable broth, and thyme. Increase the heat and bring to a boil, then turn the heat down to low. Cover and cook for 20 minutes until the celeriac is very tender.

2. Uncover and add the beans and salt. Increase the heat to medium; keep the pan uncovered and simmer for 2 minutes. Remove the thyme sprigs and turn off the heat. Add the salt and lemon juice and use an immersion blender to puree the mixture until almost smooth (a few tiny lumps is fine); you can use a food processor, too, it's just a little messier. Taste the mixture and adjust seasoning if needed with more lemon juice or salt. If the mixture seems watery, simmer over low heat and stir occasionally until the desired consistency is reached. Serve the puree piping hot, alongside chunky stews or juicy sautéed foods.

CHAPTER 11

rice & whole grains: one-pot meals & supporting roles

Rice and other grains are the real soul of food in many regions; the vegetables, the proteins, the sauces, and condiments are just garnishes. Learn to make an excellent bowl of rice and a world of cooking lands in your lap. Vegetable paella with chorizo tempeh, Persian saffron tadig, Caribbean rice with kidney beans, Indian biryani with cashews and sweet spices—maybe it's my upbringing in a rice-and-beans household, but I think one-pot, grain-based meals embellished with veggies, nuts, or even fruit is a complete meal with quality leftovers. Isn't it time for a bowl of rice?

Rice Basics

Cooking rice can sometimes seem more like magic than science; measuring the water by the knuckle, the kind of pan you use, the humidity, and age of the rice can all be factors between a just-okay rice and great rice.

Even experienced cooks say that cooking rice on the stovetop isn't exact and that results are not always consistent. However, the more you cook rice and become comfortable making it, the better it will be.

CONSIDER THE POT

Rice is cooked the world over in all kinds of vessels, but it's worth looking around your kitchen and choosing the best possible pot you've got for rice.

I recommend a heavy, stainless-steel pot with a tight-fitting lid. I'm not a fan of non-stick. Enameled cast-iron is also great for cooking rice (and other grains), as the iron is a pro at distributing the heat evenly. I don't recommend unglazed cast iron as the texture of the pot may promote sticking, and the iron can mingle with acidic ingredients (tomatoes or wine, for instance) and create some off-putting flavors.

Does your stovetop have hot spots that occasionally burn rice (or anything, really)? Consider using a burner heat diffuser, found in kitchen supply stores. It's a metal plate that sits on top of the burner, helping to create a more even distribution of heat between the burner and the bottom of a pot. There are old-fashioned diffusers that look like a perforated metal disk with a handle for ease of moving it to different burners, and there are updated, sleek disks that cover the entire burner. They come in handy especially when cooking with flimsy pots with thin bottoms or nasty range burners that seem to only have a "burn" setting.

ABOUT THAT RICE COOKER

For foolproof rice, consider purchasing a rice cooker. A thesis about rice cookers is beyond the scope of this book, but it's worth noting that if you regularly make rice more than twice a week, it may be time to consider investing in a rice cooker.

If you already own and use a rice cooker, follow your manufacturer's instructions in regards to adjusting the total liquid amount and cooking time for pilaf-style rice for any of the rice dishes in this book.

If you're a rice cooker hopeful, it can be overwhelming to browse through the online selections. Should you buy the $20 budget bucket or go bananas and buy a $300 kitchen robot that seems to do everything except serve the rice to your table?

My recommendation for a rice cooker beginner is to buy a reliable brand such as Zorushi (maybe the most established and popular brand of Japanese cookers) or Sanyo.

The price range: $50 to $80 should get you a rice cooker that will cook perfect white and brown rice.

Extras to look for: programmable rice timer,

steaming baskets for steaming vegetables or other foods while cooking rice, and a retractable cord.

SOAKED AND STRAINED

Neither soaked nor strained should describe you while preparing rice, but soaking and straining can produce results than can make you smile.

When preparing long-grain rice, in particular both white and brown basmati rice, consider soaking your rice before cooking; soaking helps produce extra-long, fluffy strands and reduces the cooking time. For best results rice should be soaked for at least 2 hours for white basmati, 4 to 6 hours for brown rice. Rinse the rice first, then stir in the cooking pot with the required amount of water. Do this overnight or before work in the morning for rice for dinner (but don't soak longer than 24 hours or the rice may sprout; sprouted rice can be mushy or bitter).

Rinsing rice is recommended for most varieties to remove excess starch and dust, but is especially useful for producing fluffier long-grain rice. To prevent any rice from slipping away when pouring the rice from the bowl, just pour the rice into a large fine-mesh metal sieve. Not a grain will be lost and it takes seconds.

WATER, WATER EVERYWHERE

The kind of rice you use will directly affect how much water you need for cooking. Interestingly enough, this mainly applies to white rice. Brown rice of most any variety requires a 1:2 ratio of rice to water; white rice varies slightly depending on the variety.

Always read the package directions on your rice and use the suggested amount of water. The amount listed in the recipe is a general guide, handy if you prefer to buy your rice in bulk.

IS YOUR RICE OF AGE?

The age of a bag of rice can determine the cooking time and amount of water needed. Rice can be "old" or "new" crop, meaning how long the rice has been around since harvest. Sometimes a bag of rice may be labeled with this information, but usually it's something you'll discover on your own by preparing that first batch of rice from the bag.

The older the rice, the less moisture it contains; it will need a longer cooking time and more liquid. But most problems happen from the opposite condition: the rice you're cooking is new (young) rice and didn't require as much water and cooking time. The result: mushy, sad, youth-gone-bad rice.

So what to do? Make a sacrificial batch of rice if you're unsure and take note of the finished product. If it needed more liquid or cooking time than suggested, it may be an older crop; use a few more tablespoons of water and cook 5 to 10 more minutes (double for both for brown rice).

Mushy or wet rice could be youthful rice full of moisture; cut down on the water by 2 to 3 tablespoons and the cooking time by a few minutes. If you're soaking young rice, reduce the total soaking time anywhere from 30 minutes to an hour.

Plain and Simple Rice

Plain rice can go with most any recipe in this book, and leftover chilled rice can be stir-fried for delicious completely new dishes you'll look forward to again and again. The following recipes make just enough to serve as a side for three to four dinners to accompany one or more entrees.

Basic Boiled Rice

Cooking rice doesn't get more basic than this: if you grew up in an ethnic household (that uses rice in its cuisine), then you probably ate it like this. This is the way my parents taught me to make rice; most of my rice recipes work this way, and once you get the hang of it, you'll find it so practical it's really the best way to make rice for two to three people if you're busy.

Boiled Long-Grain White Rice

SERVES 4, GENEROUSLY

Use this method for Carolina-type rice; it's the most common rice you'll see on supermarket shelves, nonaromatic and suitable for Latin American, Middle Eastern, and most Chinese cuisine. If you're using enriched rice, don't rinse it; check the package to see if it's been enriched.

See the following tips for other types of rice including brown, medium grain, etc.

> 1½ cups long-grain white rice
> 2¼ cups water
> ½ teaspoon salt

1. Place the rice in a fine-mesh metal sieve and rinse with cold water until the water runs clear (remember: don't rinse if it's enriched). Place in a heavy, 2-quart stainless-steel pot and add the water and salt. Cover the pot and bring to a boil over high heat.

2. Boil for 30 seconds, stir the rice a few times with a wooden spoon, and reduce the heat to low. Cover the pot with a tight-fitting lid. Leave the rice alone for 13 to 15 minutes and cook until the water is absorbed and the rice is firm but with no crunchy cores in the center of the grains. Never stir the rice as it cooks; the grains will break and become mushy. If in doubt, use a fork to lift up some of the grains and check underneath the rice to see if all of the liquid has been absorbed.

3. When the rice is done, turn off the heat and leave covered for 5 minutes. Remove the lid and use a fork to gently fluff the grains. Serve hot.

Coconut Rice: Use 1 cup of regular or reduced-fat canned coconut milk and 1¼ cups of water. If desired add a strip of organic lime peel and remove before fluffing the rice.

Sushi Rice or Medium-Grain White Rice: Decrease the water slightly to 2 cups. Rinse and cook as directed for *Boiled Long-Grain White Rice*.

Chinese-Style White Rice: Omit the salt and use a Chinese variety of long-grain white rice. Allow the rice to rest for 10 minutes, then fluff with a fork. Chinese white rice is meant to be the plain but essential supporting background for salty foods seasoned with soy sauce.

Jasmine Rice: As popular as basmati rice, this medium-grained, highly aromatic rice is a must when serving Southeast Asian cuisine. Rinse it very well and allow it to drain for about 10 minutes before boiling. Prepare as directed for *Medium-Grain White Rice*. Serve with Thai or Vietnamese cuisine and try it with Filipino and Chinese dishes, too.

Lemongrass Jasmine Rice: Rinse rice as directed for *Jasmine Rice*. Saute 1 minced shallot with 1 tablespoon of coconut oil, then add rice, water, salt, and either 2 tablespoons of prepared lemongrass or 1 stalk of pounded fresh lemongrass (see page 17). Prepare as directed for *Jasmine Rice*.

Long-Grain Brown Rice: Increase the total amount of water to 2 cups and increase the cooking time to 40 to 45 minutes (check rice after 40 minutes).

Short-Grain Brown Rice and Medium-Grain Brown Rice: Increase the total amount of water to 3 cups and increase the cooking time to 45 to 55 minutes (check the rice after 45 minutes).

Pilaf-Style White Basmati Rice

SERVES 4

Fluffy basmati rice fills the air as it cooks with a buttery aroma and has become my go-to rice for not only Asian cuisine but almost everything. Unlike short-grain or regular long-grain rice that plumps as it cooks, basmati grains grow longer. This recipe uses a brief sauté that enhances this variety of rice. Throw in a few spices for a simple rice to serve with any Indian meal.

> 1½ cups white basmati rice
> 2 teaspoons vegetable oil
> 1½ cups water
> ½ teaspoon salt

1. Place the rice in a mixing bowl, cover with 2 inches of cold water, and stir. The water will look cloudy; carefully drain and repeat three to four times. Then cover with 2 inches of water and soak for 20 minutes or up to 3 hours. Drain the rice into a fine-mesh metal sieve, stir, and air dry for 10 minutes.

2. Heat the oil over medium heat in a heavy, 2-quart stainless-steel pot. Stir in the rice and sauté for 3 minutes, until the grains look opaque. Pour in the water and salt, increase the heat to high, and boil for 30 seconds. Stir the rice and reduce the heat to low. Cover the pot

with a tight-fitting lid. Leave the rice alone for 20 minutes and never stir the rice. After 20 minutes check the rice for doneness as directed for **Boiled Long-Grain White Rice** (page 298).

3. When the rice is done, turn off the heat, and keep covered for 5 minutes. Use a fork to gently fluff apart the grains. Serve hot.

Lightly Seasoned Indian Basmati Pilaf: Here's a great basic recipe for when you need basmati rice with a little something extra. Add the following along with the water: 3 green cardamom pods, 1 stick cinnamon, 1 small carrot, peeled and finely grated. Use the cardamom pods and cinnamon sticks to garnish the rice, but don't eat!

Steamed Sticky Rice

SERVES 4

Sticky rice follows its own rules: it must be thoroughly soaked before steaming above water (never boiled). If you love Southeast Asian food, there's no replacing these slightly sweet, intensely chewy morsels of truly sticky rice.

There are traditional utensils for steaming rice, like the cone-shaped Thai woven straw basket balanced on a tall curvy pot. Though fun to look at, this setup can overwhelm small kitchens. Other methods use cheesecloth or a bamboo steamer. Ultimately, my method uses multi-tasking kitchen tools you may already have.

This no-frills method steams sticky rice in a large, fine-mesh metal sieve that should fit comfortably on top of a pot or large saucepan. I use a 7½-inch-wide sieve on top of a 2-quart pot with a few inches of boiling water, then a lid is placed on top of the sieve. The fit of the lid and sieve need not be exact, just enough to trap the steam. You may already have the right sieve and pot, and if not, for less than $20 you're all set and ready for countless other kitchen tasks. You'll avoid the tedium of plucking rice from a wicker basket or wad of cheesecloth.

1½ cups white short-grain sticky rice (sometimes called sweet rice)

1. Rinse and drain the rice as directed for **Boiled Long-Grain White Rice** (page 298), then cover it with 4 inches of water and soak for at least 2 hours. The rice will be ready to steam when an uncooked grain crumbles easily when bitten into.

2. Drain the rice into a fine-mesh metal sieve. Fill a 2-quart pot with 3 inches of water, cover, and bring to a boil over high heat. Fit the sieve on top of the pot (make sure the rice doesn't touch the water), cover the sieve with a lid that completely covers it, and steam the rice for 20 to 22 minutes. The rice is done when the grains are translucent and chewy and with no crunchy centers.

3. Serve the rice immediately. Keep it warm and store in a tightly covered container. Sticky rice should be eaten as hot as possible; as it cools it turns hard and rubbery. Cold sticky rice can be resteamed to its former sticky, yummy glory.

Crusty Persian Rice with Saffron and Pistachios

SERVES 4

Tadig is a compelling rice dish beloved in parts of the Middle East. This rice is purposefully cooked to form a crunchy, golden brown layer of crust on the bottom. Maybe you've made this crust by accident once or twice, but when done with style people love tadig so much that special Persian-style rice cookers exist solely for a perfectly toasted tadig rice crust at the touch of a button.

This recipe uses the old-fashioned stovetop method, still used by cooks the world over. Tadig excels when made with buttery basmati; it's possible to make brown rice tadig, too, but white rice makes the prettiest, best-tasting crust. Serve with **Roasted Cauliflower with Mint** *(page 285) for a light dinner for 4.*

RICE

> 1⅔ cups white basmati rice
>
> 8 cups water
>
> 1½ teaspoons sea salt

TADIG

> 1 tablespoon hot water or hot almond milk
>
> A pinch of saffron, crumbled
>
> ⅓ cup plain soy or coconut yogurt
>
> 2 teaspoons *Persian 7-Spice Blend*
> (see page 43) or use 1 teaspoon ground
> coriander, ½ teaspoon ground cinnamon,
> ½ teaspoon ground cumin

> ¼ teaspoon sea salt
>
> 4 tablespoons olive oil or melted
> nonhydrogenated vegan margarine
>
> 3 tablespoons chopped pistachios
>
> ¼ cup golden raisins (optional)

1. Place the rice in a large metal mesh strainer and thoroughly rinse with cold water. In a large, 3-quart pot bring the water to a rolling boil over high heat. Stir in the salt and then add the rice. Boil the rice for 5 minutes; remove a rice grain and check to see that it's just beginning to turn tender on the outside but still has a hard core. Drain the rice in the metal strainer again, stirring it a few times to remove any excess water.

2. While the rice is cooking, in a small cup combine the hot water with the saffron threads and set aside for 5 minutes. Stir occasionally; the color of the saffron will seep into the water.

3. In a mixing bowl combined the parboiled rice, saffron water, yogurt, 7-spice blend, salt, and half of the oil. Set aside ½ cup of this mixture, then add the pistachios and raisins, if using, to the remaining rice in the bowl. The portion of rice without the nuts will be used to form a protective layer on the bottom of the crust to prevent burned nuts or raisins during the formation of the crust.

4. Preheat a heavy, 2-quart pot, no larger than 10 inches wide, with a tight-fitting lid, over medium-high heat. Swirl the remaining oil over the bottom and 2 inches of the side of the pot. Use a wooden spoon to spread the reserved ½ cup of rice without pistachios in an even layer inside the bottom of the pot. Spread with the remaining rice with nuts. Use the bottom of a measuring cup or back of the wooden spoon to firmly press down the rice.

5. Use a chopstick to poke holes about ½ inch apart to the bottom of the rice. Spread a clean, smooth-textured kitchen towel over the top of the pot, then

place a tight-fitting lid over the towel. Gather the hanging ends of the kitchen towel so they don't drape down the sides of the pot, then use a rubber band or a kitchen clip (like the kind for clipping shut snack chip bags) to fasten the ends of the kitchen towel on top of the lid. This will trap any excess moisture and prevent it from dripping back for fluffier rice and a crisper crust.

6. Turn the heat down to medium-low and cook for 35 to 45 minutes. Check the rice by lifting the lid; the rice should have a toasted aroma and not smell burned. Or use the tip of a spatula to check the sides of the rice and see how the crust is progressing; if the rice needs more time to develop the crust, partially cover and cook another 10 to 15 minutes. Keep your nose within distance of the stove to detect any burning, but if it smells richly toasted it's likely done.

7. Remove from the heat and take off the lid and the towel. Serve tadig either of two ways: for beginners, it's best to scoop out the rice and fillings onto a platter, then use a spatula to chip away at the crusts and arrange on top of the rice. If you're a pro, place a big serving dish on top of the pan, hold on tight and flip it over. Perfectly made tadig will slip out, golden crust and all, onto the serving dish. Enjoy hot.

Potato Tadig: Another kind of tadig can be made by layering the bottom of the pot with thin slices of potato. Peel and slice 1 large potato into slices no thicker than ¼ inch. Overlap the slices on the bottom of the heated, oiled pan in a spiral pattern, then top with the rice and cook as directed. The rice won't form the crust; instead the potatoes brown into a crispy golden layer.

Tadig Tips

→ If it's taking too long to get a good crust going, increase the heat to medium-low but keep careful watch on the tagid with your nose; if you smell burning, immediately turn the heat back to low and cook only 2 to 4 minutes more.

→ Every 6 to 8 minutes, rotate the pot 90 degrees. This will help redistribute the heat for a more evenly toasted rice crust.

→ Try different pots and pans in your kitchen and see which create the best crust. Light but sturdy stainless steel is favored by some experienced tadig cooks. Cast-iron skillets and Dutch ovens are a little tricky due to their heaviness, but give it a shot if all else fails. And if you own an "always burns the rice" pan, then by all means use it for tadig!

→ Sometimes when trying to intentionally (almost) burn rice, it has a strange way of never forming a crust. No worries, you'll still have a pot of perfectly fluffy, tender basmati rice. Even after you excel at making crusty tadig, you may prefer to make basmati rice with this method for the perfectly fluffy and delectable results.

Crusty Persian Rice with Dill and Fava Beans

SERVES 4

*Big, toothsome fava beans and handfuls of fresh dill transform tadig into a wholesome, complete meal. Serve with **Harissa Carrot Salad** (page 106) or a simple tomato salad. Try it layered with potatoes as described for **Potato Tadig** (page 302).*

RICE

1⅔ cups white basmati rice

8 cups water

1½ teaspoons sea salt

CASSEROLE

4 tablespoons olive oil or melted nonhydrogenated vegan margarine

1 tablespoon *Persian 7-Spice Blend* (see page 43)

4 teaspoons lemon juice

¼ teaspoon sea salt

1 cup roughly chopped fresh dill

One 19-ounce can fava beans or 2 cups homemade cooked favas, drained and well rinsed

1. Parboil the rice as directed for the *Crusty Persian Rice with Saffron and Pistachios* (page 301).

2. Preheat a heavy, 2-quart pot with a tight-fitting lid over medium-high heat. Swirl 3 tablespoons of oil over the bottom and 2 inches of the side of the pot. In a mixing bowl combine the rice with the remaining 1 tablespoon of oil, the 7-spice blend, and the lemon juice. Use a wooden spoon to spread half of the rice over the bottom of the pot; the rice will sizzle on contact with the pot. Sprinkle half of the dill over the rice, then top with the fava beans. Scatter the remaining dill over the beans, then spread the remaining rice on top. Use the bottom of a cup or back of the wooden spoon to press down the rice.

3. Poke holes into the rice and top with a towel-covered lid as directed for the *Crusty Persian Rice with Saffron and Pistachios* (page 301). Cook as directed for tadig, checking the doneness around 35 minutes. Cook another 10 to 15 minutes if a thicker crust is desired. Serve and make sure everyone gets a piece of crust and plenty of dill and favas.

Fluffy Spiced Couscous

SERVE 4

Couscous improves dramatically when prepared a little differently from the package directions. Instead of dumping it into a pot of boiling water, the water is poured over gently toasted, spiced couscous and tightly covered. The liquid is evenly absorbed and each grain plumps up firm sans sogginess. A glass dish that comes with a tight fitting snap-on lid is ideal.

Couscous is essential for Moroccan dishes and fine for African meals that require a fast side starch.

If preparing with water, use 1 teaspoon salt; if using veggie broth decrease level of salt to ½ teaspoon or less depending on the broth.

> 1 tablespoon nonhydrogenated vegan margarine
> 1 cup couscous or whole wheat couscous
> ½ teaspoon ground coriander
> ½ teaspoon ground cumin
> ½ teaspoon ground cinnamon
> ⅛ teaspoon cayenne pepper
> ½ to 1 teaspoon salt
> 1 cup boiling water or vegetable broth

1. In a small skillet or saucepan melt the margarine. Add the couscous, spices, and salt. Stir and toast until the couscous is golden, about 2 to 4 minutes. Spread into a 9 x 13-inch baking dish.

2. Bring the water or broth to a boil and pour over the couscous. Stir and immediately cover the pan as tightly as possible. Set aside for 15 to 18 minutes. When all of the liquid has been absorbed and the grains are plump, stir with a fork until the couscous is fluffy. Serve immediately. This simple couscous can be dressed up in the following ways:

With Fruit: Add to the couscous before adding the water: ½ cup roughly chopped dates, ½ cup golden raisins, and/or ¼ cup finely chopped dried apricot.

With Nuts, Mint, and/or Preserved Lemon: Stir the following into the fully cooked couscous: 2 tablespoons chopped roasted pistachios or hazelnuts or almonds; 2 tablespoons finely chopped mint; and/or 2 teaspoons minced preserved lemon (see *Preserved Lemons, Two Ways*, page 58).

Lemony Dill Rice

SERVES 4

A typically Greek-style rice that's great served with any Mediterranean entree. I love using nontraditional but irresistable basmati rice, but any long-grain white rice will do. For best results check the suggested water amount listed on the bag of rice you're using and make adjustments for the total amount of vegetable broth.

> 1 cup long-grain white rice
> 1 small yellow onion, peeled and finely diced
> 1 small carrot, peeled and finely diced
> 1 tablespoon olive oil
> 2 cloves garlic, peeled and minced
> 1¼ cups vegetable broth
> ¼ cup lemon juice
> ½ teaspoon dried oregano
> ½ teaspoon salt
> ¼ cup finely chopped fresh dill
> A few twists of freshly ground black pepper

1. Pour the rice into a fine-mesh metal sieve, rinse, and drain. In a 2-quart pot with a tight-fitting lid, sauté the onion and carrot in the olive oil over medium heat until the onion is translucent, about 4 to 5 minutes. Stir in the garlic and fry for 45 seconds, then stir in the rice and fry for 2 minutes, stirring occasionally.

2. Stir in the vegetable broth, lemon juice, oregano, and salt. Turn the heat up to high and bring to a boil. Stir the rice a few times, reduce heat to low, and

cover tightly. Cook for 22 to 24 minutes or until all of the water has been absorbed and rice is tender. Turn off heat, add the dill and black pepper, and use a fork to fluff the rice and completely stir in the dill. Cover and let stand for 10 minutes, then serve!

chinese sticky Rice with Tempeh sausage crumbles

SERVES 6

*Mushroom-infused sticky rice with morsels of water chestnuts, shiitake mushrooms, and sweet, Chinese-style seitan sausages could become a comfort food favorite, if you didn't grow up with the homestyle Chinese dish that inspired it. For best results use a deep, well-seasoned cast-iron pot for the best chance of getting a little browned crust on the bottom, similar to **Bibimbap** (page 308). Or continue to cook the rice on low heat while you enjoy your first serving; when it's time for seconds a tasty rice crust will have formed. Serve with **Crisp Stir-Fry Greens with Veggie Oyster Sauce** (page 283) and Sriracha; sticky rice reheats flawlessly in microwave ovens for never-boring brown bag lunches.*

> 2 cups short-grain sticky rice
> 10 medium-size dried shiitake mushrooms, about 1 heaping cup or 1½ ounces
> 6 scallions, root ends trimmed
> ⅓ cup Chinese Shaoxing cooking wine (see page 13)
> 3 tablespoons soy sauce

> 2 tablespoons vegetarian stir-fry sauce (see page 13)
> 2 teaspoons toasted sesame oil
> ½ teaspoon ground white pepper
> 4 teaspoons peanut oil
> 1-inch piece peeled ginger, minced
> One 8-ounce can water chestnuts, drained, rinsed, and diced into ¼-inch-thick pieces
> 1½ cups mushroom-soaking liquid or mild vegetable broth

SAUSAGE AND TOPPING
> 1 recipe *Chinese Tempeh Sausage Crumbles*, page 53
> A handful of chopped cilantro leaves

1. Soak, rinse, and drain the sticky rice as directed for **Boiled Long-Grain White Rice** (page 298). In another bowl cover the dried mushrooms with 2 cups hot water and soak for at least 20 minutes. Drain mushrooms but reserve liquid. Strain to remove any debris. Remove the mushrooms, gently squeeze out any excess liquid, and cut away stems. Chop the mushrooms into ½-inch-thick slices. Slice the white ends of the scallion apart from the green; slice the white ends into ¼-inch pieces, then slice the green part into paper-thin slices and set aside. In a measuring cup whisk together the cooking wine, soy sauce, vegetarian stir-fry sauce, toasted sesame oil, and white pepper.

2. Use a deep, 4-quart heavy pot with a lid, preferably seasoned cast iron. Pour in the peanut oil and fry together the ginger and the white parts of the scallions for 30 seconds. Add the diced mushrooms and stir-fry for 1 minute, then add the water chestnuts and fry for 30 seconds. Stir in the drained rice and pour on the wine sauce. Stir with a rubber spatula or rice paddle to completely coat the rice

with the sauce. Pour in the mushroom-soaking liquid and bring to a boil over high heat. Stir the rice two times, reduce the heat to low, and cover tightly. Simmer for 30 to 35 minutes or until the liquid is absorbed and rice is sticky and tender.

3. While the rice cooks, prepare the **Chinese Tempeh Sausage Crumbles** and set aside ½ cup of the crumbles. When rice is done, remove the lid and sprinkle crumbles on top of the rice. Use the spatula or rice paddle and stir from the bottom up to distribute the seitan sausage throughout the rice. Partially cover and let stand for 5 minutes before serving.

4. Scoop rice into individual serving bowls. Pass around reserved sausage crumbles, green sliced scallions, and cilantro as toppings. If desired keep a small amount of rice in the pot and cook over very low heat to create a chewy, browned crust; check after 12 minutes for hot and crusty goodness.

Freekeh and Millet Pilaf

SERVES 4 AS A SIDE

Freekeh *(also known as frik) is the Middle Eastern roasted green wheat chock-full of nutrition; it's also known in Germany as* Grünkern. *I like to combine it with other grains—here, the mild millet—for a full-bodied but balanced pilaf.*

Serve with Middle Eastern or African stews or alone for a savory whole-grain breakfast. The sweetness of the raisins complements the earthiness, but leave 'em out or substitute minced apricots or dried currants, if you prefer.

If you have a baharat spice blend, either home-made (page 43) or purchased, use 1 to 2 teaspoons and add along with the coriander for an aromatic pilaf.

Note: Freekeh, especially purchased in bulk (or bought in bulk bags), is a very rustic product that sometimes may contain bits of debris, wheat chaff, and stems you don't want in your pilaf. The easiest way to remove these is to cover the freekeh with 4 inches of cold water and stir. Skim off debris that floats to the top; I use a tiny wire mesh strainer used for tea, but a large spoon works, too. When you've removed as much as possible strain the grain in a sieve and rinse with cold water.

2 shallots, peeled and minced
2 teaspoons olive oil
½ cup cracked or whole-grain freekeh, rinsed
½ cup millet
1 teaspoon ground coriander
½ teaspoon cayenne pepper
1¾ cups boiling water
½ teaspoon salt
⅓ cup raisins
½ cup chopped flat-leaf parsley or cilantro

1. In a large saucepan over medium heat, fry the shallots in the oil until golden and lightly caramelized. Add the freekeh and the millet and sauté until the millet turns light tan, about 5 minutes. Add the coriander, cayenne, boiling water, salt, and raisins and bring to a boil.

2. Reduce heat to low, cover the pan with a tight-fitting lid, and cook for 24 to 26 minutes or until all the water is absorbed and the millet and freekeh grains are tender. Turn off the heat, leave covered,

and let stand for 10 minutes. Sprinkle with parsley or cilantro and use a fork to fluff the grains. Serve hot or at room temperature.

Bulgur Wheat Mujaddara with Toasted Orzo

SERVES 6

Mujaddara, *the flawless combination of lentils, grains, and caramelized onions eaten in many variations throughout the Middle East, can be made with rice, but I prefer it with large-grain bulgur wheat. Serve this healthy one-pot meal with* **Mediterranean Chopped Salad** *(page 87) and plenty of* **Roasted Chile Pepper Harissa** *(page 42). Look for the largest grain bulgur wheat (cracked, precooked, and dried whole wheat berries) you can find; #3 bulgur has chunky grains almost the size of whole-grain buckwheat. The orzo can be replaced with any small pasta, even tiny macaroni or large-grain couscous.*

2 cups large-grain bulgur (size #3)

1 pound yellow or red onions, peeled, sliced in half and cut into ¼ thin half moons

3 tablespoons olive oil

¼ cup uncooked orzo pasta

1½ teaspoons fennel seeds

1 cup uncooked brown or green lentils

2 teaspoons ground coriander

1 teaspoon ground cumin

½ teaspoon cayenne pepper or Aleppo pepper flakes (see page 10)

1½ teaspoons sea salt

4½ cups water or vegetable broth or a combination (use less salt if using all broth)

A few twists of fresh ground black pepper

A handful of chopped flat leaf parsley

1. Pour the bulgur into a fine-mesh metal strainer and rinse with cool water. Drain well.

2. Preheat a large, heavy pot with a tight-fitting lid or a cast-iron Dutch oven over medium-high heat. Add the sliced onions and dry sauté, stirring occasionally with a wooden spoon, until the onions have reduced in bulk by about half and are starting to caramelize, about 10 to 12 minutes (starting the caramelization with a dry sauté helps speed the process). Stir in 2 tablespoons of the oil and continue to sauté until golden brown and very soft, about 5 more minutes. Set aside about ¼ cup of onion for garnish. Transfer the remaining onions to a plate and set aside.

3. Heat the remaining oil and sauté the orzo pasta for 2 minutes or until golden. Add the fennel seeds and continue to sauté for another 30 seconds. Stir in the lentils, coriander, cumin, cayenne, and salt and then pour in the water or broth. Increase the heat and bring mixture to a boil. Reduce the heat to medium-low, stir, and cover tightly. Simmer for 40 to 45 minutes, or until the lentils are almost tender. Stir in the bulgur and cook another 12 to 15 minutes or until both the lentils and bulgur are tender and all of the liquid has been absorbed.

4. Pour the sautéed onions (except for the garnish) on the bulgur, add a few twists of ground pepper, and use the wooden spoon or a spatula to stir in the onions thoroughly. Mound the mujaddara into a large serving bowl, garnish with the remaining fried onions and chopped parsley. Serve hot, or at room temperature in warm weather.

sizzling rice with veggies and chili sauce (dolsot bibimbap)

SERVES 4

Korean dolsot bibimbap is a festive piling of seasoned veggies on top of chewy rice, sizzling in a hot stone bowl that bakes a thin chewy crust; right before eating it's tossed with a sweet and completely habit-forming red chile sauce. For home kitchens there's no need for the stone bowl when a cast-iron skillet will do the job of creating the crust.

*The ingredients list may look epic, but the veggies are simply seasoned and can be prepared while the rice is cooking and the spicy red gochuchang sauce takes less than a minute to stir together. Extra seitan from the **Korean Veggie Bulgogi (Sweet Soy BBQ)** (page 249) is amazing as a topping, but I enjoy the simplicity of the spinach, sprouts, and tofu for most meals.*

RICE

> 1 recipe cooked *Sushi Rice* (page 299)
>
> 6 tablespoons toasted sesame oil , divided for two batches of bibimbap

GOCHUCHANG SAUCE

> ⅓ cup gochuchang (Korean fermented red chile paste, page 15)
>
> 2 to 3 tablespoons warm water

TOPPINGS

> *Seasoned Spinach* (recipe follows)
>
> Thin strips of *Savory Baked Tofu* (page 50)
>
> *Sesame Mung Bean Sprouts* (page 89)

ADDITIONAL GARNISH

> 1 sheet of toasted nori seaweed, cut into ¼-inch strips
>
> *Sesame Scallions* (recipe follows)
>
> Homemade kimchi (page 56) or purchased

1. Prepare rice following directions in *Sushi Rice* (page 299). Keep the hot rice covered.

2. Prepare toppings and garnish: follow the recipes for making the *Seasoned Spinach*, *Savory Baked Tofu*, *Sesame Mung Bean Sprouts*, and *Sesame Scallions* as directed. You can prepare these veggies up to 2 days in advance and store them in individual, tightly covered containers in the refrigerator.

3. Prepare the gochuchang sauce: in a small mixing bowl stir together the chile paste and water to form a smooth sauce. Add more water, a teaspoon at a time, until a consistency similar to ketchup is reached.

4. Heat a deep, 10- to 11-inch cast-iron skillet or Dutch oven over medium-high heat; it's ready to use when a drop of water flicked on the surface sizzles immediately. Using a pastry brush, brush the bottom and sides of the skillet with 2 tablespoons of the toasted sesame oil. Now using a heat-resistant rubber spatula or wooden spoon, spread *half* of the cooked rice over the entire bottom of the pan to form a thick cake. Cook the rice undisturbed and uncovered for 5 minutes.

5. Arrange the spinach, tofu, and bean sprouts in ¼ cup piles on top of the rice. Drizzle 1 tablespoon of the sesame oil over the vegetables. Cook the rice

uncovered for another 4 to 6 minutes and occasionally rotate the skillet a few times on the stovetop to evenly brown the bottom of the rice. Use a spatula to lift a portion of the rice underneath; the bottom layer touching the pan should be sizzling and forming a pale golden, crunchy crust. If desired continue to cook the rice a few minutes more until a crust dark enough to your liking has formed.

6. When ready, remove the skillet from the stove. Scatter the top with half of the nori strips and *Sesame Scallions*. Add a few spoonfuls gochuchang sauce (go easy if you're not accustomed to spicy food) and use a large metal spoon to thoroughly stir the rice, digging deep into the bottom and folding it into the chile sauce and toppings. Carefully pile servings into individual bowls and pass around additional toppings to be added as desired. Serve with kimchi.

7. Prepare the another sizzling batch of rice while you're eating the first batch of dolsot bibimbap.

Cool Bibimbap

For warm-weather meals, skip grilling the rice and top the plain, hot, boiled, short-grain rice with the seasoned veggies, tofu, and nori and pass around the gochuchang sauce. Diced avocado is an excellent unconventional topping, too!

seasoned spinach

½ pound spinach, washed and thick stems removed
2 quarts (8 cups) water
2 tablespoons soy sauce
2 teaspoons rice vinegar
2 teaspoons sugar
½ teaspoon toasted sesame oil

1. Place spinach in a large metal colander in the sink. Boil 2 quarts of water and pour over spinach to blanch the leaves. Rinse the leaves in cold water to stop the cooking. Squeeze the spinach to remove excess water and transfer to a mixing bowl.

2. Pour remaining ingredients over spinach and toss to coat with the dressing. This spinach can be made a day in advance.

sesame scallions

2 bunches scallions, root ends trimmed
1 tablespoon soy sauce
1 tablespoon rice vinegar
2 teaspoons sesame seeds
A pinch of sugar

1. Slice scallions as thin as possible on a 45-degree angle. Transfer to a mixing bowl, add remaining ingredients, and toss to coat. This is best made right before serving.

Brown Basmati Biryani with Cashews

SERVES 4

*This one-pot wonder is made with Indian spices, fresh ginger, vegetables, peas, chickpeas, and the wholesome pop of brown basmati rice. I've borrowed the precooking technique from tadig (page 302) for faster and fluffier brown basmati rice. Serve with **Cashew Yogurt Sauce** (page 66) and a chutney for a complete meal with plenty of yummy leftovers the next day.*

PRECOOKED BROWN BASMATI

    1½ cups brown basmati rice

    8 cups water

    2 teaspoons salt

BIRYANI

    2 tablespoons plus 2 teaspoons coconut oil

    ½ cup cashew pieces

    1 large red onion, peeled, sliced in half and sliced into ¼-inch-thin half-moons

    4 cloves garlic, peeled and minced

    1-inch piece peeled ginger, minced

    1 to 3 green chile peppers, finely minced

    6 green cardamom pods, lightly crushed with the side of a knife

    Two 3-inch sticks cinnamon

    2 teaspoons *Garam Masala* (page 39) or store-bought garam masala

    ½ teaspoon ground turmeric

    ½ teaspoon salt

    One 14-ounce can chickpeas, drained and rinsed, or 2 cups cooked chickpeas

    1½ cups diced cauliflower florets

    1 cup fresh or frozen green peas

1. Place the rice in a large metal mesh strainer and thoroughly rinse with cold water. In a large, 4-quart pot bring the water to a rolling boil over high heat. Stir in the salt and then add the rice. Boil the rice for 10 minutes; remove a rice grain and check to see that it's just beginning to turn tender on the outside but still has a crumbly core. Drain the rice in the metal strainer again, and shake to remove any excess water. Set aside and prepare the rest of the biryani.

2. In a small skillet over medium heat, melt the 2 teaspoons of the coconut oil, then stir in the cashews. Fry the cashews for 4 to 6 minutes or until just starting to turn golden. Transfer the nuts to a plate and set aside.

3. In a 3-quart pot over medium heat melt the remaining coconut oil, then stir in the onion and fry for 5 minutes or until softened and golden. Stir the garlic, ginger, chilies, cardamom, cinnamon sticks, garam masala, turmeric, salt, and the drained rice and fry, stirring constantly, for 5 minutes. Stir in the remaining ingredients (except for the cashews), and stir thoroughly and continue to fry for another 2 minutes.

4. Cover the pot with a tight-fitting lid, reduce heat to medium-low and cook the rice for 25 to 30 minutes. The rice is done when the grains are long and tender. Turn off heat and pick off and discard the whole spices that have risen to the top of the rice. Stir in half of the fried cashews and transfer to a serving dish. Garnish with remaining fried cashews and serve warm with a chutney or *Cashew Yogurt Sauce* (page 65).

pineapple fried rice with a thai kick

SERVES 4

Fried rice is a great workhorse for using up leftovers, including neglected rice from yesterday's takeout. This recipe is bursting with the fresh Thai flavors of lime, basil, chilies, and cilantro. Depending if you use Thai sweet soy sauce or Golden Mountain sauce, the rice will have a different character, but both are excellent and authentic. Try replacing the tofu with **Chinese Sausage Tempeh Crumbles** *(page 53) for yet another twist.*

Purchase chunks of fresh pineapple from a salad bar or use thawed, frozen chunks of pineapple.

1 recipe *Jasmine Rice* (page 299), cooked and chilled for 2 hours or overnight

1 recipe *Savory Baked Tofu* (page 50), or purchased fried or baked tofu, finely diced

3 tablespoons of peanut oil

6 scallions, white and green parts divided and finely diced

3 cloves garlic, peeled and minced

2 to 4 Thai chilies, minced

1-inch piece peeled ginger, minced

1½ cups fresh pineapple, diced into ½-inch chunks

1 red bell pepper, core and seeds removed and finely diced

2 cups snow peas, stems removed and sliced into ½-inch pieces

3 tablespoons Thai thin soy sauce (see page 19)

1 tablespoon Thai sweet soy sauce (see page 19) or Thai Golden Mountain sauce (see page 18)

½ cup lightly packed Thai basil leaves

¼ cup lightly packed chopped cilantro leaves

Lime wedges for squeezing

1. Use a fork or your fingers to break up the cold rice into smaller clumps and set aside. Have the tofu, pineapple, and the vegetables chopped and ready to go (this is a stir-fry, so the stir-fry rules apply here: see **Pad Thai with Avocado and Spicy Greens**, page 233).

2. Heat the wok over high heat and add half of the oil. Stir in the chopped white parts of the scallions, garlic, chilies, and ginger and stir-fry for 1 minute. Add the pineapple and bell pepper and stir-fry for 4 minutes or until edges of the vegetables are starting to brown.

3. Add the remaining oil, then crumble in the cold rice. Stir-fry the rice for 4 to 5 minutes; rice will start to brown. Add the snow peas and stir-fry until they turn bright green, about 2 minutes.

4. In a cup whisk together the thin soy sauce and sweet soy sauce or Golden Mountain sauce. Pour over the rice and stir. Add the tofu, green parts of scallions, basil leaves, and cilantro. Continue to stir-fry for another 2 to 3 minutes or until the scallion tops turn bright green. Turn off the heat and transfer to serving dishes. Serve the rice hot and squeeze a lime wedge over the rice before eating.

Jollof Brown Rice with Fresh Thyme

SERVES 4

*Tomato-flavored rice is a popular side in many West African menus, but it also makes a great one-pot meal served with a salad. For a complete feast, serve it with **Deluxe Tofu Vegetable Mafe** (page 160).*

For the whole-grain inclined this recipe stars brown rice. The only caveat is that brown rice boiled with additional moist ingredients can sometimes create uneven or mushy rice. To prevent that I bake this rice, for firmer, evenly cooked grains.

    1 yellow onion, peeled and minced
    1 tablespoon peanut oil or other vegetable
        oil
    4 cloves garlic, peeled and minced
    2 small hot green chilies, minced
    1 cup long-grain brown rice
    ¼ cup tomato paste
    6 sprigs fresh thyme or 1½ teaspoons dried
        thyme
    1 teaspoon salt
    2 cups boiling water
    1 cup frozen or fresh peas, preferably petit
        pois if you can find them

1. Arrange a baking rack in the center of the oven, preheat to 400°F, and have ready a 9 x 13 x 2-inch deep ceramic or metal baking dish along with enough foil to completely and tightly cover the top. Over medium heat in a deep, 12-inch skillet or wok, fry the onion in the oil until translucent and soft, about 4 to 5 minutes. Stir in the garlic and chilies, fry for another minute, and add the rice. Continue to fry the rice until the grains appear lightly toasted. Remove from the heat and spread the fried rice in the baking pan.

2. Add the tomato paste, thyme, and salt and then pour the boiling water over the rice. Stir to dissolve the tomato paste, then stir in the peas. Tightly cover with foil and bake for 25 minutes. Peel back the foil, stir twice, seal the foil again, and then turn the pan 180 degrees; this will help redistribute the heat for more even baking. Bake another 30 minutes, then remove from oven and peel back the foil. The grains should have absorbed the liquid and the rice should be firm, chewy, but not hard in the center. If the rice is still hard and looks very dry, dribble a few tablespoons of water over the rice and bake another 10 minutes or so; if the rice is very wet, loosely cover to allow a little steam to escape and continue to bake another 8 to 10 minutes. When done, remove from the oven and let stand covered for 5 minutes. Remove the thyme sprigs, fluff with a fork, and serve hot.

White Rice & Black Beans

SERVES 4 TO 6

The classic dish that often goes by the name of Christianos & Moros (or some variation thereof); without having to delve too much into the politics of the traditional name, let's just enjoy this fast and nourishing take on rice and beans that's easy

enough for a weeknight meal. Serve with your favorite hot sauce and slices of avocado and a simple green salad with ripe tomatoes.

Not all long grain white rice is the same. To ensure you'll use the correct amount of liquid, consult the package for the specific amount to use when preparing 1 cup of rice for this dish.

1 large green bell pepper

1 large yellow onion

1 to 2 green or red chile peppers, minced

4 cloves garlic, peeled and minced

3 tablespoons olive oil

1½ teaspoons ground cumin

1 teaspoon oregano

1 teaspoon dried thyme

½ teaspoon ground paprika, sweet or hot

1 cup uncooked long grain white rice

1½ cups of vegetable broth or water

One 14 ounce can black beans, drained and rinsed (2 cups cooked beans)

¾ teaspoon sea salt

2 teaspoons red wine vinegar

¼ cup finely chopped fresh cilantro

Freshly ground pepper to taste

1. Remove core and seeds from bell pepper and chile, then dice as fine as possible. Peel the onion and finely chop. In a heavy 3-quart pot over medium heat, heat the oil and add the bell pepper, onion, garlic, chiles, cumin, oregano, thyme, and paprika. Stir occasionally with a wooden spoon and cook until vegetables are very soft and golden, about 10 to 12 minutes.

2. Stir in rice and fry for another 2 minutes or until rice looks opaque and just begins to turn golden. Stir in broth, beans, salt, and vinegar, increase heat to high, and bring to a rolling boil.

3. Stir rice a few times and reduce heat to low. Cover the pot with a tight fitting lid and cook for 22 to 24 minutes or until all of the liquid has been absorbed and rice is tender. Turn off heat and keep covered for 10 minutes, then add cilantro and a few twists of ground pepper. Fluff with a fork and serve hot.

VARIATIONS

Stir in 1 cup of chopped fried finely diced **Seitan Coriander Cutlets** (page 49) along with the beans.

Use Annatto Olive Oil in place of olive oil for yellow rice!

Island Brown Rice and Peas

SERVES 6

Wholesome, delightful Jamaican rice and peas; "peas" in this classic dish are not round green peas but another term for beans such as red kidney (which give a pretty pink tint to the rice), black-eyed peas, or pigeon peas. It's a familiar combination you'll see all over the Caribbean and Latin American world, here made faster with canned beans and even more nutritious with brown rice. While considered a side dish, it's hearty enough for a whole meal as is or with any West or East Indian curry.

*If you prefer homemade beans, replacing half of the water with reserved bean cooking liquid will add more color and flavor to the rice. Make kidney beans from scratch as directed for the **Mexican Homemade Beans** on page 164.*

1 large yellow onion, peeled and finely diced

6 cloves garlic, peeled and minced

1 tablespoon coconut oil or
    nonhydrogenated vegan margarine

2 cups long-grain brown rice

2¼ cups water

One 14-ounce can coconut milk, regular or
    reduced fat

2 teaspoons dried thyme or 6 sprigs fresh
    thyme

1 teaspoon ground allspice

1¾ teaspoons sea salt

1 teaspoon ground black pepper

1 to 2 Scotch Bonnet chile peppers, left
    whole and poked with a fork 3 to 4 times

4 cups (two 14-ounce cans) cooked red
    kidney beans, black-eyed peas, or pigeon
    peas, drained and rinsed

1. In a heavy, 3-quart pot with a tight-fitting lid sauté onion, garlic, and coconut oil over medium heat until the onion is soft and golden, about 5 minutes. With a wooden spoon stir in the rice and cook for another 3 to 4 minutes or until rice is golden.

2. Stir in water, coconut milk, thyme, allspice, sea salt, and black pepper. Increase the heat to high and bring mixture to a rolling boil for 1 minute. Drop the chile pepper(s) into the rice and stir a few times, then add the beans. Reduce heat to low and cover pot with a tight-fitting lid.

3. Simmer for 55 to 65 minutes, or until the liquid is absorbed and the rice is tender. Remove from heat and let stand covered for 10 minutes. Remove chilies and thyme sprig, if using, fluff the rice with a fork, and serve hot.

colombian coconut lentil rice

SERVES 6

This Colombian side dish makes an amazing entree for us vegans, or anyone looking for a light and nourishing meatless main course. Serve alongside a crunchy cabbage salad and your favorite hot sauce.

Many Colombian dishes tend to be rather mild, so I've added the option of including nontraditional habanero peppers to heat things up.

1 cup uncooked brown or green lentils

2 cups white long-grain rice

1 tablespoon coconut oil or vegetable oil

1 large yellow onion, peeled and finely diced

3 cloves garlic, peeled and minced

2 teaspoons ground cumin

¼ teaspoon ground black pepper

¼ teaspoon cayenne pepper

1¼ cups water

One 14-ounce can coconut milk, regular or
    reduced fat (the latter works well here)

1 teaspoon sea salt

1 to 2 habanero chile peppers (optional)

1. In a small bowl soak lentils with 1 cup of hot water for 30 minutes. Drain off excess liquid. Rinse and drain rice according to **Boiled Long-Grain White Rice** (page 298) directions.

2. About 15 minutes into soaking the lentils, heat the coconut oil in a heavy, 4-quart pot over medium heat. Use a wooden spoon to stir in the onion and garlic and fry until onion is soft and golden, about 4 to 5 minutes. Stir in the rice and fry for another 3 minutes, or until rice is toasted and just starting to turn golden.

3. Stir in the spices, then add the water and bring to a simmer, stirring constantly. Add the lentils, coconut milk, and salt and increase heat to high. If using habanero chilies, pierce the whole chilies several times with a fork and add to the pot. Bring mixture to a rolling boil, stir one more time, then reduce heat to low and cover the pot with a tight-fitting lid.

4. Simmer the rice for 28 to 32 minutes, or until the liquid has been absorbed and rice and lentils are tender. If the liquid is absorbed before the lentils or rice are tender, drizzle in ½ cup of hot water, cover, and cook for another 5 to 10 minutes. Remove from heat and let stand covered for 10 minutes. Uncover, remove and discard habanero if using, fluff rice with a fork, and serve.

Mexican Red Rice

SERVES 4

Make this red pilaf-style rice to serve alongside any Latin dish, but especially Mexican dishes; while not completely authentic, it's a welcome side with beans, roasted tofu, or seitan. It's best served simply as is, but you can stir in ½ cup of corn kernels or finely diced carrot along with the broth for confetti-like fiesta rice.

1 cup long-grain white rice

2 teaspoons olive oil

2 cloves garlic, peeled and minced

1 small yellow onion, peeled and finely diced

1 jalapeño or serrano chile, minced

1½ cups vegetable broth

4 teaspoons tomato paste

½ teaspoon ground cumin

½ teaspoon sea salt

3 tablespoons finely chopped fresh cilantro

1. Rinse and drain rice as directed for **Boiled Long-Grain White Rice** (page 298). In a 2-quart pot heat the olive oil over medium heat, add the garlic, and fry for 30 seconds. Stir in the onion and chile and fry, stirring occasionally, for 4 minutes or until the onion is soft and golden.

2. Stir in the rice and fry for 2 minutes; the rice grains will turn slightly translucent on the edges. In a 2-cup liquid measuring cup whisk together the vegetable broth, tomato paste, cumin, and salt, stir into the rice, and increase the heat to high. Bring to a boil for 1 minute, then turn heat down to low. Stir the rice one more time, cover the pot with a tight-fitting lid, and cook for 20 to 24 minutes or until all of the liquid has been absorbed and the rice is very tender. Turn off the heat, leave the pot covered, and set aside to rest for 5 minutes.

3. Uncover, sprinkle the top with cilantro, and use a fork to fluff the rice. Serve hot.

Red Brown Rice: Long-grain brown rice can be used for this recipe; it just requires more liquid and a longer cooking time. Increase the broth to 4 cups total and lengthen the cooking time to 45 to 55 minutes; check the rice around 45 minutes to see if the water has been absorbed and the grains are tender.

artichoke skillet paella with chorizo tempeh crumbles

SERVES 4 TO 6

A famous Spanish dish, paella is a massive pan of almost creamy, delicately seasoned saffron rice studded with all manner of toppings. Sometimes making paella can seem intimidating, but sans the seafood and animal products the total cooking time is reduced and the chorizo crumbles can be made in advance.

The other factors that makes paella seem complex are a special pan and an open fire; a 2-inch-deep by 12-inch-wide skillet and your stovetop are the hardworking paella tools you already own (at least the stove part maybe?). Paella is a bountiful dish, an ideal reason to gather the tribe for a relaxing weekend supper.

Paella needs starchy, short-grain white rice to do its thing; Spanish Valencia ("bomba" variety rice is best) is the quintessential rice for paella but can be difficult to find. Italian Arborio rice is a good substitute; the results will be softer and creamier than Spanish short-grain but delicious still. If you're desperate for paella and short on resources, Japanese short-grain sushi rice can stand in; though sticky, it cooks up chewy and creamy in the paella broth.

4 tablespoons olive oil

One 10-ounce jar artichoke hearts, well drained, or one 10-ounce bag frozen artichoke hearts, thawed and drained

1 large yellow onion, peeled and finely diced

6 cloves garlic, peeled and minced

2 red or yellow bell peppers (or one of each), cores and seeds removed and diced into ½-inch pieces

⅓ cup dry white wine

2 cups short-grain white rice such as Spanish Valencia, Italian Arborio, or Japanese sushi rice, rinsed and drained (see **Boiled Long-Grain White Rice** on page 298 for washing method)

4 cups vegetable broth (golden "chicken" flavor is recommended)

4 ripe roma tomatoes, seeded and finely diced, or 1 cup canned diced tomatoes

A generous pinch of saffron threads (about ¼ teaspoon), crushed

1½ teaspoons dried thyme

¾ teaspoon sea salt

½ teaspoon sweet or hot smoked paprika

½ teaspoon ground cumin

2 bay leaves

½ recipe **Chorizo Tempeh Crumbles** (page 52)

2 tablespoons lemon juice

1½ cups frozen green peas

½ cup pearl onions, either from a jar (drained and rinsed) or frozen (don't thaw)

½ cup chopped parsley

Lemon wedges for squeezing over paella

If you'd rather use purchased vegan chorizo for the paella for a faster dish, look for firm, sliceable sausage (Field Roast makes the tastiest and easiest to use chorizo) and avoid the squishy, greasy kind. Or use your favorite spicy sausage links. For the best flavor, sauté thin slices of sausages for 1 to 2 minutes to lightly brown the exterior before using in the paella.

1. Heat 1 tablespoon of the oil in a 2-inch-deep, 12-inch-wide skillet. Slice the artichoke hearts into quarters and use a paper towel to pat away any moisture. Add the artichokes to the pan and fry, stirring occasionally, for about 4 minutes or until the edges are browned. Transfer the artichokes to a plate and set aside.

2. Add the remaining oil, then stir in the onion and fry for 4 minutes. Stir in the garlic and bell peppers and fry another 5 minutes, then stir in wine and simmer for 2 minutes. Add the rice and fry, stirring occasionally, for 2 minutes.

3. Stir in the vegetable broth, tomatoes, saffron, thyme, salt, paprika, cumin, and bay leaves. Increase the heat to high and bring to a rolling boil, then reduce the heat to low. This next step is important: do not cover the pan. Gently tuck the artichokes into the rice. Simmer the uncovered rice on low heat for 18 to 20 minutes and do not stir. Occasionally rotate the pan about 45 degrees on the top of the stove to help evenly distribute the heat throughout the rice as it cooks.

4. At around 18 minutes the rice should be mostly tender and almost all of the liquid should be absorbed, with some thick liquid bubbling around the edges and spaces between the rice. If the rice still has crunchy cores and most of the liquid has been absorbed, add another ½ cup of vegetable broth and continue to simmer for another 5 minutes; if the rice has enough moisture, don't add additional broth but continue to simmer.

5. When the inner layer of rice is creamy and the liquid has been absorbed, sprinkle the top of the rice with the chorizo tempeh, lemon juice, peas, and pearl onions. Partially cover the skillet and cook for 3 minutes, or until the pearl onions and peas are hot. Remove the lid and gently stir the top of the rice with a fork; if a thin, browned crust forms on the bottom of the paella, congratulations, you've just made *soccorat*, the much-sought-after bottom crust of a well-crafted paella. If not and you'd like some, increase the heat to medium-low and continue to cook uncovered for another 3 to 5 minutes, but watch carefully to prevent any burning. Remove the bay leaves, sprinkle with parsley, and serve the paella hot with lemon wedges for squeezing onto individual servings.

CHAPTER 12:

sweet Beginnings

Undeniably, the world has a sweet tooth (some places bigger than others).

If you've cooked meals from the recipes in this book, you're possibly craving a little something sweet, either as a midday snack paired with tea (as many Asian sweets are enjoyed) or as a dessert for a traditional grand finale. For busy chefs, pears poached in a range of global teas are a light dessert for any level of cooking expertise. For the ambitious, I'm crazy about the simplified French tart tatin or that irresistible syrupy filo pie stuffed with nuts, baklava, or whimsical sweet rice mochi dumplings wrapped around a red bean ice cream filling.

If choices weren't hard enough, I'll suggest my favorite dessert in this book—a relaxed bar cookie spin on tender, melt-in-your-mouth

Middle Eastern mamouls, a delicate semolina cookie with a rose-water scented date filling. If a slice of cake is more your style, choose from a dairy-free citrusy Italian ricotta cheesecake and a slim, flourless chocolate torte punched up with Ethiopian spices. Perhaps the most important lesson to be learned from sampling the great cuisines of the world: that there *is* a dessert for every sweet tooth on the planet.

Tenacious Tart Tatin (French Caramelized Apple Tart)

MAKES ONE 9½-INCH TART

Tart tatin is the ultimate French country dessert, a sophisticated, not-too-sweet tart of meltingly soft apple braised in dark amber caramel on a tender pastry crust. It's a departure from American apple pie: rustic, glossy, and without spices, the flavors of bittersweet caramel and caramelized apples shine through brightly.

Making tart tatin can be a challenge for beginners. There's the flipping of a heavy, hot pan and rolling out a fragile crust, but my veganized take uses friendlier tactics. The olive oil shortbread crust (olive oil is amazing paired with apples) is pressed, not rolled, into a pan, and the apples are fully caramelized on the stovetop then arranged on top of the prebaked crust. It's still faithful to the original, but requires less dexterity on the chef's part. And it's one of my top go-to desserts to impress.

It's essential to use the freshest, firmest, tart cooking apples here; the intense cooking in the caramel turns overly soft, old apples into applesauce. That's also why the apples are cut into thick quarters; they will shrink down dramatically cooked in bubbling caramel.

Use the widest, deepest skillet you own for caramelizing the apples. The rapidly boiling caramel over high heat is intense but will go smoothly using

a 12-inch skillet (stainless steel is best) that's at least 2 inches deep.

Store the frozen, unbaked crust up to a week in the freezer and bake as needed. To bake the crust in advance, store it (still in the pan) in a loosely covered container for up to 1 day.

OLIVE OIL SHORTBREAD CRUST
- ½ cup olive oil
- 1⅔ cups all purpose flour
- 3 tablespoons confectioners' sugar
- ½ teaspoon salt
- 1 to 2 tablespoons plain almond milk

CARAMEL APPLE TOPPING
- 6 large, firm, tart cooking apples (about 2½ to 3 pounds) like Granny Smith, Braeburn, or Fuji
- 6 tablespoons nonhydrogenated vegan margarine
- ¾ cup sugar
- 2 tablespoons brandy, apple brandy (Calvados), or cognac
- Vegan vanilla ice cream, optional

1. Freeze the olive oil an hour before making the crust. Pour into a plastic container and freeze until semi-solid, about the consistency of a soft sorbet. If too solid, remove from the freezer and stand at room temperature until it melts slightly.

2. Lightly oil a 9- to 10-inch springform cake pan or tart pan with a removable bottom. Sift the flour, confectioners' sugar, and salt together in a mixing bowl. Add the semi-frozen olive oil in spoonfuls. Use half at first and cut it into the flour using a fork or a pastry cutter. Add the remaining oil and mix until the flour looks crumbly. Drizzle in 1 tablespoon of almond milk and stir until the dough holds together

when squeezed between your fingers. If it's too crumbly, add additional tablespoons of milk, one at a time, until the dough holds together. Firmly press the dough into the pan, shaping a slightly raised edge along the sides of the pan. Using a fork, poke holes all over the dough and freeze for 30 minutes. Preheat oven to 350°F and place the crust on a large, rimmed baking sheet. Bake for 16 to 18 minutes or until firm. Remove from oven and transfer to a cooling rack. When ready to top with apples, remove either the outer ring of the springform pan or tart pan.

3. While the crust is baking, core and peel the apples and slice into quarters. In a deep, 12-inch skillet over medium heat, melt the margarine, then sprinkle the sugar in an even layer and stir a few times. Arrange the apple quarters on top in a single layer, cut side facing down, squeezing in the slices if necessary; as they cook, they'll shrink to fit, just like a good pair of jeans.

4. Turn the stove burner to high heat. Cook the apples, occasionally rotating the pan on the stovetop to evenly distribute the heat, for 10 to 12 minutes until most of the bubbling juices are a deep amber color. Keep the pan moving to prevent any one corner of the caramel from turning too dark or burning too fast. Turn off the heat and use tongs to turn each piece over and coat it completely with caramel; some dark, almost burned spots on the apples are desirable. If the apples are very soft use a large metal spoon to flip. Return the heat to high and continue to cook for 3 to 5 minutes or until all the apples are coated and the bubbling caramel has darkened to a slightly deeper shade of amber. It's important to cook the caramel down to a deep amber color to make it less sweet and slightly bitter, the way a proper caramel should taste. But watch it closely and never walk away from boiling caramel—it is prone to rapidly transforming from very dark to suddenly burning!

5. Turn off the heat and, using tongs or the large metal spoon, place one slice at a time in a spiral pattern on top of the crust; start from the outside edge and work towards the center, overlapping the apples and using the remaining slices to fill the gap in the center of the tart. Back on the stove, turn the heat to medium, and stir the brandy into the juices in the pan and simmer for 30 seconds. Turn off heat, stir the sauce a few times, and drizzle it over the tart.

6. Cool the tart for 12 minutes before serving. Slice with a thin, sharp knife and serve with vegan vanilla ice cream. Tart tatin is best consumed within a day of preparing; store the tart chilled and loosely covered. Gently reheating chilled slices will enhance the flavor.

With Sea Salt: Sprinkle a few grains of high-quality salt such as Maldon or Himalayan pink over the tart as it cools. But go easy on the salt and use less than ⅛ teaspoon at the most, preferably even less.

Tenacious Tart Tatin (French Caramelized Apple Tart), page 321

walnut spice sticky cake

MAKES ONE 9 X 13-INCH SHEET CAKE

A wholesome, sticky cake bursting with some of the most popular flavors in Greek sweets: walnuts, cinnamon, cloves, oranges, and even olive oil. Enjoy this rustic cake as a homestyle dessert or as an aromatic coffee cake at brunch. Barley flour is a common sight in Greek baked goods and, though a whole-grain flour, it gives this cake a delicate crumb and nutty flavor; nutritious whole spelt flour can also be used. With any cake, but especially ones made with whole-grain flour, mix the batter just long enough to moisten; mixing by hand is the best way to avoid overmixing.

The orange juice syrup topping gives the cake a pretty sheen and makes it soft and tender. It also helps keep the cake fresh longer.

> 1¼ cups barley flour or spelt flour
> 1 cup all-purpose flour
> 2 teaspoons baking powder
> ½ teaspoon baking soda
> 1½ teaspoons ground cinnamon
> ½ teaspoon ground cloves
> ¼ teaspoon ground nutmeg
> ½ teaspoon salt
> One 6-ounce cup vanilla or lemon soy
>   yogurt (¾ cup plus 2 tablespoons)
> ⅔ cup plain or vanilla soy milk
> 2 tablespoons ground flaxseeds
> Finely grated zest from one organic orange
> ½ cup orange juice
> ⅓ cup extra-virgin olive oil

> 1 teaspoon pure vanilla extract
> ¾ cup sugar
> 1¼ cups chopped walnuts

ORANGE SYRUP

> ⅔ cup orange juice
> ⅓ cup sugar
> ⅓ cup water
> 1 cinnamon stick
> 4 cloves

1. Cut a rectangle of parchment paper to fit into the bottom of a 9 x 13 x 2-inch metal baking pan or a 9-inch springform pan, place it on the bottom, and spray the insides of the pan generously with olive oil. Preheat an oven to 350°F. In a large mixing bowl sift together barley or spelt flour, all-purpose flour, baking powder, baking soda, all of the ground spices, and salt and form a well in the center.

2. In another bowl whisk together until smooth the soy yogurt, soy milk, flaxseeds, orange zest, orange juice, olive oil, vanilla, and sugar. Pour this liquid mixture into the center of the dry ingredients and use a rubber spatula or wooden spoon to fold the dry ingredients into the wet only long enough to moisten; don't overmix. Fold in 1 cup of the chopped walnuts, spread the batter into the pan (no need to spread into the corners of the pan; it expands during baking), and sprinkle the remaining ¼ cup of walnuts on top of the batter. Bake for 36 to 38 minutes or until a toothpick inserted into the center of the cake comes out clean (a few moist crumbs are okay).

3. While the cake is baking, prepare the syrup. Combine all of the ingredients in a saucepan and bring to a vigorous boil over medium heat, stirring

WALNUT SPICE STICKY CAKE

occasionally. Boil for 3 to 5 minutes or until the sugar has dissolved, reduce heat to low, and simmer for 10 minutes. The syrup should be thin (not thick like pancake syrup). Remove from heat to cool.

4. When syrup has cooled down slightly, remove cloves and cinnamon stick, then pour syrup evenly over the cake while it's hot. When cake is completely cool use a thin, sharp serrated knife to slice into wedges. Store cake tightly covered at room temperature.

pumpkin churros

MAKES ABOUT 2 DOZEN SMALL CHURROS

Stop the presses: pumpkin churros are in la casa! Light and crispy on the outside, creamy and soft in the center, and kissed with a coating of cinnamon sugar, these will be your new favorite autumn treat. The churros I grew up with were not the long sticks most North Americans may be familiar with via Mexican cuisine; these little guys are the crisp, plump loops you'll find throughout South America and Spain. Hot chocolate made with rice or almond milk is the ideal companion, but hot spiced apple cider or a pumpkin-spiced cup of coffee is fine, too.

I rarely deep-fry at home, but the occasional churro (and tostone) is the exception. The best deep-frying vessel for home is a cast-iron soup pot or wok, but any heavy pot with sides at least 4 inches high is okay. The choice of oil is flexible, too: a freshly poured batch is best, Peanut oil makes the tastiest fried treats, but a canola or a vegetable oil blend is a thrifty choice. Since the dough is quickly made

and squeezed through a pastry bag directly into oil, there's no rolling, cutting, rising, or shaping at all. Churros are the fastest, easiest homemade donut, as spontaneous as you are.

FRYING AND COATING

Cinnamon sugar: ⅓ cup sugar plus
⠀½ teaspoon ground cinnamon
Mild vegetable oil for deep-frying, enough
⠀for about 2½ inches

CHURRO DOUGH

¾ cup all-purpose flour
1 tablespoon cornstarch
¼ teaspoon baking powder
¼ teaspoon ground nutmeg
¼ teaspoon salt
¾ cups water
2 tablespoons dark brown sugar
⅔ cup pumpkin puree
1 tablespoon nonhydrogenated vegan
⠀margarine

1. Stir together sugar and cinnamon on a dinner plate. On another plate spread layers of paper towels or crumpled brown paper bags and keep it next to the stove.

2. In a deep, cast-iron pot pour about 2½ inches of oil. Heat the oil over medium-high heat; the oil is ready when it's rippling and a small chunk of bread fries up golden immediately. If you have a thermometer the oil should be at 350°F.

3. Meanwhile, in a mixing bowl combine flour, cornstarch, baking powder, nutmeg, and salt. In a large saucepan over medium heat bring to an active simmer the water, brown sugar, and pumpkin puree, then stir in the margarine. Turn heat down to low and slowly pour in a little of the flour mixture at a time, mixing constantly with a large fork (don't

use a wire whisk; the dough will stick to the wires). When the dry ingredients are moistened, turn off the heat and switch to a rubber spatula. Continue to stir the dough until smooth.

4. Fit a very large pastry bag with a large star-tipped nozzle; the end of the tip should be at least ¼ inch wide. When dough is cool enough to handle, use the rubber spatula to pack the dough into the bag. Firmly twist the top of the bag and squeeze the dough through the nozzle. Squeeze a length of dough about 4 to 5 inches long into the hot oil, either looping the ends together or making a straight line. It may be helpful to use kitchen scissors to snip off the dough before it lands in the oil. Fry four to five churros at a time but don't crowd the pan.

5. If you don't feel comfortable lowering dough directly into hot oil, squeeze a dough loop onto plastic wrap, then carefully lift it into the oil. Fry for 2 to 3 minutes until churros are puffed and golden, turning over once with a wire skimmer. Transfer to the paper-lined plate to drain. After cooling for 1 minute, flip warm churros a few times in the cinnamon sugar and serve warm.

Orange Blossom Hazelnut Baklava

MAKES ONE 13 × 9-INCH PIE, SERVING AT LEAST 8 TO 10

To know baklava is to yearn for it: a meltingly crisp confection of sticky syrup, golden filo, and crunchy nuts is love at first bite. Baklava is enjoyed in many forms through the Mediterranean and Middle East and makes an ideal ending to meals of those cuisines. Or savored with afternoon coffee or as an elegant brunch finale.

Walnuts are a must, but phenomenal baklava includes hazelnuts (and maybe almonds and shelled green pistachios), chopped very finely. The best fillings are almost sandy, but not powdered and definitely not nut butter. The syrup is spiked with delicate orange flower water; rose water is a close second choice. Either way this baklava is gorgeous.

ORANGE FLOWER SYRUP

- ¾ cup sugar
- ¾ cup water
- ½ cup agave nectar
- 2 tablespoons lemon juice
- 1 teaspoon orange flower water or food-grade rose water (see page 10)

FILLING

- 1 cup very finely chopped walnuts
- 1 cup very finely chopped hazelnuts (skins removed, see sidebar for technique), or a mix of hazelnuts and blanched almonds
- ½ teaspoon ground cinnamon
- ¼ teaspoon ground nutmeg or cloves
- 2 tablespoons sugar
- 2 tablespoons melted nonhydrogenated vegan margarine

FILO

- 8 tablespoons (½ cup or 1 stick) of nonhydrogenated vegan margarine, melted
- ½ cup olive oil
- 1 pound frozen filo dough, approximately twenty 13 x 18-inch sheets, completely thawed (you will have some leftover sheets)

1. Prepare the syrup and the filling first. In a large saucepan combine all of the syrup ingredients except the orange flower water and boil over high heat for 2 minutes. Reduce the heat to medium and simmer for 10 minutes, swirling the pan occasionally. Turn off the heat, stir in the orange flower water, and remove from the burner. For the filling, in a mixing bowl thoroughly combine all of the ingredients.

2. Preheat the oven to 350°F. In a large cup, stir together the margarine and olive oil. Generously brush the insides of a 9 x 13 x 2-inch ceramic or metal baking pan with olive oil. Follow the filo-handling directions for spinach pie on page 255, slicing the sheets in half (or whatever size necessary) to fit inside the baking pan. Arrange a sheet of trimmed filo into the bottom of the pan.

3. Use a pastry brush to lightly brush the filo with the margarine mixture, top with another sheet, and repeat for ten layers. Spread half of the filling evenly over the filo. Top with another eight sheets of oiled filo dough, then spread the remaining filling on top. Cover this with a final ten sheets of oiled filo and gently press down.

4. Using one hand to press down on the filo to steady, with the other hand use a sharp, serrated knife and, all the way to the bottom, cut the pie into diamonds or squares about 2 inches wide. Bake for 18 minutes, then remove the baklava from the oven. Pour the leftover oil mixture evenly over the top and bake another 22 to 26 minutes or until the top is golden and lightly puffed. Transfer to a cooling rack and let stand for 5 minutes.

5. Use a spoon and carefully pour the syrup *only* in between the slices. Avoid pouring it directly on top of the baklava; this will keep the top layers of the filo flakey. It may look like there's a lot and the syrup may pool between the slices at first, but it will eventually sink in. Set the baklava aside for at least 1½ hours; the syrup needs time to soak into the pastry. Baklava is a delight served slightly warm, so consider gently toasting cold baklava before serving. All that syrup will keep the bakalava fresh for at least 3 days, if it remains that long. Store loosely covered at room temperature.

Flower Water Baklava: Replace orange flower water with rose water or use a teaspoon of both for a really lovely aromatic baklava.

Chocolate Baklava: Stir 3 ounces of finely chopped, semi-sweet chocolate into the filling before laying inside the filo.

Nudie Nuts

To remove the skins from hazelnuts, gently toast them at 300°F for 10 to 14 minutes until fragrant and the skins are cracked. Pour into a rough-textured clean kitchen towel, wrap into a tight hobo-style pouch with one hand, and use the other hand to vigorously massage the pouch. The hazelnuts rubbing against each other will slough off the skins, plus the steam will loosen them, too. Continue for about 5 minutes, shake the pouch a few times, and carefully open. Most of the skins will sink underneath the peeled nuts; little bits of skin may remain but that's okay. Pick out the hazelnuts and shake the towel in the garbage, sink, or outside in the garden (but probably not out your apartment window!).

Orange Blossom Hazelnut Baklava, page 327

carrot semolina Halva

MAKES ONE 8-INCH ROUND HALVA

Halva is a name for a wide range of sweet, buttery, Indian pudding-like desserts (but not to be confused with Middle Eastern sesame halva candy). Two popular halvas, brilliant orange carrot halva and comforting semolina halva, join forces here for a mellow pudding that feels exotic and familiar at the same time; once chilled it can be sliced up into little squares, or serve it warm scooped into parfait glasses. Prepare it with half the sugar for a nourishing breakfast treat.

3 tablespoons nonhydrogenated vegan margarine

2 large carrots, peeled and finely grated (about 1½ cups grated, firmly packed)

3 tablespoons brown sugar

2 cups water

⅔ cup sugar

¾ teaspoon ground cardamom

¼ teaspoon salt

A pinch of ground nutmeg

⅓ cup golden raisins

½ cup fine semolina flour

½ teaspoon pure vanilla extract

¼ cup sliced almonds or cashew halves

1. In a large saucepan over medium heat melt the margarine and stir in the carrots. Sauté the carrots for 3 minutes until softened and juicy, then sprinkle with brown sugar. Sauté another 2 to 3 minutes until the carrots look slightly caramelized. Turn off the heat and transfer the carrots to a bowl. Lightly oil an 8-inch round cake pan.

2. Add the water to the saucepan and bring to a boil over high heat. Stir in the sugar, cardamom, salt, nutmeg, raisins, and sautéed carrots and simmer for 1 minute or until the sugar is dissolved, then turn the heat down to low. Stirring constantly with a whisk, slowly pour in the semolina. Continue to stir until the semolina is very thick and bubbling; you may want to switch to a wooden spoon or heat-resistant silicone spatula to stir the thickening semolina. Cook for 2 minutes, stirring the entire time, then turn off the heat. The finished semolina will have the consistency of thick, sticky dough. Stir in the vanilla extract. Spread the mixture into the oiled cake pan and sprinkle the almonds on top.

3. Set halva aside to cool for 30 minutes. Use a sharp knife to slice into 1-inch squares and serve. A plastic knife dipped into water is also an easy way to cut neat squares of halva.

4. Alternatively, you can serve the halva still warm as a pudding. Scoop the freshly made halva into serving bowls or parfait cups, sprinkle each serving with almonds, and serve warm.

Rose water Date semolina squares

MAKES ONE 8 X 8-INCH PAN OF DATE-FILLED BARS

Mamouls are buttery Middle Eastern cookies, traditionally shaped like little mounds with pretty patterns pressed on top and filled with aromatic sweet fillings. Special molds are used to press the cookies into shapes and patterns, but for the rest of us without mamoul molds, pressing the sandy semolina dough and rose water–scented date filling into a brownie pan is neat and easy enough for novice bakers. The result is exotic bar cookies, a rich finish to Middle Eastern feasts or for afternoon breaks with hot mint tea. Served warm, this is my favorite dessert in this book, period.

FILLING

1 pound dates without pits, soaked in hot
    water for 20 minutes
¼ cup sugar
1 teaspoon ground cinnamon
1 teaspoon rose water or orange flower
    water (see page 10)
¼ teaspoon ground cardamom

SEMOLINA PASTRY

½ cup nonhydrogenated vegan margarine,
    slightly softened (but not melty or
    greasy)
¼ cup nonhydrogenated shortening
⅔ cup powdered sugar
1½ teaspoons pure vanilla extract
½ teaspoon finely grated lemon rind or
    ¼ teaspoon lemon extract
1½ cups all-purpose flour
1¼ cups fine semolina flour
¼ teaspoon baking powder
A pinch of salt

TOPPING

2 tablespoons finely chopped pistachios
1 tablespoon powdered sugar

1. Make the filling first: drain the dates in a mesh sieve, pressing them down to remove any excess water. Transfer them to a food processor and pulse with the remaining filling ingredients into a thick paste; scrape down the sides of the processor often with a rubber spatula.

2. Preheat the oven to 350°F. Line the bottom of an 8-inch-square brownie pan with foil up to the edges of the pan and fold about 1 inch of foil over the sides of the pan. Spray the bottom with a light coating of cooking oil spray.

3. With a handheld mixer or standing mixer, in a large bowl cream together the margarine and shortening. Scrape the sides of the bowl frequently and beat until the mixture is fluffy, about 2 minutes. Beat in the powdered sugar, then the vanilla extract and lemon rind. Add the flour, semolina flour, baking powder, and salt and use a fork or a pastry cutter to cut the dry ingredients into the margarine mixture and make a sandy dough.

4. Pour half of the dough into the lined pan and firmly press it into an even layer in the bottom of the pan. Drop spoonfuls of the date filling over the dough, then lightly moisten fingertips and press the filling into an even layer all the way to the edges of the pan. Crumble the remaining dough over the date filling and press down all the way to the edges of the pan. Sprinkle the top with the chopped pistachios and gently press on the top.

5. Bake for 30 minutes or until the top is a pale yellow color and feels firm. Cool for 15 minutes, then grab the foil on the edges of the pan and lift the entire pastry out of the pan. Gently peel the foil away from the sides of the pastry and use a sharp knife to slice into sixteen small squares (or smaller squares, as these are very rich). Sprinkle the squares with powdered sugar. Serve warm or stored in a tightly covered container at room temperature; the squares will stay fresh for up to a week.

vanilla coconut sticky rice with mango

SERVES 3 TO 4

Perhaps even better than pie à la mode, the enticing combination of warm, pudding-like coconut sticky rice topped with cool mango is easy to make at home . . . maybe a little too easy—for a tempting weekend breakfast treat, too. A touch of vanilla extract or pandan leaf with its nutty-vanilla aroma adds another dimension to this Thai restaurant dessert classic. Don't limit yourself to mango, either; try topping the sticky coconut rice with thin slices of banana, kiwi, pineapple, strawberries, or even a scoop of chocolate coconut vegan ice cream!

The sticky rice needs time to soak up the sweetened coconut milk, so plan at least 30 minutes between finishing the rice and serving it; the longer the rice is left alone to absorb the coconut milk, the firmer it will be. If making Pad Thai or a stir-fry for dinner, make the coconut rice first and set it aside; once the dinner plates are cleared, it will be ready for dessert. To reheat the coconut rice, transfer to a covered glass dish and microwave for 1 to 1½ minutes, stopping to occasionally stir. Don't reheat it to piping hot; get it only warm enough to be soft and gooey.

> 1 cup uncooked sticky rice, soaked and prepared as directed on page 300 and see directions below
> 1⅓ cups canned coconut milk, regular or reduced fat

⅓ cup sugar

1 tablespoon brown sugar

¼ teaspoon sea salt

Two 4-inch pieces of frozen pandan leaf or ½ teaspoon pandan extract (see page 18) or pure vanilla extract

COCONUT SAUCE

½ cup coconut milk (remaining from 14-ounce can)

1 tablespoon sugar

2 teaspoons lime juice

¼ teaspoon cornstarch

1 ripe mango, peeled as described page 77, then sliced into thin, ¼-inch slices

2 teaspoons *Toasted Rice Powder* (page 41), for a little crunch on top (optional)

1. Steam the sticky rice as directed page 300; for more pandan flavor, layer a few pandan leaves in the sieve before adding the rice. Discard the leaves after the rice is done.

2. While the rice is steaming, in a large saucepan over medium heat whisk together the coconut milk, sugar, brown sugar, and sea salt. Bring to a rapid simmer, add the pandan leaves, and reduce the heat to low. Partially cover and simmer the coconut milk for 10 minutes and stir occasionally. Turn off the heat, cover, and set aside until the rice is done steaming. If you're using pandan or vanilla extract, whisk it into the coconut milk mixture after you've turned off the heat. Just before the rice is done steaming (check it to see if the grains are soft), reheat the coconut milk for 1 minute over high heat.

VANILLA COCONUT STICKY RICE WITH MANGO

3. When the rice is done (the grains are sticky and chewy), transfer the hot rice to a mixing bowl. Pour the reheated coconut milk over the rice and discard the pandan leaf, if using. Use a wooden spoon, rice paddle, or rubber spatula to vigorously stir the rice for 2 minutes. Cover the bowl tightly with plastic wrap and set aside for 30 minutes, or until the coconut milk has been absorbed by the rice. The rice will resemble a very thick rice pudding.

4. Make the coconut sauce: in a small saucepan whisk together the remaining coconut milk, sugar, lime juice, and cornstarch. Stirring constantly, simmer over medium heat for 2 minutes or until thickened. To serve, peel and slice the mango. Use a rubber spatula or rice paddle and mound rice into a large serving dish or a few smaller bowls for individual servings, then arrange mango slices on top. Drizzle with coconut sauce, sprinkle with **Toasted Rice Powder**, if using, and serve warm.

Red Bean Ice Cream Mochi Dumplings

MAKES 24 MINI DUMPLINGS

(SOY FREE, IF SOY FREE ICE CREAM IS USED)

Mochi *(sweet, chewy rice dough) is fun and easy to make at home with the help of a microwave. Wrap it around ice cream, and you have one of my favorite ice cream treats in the palm of your hand and a fitting finale to any Japanese meal.*

Red bean is as endearing as chocolate in the world of Asian ice cream and still the best flavor for these playful treats. A little store-bought sweetened red beans (easy to find anywhere you find the mochiko flour) and ordinary vegan vanilla ice cream will get you closer to red bean ice cream mochi in minutes. Even faster, scoop any flavor directly out of the pint: green tea, chocolate, coconut, strawberry, or mango . . . any flavor of mochi is a go!

Note that this mochi must be cooked in the microwave to get the right consistency. Cooking on the stovetop won't work for this recipe.

RED BEAN VEGAN ICE CREAM

    1 pint vegan vanilla ice cream (preferably coconut-based), slightly softened
    ½ cup lightly mashed sweetened adzuki beans (see next page)

MOCHI WRAPPERS

    1 cup water
    ⅓ cup sugar
    1¼ cups glutinous-rice flour (mochiko flour, see next page)
    1 teaspoon vanilla, coconut, or almond extract
    A pinch of salt
    ¼ cup mashed sweetened adzuki beans
    ¼ cup or more cornstarch for dusting

1. Line the 24 cups of a metal mini cupcake pan with plenty of plastic wrap; use several pieces, enough to easily press the plastic loosely into each of the cups. If you have a silicone cupcake pan use that instead but don't line with plastic wrap; the ice cream will pop out without the plastic.

2. Empty the softened ice cream into a mixing bowl. Use a rubber spatula to thoroughly mix the

beans into the softened ice cream. The ice cream will rapidly melt, so work quickly. Use the rubber spatula to smooth the ice cream into each cup, then cover with plastic wrap. Freeze the pan until the ice cream is completely solid, at least 2 hours or overnight.

3. For the mochi wrappers, stir the water and sugar together in a 1-quart glass bowl until mostly dissolved. Stir in the mochiko flour, vanilla extract, salt, and adzuki beans; stir into a paste. Cover the bowl with plastic wrap and microwave for 2 minutes on high heat. Remove the plastic wrap; the dough will be thick and sticky. Use a rubber spatula to vigorously stir for about 1 minute. Cover with plastic wrap and microwave for another 1 minute on high. The dough should now be very stiff and thick; if not, cover and microwave for another 20 to 30 seconds. Remove the plastic and give the dough another vigorous stir for about 20 seconds. The dough will look thick and gummy, but that's okay!

4. Generously dust a work surface with cornstarch. Scoop the hot mochi dough onto the work surface and dip your fingers in cornstarch. Press and stretch mochi into an oblong shape. If the mochi is too hot to handle, cool for a minute, but do try to work when the mochi is warm for best results. Flip the mochi a few times and sprinkle the other side with cornstarch while stretching it. When you've stretched it as thin as possible without tearing it, use a rolling pin dusted with cornstarch to roll it even thinner, less than ¼ inch. If the mochi starts to stick at any time dust it immediately with cornstarch.

5. Use a 3¼-inch round cookie cutter and cut out twenty-four circles; you can also roll out the dough scraps one more time to cut out more circles. Remove the ice cream cups from the freezer, uncover, and pull out the plastic to remove the ice cream scoops. To assemble a mochi dumpling, place an ice cream scoop, rounded side down, in the cen-

ter of a mochi wrapper. Quickly fold the edges over the flat-bottomed end of the ice cream, pressing together the edges to seal. Set the mochi seal side down on a tray lined with plastic or waxed paper. If the unwrapped ice cream scoops begin to get melty, keep half of the scoops in the freezer as you work for a constant supply of firm ice cream.

6. Cover the mochi ice cream in the tray with plastic wrap. Return to the freezer and freeze until solid. Ice cream mochi dumplings are best served slightly thawed, about 1 to 1½ minutes out of the freezer. Store frozen in tightly covered containers or zip-top plastic bags.

Look for canned sweetened red adzuki beans and mochiko flour at pan-Asian, Japanese, or Korean grocery stores. Purchase a 14-ounce can for this recipe: you'll have a little extra bean paste, but you may have extra mochi dough as well, great for making traditional little red bean mochi. Scoop 2 teaspoons of paste into a mochi wrapper, fold into a half-moon, and seal. Store tightly covered and chilled until ready to nibble on with a cup of green tea.

Mochi Green Tea Ice Cream Dumplings: Stir 1 to 3 teaspoons of unsweetened matcha green tea powder into the softened ice cream.

Mochi Wrapper Variations: For flavored mochi wrappers, omit the adzuki beans and stir into the mochiko flour ONE of the following: 1½ teaspoons unsweetened matcha green tea powder; 2 tablespoons cocoa powder plus an additional 2 tablespoons of sugar (in addition to the ⅓ cup); a few drops of beet or carrot juice for pastel pink or orange mochi!

Chai Tea Poached Pears with Ginger Yogurt

SERVES 4

(SOY FREE, IF COCONUT YOGURT IS USED, AND LOW FAT, IF MADE WITHOUT COCONUT YOGURT)

Looking for an elegant dessert that's easy on busy cooks? Then pears poached in spiced tea and swirled with a cool gingery soy yogurt impress without much (kitchen) distress. Chai tea makes these pears especially aromatic, but switch up the choice of tea to fit the cuisine.

If you prefer to use loose-leaf tea, use 2 rounded tablespoons of tea. Pack it into a paper liner or fine-mesh tea ball; if any leaves leak out, strain the liquid a few times before reducing.

TEA PEARS
    3½ cups water
    ¾ cup sugar
    4 bags chai tea blend
    Two 3-inch cinnamon sticks
    4 firm bosc pears
    1 tablespoon lemon juice

YOGURT
    2 cups vanilla or lemon, soy or coconut
        yogurt
    2 tablespoons chopped candied ginger

1. In a 2-quart saucepan combine the water and sugar. Bring to a boil over medium high heat; when the sugar has dissolved reduce heat to medium-low. Add the tea bags and cinnamon sticks and simmer for 5 minutes, then remove the tea bags. Stir in the lemon juice.

2. Meanwhile, use a vegetable peeler and peel the pears; keep a bowl of cool water handy to soak the peeled pears to prevent browning while peeling the remaining pears. Slice the peeled pears in half, then use a metal measuring tablespoon to scoop out the seeds in the center. Lower the pears into the pot and simmer for 18 to 22 minutes or until pears are tender but not falling apart.

3. Use a slotted spoon to remove the pears and transfer to a bowl. Continue to simmer the remaining liquid for 20 minutes, or until the liquid has reduced and looks slightly syrupy. Turn off the heat and set aside to cool.

4. To prepare the yogurt, pulse the yogurt with the ginger in a blender until smooth. Serve pears either at room temperature or chilled; place a pear half in a small serving bowl, drizzle with a few spoonfuls of tea syrup, then drizzle with the ginger yogurt or pass the yogurt around in a separate serving dish.

Thai Tea Pears: Use a Thai red tea blend: the vanilla chai flavors and red color work beautifully with the pears.

Rooibos Chai Pears: A rooibos chai blend is a caffeine-free, full-bodied red herbal tea blended with chai spices, usually available in natural food stores. Simmered with pears, it makes a light finish to an African meal.

Vanilla Kukicha Pears: Kukicha is a delectable Japanese tea made from the lightly roasted twigs (not leaves) of tea plants. It has a warm, toasted aroma that's scrumptious with pears. Stir ½ teaspoon of vanilla extract into the syrup after it's done simmering.

Almond Oolong Pears: Oolong, my favorite Chinese tea, has a sweet, biscuity finish and a rich brown color. Stir ½ teaspoon almond extract into the syrup right before pouring on the pear halves and scatter a few sliced toasted almonds on each pear before serving.

Italian cashewcotta cheesecake

MAKES ONE 8-INCH CHEESECAKE OR FOUR
4-INCH MINI CHEESECAKES

Italian cheesecakes are a refreshing departure from the brick-solid, American-style confections; this cashew-and-tofu-based creamy treat has a slightly grainy texture not unlike Italian ricotta cheesecakes. Though two cups of powdered sugar may sound like a lot, this cheesecake remarkably tastes less sweet than its American counterpart. The aromatic touch of citrus and almond extracts combined with no crust or toppings makes this an easy favorite. Serve it slightly warm after baking, or chill overnight for a deeper flavor and firmer texture.

This style of cheesecake doesn't need a topping, but for those who can't bear the thought of a naked cheesecake I've included one of fresh strawberries kissed with a touch of balsamic vinegar.

Extra-firm silken tofu is the best choice for this cake. Firm silken tofu (both boxed and refrigerated water packed) can also be used; the texture of the cake may be slightly softer.

1 cup unroasted, unsalted cashews

24 ounces extra-firm silken tofu (Mori-Nu boxed tofu recommended), drained

2 tablespoons coconut oil, softened

2 cups powdered sugar

2 tablespoons lemon juice

1 tablespoon white rum or brandy

1 tablespoon cornstarch

2 teaspoons pure vanilla extract

1 teaspoon almond extract

½ teaspoon orange extract or grated zest from 1 orange

½ teaspoon lemon extract or grated zest from 1 lemon

¼ teaspoon salt

2 tablespoons powdered sugar, for sprinkling (optional)

Fresh Balsamic Strawberry Topping (optional, recipe follows)

The size of the pan is important here for a cheesecake with a pleasing height; 9- or 9½-inch pans will produce a thinner—though still delicious—cake. Reduce baking time by 10 to 12 minutes depending on the size of the pan.

1. In a small bowl cover the cashews with 2 inches of hot water and soak overnight or until cashews are very soft and no hard bits remain.

2. Preheat the oven to 350°F and spray the insides of an 8-inch round baking pan or four 4-inch mini-springform pans with cooking oil spray. Line

the bottom with a round of parchment paper cut to fit the bottom of the pan.

3. Drain the cashews, transfer them to a blender, and add the tofu and coconut oil. Pulse until the mixture is completely smooth; depending on how powerful the blender is this can take 1 to 3 minutes. Add the remaining ingredients, except for the 2 tablespoons of powdered sugar, pulse until very smooth, and use a rubber spatula to scrape down the sides of the blender frequently.

4. Pour the batter into the prepared pan and use a rubber spatula to get every last drop of the batter from the blender into the pan. Lift the pan a few inches off the kitchen counter and drop a few times to help release some of the larger air bubbles from the batter. Bake for 50 to 55 minutes, or until the top of the cake feels firm and the edges are just starting to turn golden. For mini-cheesecakes, bake for 25 minutes, check the top of the cakes for firmness, and continue to bake for 5 to 8 minutes longer if necessary.

5. Remove from the oven and set on a wire rack to cool for 25 minutes. Run a knife around the edges of the cake and stretch a piece of plastic wrap on top of the pan. Place a large dish on top of the pan and invert the cake pan. Tap the bottom of the pan a few times to release the cake, lift the pan, and peel off the parchment paper. Now place a serving dish on top of the cake and invert one more time, then remove the plastic wrap from the top of the cake. If using mini-springform pans, remove the outer ring and use a spatula to lift cakes off the metal bottoms and transfer to serving plates. Optional: sprinkle the top with the 2 tablespoons of powdered sugar (sift the powder through a wire mesh sieve and gently

tap it over the top of the cake for a pretty dusting). Store the cheesecake tightly wrapped in the refrigerator. For cleaner slicing of this cake, try using a plastic knife.

Fresh Balsamic Strawberry Topping

MAKES ABOUT 2 CUPS

A fresh and juicy strawberry topping to spoon on top of individual slices of cheesecake. This can be made up to 2 hours before serving the cake, but use it to top the cake right before serving.

1 pint fresh strawberries
2 tablespoons sugar
2 teaspoons good-quality balsamic vinegar
   or white balsamic vinegar

1. Clean the strawberries and remove the stems. Slice them into thin, ¼-inch slices and combine with remaining ingredients. Set aside for 3 minutes before serving.

2. To use frozen strawberries, slice unthawed berries, combine with the remaining ingredients, and stir occasionally until the berries are completely thawed.

ITALIAN CASHEWCOTTA CHEESECAKE, PAGE 337

Ethiopian chocolate flourless torte

MAKES ONE 8-INCH TORTE

This slim, naturally gluten-free cake packs a punch of velvety chocolate and a hint of smoky berbere spice; bake this elegant dessert while dinner is cooking on the stovetop and serve it still warm garnished with a light dusting of cocoa powder. But don't underestimate this slim torte: one slender slice packs a full-bodied chocolate punch, ideally paired with a scoop of high-quality vegan vanilla or coconut ice cream. While not authentic to Ethiopian cuisine, chocolate is a language that everybody understands.

Substitute the berbere spice blend with cayenne or ancho chile powder for a **Mexican Chocolate Torte** *(see below), one of the "new" classic American dessert flavors.*

For best presentation, plate the torte on a serving dish that's perfectly flat. Even a slightly curved dinner plate will create a depression in the center of this slender cake.

⅔ cup semi sweet chocolate chips

½ cup plus 2 teaspoons unsweetened cocoa powder

12 ounces extra firm silken tofu (Mori Nu boxed tofu recommended)

¾ cup sugar

½ cup ground almonds or hazelnuts

2 tablespoons cornstarch

1 teaspoon pure vanilla extract

½ teaspoon almond extract

1½ teaspoons ground cinnamon

½ teaspoon ground **Berbere Spice Blend** (see page 44)

A pinch of salt

1. Preheat oven to 350°F and line an 8-inch round baking pan with a round of parchment paper cut to fit the bottom. Spray the insides with cooking oil spray.

2. Melt the chocolate chips: the easiest and fastest way is to pour the chips into a glass bowl and microwave on high for 1 minute to melt some of the chips. Move the half-melted chips around with a rubber spatula, then return to the microwave for 40 seconds and stir again until all of the chips are melted; if necessary microwave for another 20 to 30 seconds until all of the chips are soft and easy to stir.

3. Set aside the 2 teaspoons of cocoa powder for decorating the torte, then in a blender combine the remaining ingredients and pulse until smooth, scraping the sides of the blender frequently. Add the melted chocolate and pulse until completely blended. Pour into the prepared pan and use a rubber spatula to get every last drop of the batter into the pan. Smooth the top of the torte and bake for 42 to 45 minutes, or until the top of the cake feels firm.

4. Remove the torte from the oven and set it on a wire rack to cool for 15 minutes. Run a knife around the edges of the torte, place a serving dish on top of the pan, and invert the cake pan. Tap the bottom of the pan a few times to release the torte, lift the pan, and peel off the parchment paper. Sprinkle the top with cocoa powder (for best results sift the powder through a wire mesh sieve and gently tap it over the top of the cake for a pretty, even coating of powder).

5. Serve the torte warm. Loosely covered and chilled, the torte tastes best if eaten within 2 days. To reheat, microwave for 20 to 25 seconds or until slightly warm in the center of the torte.

Mexican Chocolate Torte: Omit the *Berbere Spice Blend* and substitute 1 teaspoon cinnamon and ½ teaspoon Mexican chile powder, ancho chile powder or cayenne pepper.

PART 3

menus

online resources

recipes by icon

thanks & acknowledgments

metric conversions

index

about the author

Menus

Vegan food is the ultimate fusion cuisine! Go for it and serve that African rice dish with a Sri Lankan curry alongside a Mexican salsa and wrap it up with pears poached in Thai tea. It's your world; we're just lucky enough to dine in it.

Sri Lankan Curry Party
Coconut Chile Relish (*Pol Sambol*), page 69
Sri Lankan Coconut Roti, page 193
Steamed jasmine rice, page 299, and/or string
    hoppers (Sri Lankan rice noodle patties,
    available at some Southeast Asian markets)
Whole Cashew Curry, page 140

Japan by Way of the East Village
Ninja Carrot Ginger Dressing with simple green
    salad, page 84
Sensei Tofu Hijiki Burgers with steamed short-
    grain brown rice, page 248
Red Bean Ice Cream Mochi Dumplings, page 334

International Super Bowl Party
Garlic Chive Seitan Potstickers, page 171
Whipped Garlic Dip (*Toum*), page 63, with grilled
    white or whole wheat pita
Filo Samosas, page 209, with Tamarind Date
    Chutney, page 59
Jamaican Curry Seitan Patties, page 213, (make
    small, 3-inch "cocktail" size or slice patties
    in half)
Crispy Plantains with East Meets West Chocolate
    Mole Dip, page 290

Pierogi Are Everything, Everything Is Pierogi
Potato Pierogi with Fried Onions, page 173,
    pick three of the following: Sauerkraut

Mushroom, page 176; Celeriac, page 176;
    Spinach and Dill, page 176; Roasted Garlic and
    Horseradish, page 176
All-natural unsweetened applesauce (preferably
    organic), either store-bought or homemade
Sour Dilly Cream, page 71
Roasted Beet Salad with Dill Vinaigrette, page 103

Mostly Korean Year-Round BBQ
Fast Lane Cabbage Kimchi, page 56
Sesame Mung Bean Sprouts, page 89
Korean Veggie *Bulgogi* (Sweet Soy BBQ), page 249
Large, crisp romain lettuce leaves for wrapping
Korean soybean garlic paste or gochuchang paste
    (see page 15)
Steamed short-grain white or brown rice, page 299
Red Bean Ice Cream Mochi Dumplings, page 334

Southeast Asian Brunch
Scrambled Tofu Breakfast Bahn Mi, page 109
Mock Nuoc Cham, page 67
Golden Coconut Crepes (Vietnamese *Banh Xeo*),
    page 207
Vanilla Coconut Sticky Rice with Mango, page 332

Japanese Soul Food Dinner
Tonkatsu Sauce, page 70
Sesame Panko Tempeh Cutlets (Tempeh *Katsu*),
    page 246
Thinly shredded green cabbage

Lemon wedges for squeezing
Steamed short-grain Japanese rice, page 299, or
soba noodles dressed with sesame oil and a
shake of tamari

Dumplings, Everywhere, Dumplings
Steamed BBQ Seitan Buns (*Char Siu Seitan Bao*),
page 197
Shanghai Kale Dumplings in Sesame Sauce,
page 179
Momo Dumplings with Spicy Sesame Tomato
Sambal and Cabbage Slaw, page 184
Afghan Pumpkin Ravioli with Spicy Tomato Sauce,
page 183
Kimchi and Tofu Manju Dumplings, page 181

Clash of the Islands (Greek versus Caribbean)
Greek Creamy Lemon Rice Soup (*"No"* govlemano),
page 127
Jerk-Roasted Seitan Strips, page 271
Lemon Garlic Potatoes, page 285
Braised Greens with Lemon and Olive Oil, page 293
Favorite habanero hot sauce

Moms Love Thai Food (Mother's Day Lunch)
Tom Yum Noodle Soup, made without noodles
as a light starter, page 217
Avocado Mango Cashew Salad, page 78
Red Curry with Kabocha and Potatoes, page 144
Steamed sticky rice or boiled jasmine rice (see
page 299)
Chai Tea Poached Pears with Ginger Yogurt—Thai
Tea variation, page 336

Middle Eastern Summertime Brunch
Roasted Chile Pepper Harissa Paste, page 42
Eggplant Shakshuka with Green Tahini Sauce,
page 153
Mediterranean Chopped Salad, page 87
Orange Blossom Hazelnut Baklava, page 327

Dips and Spreads Make the Meal (Finger-Food Menu of Tasty, Spreadable Things)
Soft Red Lentil Kibbe with Fresh Herbs, page 111
Creamy Walnut Red Pepper Spread (*Muhamarra*),
page 95
Garlicky Potato Dip (*Skordalia*), page 93
Cultured Cashew Spread with French Herbs, page 94
Warm pita bread, crackers, and crudité

Dads Love Seitan, Potatoes, Beer, and Endive (Father's Day Lunch)
Bittersweet Apple and Endive Salad, page 87
Beer-Bathed Seitan Stew and Oven Pommes Frites,
page 156
Tenacious Tart Tatin with your favorite vegan
vanilla ice cream, page 321

Nobody Beats the Mediterranean Mezze Cocktail Party
Very Nice Chickpea Crepes (French *Socca*), page 205
Crispy Oven Fried Eggplant and Zucchini with
Skordalia, page 283
Soft Red Lentil Kibbe with Fresh Herbs, page 111,
and pita and romain lettuce leaves for dipping
Sweet Autumn Toasted Pita and Kale Salad,
page 100, or Pistachio Date Quinoa Salad,
page 89

Pan-Asian Summer Bento Lunchbox
Savory Baked Tofu, page 50, sliced into bite-size
triangles
Curried Avocado Summer Rolls, page 82

Olive Oil Harissa Paste, page 43
Roasted Cauliflower with Mint, page 285
Rose Water Date Semolina Squares, page 330

Ooo La La, Le French Menu
French Farmhouse Asparagus Bisque, page 123
Red Wine–Braised Leeks and Mushrooms, page 265
Luscious White Bean and Celery Root Puree,
    page 294
Dinner crepes, from Your International House of
    Dinner Crepes, page 203
Tenacious Tart Tatin, page 321

Homestyle Chinese Takeout Menu
Zen Spinach Wonton Soup, page 117
Crisp Stir-Fry Greens with Veggie Oyster Sauce,
    page 283
Spicy Saucy Soft Tofu (*Ma-Po* Tofu), page 150
Steamed Long-Grain White Rice, page 298

The Kickin' Tacos & Churros Birthday Dinner
Pickled Red Onions, page 62
Pumpkin Seed Mole Dip (*Sikil Pak*), page 92
Mexican Chopped Salad, page 102
Sweet and Savory Jackfruit Carnitas Tacos
    with a toppings bar, page 105
Pumpkin Churros, page 326

Indian Thanksgiving
Rhubarb Cranberry Chutney, page 68
Tomato Dill Apple Raita, page 66
Masala Potato Soup, page 121
Ginger Tomato Chickpeas (*Chole* or *Chana Masala*),
    page 135
Golden Tandoori Tofu, page 268
Pilaf-Style White Basmati Rice, page 299
Carrot Semolina Halva, page 330

Filipino Latino Midwinter Dinner
Watercress Coconut Lumpia Spring Rolls, page 176
Tofu and Potato Adobo Stew, page 148
Jasmine rice, page 299
Pumpkin Churros with your favorite vegan
    coconut ice cream, page 326

African Latin Mashup Feast
Ginger Peanut Squash Soup, page 128
Mexican Chopped Salad, page 102
Yassa Lemon Mustard Tofu, page 270
Coconut Rice, page 298
Chai Tea Pears with Ginger Yogurt—Rooibos Chai
    variation, page 336

Online resources

It's no longer crazy to imagine shopping for groceries on your computer. Unusual spices and vegan staples such as vital wheat gluten flour are easier than ever to buy online, often at great prices. Below are a few online resources you may find useful.

KALUSTYANS.COM *The place to find every spice, seasoning blend, dried herb, specialty beans, grains, and delicacies from afar. If ever in NYC, do yourself a favor a wander around the tidy little isles of the original store on Lexington Avenue and just try to resist bringing home 4 different kinds of smoked paprika.*

PENZEYS.COM *Another good source for spices, with brick and mortar locations across the U.S.*

BOBSREDMILL.COM *Get your vegany vegan nutritional yeast and vital wheat gluten in big bags!*

RECIPES BY ICON

(123) BEGINNER COOKING

Try this if you're a kitchen novice: recipe has fewer steps beyond chopping or prepping the ingredients or is straightforward in putting together.

GLUTEN FREE

No wheat or barley. Be sure to use gluten-free soy sauce in these recipes (such as gluten-free tamari) when soy is mentioned in the ingredients.

🔵 LOWER FAT

Recipe has 1 tablespoon or less of added oil, no nuts, no avocado.

ⓢ ON A BUDGET

Cheaper ingredients, especially when seasonal produce is used.

RICE AND WHOLE GRAINS: ONE-POT MEALS AND SUPPORTING ROLES

SWEET BEGINNINGS

④⑤ QUICK & EASY

Under 45 minutes from start to finish. Does not include preparing other recipes needed for the final recipe or presoaking of beans or nuts.

SPICE BLENDS

THE THREE PROTEIN AMIGOS: TOFU, SEITAN, AND TEMPEH

PICKLES, CHUTNEYS & SAUCIER SAUCES

SALADS, SPREADS & SANDWICHES

SIT BACK & SIMMER

Majority of cooking time is inactively spent on the stovetop or in the oven, so you can relax.

Ⓢ SOY FREE

No tofu, tempeh, miso, soy sauce. Margarine may be listed, so be sure to use a soy-free vegan margarine. As of this writing Earth Balance has a product in its line of vegan "buttery spread" that is soy free.

Thanks & Acknowledgments

Going all the way back *Vegan Cupcakes Take Over the World*, having my recipes tested by real people in their real-life kitchens has always been a big part of what makes my cookbooks labors of love.

The following home chefs of all levels helped make these recipes what they are today. Many of them are food bloggers too! Thanks so much all of you for lending a hand and getting the dishes a little dirty.

Danielle Aquilino, aveganfoodsnob.blogspot.com

Andy Artz

Erin Barnes

Deb Bervoix (ninety recipes tested!)

Helen Bird, parisvegan.com

Olivia Boatwright (tested ninety-one recipes!)

Carly Bogen and Jenna McDavid

Rebecca Bosford

Diane Buendia, leiterfraugutentag.blogspot.com

Jamie C., theradioactivevegan.blogspot.com

Tiffany Cadiz, breadwithoutbutter.blogspot.com

Kelly Cavalier (tested ninety-six recipes, whoa!), threeandahalfvegans.blogspot.ca

Lesley Clarke

Ellie Collier, ellieheartscrafts.wordpress.com

Lindsay Cornish

Jeni Dick, hungryveganrunner.wordpress.com

Craig Dugas, inspiredeats.com

Jessie Dugas

Emma Ekberg, blog.emmaekberg.se

Christine Fisher

Angela Fortezza-Soto

Benoit Fournier

Caroline Frasier

Tracy Fryer

Katya Galbis, veggisima.com

Denise Ganley

Amy Gedgaudas, tahinitoo.wordpress.com

Erin Goddard, meet-the-wikos.com

Rachel Hallows

Isabella Hammer

Rose Hermalin

Katherine Maria Howell

Cindy Hui, LookyTasty.com

Teressa Jackson

Shannon Jacobs

Caitlin Johnson, CornfieldsandCookies.wordpress.com

Amre Klimchak

Trine Kofoed

Jeff Koon, vegansortof.com

Kim Korstjens

SaraJane Kramer, veganchicksrock.blogspot.ca

Nicholas Kuhlman

Lee Ann L.

Lisa L.

Ted Lai

Yvonne Lamberti, veggiesandstitches.blogspot.de

Laura K. Lawless, TheVeggieTable.com

Jackie Lealess

Hilary Lear

Yona Lesorgen

Kim Logan

Janet Malowany, tastespace.wordpress.com

Amey Mathews, veganeatsandtreats.blogspot.com

Melanie Martin

Megan McClellan

Laura "Queen of the Drunken Noodle" McGowan

Kim Michael

Melissa Montovani

Betsy Mullins-Urwin

Jess Nadel, cupcakesandkale.blogspot.com

Cadry Nelson, cadryskitchen.com

Mel Nicholas, veganisethis.blogspot.com (oh my, 89 recipes tested!)

Lindsay Oakes

Thalia C. Palmer

Grace Parikh

Ray Parrish

Jessie Pascoe, jessiepascoe.tumblr.com

Vivian Peterson

Stephanie Philpott-Jones (P-J)

Gabrielle Pope

Rebekah Reid, beckystastyplanet.blogspot.com

Monique Rijks-Surette, forkoffheartdisease.wordpress.com

Dayna Rozental, seitansaiddance.blogspot.com

Kimberly Roy

Nita Ruggiero

Amanda Sacco (the *Veganomicon* testing queen!)

Jackie Smith

Timberly Stephens

Kelly Sullivan, KZCakes.com

Stacy Swartz-Thomas and Chris Thomas

Bonnie Taffer

Tamar Tamler

Stephanie Taylor

Kristen Thomas

Leinana Two Moons

Cheryl van Grunsven, vandanoindustries.wordpress.com

Maris Wagener

Lowrie Ward

Claudia Weber

Kathryn Weber

Angela Wheaton, chocolatesushidragon.blogspot.co.uk

Angela White

Laurie Wing, littleurbanfarm.wordpress.com

Mat Winser

Abby Wohl, RN

Liz Wyman, cookingtheveganbooks.com

Also a thousand thanks to . . .

John Stavropolous, illustrator and all around life-support system during this two-year tour of vegan world food duty.

Keren Form and Catherine Yang for Chinese inspiration and lessons of *toban djan* and wok stir frying. Many thanks to Danaher Dempsey for his lessons on Sri Lankan edibles, and Shyaporn Theerakulstit for Thai food and wok tips. Go do yourself a favor and watch Shy's (not food, just pure awesome) videos on YouTube right now. Special thanks to my cooking assistant Timberly Stephens.

My Omaha team of Isa Chandra Moskowitz (photographer, stylist, post punk sistah, theppk.com), John "the Lazy Vegan" McDevitt, food-stylist warrior Jessica Joyce, Justine Limoges, and chef Daniel Ocanto with his mad knife skillz. Also thanks to Kjell Peterson, whose pottery graces many of these photographs (kjellpeterson.com). And Fizzle, Avocado, and Kirby for the hugs and kitty sass.

I'd also like to thank my editor at Da Capo Renee Sedliar, project manager Christine E. Marra, Marco Pavia, and my agent, Marc Gerald.

Plus special thanks to Katie McHugh, The Veganauts, and Team Cardamom.

And finally, a thousand thanks to my adventuring party of proofreaders, who fearlessly marched through a weekend of Pain and Pizzas (and vegan brunch!): Donna Ansari, Saif Ansari, Rob Bohl, John Carimando, Michael Cooper, Joanna Corcoran, Luke Crane, Radek "Sir Brinesalot" Drozdalski, Bret Gillan, joss, James Mendez Hodes, Carly Knight, Adam Liebling, Erica Manney, Ryan Roth, Daniel Scribner, Melissa Allen Spangenberg, Jared Sorenson, and Graham Walmsley.

metric conversions

The recipes in this book have not been tested with metric measurements, so some variations might occur. Remember that the weight of dry ingredients varies according to the volume or density factor: 1 cup of flour weighs far less than 1 cup of sugar, and 1 tablespoon doesn't necessarily hold 3 teaspoons.

OVEN TEMPERATURE EQUIVALENTS, FAHRENHEIT (F) AND CELSIUS (C)	
100°F	= 38°C
200°F	= 95°C
250°F	= 120°C
300°F	= 150°C
350°F	= 180°C
400°F	= 205°C
450°F	= 230° C

GENERAL FORMULA FOR METRIC CONVERSION	
Ounces to grams	multiply ounces by 28.35
Grams to ounces	multiply grams by 0.035
Pounds to grams	multiply pounds by 453.5
Pounds to kilograms	multiply pounds by 0.45
Cups to liters	multiply cups by 0.24
Fahrenheit to Celsius	subtract 32 from Fahrenheit temperature, multiply by 5, divide by 9
Celsius to Fahrenheit	multiply Celsius temperature by 9, divide by 5, add 32

VOLUME (DRY) MEASUREMENTS	
¼ teaspoon	= 1 milliliter
½ teaspoon	= 2 milliliters
¾ teaspoon	= 4 milliliters
1 teaspoon	= 5 milliliters
1 tablespoon	= 15 milliliters
¼ cup	= 59 milliliters
⅓ cup	= 79 milliliters
½ cup	= 118 milliliters
⅔ cup	= 158 milliliters
¾ cup	= 177 milliliters
1 cup	= 225 milliliters
4 cups or 1 quart	= 1 liter
½ gallon	= 2 liters
1 gallon	= 4 liters

VOLUME (LIQUID) MEASUREMENTS		
1 teaspoon	= ⅙ fluid ounce	= 5 milliliters
1 tablespoon	= ½ fluid ounce	= 15 milliliters
2 tablespoons	= 1 fluid ounce	= 30 milliliters
¼ cup	= 2 fluid ounces	= 60 milliliters
⅓ cup	= 2⅔ fluid ounces	= 79 milliliters
½ cup	= 4 fluid ounces	= 118 milliliters
1 cup or ½ pint	= 8 fluid ounces	= 250 milliliters
2 cups or 1 pint	= 16 fluid ounces	= 500 milliliters
4 cups or 1 quart	= 32 fluid ounces	= 1,000 milliliters
1 gallon	= 4 liters	

WEIGHT (MASS) MEASUREMENTS		
1 ounce	= 30 grams	
2 ounces	= 55 grams	
3 ounces	= 85 grams	
4 ounces	= ¼ pound	= 125 grams
8 ounces	= ½ pound	= 240 grams
12 ounces	= ¾ pound	= 375 grams
16 ounces	= 1 pound	= 454 grams

LINEAR MEASUREMENTS	
½ in	= 1½ cm
1 inch	= 2½ cm
6 inches	= 15 cm
8 inches	= 20 cm
10 inches	= 25 cm
12 inches	= 30 cm
20 inches	= 50 cm

INDEX

JOHN STAVROPOULOS

about the author

TERRY HOPE ROMERO is the author and co-author of bestselling vegan cookbooks *Veganomicon: The Ultimate Vegan Cookbook, Vegan Cupcakes Take Over the World, Vegan Cookies Invade Your Cookie Jar, Vegan Pie in the Sky,* and *Viva Vegan!* Terry has also presented informative and lively cooking demonstrations and talks to hungry crowds at food festivals and conferences the world over, in Paris, New York City, Boston, Toronto, and many more places.

Terry also contributes to *VegNews* with her *Hot Urban Eats* column and has hosted the public access vegan cooking show the *Post Punk Kitchen.* She also holds a certificate in Plant Based Nutrition from Cornell University.

Terry lives, cooks, and eats in Queens, NYC, and can be found on the web at veganlatina.com.